2007
The Supreme Court Review

2007
The

"Judges as persons, or courts as institutions, are entitled to
no greater immunity from criticism than other persons
or institutions . . . [J]udges must be kept mindful of their limitations and
of their ultimate public responsibility by a vigorous
stream of criticism expressed with candor however blunt."
—*Felix Frankfurter*

". . . while it is proper that people should find fault when
their judges fail, it is only reasonable that they should recognize the
difficulties. . . . Let them be severely brought to book,
when they go wrong, but by those who will take the trouble
to understand them."
—*Learned Hand*

THE LAW SCHOOL

THE UNIVERSITY OF CHICAGO

Supreme Court Review

EDITED BY

DENNIS J. HUTCHINSON

DAVID A. STRAUSS

AND GEOFFREY R. STONE

 THE UNIVERSITY OF CHICAGO PRESS

CHICAGO AND LONDON

INTERNATIONAL STANDARD BOOK NUMBER: 978-0-226-36252-6

LIBRARY OF CONGRESS CATALOG CARD NUMBER: 60-14353

THE UNIVERSITY OF CHICAGO PRESS, CHICAGO 60637

THE UNIVERSITY OF CHICAGO PRESS, LTD., LONDON

The paper used in this publication meets the minimum requirements of American National Standard for Information Sciences–Permanence of Paper for Printed Library Materials, ANSI Z39.48-1984. ∞

TO SAUL LEVMORE

*Dean
and master teacher,
scholar, and colleague*

CONTENTS

DAVID J. GARROW

SIGNIFICANT RISKS: GONZALES v CARHART AND THE FUTURE OF ABORTION LAW

The Supreme Court's five-to-four upholding of the facial constitutionality of the Partial-Birth Abortion Ban Act (PBABA) of 2003
in April 2007 represented at least a symbolic break from its previous
major abortion ruling, *Stenberg v Carhart*, in 2000. The Court's
grant of certiorari in *Gonzales v Carhart* was announced on Justice
Samuel A. Alito's first public day on the bench, February 21, 2006,
and most commentators believed that Alito's replacement of Justice
Sandra Day O'Connor, who had cast the decisive fifth vote when
Stenberg narrowly voided a Nebraska law banning "partial-birth"
abortions, promised a different outcome in this case. That proved
correct, yet the crucial Justice, and author of an unusually intriguing
majority opinion, was Anthony M. Kennedy, who was challenged
to square his angry dissent in *Stenberg* with his insistent, ongoing
support for his reading of the landmark controlling opinion in
Planned Parenthood of Southeastern Pennsylvania v Casey, which he
had so famously—or infamously—joined fifteen years earlier in June
1992. Kennedy's opinion in *Gonzales v Carhart* drew considerable
editorial obloquy,[1] but a close and open-minded reading of the

David J. Garrow is Senior Research Fellow, Homerton College, University of Cambridge.

AUTHOR'S NOTE: Thanks to Jan Crawford Greenburg, Arthur Hellman, and Dennis J.
Hutchinson for helpful reactions and recommendations.

[1] See, e.g., Charles Fried, *"The Supreme Court Phalanx": An Exchange*, New York Review
of Books (Dec 6, 2007) (available at http://www.nybooks.com/articles/20877) (asserting

decision suggests that the ruling represents as narrow as possible an upholding of PBABA. Such a reading also indicates that Kennedy's insistence that he has remained entirely true to what he said and signed onto in *Casey* is a highly credible contention that his critics have failed to consider carefully or fairly. Furthermore, a thorough and inclusive review of *Gonzales v Carhart*'s actual impact—upon the medical practice of abortion, upon abortion politics and legislation, and upon abortion litigation to date—reveals that in all three arenas the decision has had and likely will continue to have far more modest consequences than many critics and commentators initially proclaimed.

I

The origins of the federal PBABA of 2003 reach back to 1993, the year after the Supreme Court's stunning but explicitly circumscribed reaffirmation of the core holding of *Roe v Wade* in *Planned Parenthood v Casey*. Early that year, abortion opponents began to publicize an unpublished seminar paper that an Ohio abortion provider, Dr. Martin Haskell, had presented at a National Abortion Federation meeting in September 1992. In it, Dr. Haskell had described in full medical detail a procedure he used for late second-trimester abortions that differed significantly from the standard second-trimester procedure of dilation and evacuation, or "D&E." Haskell's approach was to remove the fetus as intact as possible, and he introduced the new name dilation and extraction, or "D&X," for his procedure. The key to Haskell's method was what he termed "fetal skull decompression," so that the largest part of the fetus could fit through the cervical os rather than require piecemeal removal as in a standard D&E.[2]

By midyear, abortion opponents' efforts to draw attention to Haskell's method were receiving prominent news coverage in the medical trade press, which also reported that another physician, Dr.

---

that "Justice Kennedy's decision is incompatible not only with precedent but with his own strongly expressed profession of principle").

[2] See Jenny Westberg, *Grim Technology for Abortion's Older Victims*, Life Advocate (February 1993) (available at http://www.lifeadvocate.org/arc/arc.htm); Martin Haskell, *Dilation and Extraction for Late Second Trimester Abortion* (Sept 13, 1992), in *Second Trimester Abortion: From Every Angle* 27–33 (1992), cited in David J. Garrow, *Liberty and Sexuality: The Right to Privacy and the Making of Roe v. Wade* 719, 966 n 29 (updated ed 1998). Perhaps surprisingly, no PDF copy of Haskell's paper is universally available. See, however, *2nd Trimester Abortion: An Interview with W. Martin Haskell, M.D.*, Cincinnati Medicine 18–19 (Fall 1993).

James T. McMahon of Los Angeles, used the same procedure and termed it "intact D&E." Both doctors explained to *American Medical News*, published by the American Medical Association, that intact as opposed to dismembered evacuation minimized the dangers of perforation, tearing, or hemorrhaging for the woman, notwithstanding how intact removal "makes some people queasy." Dr. McMahon explained his perspective: "Once you decide the uterus must be emptied, you then have 100% allegiance to maternal risk. There's no justification to doing a more dangerous procedure because somehow this doesn't offend your sensibilities as much."[3]

Two years passed before abortion opponents initiated a move that brought Haskell and McMahon's method to widespread public attention, a time span which included the enactment of the Freedom of Access to Clinic Entrances (FACE) Act of 1994, the most significant abortion-rights measure ever passed by the U.S. Congress. In early June 1995, Douglas Johnson, federal legislative director of the National Right to Life Committee (NRLC), told the *Washington Times* that Florida Republican Representative Charles T. Canady, chairman of the House Judiciary Committee's subcommittee on the Constitution, would soon be introducing a bill to ban what Johnson called "partial-birth" or "brain suction" late-term abortions.[4] Johnson's announcement, and the *Times*' story, marked the very first public appearance of the "partial-birth" label. In later interviews, Keri Harrison Folmar, an assistant counsel to Canady's subcommittee and former NRLC staffer who actually drafted Canady's bill, recalled how she, Johnson, and Canady came up with the "partial-birth" phrase while also considering a handful of other possible names—"partial-delivery abortion" as well as "brain suction abortion"—for the procedure they hoped to ban. "We called it the most descriptive thing we could call it," Folmar explained. "We wanted a name that rang true."[5]

On June 8, Canady and Nevada Republican Representative Barbara Vucanovich circulated a "Dear Colleague" letter seeking cosponsors for the bill, and on June 14 Canady introduced H.R. 1833, the Partial-Birth Abortion Ban Act of 1995. It authorized up to two

---

[3] Diane M. Gianelli, *Shock-Tactic Ads Target Late-Term Abortion Procedure*, American Medical News 3 (July 5, 1993).

[4] Joyce Price, *Pro-Life Attack on Partial Birth Abortion Bears Fruit*, Washington Times A4 (June 4, 1995).

[5] Cynthia Gorney, *Gambling with Abortion*, Harper's Magazine 33, 38 (Nov 2004).

years in prison for any doctor who "partially vaginally delivers a living fetus before killing the fetus and completing the delivery." The very next day Canady convened a subcommittee hearing on his bill that featured detailed medical testimony both for and against the measure, and within little more than twenty-four hours the phrase "partial-birth abortion" was in the pages of scores of newspapers all across the United States.[6] It represented the beginning of an important turning point in the abortion debate, a strategic innovation which put the abortion-rights proponents who had triumphed in *Casey* and then with FACE constantly on the political defensive for the next twelve years.

Canady's bill passed the House on November 1, 1995, by a vote of 288 to 139, and, after a hearing that featured three additional doctors, the Senate approved an amended version by a margin of 54 to 44 on December 7. The House ratified that measure by 286 to 129 on March 27, 1996, after conducting an additional hearing, but President Clinton vetoed it on April 10. While the House in September mustered an override vote of 285 to 137, a Senate tally of 58 to 40 fell well short of the necessary two-thirds.

The following spring, at the outset of the new 105th Congress, after a joint House-Senate hearing that featured six interest-group spokespersons and one physician, the House again approved a Partial-Birth Abortion Ban bill, H.R. 1122, which incorporated the same description of the banned procedure as used in Canady's 1995 measure. The House vote of 295 to 136 on March 20, 1997, was soon followed by Senate passage of a slightly amended bill on a tally of 64 to 36. The House approved that version in October 1997 by 296 to 132, but two days later President Clinton again exercised his veto power. In July 1998, the House overrode the president by 296 to 132, but in September 1998 a Senate roll call of 64 to 36 fell three votes short of an override.

In the fall of 1999, the Senate passed S. 1692, a Partial-Birth Abortion Ban bill that featured a revised and expanded description

---

[6] In the nation's premier newspapers, the phrase first appeared in the *Washington Post* on June 14, and two days later in the *New York Times*. See Kevin Merida, *Antiabortion Measures Debated; House Republicans Push for New Restrictions in Several Areas*, Washington Post A4 (June 14, 1995); and Jerry Gray, *Emotions High, House Takes Up Abortion*, New York Times A19 (June 16, 1995). See also Tamar Lewin, *Method to End 20-Week Pregnancies Stirs a Corner of the Abortion Debate*, New York Times A10 (July 5, 1995).

of the procedure it sought to prohibit,[7] by a vote of 63 to 34. In April 2000, the House approved a similar bill, H.R. 3660, by 287 to 141, but efforts to reconcile the measures in conference ended once the *Stenberg* decision was handed down on June 28.[8]

Two years then passed before action resumed with Ohio Republican Representative Steve Chabot's introduction of H.R. 4965 on June 19, 2002. In the interim, of course, President Clinton had left office and George W. Bush had become president. Almost equally important, Chabot's bill included a fifteen-page, thirty-paragraph section of congressional "Findings" aimed at rebutting, and trumping, much of the fact-finding and analysis contained in the *Stenberg* majority opinion. In particular, those findings included a declaration that "a partial-birth abortion is never necessary to preserve the health of a woman."[9] In addition, Chabot's bill also employed a significantly different and more anatomically detailed definition of the targeted procedure. Now a "partial-birth abortion" was one in which a doctor

> (A) deliberately and intentionally vaginally delivers a living fetus until, in the case of a head-first presentation, the entire fetal head is outside the body of the mother, or, in the case of a breech presentation, any part of the fetal trunk past the navel is outside the body of the mother, for the purpose of performing an overt act that the person knows will kill the partially delivered living fetus; and
>   (B) performs the overt act, other than completion of delivery, that kills the partially delivered living fetus . . . .[10]

Three weeks later, a brief House hearing heard two doctors testify in favor of the measure, and two weeks after that the House passed

---

[7] S 1692, 106th Cong, 1st Sess, defined the "partial-birth" procedure as "an abortion in which the person performing the abortion deliberately and intentionally (a) vaginally delivers some portion of an intact living fetus until the fetus is partially outside the body of the mother, for the purpose of performing an overt act that the person knows will kill the fetus while the fetus is partially outside the body of the mother; and (b) performs the overt act that kills the fetus while the intact living fetus is partially outside the body of the mother."

[8] The state statute voided by *Stenberg*, Neb Rev Stat Ann § 28-326(9) (Supp 1999), defined a prohibited "partial-birth" abortion as "deliberately and intentionally delivering into the vagina a living unborn child, or a substantial portion thereof, for the purpose of performing a procedure that the person performing such procedure knows will kill the unborn child."

[9] HR 4965, 107th Cong, 2d Sess, § 2(13).

[10] Id at § 3(b)(1).

the bill on a vote of 274 to 151. The Senate did not act on it, and so in February 2003, Representative Chabot and Senator Rick Santorum reintroduced the legislation as H.R. 760 and S. 3 in the new 108th Congress. The Senate passed a slightly amended S. 3 on March 12 by 64 to 33, and, after a very brief, one-doctor hearing on March 25, the House approved H.R. 760 by 282 to 139 in early June. Following a conference committee report, in October the two houses approved S. 3 by votes of 281 to 142 and 64 to 34. President Bush signed the Partial-Birth Abortion Ban Act into law on November 5, 2003.[11]

II

The nine years of public and congressional debate that culminated with President Bush signing legislation equivalent to that which President Clinton twice had vetoed demonstrated sustained and overwhelming majority support for the federal criminalization of a medical procedure that the *Stenberg* majority had concluded was sometimes necessary to protect pregnant women's health. That looming conflict led reproductive rights litigators to file three separate but coordinated constitutional challenges to PBABA—in federal district courts in Nebraska, New York City, and San Francisco—even before President Bush signed the measure into law.[12] In Nebraska, Judge Richard G. Kopf—who previously had presided over the trial in *Stenberg*—issued a temporary restraining order (TRO) covering the four physician plaintiffs who practiced in his state within hours of the president's signature.[13] The following day, ruling in the New York case filed by the National Abortion Federation, whose members included hundreds of doctors all across the entire country, Judge Richard C. Casey issued a similar TRO whose effect was nationwide.[14]

---

[11] Succinct but comprehensive summary accounts of congressional activity on partial-birth abortion bills from 1995 through 2003 appear in both U.S. House of Representatives, *Partial Birth Abortion Ban Act of 2003*, Report 108-58, 108th Cong, 1st Sess, 12–14, and Jay Alan Sekulow, et al, Amicus Brief of the American Center for Law and Justice, et al, *Gonzales v Carhart*, No 05-380 (filed May 22, 2006), 18–25.

[12] Sheryl Gay Stolberg, *3 Suits Filed to Block an Abortion Bill That Bush Intends to Sign*, New York Times A30 (Nov 1, 2003).

[13] *Carhart v Ashcroft*, 287 F Supp 2d 1015 (D Neb 2003). See also *Carhart v Ashcroft*, 292 F Supp 2d 1189 (D Neb 2003) (continuing the temporary restraining order indefinitely).

[14] *National Abortion Federation v Ashcroft*, 287 F Supp 2d 525 (SD NY 2003). Although unreported, an additional TRO also was issued in the San Francisco case. See *Planned Parenthood Federation of America v Ashcroft*, 320 F Supp 2d 957, 967 (ND Cal 2004).

As judges Kopf and Casey both highlighted,[15] PBABA's most glaring contradiction with *Stenberg* lay in the act's lack of a statutory exception for instances in which the banned procedure could protect a pregnant woman's health. Writing for the *Stenberg* majority, Justice Stephen G. Breyer had stated that Nebraska "fails to demonstrate that banning D&X without a health exception may not create significant health risks for women, because the record shows that significant medical authority supports the proposition that in some circumstances, D&X would be the safest procedure."[16] Breyer went on to note that the District Court—Judge Kopf—had "agreed that alternatives, such as D&E and induced labor, are 'safe' but found that the D&X method was significantly *safer* in certain circumstances."[17] Observing that "a statute that altogether forbids D&X creates a significant health risk," the *Stenberg* majority went on to hold that "where substantial medical authority supports the proposition that banning a particular abortion procedure could endanger women's health, *Casey* requires the statute to include a health exception." This, the majority added, was "simply a straightforward application" of *Casey*'s own holding.[18] However, in an additional concurrence, Justice O'Connor stated that "[i]f there were adequate alternative methods for a woman safely to obtain an abortion before viability, it is unlikely that prohibiting the D&X procedure alone would 'amount in practical terms to a substantial obstacle to a woman seeking an abortion,'" the standard declared in *Casey*.[19]

On March 29, 2004, trials commenced in all three cases and lasted between two and three weeks apiece. Each of the three district judges heard testimony from between twelve and eighteen different doctors, and, following the trials, the three judges issued opinions that ran to 58, 79, and 270 pages (Judge Kopf) in the Federal Supplement. All three courts held PBABA unconstitutional, and all three jurists found its lack of a health exception to be a fatal flaw pursuant to *Stenberg* and *Casey*. First to announce her decision was Judge Phyllis J. Hamilton of the Northern District of California, who, in words that directly echoed *Stenberg*, found that "intact D&E is in fact the safest medical option for some women in some cir-

---

[15] 287 F Supp 2d at 1016, 287 F Supp 2d at 526.
[16] *Stenberg v Carhart*, 530 US 914, 932 (2000).
[17] Id at 934 (quoting 11 F Supp 2d at 1125–26).
[18] Id at 938.
[19] Id at 950 (quoting 505 US at 884).

cumstances" and that "under certain circumstances" it is "signifi-cantly safer than D&E by disarticulation."[20]

Judge Hamilton also held that PBABA's wording, like that of the Nebraska statute struck down in *Stenberg*, was sufficiently inclusive to cover nonintact D&Es and thereby violate *Casey*'s "substantial obstacle" standard,[21] and that the statute was unconstitutionally vague,[22] but she voiced barely concealed contempt for the medical evidence Congress relied upon to justify PBABA's lack of a health exception. Summarizing the congressional hearing record from 1995 through 2003, she observed that "over a period of approxi-mately eight years, Congress entertained live testimony from a total of eight physicians, six of whom supported the ban."[23] Judge Ham-ilton further asserted, with reference to a 1998 opinion article in the *Journal of the American Medical Association* coauthored by two physicians, one of whom had testified before Congress and the other of whom was a government witness in all three PBABA trials, that "[m]any of the congressional 'findings' mirror substantially the con-clusions reached in Dr. Sprang's article."[24] She added that "this court indicated at trial that it found the article itself to be lacking in trustworthiness."[25] Looking in particular at congressional activity in 2002–2003, Judge Hamilton concluded that "at the time that it made its findings, Congress did not have before it any *new* medical evidence or studies not available to both the district court and Su-preme Court in *Stenberg*, at the times the courts issued their de-cisions."[26] All in all, she found, "Congress's conclusion that the procedure is never medically necessary is not reasonable and is not based on substantial evidence."[27]

In late August 2004, Judge Casey in Manhattan issued his decision

---

[20] *Planned Parenthood Federation of America v Ashcroft*, 320 F Supp 2d 957, 1002 (ND Cal 2004).

[21] Id at 971.

[22] Id at 977–78.

[23] Id at 1019. See also Neal Devins, *Tom DeLay: Popular Constitutionalist?* 81 Chi Kent L Rev 1055, 1060 (2006) (describing how "[a]n increasingly ideological, increasingly po-larized Congress sees hearings as staged events in which each side can call witnesses who will explain their views to the public," rather than call "nonpartisan witnesses").

[24] Id (referencing M. LeRoy Sprang and Mark G. Neerhof, *Rationales for Banning Abor-tions Late in Pregnancy*, 280 JAMA 744 [1998]).

[25] Id at 1019–20.

[26] Id at 1023.

[27] Id at 1024.

and likewise targeted the inadequacy of Congress's fact-finding. "Congress did not hold extensive hearings, nor did it carefully consider the evidence before arriving at its findings," he wrote. "Even the Government's own experts disagreed with almost all of Congress's factual findings" in their testimony at trial.[28] In particular, Judge Casey observed, "[t]here is no consensus that D&X is never medically necessary, but there is a significant body of medical opinion that holds the contrary."[29] His conclusion was almost identical to Judge Hamilton's: "Congress's factfindings were not reasonable and based on substantial evidence."[30]

In early September 2004, Judge Kopf rendered the last of the District Court decisions. Much like the other two jurists, he too concluded that "the congressional record proves the opposite of the Congressional Findings."[31] In particular, Congress's assertion that a medical consensus existed that the partial-birth procedure was never necessary to protect a woman's health "is both unreasonable and not supported by substantial evidence," Judge Kopf found.[32] Indeed, "the trial evidence established that a large and eminent body of medical opinion believes that partial-birth abortions provide women with significant health benefits in certain circumstances."[33] The evidence further demonstrated "that Congress was wrong, and unreasonably so," in its findings, for "the overwhelming weight of the trial evidence proves that the banned procedure is safe and medically necessary in order to preserve the health of women under certain circumstances." In fact, "the banned procedure is, sometimes, the safest abortion procedure to preserve the health of women," Judge Kopf found.[34]

The Justice Department appealed all three adverse district court rulings to their respective circuit courts of appeal, and in July 2005, an Eighth Circuit panel became the first to rule when it affirmed Judge Kopf's decision. Quoting from *Stenberg*, the panel unani-

---

[28] *National Abortion Federation v Ashcroft*, 330 F Supp 2d 436, 482 (SD NY 2004).

[29] Id.

[30] Id at 488.

[31] *Carhart v Gonzales*, 331 F Supp 2d 805, 1012 (D Neb 2004).

[32] Id at 1015.

[33] Id at 1016.

[34] Id at 1016, 1017. Judge Kopf held the act unconstitutional both for its lack of a health exception and because it contravened *Casey* and *Stenberg*'s "undue burden" standard. Id at 1048, 1031.

mously held that "[w]e believe the appropriate question is whether 'substantial medical authority' supports the medical necessity of the banned procedure."[35] Thus, "when 'substantial medical authority' supports the medical necessity of a procedure in some instances," the panel concluded, "*Stenberg* requires the inclusion of a health exception."[36]

In late September, the Solicitor General petitioned the Supreme Court to hear the government's appeal in *Gonzales v Carhart*. He asserted that in passing PBABA, the Congress had acted "on the basis of a different (and fuller) evidentiary record" than the *Stenberg* court had had before it.[37] In addition, he asserted that *Stenberg* had established that "the critical question was whether the statute being challenged would pose '*significant* health risks for women.'"[38] In a subsequent reply brief in early December, the Solicitor General suggested that Congress had considered "the latest and best available medical evidence" before passing PBABA.[39] He further asserted that "the correct inquiry" in the case at hand "is simply whether there was sufficient evidence to suggest that *Congress's* determination was reasonable" when it adopted the statute.[40]

Before the Court acted on the petition, both the Second and Ninth Circuits issued their decisions on the same day. The Ninth Circuit ruling, written by Judge Stephen Reinhardt, affirmed the District Court's judgment on all points.[41] The Second Circuit decision, written by Judge Jon O. Newman and joined in full by Chief Judge John M. Walker, Jr., featured both an energetic dissent by Judge Chester J. Straub and, more importantly, a perceptive and significant additional concurrence by Judge Walker.[42] Acknowledging how his court was required to follow *Stenberg*, Judge Walker

---

[35] *Carhart v Gonzales*, 413 F3d 791, 796 (8th Cir 2005).

[36] Id at 796, 797. The Eighth Circuit did not reach Judge Kopf's conclusion that the act also constituted an undue burden. Id at 803–04.

[37] Paul D. Clement, Petition for a Writ of Certiorari, *Gonzales v Carhart*, No 05-380 (filed Sept 23, 2005), 17.

[38] Id at 20 (quoting 530 US at 932 and adding emphasis).

[39] Paul D. Clement, Reply Brief for the Petitioner, *Gonzales v Carhart*, No 05-380 (filed Dec 2, 2005), 3.

[40] Id at 8. In a footnote, quoting from *Turner Broadcasting System v FCC*, 520 US 180, 195 (1997) and adding emphasis, Clement explained that "the precise inquiry is whether, 'in formulating its judgment, Congress has drawn *reasonable inferences* based on substantial evidence.'" Id at 8 n 4.

[41] *Planned Parenthood Federation of America v Gonzales*, 435 F3d 1163 (9th Cir 2006).

[42] *National Abortion Federation v Gonzales*, 437 F3d 278 (2d Cir 2006).

nonetheless harshly criticized that decision, emphasizing how *Stenberg*'s analysis of a ban on the D&X procedure "equates the denial of a potential health benefit (in the eyes of some doctors) with the imposition of a health risk and, in the process, promotes marginal safety above all other values."[43] In so doing, *Stenberg* "denies legislatures the ability to promote important interests above the conferral upon some citizens of a marginal health benefit."[44] On the other hand, Judge Walker stressed, there was "substantial evidence that, even if the D&X procedure is wholly prohibited, a woman can obtain a safe abortion in almost every conceivable situation." At most, a ban on D&Xs "might deny some unproven number of women a marginal health benefit," he contended.[45]

At the same time, Judge Walker also noted, just as all three trial judges had, the glaring contradictions that underlay PBABA's findings. When Representative Chabot first introduced the bill in June 2002, "complete with the same detailed factual findings that were ultimately enacted into law," Judge Walker observed, Congress had not yet conducted any relevant post-*Stenberg* hearings, and thus in actuality "had not considered any new evidence" whatsoever.[46] In response, Judge Straub asserted that "it is irrelevant that the text of the Act was introduced prior to hearings," for "[w]e are not empowered to review Congress's internal procedures or methods."[47]

Two weeks after the Second and Ninth Circuit rulings, the Solicitor General filed a supplemental brief highlighting Judge Walker's critical statement about how *Stenberg*'s approach to partial-birth bans "promotes marginal safety above all other values."[48] One week later the Supreme Court unsurprisingly granted certiorari,[49] and when the Solicitor General subsequently filed a petition for certiorari in the Ninth Circuit case, asking that it be held pending

---

[43] Id at 291.

[44] Id at 292.

[45] Id at 296.

[46] Id at 293 n 9.

[47] Id at 300 n 11 (citing *U.S. v Ballin*, 144 US 1 [1892]).

[48] Paul D. Clement, Supplemental Brief for the Petitioner, *Gonzales v Carhart*, No 05-380 (filed Feb 14, 2006), 5.

[49] *Gonzales v Carhart*, 546 US 1169 (2006). See also Linda Greenhouse, *Justices to Review Federal Ban on Disputed Abortion Method*, New York Times A1 (Feb 22, 2006) (observing that "[a] lower court's invalidation of a federal statute has an almost automatic claim on the justices' attention").

the Court's decision in *Gonzales v Carhart*,[50] the Court instead granted certiorari in *Gonzales v Planned Parenthood Federation of America* as well.[51] In mid-August the Court scheduled oral arguments in both cases for November 8, 2006.

Shortly before the Court added the Ninth Circuit case to its argument calendar, Solicitor General Paul D. Clement had filed his merits brief in *Gonzales v Carhart*. He asserted that the evidence "at most suggests that partial-birth abortion may be *marginally* safer than more common abortion procedures in some narrow circumstances," and he highlighted how "one of the express purposes of the Act is to 'draw a bright line that clearly distinguishes abortion and infanticide.'"[52] More boldly, the Solicitor General also contended that "[t]o the extent that the Court concludes that *Stenberg* compels the conclusion that the Act is facially invalid, however, *Stenberg* should be overruled."[53]

"To be sure," the Solicitor General admitted, "some language in the Court's opinion in *Stenberg*"—namely, the "substantial medical authority" standard identified and adopted by the Eighth Circuit panel below—"could be read, in isolation, to suggest that a statute prohibiting a particular abortion procedure would be unconstitutional as long as there is *conflicting evidence* as to whether the statute at issue would create significant health risks."[54] But "the proper understanding" of *Stenberg*, Clement continued, would require that the plaintiffs "must actually prove that the regulation at issue would create significant health risks for women" and thus that the absence of a health exception would represent an undue burden.[55] In a footnote, the Solicitor General underscored how repeatedly *Stenberg* had employed the word "significant,"[56] and he asserted that the applicable standard should be whether a regulation creates "signif-

---

[50] Paul D. Clement, Petition for a Writ of Certiorari, *Gonzales v Planned Parenthood Federation of America*, No 05-1382 (filed May 1, 2006), 2. See also Paul D. Clement, Reply Brief for the Petitioner, *Gonzales v Planned Parenthood Federation of America*, No 05-1382 (filed May 25, 2006), 1 (same).

[51] *Gonzales v Planned Parenthood Federation of America*, 126 S Ct 2901 (2006).

[52] Paul D. Clement, Brief for the Petitioner, *Gonzales v Carhart*, No 05-380 (filed May 22, 2006), 10, 11 (quoting Act § 2[14][G]).

[53] Id at 11.

[54] Id at 16–17.

[55] Id at 18.

[56] Id at 19 n 3 (quoting 530 US at 931, 932, 938).

icant health risks in a large fraction of its applications."[57]

Clement repeated his earlier claim that "Congress made its findings based on a more recent, and more robust, evidentiary record," and he again reiterated that the Court should determine only "whether there is sufficient evidence to suggest that *Congress's* determination was reasonable."[58] The medical evidence indicated that "any differences in safety are debatable and sufficiently marginal" and that "substantial evidence supported Congress's ultimate finding that partial-birth abortion is never necessary to preserve the mother's health."[59] Absent proof that a partial-birth ban would create "significant health risks," it would not constitute an undue burden. In closing, Clement declared that "[t]he protection of innocent human life—in or out of the womb—is the most compelling interest the government can advance."[60]

The merits briefs filed by the Center for Reproductive Rights (CRR), in the Nebraska case, and Planned Parenthood Federation of America (PPFA) as the lead appellee in the Ninth Circuit case, both took dead aim at PBABA's underlying legislative infirmities. CRR declared that "the congressional findings were not reasonable," while PPFA termed them "patently unreasonable."[61] Hoping to highlight PBABA's contradiction of *Stenberg* in a manner that might most motivate Justices such as Anthony Kennedy to void the statute, CRR asserted that "Congress has not merely promulgated a measure that poses a significant threat to women's health," but also "has issued a rebuke to this Court, challenging its pre-eminence as the branch of government whose duty it is 'to say what the law is.'"[62]

Claiming that PBABA "must be struck down unless the Court overturns *Stenberg*," CRR emphasized *Stenberg*'s finding that "substantial medical authority" attested to how such a ban could endanger women's health.[63] It quoted Judge Kopf's conclusion that

---

[57] Id at 20. See also id at 26 (reiterating the phrase "significant health risks").

[58] Id at 29, 31.

[59] Id at 39, 40.

[60] Id at 40, 41.

[61] Priscilla J. Smith, Brief of Respondents, *Gonzales v Carhart*, No 05-380 (filed Aug 10, 2006), 2; Eve C. Gartner, Brief of Planned Parenthood Respondents, *Gonzales v Planned Parenthood Federation of America*, No 05-1382 (filed Sept 20, 2006), 24.

[62] Smith, Brief of Respondents, 15 (quoting *Marbury v Madison*, 5 US [1 Cranch] 137, 177 [1803]).

[63] Id at 16, 18.

trial evidence demonstrated that "a large and eminent body of medical opinion" supported that finding, and it reached out to embrace the additional holding that the Ninth Circuit, unlike the Eighth, had rendered, arguing that PBABA's "definition of 'partial-birth abortion' does not clearly distinguish between D&E and intact D&E procedures in a way that would allow physicians to control their actions during a D&E to prevent them from running afoul of the Act."[64]

PPFA's brief repeatedly stressed how intact abortions were "meaningfully safer" and "significantly safer" than other alternatives, and it highlighted Judge Hamilton's finding that the procedure was "the safest medical option for some women."[65] It stated that "there is more and better evidence of 'substantial medical evidence' here than in *Stenberg*" and made a passing reference to "the primacy of maternal health" while also arguing that "the scienter provisions do not limit the Act in a manner on which physicians can rely."[66] Most notably of all, however, it quoted from *Casey* a phrase which Justice Kennedy also had cited in his opinion for the Court in *Lawrence v Texas* to remind the Justices that "[w]hile the Act serves an interest in promoting a moral judgment against intact D&E, this Court has repeatedly held that its 'obligation is to define the liberty of all, not to mandate our own moral code.'"[67]

In his reply brief, the Solicitor General evinced a decidedly more defensive tone while nonetheless continuing to insist upon what he termed "Congress's superior capacity to root out raw data."[68] Seeking to minimize the import of Judge Hamilton and Judge Kopf's evaluations of the medical testimony their courts had taken, Clement maintained that "[t]he constitutionality of nationwide legislation properly depends on the credibility judgments of Congress, not those of individual district court judges."[69] He contended that PBABA "denies no woman the ability to obtain a safe abortion,"

---

[64] Id at 34, 38.

[65] Gartner, Brief of Planned Parenthood Respondents, i, 10, 15.

[66] Id at 23, 24, 43.

[67] Id at 32 (quoting 505 US at 850 and 539 US at 571).

[68] Paul D. Clement, Reply Brief for the Petitioner, *Gonzales v Carhart* and *Gonzales v Planned Parenthood Federation of America*, Nos 05-380 and 05-1382 (filed Oct 25, 2006), 7 n 3. That note went on to acknowledge that "Congress held two post-*Stenberg* hearings in which it heard testimony from two physicians . . . who had not previously testified . . . and received new documentary evidence."

[69] Id at 11.

and tellingly argued that "respondents appear to concede that standard D&E abortions are generally safe."[70] He avowed that "partial-birth abortion is not safer than other types of abortion either generally or in any specific circumstances," and he quoted Justice Kennedy's statement in dissent in *Stenberg* that federal courts "are ill-equipped to evaluate the relative worth of particular surgical procedures."[71] Clement also insisted that PBABA "unambiguously excludes standard D&E abortions" and "does not reach partial-birth abortions carried out by physicians who had intended to perform standard D&E abortions instead" but instead found themselves confronted with a fetal evacuation that went beyond PBABA's anatomical landmarks.[72]

III

When oral arguments in first *Gonzales v Carhart* and then *Gonzales v Planned Parenthood Federation of America* both took place on November 8, 2006, Justice Breyer posed a suggestive early question to Solicitor General Clement. "If medical opinion is divided," Breyer asked, "could this Court say 'this use of the procedure, we enjoin the statute to permit its use but only where appropriate medical opinion finds it necessary for the safety or health of the mother?'"[73] Knowledgeable observers understood Justice Breyer to be alluding, although not by name, to the Court's unanimous resolution ten months earlier of *Ayotte v Planned Parenthood of New England*, an abortion case in which a New Hampshire parental notification statute failed to include an exception for instances in which an immediate abortion was necessary to protect a pregnant minor's health.[74] There, in Justice O'Connor's final opinion before she left the bench, the Court had explained that "[w]e prefer . . . to enjoin only the unconstitutional applications of a statute, while leaving

---

[70] Id at 1, 18.

[71] Id at 15, 21.

[72] Id at 25. See also Paul D. Clement, Brief for the Petitioner, *Gonzales v Planned Parenthood Federation of America*, No 05-1382 (filed Aug 3, 2006), 32 (stating that PBABA "applies only where the person performing the abortion has the specific intent, at the outset of the procedure, to deliver the requisite portion of the fetus for the purpose of performing the ultimate lethal act").

[73] Transcript of Argument, *Gonzales v Carhart*, No 05-380 (Nov 6, 2006), 19.

[74] 546 US 320 (2006).

other applications in force."[75] The Court had remanded the case so that a more narrowly drawn injunction might be entered in place of the lower courts' previous invalidation of the statute.[76]

Clement parried Justice Breyer's suggestion, noting that some doctors preferred to use the D&X procedure for every late second-trimester abortion, not just specific ones, but Breyer reiterated his point "that there has to be a significant body of medical opinion that says that this is a safer procedure and necessary for the safety of the mother" in particular, identifiable circumstances.[77] Justice Kennedy then asked the Solicitor General how "an as-applied challenge could be brought if we sustain" PBABA against the present preenforcement facial challenges. "I have read all the doctors' testimony in this case, hundreds of pages," Kennedy explained, and was "trying to imagine how an as-applied challenge would be really much different from what we have seen already." Clement replied that in the future doctors "might come in and target their challenge to particular conditions."[78]

When Priscilla Smith of CRR came to the podium, she was able to utter just two sentences before Justice Kennedy interrupted. "In those cases where intact D&Es or D&Xs are performed," he asked, "in how many of those instances is there serious health risk to the mother that requires the procedure as opposed to simply being an elective procedure?" No statistics were available, Smith replied, and a few moments later Kennedy intervened again to ask "[i]f there is substantial evidence that other procedures or alternate procedures are available," what obstacles precluded their usage?[79] Kennedy grasped "the government's argument that there are alternative

---

[75] Id at 328–29. The *Ayotte* Court acknowledged that this preference had not governed its most recent prior abortion case, as "the parties in *Stenberg* did not ask for, and we did not contemplate, relief more finely drawn" than the voiding of the entire Nebraska partial-birth ban statute. Id at 331.

[76] Id at 331–32. Following New Hampshire's June 2007 repeal of the statute, the District Court dismissed the case as moot. See *Planned Parenthood of Northern New England v N.H. Attorney General*, 2007 WL 329709 (D NH 2007); see also Pam Belluck, *New Hampshire to Repeal Parental Notification Law*, New York Times A22 (June 8, 2007); Norma Love, *N.H. Repeals Parental Notice Law*, Union Leader (Manchester) A2 (June 30, 2007).

[77] Transcript of Argument (cited in note 73), 20. See also Jeffrey Rosen, *Partial Solution*, New Republic 8 (Dec 11, 2006) (highlighting Justice Breyer's effort to point the Court toward "allowing the federal ban to be enjoined only for specific categories of medical conditions in which substantial numbers of doctors believe that D&X abortions are safer than D&E abortions").

[78] Id at 21, 23.

[79] Id at 28–29, 30.

mechanisms," but when Chief Justice John G. Roberts, Jr., asked whether a marginal benefit in safety would be enough to save the procedure from proscription, Smith responded that "I don't believe a marginal benefit in safety is enough and I don't believe that's what we have here."[80] Toward the end of her time, Justice Kennedy asserted that "[i]t seems to me that your argument is that there is always a constitutional right to use what the physician thinks is the safest procedure," but Smith immediately demurred, explaining that pursuant to *Stenberg* and *Casey* there has to be "a substantial body of medical opinion, an objective standard that in fact supports the use of that procedure."[81]

At the very outset of his argument in the second case, the Solicitor General pointed out that "if a doctor really thinks the D&X procedure is the way to go, he can induce fetal demise at the outset of the procedure" and thereby not fall within PBABA's explicit prerequisite that its prohibition applies only in cases of *living* fetuses.[82] "If you look through the record on this point," Clement continued, "I think you will not find any testimony that supports a significant risk from that injection" which would induce fetal demise—"the risks are not significant."[83] Seeking to portray his adversaries' stance as extreme, Clement stated that "it's very clear that their position is one of zero tolerance for any marginal risk to maternal health." That immediately led Justice Kennedy to muse about the meaning of "significant,"[84] but Clement soon returned to his characterization of the appellees' arguments, noting that "their doctors don't think that this is a safer procedure in rare cases, they think it's a safer procedure every single time." In essence, "it's just a question ultimately of whether you're going to defer to individual doctors' judgments," Clement contended. "[T]he question is, when you have a perfectly safe alternative, and you have some doctors who like to do it a different way, can Congress countermand

---

[80] Id at 31, 36–37. In subsequent colloquies, Smith erroneously stated that "doctors perform the same dilation protocols whether they are going to perform a D&E or an intact D&E" and that "they are always looking for a minimal amount of dilation." Id at 40, 41.

[81] Id at 50.

[82] Transcript of Argument, *Gonzales v Planned Parenthood Federation of America*, No 05-1382 (Nov 8, 2006), 4.

[83] Id at 5.

[84] Id at 6.

the doctors' judgment or do the doctors get the final word?"[85]

Justice Kennedy quizzed the Solicitor General on the statute's intent requirement, commenting that "that's important to me because . . . in reading the medical testimony it seemed to me that D&Es . . . result in intact deliveries quite without the intent of the doctor." He challenged Clement that "you pin your whole case on the availability of D&E even though D&Es sometimes inadvertently turn into intact D&Es," but Clement reassured him that "the statute requires the intent at the outset of the procedure."[86]

When PPFA's Eve Gartner's turn came, she warned the Court that with the fetal demise alternative, "the injection procedure carries significant risks for some women." She stated that D&X is "a procedure that is not marginally safer but significantly safer" than a standard D&E, an assertion that immediately led Chief Justice Roberts to ask whether the difference between "marginally safer and significantly safer" was constitutionally meaningful.[87] Like Priscilla Smith, Gartner too answered that "[m]arginal safety would not be enough," but she emphasized that "what Congress has done here is take away from women the option of what may be the safest procedure for her."[88]

In rebuttal, Paul Clement reminded the Court that if it "allows this statute to go into operation, it will not foreclose the possibility of a future pre-enforcement as-applied challenge that focuses on particular medical conditions."[89] His closing words eloquently summarized the government's position: "fetal demise that takes place in utero is one thing. That is abortion as it has been understood. But this procedure, the banned procedure, is something different. This is not about fetal demise in utero. This is something that is far too close to infanticide for society to tolerate."[90]

IV

Experienced observers of the Court believed Justice Kennedy's comments at argument "suggested that he had not made up

---

[85] Id at 14–15.

[86] Id at 16, 25.

[87] Id at 42, 43, 44.

[88] Id at 44, 46.

[89] Id at 51–52.

[90] Id at 53.

his mind" about PBABA's constitutionality notwithstanding his extremely forceful dissent six years earlier in *Stenberg*.[91] In that opinion, Kennedy repeatedly employed the pejorative label "abortionist" to characterize physicians covered by the Nebraska statute[92] while declaring that "[s]tates may take sides in the abortion debate and come down on the side of life."[93] He endorsed "Nebraska's right to declare a moral difference between the procedures" used in D&X and D&E abortions because "D&X perverts the natural birth process to a greater degree than D&E."[94] Emphasizing that "as an ethical and moral matter D&X is distinct from D&E," Kennedy went on to say that "[n]o studies support the contention that the D&X abortion method is safer than other abortion methods."[95] Indeed, "[s]ubstantial evidence supports Nebraska's conclusion that its law denies no woman a safe abortion. The most to be said for the D&X is it may present an unquantified lower risk of complication for a particular patient but that other proven safe procedures remain available even for this patient."[96]

Justice Kennedy's *Stenberg* dissent also criticized what he termed the majority's "physician-first view." States are "entitled to make judgments where high medical authority is in disagreement," he wrote, and the majority's "immense constitutional holding" required complete deference to individual physicians' unfettered preferences.[97] "[M]edical procedures must be governed by moral principles having their foundation in the intrinsic value of human life, including life of the unborn," Kennedy preached. By confronting "an issue of immense moral consequence," Kennedy declared, Nebraska had targeted "a procedure many decent and civilized people find so abhorrent as to be among the most serious of crimes against human life."[98]

---

[91] Linda Greenhouse, *Justices Hear Arguments on Late-Term Abortion*, New York Times A25 (Nov 9, 2006). See also Lyle Denniston, *Commentary: Kennedy Vote in Play on Abortion*, Scotusblog (Nov 8, 2006) (available at http://www.scotusblog.com/wp/commentary-and-analysis/commentary-kennedy-vote-in-play-on-abortion/); Joan Biskupic, *Abortion Case Draws Throngs to High Court*, USA Today A3 (Nov 9, 2006); and Charles Lane, *No Pointers to Ruling in Abortion Case*, Washington Post A3 (Nov 9, 2006).

[92] 530 US at 957, 959, 960, 964, 965.

[93] Id at 961.

[94] Id at 962–63.

[95] Id at 963, 966.

[96] Id at 967.

[97] Id at 969–70, 978.

[98] Id at 979. See also *Hill v Colorado*, 530 US 703, 765, 780, 790 (2000) (Kennedy, J,

Despite the uncertain impression conveyed by Justice Kennedy's comments at oral argument, when the decision in *Gonzales v Carhart* came down on April 18, 2007, he was the author of a five-man majority opinion also joined by Justices Antonin Scalia, Clarence Thomas, Samuel Alito, and Chief Justice Roberts.[99] At the very outset, Kennedy stressed that the PBABA was both "more specific" and "more precise" than the Nebraska statute voided in *Stenberg*.[100] In contrast to his dissent there, Kennedy now spoke of "abortion doctors"[101] and a mention of "the unborn child's development" was balanced by references to "embryonic tissue," "the fetus," and "the entire fetal body."[102]

As his majority included two Justices who had dissented angrily in *Casey*, Scalia and Thomas, Kennedy carefully explained how among the principles "[w]e assume . . . for the purposes of this opinion" was *Casey*'s conclusion that states "may not impose . . . an undue burden" on a woman's right to secure a pre-viability abortion. But he emphasized that *Casey* "struck a balance" between that right and the state's prerogative to "'express profound respect for the life of the unborn,'" a "balance that was central to its holding."[103] He then proceeded, by means of a painstaking analysis of PBABA's precise language, to reject the appellees' contentions that the statute's medical terminology was both unconstitutionally vague and might also prohibit standard D&Es, a breadth of coverage which even the government acknowledged "would impose an undue burden."[104]

Kennedy explained, just as the Solicitor General had emphasized at argument, that "[t]he Act does not restrict an abortion procedure involving the delivery of an expired fetus."[105] Furthermore, § 3(b)(1) expressly stated, Kennedy continued, that "the overt act causing the fetus' death must be separate from delivery. And the overt act must

---

dissenting) (calling abortion "a profound moral issue," suggesting abortion may be "a profound moral wrong" and terming abortion an act of "profound moral consequence").

[99] 127 S Ct 1610 (2007).

[100] Id at 1619.

[101] Id at 1625, 1631, 1632.

[102] Id at 1620, 1621.

[103] Id at 1626, 1627 (quoting 505 US at 877). See also *Hill v Colorado*, 530 US 703, 791 (Kennedy, J, dissenting) (invoking "the reasoned, careful balance" which Kennedy said "was the basis for the opinion in *Casey*").

[104] Id at 1627.

[105] Id.

occur after the delivery to an anatomical landmark. This is because the Act proscribes killing 'the partially delivered fetus,'" which meant "has been delivered" already.[106] What's more, Kennedy said, the statute's specification that a doctor act "deliberately and intentionally" meant that "[i]f a living fetus is delivered past the critical point by accident or inadvertence, the Act is inapplicable."[107]

Earlier in his opinion, Kennedy had highlighted how "[d]octors who attempt at the outset to perform intact D&E may dilate for two full days,"[108] a statement which echoed the Solicitor General's comment during oral argument that "the differences between the two procedures are probably most manifest in the dilation regimen."[109] Now Kennedy again reiterated that "a doctor performing a D&E will not face criminal liability if he or she delivers a fetus beyond the prohibited point by mistake" and emphasized that "[t]he scienter requirements narrow the scope of the Act's prohibition and limit prosecutorial discretion."[110] He stressed that PBABA "does not prohibit the D&E procedure in which the fetus is removed in parts," and underscored that "[t]he Act's intent requirements . . . limit its reach to those physicians who carry out the intact D&E after intending to undertake both steps"—the delivery then followed by the overt act—"at the outset." Kennedy then again repeated that "[i]f the doctor intends to remove the fetus in parts from the outset, the doctor will not have the requisite intent to incur criminal liability."[111]

Kennedy's insistent repetitiveness reflected an intense desire to draw as bright a line as possible between criminally prohibited conduct and medical procedures doctors could employ without worry. He restated how PBABA "departs in material ways from the statute in *Stenberg*," and graphically if not gratuitously explained that "D&E does not involve the delivery of a fetus because it requires the removal of fetal parts that are ripped from the fetus as they are pulled through the cervix."[112] A "standard D&E does not involve

---

[106] Id at 1627–28.

[107] Id at 1628.

[108] Id at 1621.

[109] Transcript of Argument, *Gonzales v Planned Parenthood Federation of America* (cited in note 82), 11.

[110] *Gonzales v Carhart*, 127 S Ct at 1628, 1629.

[111] Id at 1629.

[112] Id at 1630.

a delivery followed by a fatal act," he again expounded, and "an intact delivery is almost always a conscious choice rather than a happenstance."[113]

The majority opinion's prescription was clear: "those doctors who intend to perform a D&E that would involve delivery of a living fetus to one of the Act's anatomical landmarks must adjust their conduct to the law by not attempting to deliver the fetus to either of those points."[114] Kennedy then addressed how PBABA, on its face, did not violate *Casey*'s "substantial obstacle" test, and he also reiterated, quoting *Casey*'s three-Justice plurality, that simply because a law "'has the incidental effect of making it more difficult or more expensive to procure an abortion cannot be enough to invalidate it.'"[115] That plurality's explicit recognition that the state can express "its own regulatory interest in protecting the life of the fetus that may become a child," Kennedy asserted, "cannot be set at naught by interpreting *Casey*'s requirement of a health exception so it becomes tantamount to allowing a doctor to choose the abortion method he or she might prefer. Where it has a rational basis to act, and it does not impose an undue burden, the State may use its regulatory power to bar certain procedures and substitute others, all in furtherance of its legitimate interests in regulating the medical profession in order to promote respect for life, including life of the unborn."[116]

That latter sentence represented the true crux of the majority's holding, and Kennedy expressly grounded it not on the protection of fetal life, but on the state's interest in controlling the particular methods by which fetal life legally could be taken. That holding also reaffirmed the continuing validity and applicability of *Casey*'s decisive undue burden test, and, in conjunction with the majority's earlier acknowledgment that a ban which covered standard D&E procedures would indeed violate that standard,[117] thus created a serious if not fatal impediment to this opinion serving as a direct stepping stone toward further prohibitions of second-trimester abortions.

However, Kennedy immediately added that "for many, D&E is

---

[113] Id at 1631, 1632.

[114] Id at 1632.

[115] Id at 1632, 1633 (quoting 505 US at 874).

[116] Id at 1633.

[117] See text at note 104.

a procedure itself laden with the power to devalue human life."[118] Then he proceeded to deliver several memorable paragraphs of sermonic dicta. "Respect for human life finds an ultimate expression in the bond of love the mother has for her child," he began. "While we find no reliable data to measure the phenomenon, it seems unexceptionable to conclude some women come to regret their choice to abort the infant life they once created and sustained. See Brief for Sandra Cano et al. as *Amici Curiae* in No. 05–380, pp. 22–24. Severe depression and loss of esteem can follow. See *ibid*."[119]

Kennedy's citation of that amicus brief was notable and revealing, but far from odd or extraordinary. The three referenced pages consisted almost entirely of footnote material, quoting from some of the 178 affidavits excerpted in the brief's own ninety-six-page appendix, in support of just two sentences of actual text. Explaining that those women had been asked, "How has abortion affected you?" the two sentences stated that "Typical responses . . . included depression, suicidal thoughts, flashbacks, alcohol and/or drug use, promiscuity, guilt, and secrecy. Each of them made the 'choice' to abort their baby, and they have regretted their 'choices.'"[120] No one sought to demonstrate that these women's declarations were either fraudulent or dishonest, and the scores of affidavits certainly supported the brief's emphasis on what it called "the adverse emotional and psychological effects of abortion" and its claim that "abortion in practice hurts women's health."[121]

No jurist ought to be denounced or demonized for considering real women's real testimonies with the utmost seriousness while judging an abortion case, whether in 2007 or in 1971,[122] and Justice Kennedy certainly was attempting to do just that. "In a decision so fraught with emotional consequence," he then went on, doctors

---

[118] *Gonzales v Carhart*, 127 S Ct at 1633.

[119] Id at 1634.

[120] Linda Boston Schlueter, Brief of Sandra Cano, et al, *Gonzales v Carhart*, No 05-380 (filed May 22, 2006), 22–24. For a discussion of this brief prior to Justice Kennedy's citation of it, see Reva B. Siegel, *The New Politics of Abortion: An Equality Analysis of Woman-Protective Abortion Restrictions*, 2007 U Ill L Rev 991, 1025–26 n 142.

[121] Id at 1, 2.

[122] See, e.g., Nancy Stearns, Brief Amicus Curiae on Behalf of New Women Lawyers, et al, *Roe v Wade* and *Doe v Bolton*, Nos 70-18 and 70-40 (filed Aug 2, 1971), 7 (arguing that "[c]arrying, giving birth to, and raising an unwanted child can be one of the most painful and long-lasting punishments that a person can endure").

might understandably believe it in a patient's best interest "not to disclose precise details of the means that will be used."[123] Kennedy's reference to "emotional consequence" directly echoed a passage from *Casey*—"Abortion is a unique act. It is an act fraught with consequences for others: for the woman who must live with the implications of her decision . . ."—that five Justices there had endorsed.[124] But with regard to doctors not detailing the "means that will be used," Kennedy continued, it is "precisely this lack of information concerning the way in which the fetus will be killed that is of legitimate concern to the State."[125] After quoting *Casey*'s characterization of abortion as "a decision that has such profound and lasting meaning,"[126] Kennedy then opined that "[t]he state has an interest in ensuring so grave a choice is well informed. It is self-evident that a mother who comes to regret her choice to abort must struggle with grief more anguished and sorrow more profound when she learns, only after the event . . . that she allowed a doctor to pierce the skull and vacuum the fast-developing brain of her unborn child, a child assuming the human form."[127]

Kennedy's language may have been purposely graphic, but it also once again directly echoed a passage from *Casey*: "In attempting to ensure that a woman apprehend the full consequences of her decision, the State furthers the legitimate purpose of reducing the risk that a woman may elect an abortion, only to discover later, with devastating psychological consequences, that her decision was not fully informed."[128] Yet notwithstanding his gratuitous language, Kennedy proceeded toward what in its essence would be an exceptionally constricted affirmance of PBABA's facial constitutionality. "The prohibition in the Act would be unconstitutional, under precedents we here assume to be controlling," he again qualified, "if it 'subject[ed] [women] to significant health risks,'"[129] a phrase which

---

[123] *Gonzales v Carhart*, 127 S Ct at 1634.

[124] 505 US at 852. See also *Hill v Colorado*, 530 US 703, 791 (2000) (Kennedy, J, dissenting) (also quoting *Casey*'s "fraught with consequences" language).

[125] *Gonzales v Carhart*, 127 S Ct at 1634.

[126] Id (quoting 505 US at 873).

[127] Id. See also *Hill v Colorado*, 530 US 703, 792 (Kennedy, J, dissenting) (calling abortion "one of life's gravest moral crises").

[128] 505 US at 882.

[129] *Gonzales v Carhart*, 127 S Ct at 1635.

he drew most directly from *Ayotte*[130] and indirectly from *Casey*.[131] Whether PBABA "creates significant health risks for women has been a contested factual question," Kennedy acknowledged, and "both sides have medical support for their position," he claimed.[132] "There is documented medical disagreement over whether the Act's prohibitions would ever impose significant medical health risks on women," and "[t]he question becomes whether the Act can stand when this medical uncertainty persists."[133]

"The State's interest in promoting respect for human life at all stages in the pregnancy," Kennedy stated, meant that it could mandate "reasonable alternative procedures" as it "need not give abortion doctors unfettered choice . . . nor should it elevate their status above other physicians in the medical community."[134] All in all, "the medical uncertainty over whether the Act's prohibition creates significant health risks provides a sufficient basis to conclude in this facial attack that the Act does not impose an undue burden," Kennedy concluded. "Alternatives are available."[135] For one, "[i]f the intact D&E procedure is truly necessary in some circumstances, it appears likely that an injection that kills the fetus is an alternative." In addition, since, with standard D&Es, PBABA "allows . . . a commonly used and generally accepted method, so it does not construct a substantial obstacle to the abortion right."[136]

Finally, toward the very end of the majority opinion, Justice Kennedy addressed the question that had dominated so much of the two cases' earlier litigation and briefing. "[W]e do not in the circumstances here place dispositive weight on Congress' findings," he wrote. "The Court retains an independent constitutional duty to review factual findings where constitutional rights are at stake."[137] He acknowledged that "some recitations in the Act are factually incorrect," including Congress's finding that "there existed a medical consensus that the prohibited procedure is never medically nec-

---

[130] See 546 US at 328 ("it would be unconstitutional to apply the Act in a manner that subjects minors to significant health risks").

[131] See 505 US at 880.

[132] *Gonzales v Carhart*, 127 S Ct at 1635.

[133] Id at 1636.

[134] Id.

[135] Id at 1637.

[136] Id.

[137] Id.

essary. The evidence presented in the District Courts contradicts that conclusion," and "[u]ncritical deference to Congress' factual findings in these cases is inappropriate."[138]

Nonetheless, Kennedy said, "[c]onsiderations of marginal safety, including the balance of risks, are within the legislative competence when the regulation is rational and in pursuit of legitimate ends." Thus, "if some procedures have different risks than others, it does not follow that the State is altogether barred from imposing reasonable regulations."[139] PBABA was not facially invalid "where there is uncertainty over whether the barred procedure is ever necessary to preserve a woman's health, given the availability of other abortion procedures that are considered to be safe alternatives." Lastly, Kennedy emphasized, physicians could mount "pre-enforcement, as-applied challenges" to PBABA "if it can be shown that in discrete and well-defined instances a particular condition has or is likely to occur in which the procedure prohibited by the Act must be used."[140]

Only a single, very brief concurring opinion by Justice Thomas, joined by Justice Scalia, was appended to Anthony Kennedy's insistently detailed and tightly delimited opinion for the Court. Thomas reiterated his view that "the Court's abortion jurisprudence, including *Casey* . . . has no basis in the Constitution," but he then went on to add that the issue of "whether the Act constitutes a permissible exercise of Congress' power under the Commerce Clause is not before the Court" since the challengers had never raised that question.[141] Several earlier law review articles had analyzed PBABA's constitutional vulnerability in light of *United States v Lopez* and *United States v Morrison*,[142] but, as Neal Devins has highlighted, during congressional consideration of the legislation, "the bill's federalism implications" received "no meaningful attention."[143] Senator Dianne Feinstein, Democrat of California, "was

---

[138] Id at 1637–38 (internal citation omitted).

[139] Id at 1638.

[140] Id.

[141] Id at 1640 (Thomas, J, concurring).

[142] See Allan Ides, *The Partial-Birth Abortion Act of 2003 and the Commerce Clause*, 20 Const Comm 441 (2003–04); Robert J. Pushaw, Jr., *Does Congress Have the Constitutional Power to Prohibit Partial-Birth Abortion?* 42 Harv J Leg 319 (2005). See also Brannon P. Denning, *Gonzales v Carhart: An Alternate Opinion*, 2006–2007 Cato Supreme Ct Rev 167.

[143] Neal Devins, *How Congress Paved the Way for the Rehnquist Court's Federalism Revival: Lessons from the Federal Partial Birth Abortion Ban*, 21 St John's J Leg Comm 461, 464, 466 (2007).

the only lawmaker to suggest that the bill was inconsistent with Rehnquist Court federalism decisions."[144] Thomas's concurrence raised the surprising possibility that a broader-gauged constitutional attack on PBABA might have attracted an unexpected vote to strike down the statute, but at a minimum it suggested that Thomas aspires to a consistent application of his constitutional principles irrespective of their impact on his presumed policy preferences.

Justice Ruth Bader Ginsburg's dissent, joined by Justices John Paul Stevens, David H. Souter, and Stephen G. Breyer, called the majority's decision "alarming" and preposterously alleged that it "refuses to take *Casey* and *Stenberg* seriously."[145] Asserting that Justice Kennedy's opinion employed "flimsy and transparent justifications" to uphold PBABA, Ginsburg complained that the act failed to further the government's professed interest in protecting fetal life since "[t]he law saves not a single fetus from destruction, for it targets only a *method* of performing abortion."[146] Failing to confront fairly and frontally Kennedy's argument that government's interest in regulating the practice of medicine allowed it to draw a moral bright line between different methods of fetal demise,[147] Ginsburg instead mused rhetorically that "[o]ne wonders how long a line that saves no fetus from destruction will hold up in the face of the Court's 'moral concerns.'"[148] Ginsburg did accurately identify that "the Court determines that a 'rational' ground is enough to uphold the Act,"[149] and she conceded that the majority opinion did not "foreclose entirely a constitutional challenge" at a later time to PBABA. "One may anticipate that such a preenforcement challenge will be mounted swiftly," she rather suggestively declared.[150] In conclusion, she stated that "[a] decision so at odds with our jurisprudence should not have staying power" and asserted that "the notion" that PBABA "furthers any legitimate governmental interest is, quite simply, irrational."[151]

---

[144] Id at 466.

[145] *Gonzales v Carhart*, 127 S Ct at 1641 (Ginsburg, J, dissenting).

[146] Id at 1646, 1647.

[147] See text at note 116 (quoting 127 S Ct at 1633).

[148] *Gonzales v Carhart*, 127 S Ct at 1650 (Ginsburg, J, dissenting) (quoting 127 S Ct at 1633).

[149] Id (quoting 127 S Ct at 1633, 1638).

[150] Id at 1651, 1652.

[151] Id at 1653.

V

When the decision in *Gonzales v Carhart* came down on the morning of April 18, many reactions were eminently predictable even if not particularly perceptive. Jay Sekulow of the American Center for Law and Justice, who had filed a substantive amicus brief in defense of PBABA, praised the ruling as "a monumental victory for the preservation of human life."[152] On the other hand, Dr. Douglas W. Laube, president of the American College of Obstetricians and Gynecologists, denounced the decision as "shameful and incomprehensible."[153] Far more accurately, attorney Bonnie Scott Jones of CRR castigated the majority for "directly overturning *Stenberg*'s mandate to protect women's health in the face of medical uncertainty" and warned that the holding "opens the door for legislatures to dictate medical treatment in virtually any area of medical practice."[154]

Among ostensibly less partisan observers, discernment also varied greatly. The dean of Supreme Court journalists, Lyle Denniston, quickly pronounced that *Gonzales v Carhart* was "a decision that surely is on a par, historically, with *Roe v Wade*," and predicted that the ruling "guarantees" further litigation to establish "whether anything remains legally and practically speaking of the constitutional right to abortion."[155] He opined that the case "almost certainly will infect relations among the Justices for some time to come" and that "the Court's work as a collegial institution may well suffer." Denniston added that "the decision's treatment of abortion precedents gives the impression that the work the Justices do . . . may not have any real enduring effect, if even one new Justice arrives." He

---

[152] Tony Mauro, *High Court Upholds Ban on "Partial Birth" Abortion*, Legal Times (April 19, 2007) (available at http://www.law.com/jsp/article.jsp?id=1176887056341) (quoting Sekulow).

[153] Dr. Douglas W. Laube, *ACOG Statement on the U.S. Supreme Court Decision Upholding the Partial-Birth Abortion Ban Act of 2003* (April 18, 2007) (available at http://www.acog.org/from_home/publications/press_releases/nr04-18-07.cfm). See also R. Alta Charo, *The Partial Death of Abortion Rights*, 356 New England J Med 2125 (2007); Michael F. Greene, *The Intimidation of American Physicians—Banning Partial-Birth Abortions*, 356 New England J Med 2128 (2007); and George J. Annas, *The Supreme Court and Abortion Rights*, 356 New England J Med 2201 (2007).

[154] Bonnie Scott Jones, *A Sharp Reversal* (April 18, 2007) (available at http://www.scotusblog.com/wp/commentary-and-analysis/a-sharp-reversal-commentary-from-the-center-for-reproductive-rights/).

[155] Lyle Denniston, *Commentary: Some Consequences of Carhart II* (April 18, 2007) (available at http://www.scotusblog.com/wp/uncategorized/commentary-some-consequences-of-carhart-ii/).

did briefly acknowledge that Justice Kennedy's majority opinion "read like a narrow, perhaps even cautious decision," but he nonetheless insisted that it "makes a substantial revision of the present law of abortion."[156]

In contrast, other first-day news reports emphasized "the Court's balancing of the various interests" and highlighted as "[m]ost notable" Justice Kennedy's emphasis on "ethical and moral concerns."[157] As Yale law professor Jack Balkin accurately stressed, "[t]he actual interest the Court is asserting is not the interest in protecting potential life but rather an interest in not having the life of fetuses ended in ways that the legislature regards as particularly gruesome."[158] In addition, with regard to Justice Kennedy's weighty concern for the emotional consequences women could subsequently suffer once they fully understood what an intact abortion entailed, both Balkin and Columbia law professor Michael Dorf rightly pointed out how, in Balkin's words, "the appropriate remedy . . . would be *informing* the women about the nature of intact D&E, not preventing the women from choosing whether to undergo the procedure."[159] Balkin also suggested that Kennedy's emphatic anxiety about the adverse mental health consequences of abortion "might lead states to pass a wide range of new laws under the rubric of 'informed consent' that would require doctors to show women the results of ultrasound imaging of the fetus before it is aborted, to describe in gruesome detail how the fetus will be terminated, dismembered and removed," etc.[160]

---

[156] Id.

[157] Linda Greenhouse, *In Reversal, Justices Back Ban on Method of Abortion*, New York Times A1 (April 19, 2007).

[158] Jack Balkin, *Gonzales v Carhart—Three Comments* (April 18, 2007) (available at http://balkin.blogspot.com/2007/04/gonzales-v-carhart-three-comments.html).

[159] Id. See also Michael C. Dorf, *Supreme Court Partial Birth Abortion Ruling* (April 18, 2007) (available at http://michaeldorf.org/2007/04/supreme-court-partial-birth-abortion .html). Additionally see Joanna Grossman and Linda McClain, *New Justices, New Rules: The Supreme Court Upholds the Federal Partial-Birth Abortion Ban Act of 2003*, Findlaw (May 1, 2007) (available at http://writ.lp.findlaw.com/commentary/20070501_mcclain.html), and Joanna Grossman and Linda McClain, *Gonzales v. Carhart: How the Supreme Court's Validation of the Federal Partial-Birth Abortion Ban Act Affects Women's Constitutional Liberty and Equality*, Findlaw (May 7, 2007) (available at http://writ.lp.findlaw.com/ commentary/ 20070507_mcclain.html) (both highlighting how Justice Kennedy's emphasis upon "emotional consequence" directly echoed *Planned Parenthood v Casey*).

[160] Jack Balkin, *The Big News About Gonzales v Carhart—It's the Informed Consent, Stupid* (April 19, 2007) (available at http://balkin.blogspot.com/2007/04/big-news-about-gonzales-v-carhart.html).

VI

While quickly composed newspaper editorials denounced the "fundamental dishonesty"[161] of an "unconscionable" decision,[162] more assiduous journalists interviewed experienced physicians and reported that the ruling "as a practical matter, is unlikely to have much of an effect" on the actual performance of abortions.[163] Citing data that the Alan Guttmacher Institute first published in 2003,[164] reporters highlighted how an estimated total of only 2,200 intact procedures had been performed in 2000, by just thirty-one abortion providers.[165] That represented less than one-fifth of 1 percent—0.17—of all U.S. abortions, and in part reflected not only how the U.S. abortion rate had dropped by 22 percent between 1987 and 2002,[166] but also how the proportion of abortions taking place in the second trimester of pregnancy—at thirteen weeks' gestation or later—had declined to only 11 percent of all abortions by 2001.[167] In the preceding decade, the proportion of abortions performed during the first eight weeks of pregnancy had risen from 52 to 59 percent of all procedures,[168] and for second trimester abortions, standard D&Es were used for 99 percent at thirteen to fifteen weeks, 94.6 percent at sixteen to twenty weeks, and 85 percent at twenty-one or more weeks in 2000.[169]

---

[161] *Denying the Right to Choose*, New York Times A26 (April 19, 2007).

[162] *A U-Turn on Abortion*, Los Angeles Times (April 19, 2007) (available at http://www.latimes.com/news/opinion/la-ed-abortion19apr19,0,4748632.story?coll=la-opinion-leftrail).

[163] Gina Kolata, *Anger and Alternatives on Abortion*, New York Times A11 (April 21, 2007). See also David J. Garrow, *Don't Assume the Worst*, New York Times A15 (April 21, 2007) (stating that the "extremely limited" ruling will affect only a "tiny percentage" of abortions).

[164] Lawrence B. Finer and Stanley K. Henshaw, *Abortion Incidence and Services in the United States in 2000*, 35 Perspectives on Sexual and Reproductive Health 6, 13 (2003).

[165] David Brown, *Data Lacking on Abortion Method*, Washington Post A8 (April 19, 2007).

[166] Lawrence B. Finer, et al, *Reasons U.S. Women Have Abortions: Quantitative and Qualitative Perspectives*, 37 Perspectives on Sexual and Reproductive Health 110 (2005). See also Rachel K. Jones, et al, *Abortion in the United States: Incidence and Access to Services, 2005*, 40 Perspectives on Sexual and Reproductive Health 6 (2008).

[167] Lawrence B. Finer, et al, *Timing of Steps and Reasons for Delays in Obtaining Abortions in the United States*, 74 Contraception 334 (2006). In 1999, only 1.5 percent of all abortions, or a total of 9,643, were performed at or after 21 weeks' gestation. See Stephen T. Chasen, et al, *Dilation and Evacuation at >20 Weeks: Comparison of Operative Techniques*, 190 Am J Obstetrics and Gynecology 1180 (2004).

[168] Id.

[169] Phillip G. Stubblefield, et al, *Methods for Induced Abortion*, 104 Obstetrics and Gynecology 174, 179 (2004).

As a small number of diligent journalists soon highlighted, most physicians who previously had performed intact D&Es quickly concluded that the best way to cope with the Supreme Court's decision would be to insure that fetuses whom they desired to remove largely intact were no longer "living" prior to when delivery commenced. As Dr. Eve Espey of the University of New Mexico told David G. Savage of the *Los Angeles Times*, "most are planning on going to fetal injections" so as to insure prior fetal demise.[170] Indeed, two clinical research reports published in major medical journals in the years before PBABA's passage had previously detailed how almost all physicians who performed late-term abortions already chose to induce fetal death before delivery by injecting the drug digoxin into the amniotic sac so as to end fetal cardiac function.[171] The studies explained that proper placement of the injection needle could be confirmed by the aspiration of amniotic fluid, and that subsequent fetal heart activity could be monitored by ultrasound.[172] Doctors administered the digoxin a day before performing delivery, usually in conjunction with the insertion of osmotic laminaria intended to obtain wide dilation of the cervix.[173] Physicians preferred to induce prior fetal death for both medical and emotional reasons. After the fetus dies, "[t]he result is soft, macerated tissue, which many clinicians believe eases evacuation of the fetus and decreases procedure duration," one article explained.[174] In addition, over 90 percent of patients "stated a strong preference for fetal demise before abortion."[175]

---

[170] David G. Savage, *Enigmatic Jurist Recasts the Debate on Abortion*, Los Angeles Times A22 (April 22, 2007).

[171] Rebecca A. Jackson, et al, *Digoxin to Facilitate Late Second-Trimester Abortion: A Randomized, Masked, Placebo-Controlled Trial*, 97 Obstetrics and Gynecology 471 (2001) ("in our nonrandom telephone survey of 20 D&E providers nationwide, 95% reported its routine use for terminations at or after 20 weeks gestation"); Eleanor A. Drey, et al, *Safety of Intra-Amniotic Digoxin Administration Before Late Second-Trimester Abortion by Dilation and Evacuation*, 182 Am J Obstetrics and Gynecology 1063 (2000).

[172] Jackson, et al, 97 Obstetrics and Gynecology at 472 (cited in note 171).

[173] Stubblefield, et al, 104 Obstetrics and Gynecology at 179 (cited in note 169), expressly states that an intact D&E "requires 2 or more days of laminaria treatment to obtain wide dilation of the cervix." See also Finer and Henshaw, 35 Perspectives on Sexual and Reproductive Health at 13 n (cited in note 164), who likewise state that intact procedures entail "deliberate dilation of the cervix, usually over several days."

[174] Jackson, et al, 97 Obstetrics and Gynecology at 471 (cited in note 171). See also National Abortion Federation, *2007 Clinical Policy Guidelines* (available at http://www.prochoice.org/pubs_research/publications/downloads/professional_education/cpgs_2007.pdf), 20 n 16 ("In addition to achieving fetal demise, fetocidal agents induce softening of fetal cortical bones").

[175] Id at 475. See also Drey, et al, 182 Am J Obstetrics and Gynecology at 1063 (cited in note 171) ("both the patient and the clinician may prefer to abort a dead fetus").

The first of the two clinical studies stated that "there are no reports of maternal side effects or complications as a result of this use of digoxin" and concluded that "digoxin injection appears safe."[176] The second article noted that contraindications for the use of digoxin included renal failure and uncontrolled hyperthyroidism, and reported that approximately 15 percent of patients experienced subsequent vomiting.[177] However, it too concluded that "[t]here were no complications associated with intra-amniotic injection."[178]

In the wake of *Gonzales v Carhart*, Dr. Nancy Stanwood, an assistant professor at the University of Rochester Medical Center, told the *Los Angeles Times'* David Savage that "[w]e physicians will make some slight changes in our practice. An injection for the fetus adds another risk to woman's health, and it means added time and money. But if that's what's necessary, that's what we will do."[179] Within weeks of the decision, Planned Parenthood Federation of America (PPFA) altered its *Manual of Medical Standards and Guidelines*, which PPFA lawyers explain "govern all of our affiliates,"[180] to require that "digoxin must be given for all pregnancy terminations at 20 weeks or more" as well as at eighteen and nineteen weeks' gestation if advance osmotic dilation of the cervix is initiated.[181] PPFA's *Manual* expressly states that "using digoxin for fetal demise is safe for the woman."[182]

In the months following the *Gonzales* decision, several other journalists confirmed and enriched those initial indications of how late-term abortion providers would cope with PBABA's strictures. Dr. Eleanor A. Drey of the University of California, San Francisco, a coauthor of the two digoxin studies, told Rebecca Vesely of the *Oakland Tribune* that some providers were using digoxin for pro-

---

[176] Drey, et al, 182 Am J Obstetrics and Gynecology at 1063, 1066 (cited in note 171). See also National Abortion Federation, *2007 Clinical Policy Guidelines* at 20, n 16 (cited in note 174) (calling intra-amniotic digoxin and similar injections "safe, effective regimens").

[177] Jackson, et al, 97 Obstetrics and Gynecology at 472, 474 (cited in note 171).

[178] Id at 474.

[179] Savage, *Enigmatic Jurist* (cited in note 170).

[180] E-mail message from Eve C. Gartner (Deputy Director, Public Policy Litigation and Law, PPFA) to David J. Garrow, Nov 28, 2007 (on file with the author).

[181] Planned Parenthood Federation of America, *PPFA Manual of Medical Standards and Guidelines*, May 2007. This manual unfortunately is not publicly available, but its May 2007 *Digoxin Injection* update is on file with the author.

[182] Id.

cedures as early as fourteen weeks' gestation.[183] Dr. Drey noted that fetal death could also be achieved by cutting the umbilical cord, but that no clinical data existed on the safety or efficacy of that practice. "There's no nice way of having a second trimester abortion and no nice way to talk about it," Drey explained. Her university's clinic at San Francisco General Hospital would continue to perform noninjection second trimester D&Es, she said, but "[w]e'll have fewer observers in the room and we will document the procedure as 'standard D&E.'"[184]

Most second-trimester providers, however, did expand their use of digoxin. In Michigan, Northland Family Planning, which operates three clinics in Detroit's suburbs, previously had used injections from twenty weeks' gestation "because doctors felt it made removal of the fetus easier" but now employed them as early as fourteen weeks.[185] WomanCare, with six clinics across Michigan, began using digoxin for every abortion from eighteen weeks' gestation. "It's awful. It's unnecessary. It's dangerous. It's more complicated. It makes the woman go through another procedure that's not necessary," Dr. Alberto Hodari told the *Detroit News*.[186] In Massachusetts, four major Boston-area hospitals began using digoxin from approximately twenty weeks' gestation, with Dr. Michael F. Greene, director of obstetrics at Massachusetts General, telling the *Boston Globe* that the injections are "trivially simple" and, in the *Globe*'s words, "add no risk."[187] At Oregon Health and Science University in Portland, digoxin injections were now required from twenty weeks' gestation, Professor Mark Nichols told the *Globe*. In addition, medical and nursing students "are no longer invited to watch later-term abortions, for fear one might misinterpret the procedure and lodge a criminal complaint," the *Globe* added.[188]

When all of the most revealing and well-informed medical commentary is considered, the conclusion that *Gonzales v Carhart* has

---

[183] Rebecca Vesely, *Courts Force New Abortion Methods*, Oakland Tribune (June 4, 2007) (available at http://findarticles.com/p/articles/mi_qn4176/is_20070604/ai_n19199832/print).

[184] Id.

[185] Kim Kozlowski, *Abortion Procedure Fuels Debate*, Detroit News (July 30, 2007) (available at http://cul.detmich.com/detnews_jul30_2007/detnews_jul30_2007.html).

[186] Id. See also Carole Joffe, *The Abortion Procedure Ban*, Dissent 57, 58 (Fall 2007).

[187] Carey Goldberg, *Shots Assist in Aborting Fetuses*, Boston Globe (Aug 10, 2007) (available at http://www.boston.com/news/local/articles/2007/08/10/shots_assist_in_aborting_fetuses/).

[188] Id.

done little more than require the modest number of physicians who perform intact D&Es to utilize in all late second-trimester procedures an injection protocol that most of them already used and that credible clinical studies hold to be completely safe seems almost impossible to avoid. In light of both PBABA's own requirement that its prohibition applies only in cases of "living" fetuses, and Justice Kennedy's insistent articulation of a bright-line intent test, there frankly appears to be virtually no practical possibility that a plausible criminal prosecution under PBABA could be mounted by any U.S. attorney and the U.S. Department of Justice anywhere in the country. Doctors' own rational and understandable safeguards, such as now drastically minimizing the number of firsthand witnesses to any late-term abortion, further insulate physicians from any credible worries that a criminal indictment will ever be brought alleging a violation of PBABA's prohibition.

VII

If the medical consequences of *Gonzales v Carhart* now appear to be far more modest than activists and editorialists initially proclaimed, the decision's political impact also may be far more limited than some observers at first predicted. One week after the ruling, National Public Radio (NPR) asked PBABA's strategic and spiritual godfather, Douglas Johnson of the National Right to Life Committee (NRLC), where abortion opponents would turn next. In reply, Johnson noted that nine states—within days Georgia would become the tenth—already required abortion providers "to offer the woman an opportunity to view an ultrasound before she proceeds. I think you'll see more states adopting that type of legislation." Given the emphasis Justice Kennedy's opinion placed on pregnant women's understanding of the consequences of abortion, "I think that bodes well for these ultrasound full disclosure bills . . . allowing the woman the opportunity to see the ultrasound," Johnson added.[189]

Johnson's focus on fetal ultrasound appeared to signal a strikingly narrow and indeed cautiously incremental short-term agenda. However, William Saletan, a savvy abortion politics analyst, perceptively

---

[189] National Public Radio, *Morning Edition* (April 26, 2007) (available at http://www.npr.org/templates/story/story.php?storyId=9843340). See also Patrik Jonsson, *Ultrasound: Latest Tool in Battle Over Abortion*, Christian Science Monitor (May 15, 2007) (available at http://www.csmonitor.com/2007/0515/p03s03-ussc.htm).

highlighted the underlying tension between *Gonzales*'s reliance on where fetal demise occurs—inside or outside the womb—and abortion opponents' new emphasis on fetal imaging rather than "partial-birth." Ultrasound, Saletan explained, "has exposed the life in the womb to those of us who didn't want to see what abortion kills. The fetus is squirming, and so are we."[190] A policy focus on ultrasound shifts political debates away from abortion techniques to fetal growth, and from what happens when a fetus is *removed* from the womb, whether intact or in parts, to what is happening *within* the womb prior to the onset of *every* abortion procedure. Indeed, Saletan acknowledged, in comparison to various state efforts to force medically distorted, government-drafted screeds upon abortion patients under the guise of "informed consent," "ultrasound is the least onerous"[191] and perhaps the most objective and reasonable as well.

NRLC's incrementalist agenda meshed well with public opinion soundings taken soon after *Gonzales* came down. Respondents to a Gallup poll in early May 2007 were asked whether "a specific abortion procedure known as 'late term' abortion or 'partial birth' abortion . . . should be legal or illegal," and 72 percent said "illegal" versus only 22 percent who chose "legal."[192] In contrast, only 35 percent of those same respondents answered affirmatively when asked, "Would you like to see the Supreme Court overturn its 1973 *Roe* versus *Wade* decision concerning abortion, or not?" Fifty-three percent said no, although those numbers represented a significant shift from January 2006, when 66 percent had answered no and just 25 percent said yes.[193]

---

[190] William Saletan, *Window to the Womb*, Washington Post B2 (April 29, 2007).

[191] Id.

[192] See Jeffrey M. Jones, *Slim Majority Approves of Supreme Court Following Partial-Birth Ruling*, Gallup News Service (May 15, 2007) (available at http://www.gallup.com/poll/27592/Slim-Majority-Approves-Supreme-Court-Following-PartialBirth-Ruling.aspx), and *Abortion and Birth Control* (available at http://www.pollingreport.com/abortion.htm). A Pew Research Center poll, conducted during August 2007 and using the exact same language as the Gallup question, showed 75 percent of more than 3,000 respondents choosing "illegal" and only 17 "legal" (available at http://www.pollingreport.com/abortion.htm). In contrast, an ABC News/*Washington Post* poll conducted in mid-July 2007 used a very differently and perhaps less clearly worded question—"The Supreme Court recently upheld a federal restriction on the procedure known as partial birth abortion, banning the procedure except when a woman's life is at risk. Do you approve or disapprove of this decision?"—that resulted in only 55 percent of respondents choosing "approve" versus 43 percent who said "disapprove" (also available at http://www.pollingreport.com/abortion.htm).

[193] Gallup Poll, May 10–13, 2007, and Jan 20–22, 2006 (available at http://www.pollingreport.com/abortion.htm).

Analyzing the more detailed results of the May 2007 poll, Gallup's Lydia Saad underscored how a total of 58 percent of respondents indicated they "think abortion should either be limited to only a few circumstances or illegal in all circumstances." In contrast, only 41 percent "think it should be legal in all or most circumstances."[194] She pointed out how "relatively few Americans are positioned at either extreme of the spectrum of beliefs—saying abortion should be legal in either all circumstances (26%) or illegal in all circumstances (18%)," and she likewise highlighted how "[j]ust 16%" said "they will only vote for candidates for major offices who share their views on abortion."[195] The CBS News/*New York Times* poll similarly asked respondents to choose from among three options: "Abortion should be generally available to those who want it; or, abortion should be available, but under stricter limits than it is now; or, abortion should not be permitted." In mid-May 2007, 37 percent of respondents answered "stricter limits" and 21 percent chose "not permitted"—a 58 percent total that matched Gallup's figure. Those answering "generally available" came to 39 percent in May, rose to 41 percent in mid-July 2007, but declined to 34 percent by early September 2007, as opposed to a total of 64 percent choosing either "stricter limits" (39) or "not permitted" (25).[196]

Those poll results clearly signaled that an incrementalist strategy aiming at "stricter limits" would continue to produce far more successful results for abortion opponents than any "absolutist" focus on outlawing all abortions or reversing *Roe v Wade*. Nonetheless, in late May a significant number of "absolutist" advocates publicly denounced right-to-life leaders such as Dr. James C. Dobson, chairman of Focus on the Family, who had praised and celebrated the *Gonzales* ruling. Emphasizing, like Justice Ginsburg's dissent, that "this ban cannot prevent a *single* abortion," they angrily complained about how "many national ministries have spent years using the PBA ban to motivate financial donations, all the while *misrepre-*

---

[194] Lydia Saad, *Public Divided on "Pro-Choice" vs. "Pro-Life" Labels*, Gallup News Service (May 21, 2007) (available at http://www.gallup.com/poll/27628/Public-Divided-Pro Choice-vs-ProLife-Abortion-Labels.aspx).

[195] Id. The partisan breakdown on that latter question was 17 percent for Republicans and 14 percent for Democrats.

[196] CBS News/*New York Times* Poll, May 18–23, 2007, July 7–17, 2007, and Sept 4–9, 2007 (available at http://www.pollingreport.com/abortion.htm).

senting the legal effect of the ban."[197] The absolutists decried *Gonzales*'s careful distinctions between different methods of abortion as "more wicked than *Roe*,"[198] and Colorado Right to Life president Brian Rohrbough, a leading absolutist, deplored how "[t]he broader movement is claiming that we're saving lives, and we're not."[199]

The absolutists' fury toward the major national antiabortion groups was reminiscent of the outrage that gripped a significant portion of the right-to-life movement in the late 1980s after it became clear that not even the outspokenly "pro-life" presidency of Ronald Reagan would lead to any federal constitutional amendment or statute that would reverse or undercut *Roe*. That intense disillusionment spiraled downward into terrorist attacks that took the lives of three doctors, three other clinic personnel, and one law enforcement officer before dissipating in the wake of the 1994 enactment of the federal Freedom of Access to Clinic Entrances Act,[200] but in 2007 the new anger was instead channeled into efforts to propose and pass state constitutional amendments that would proclaim fertilized embryos to be "persons" in the eyes of the law. Such a declaration of fetal personhood would contradict federal constitutional protection of a woman's right to choose abortion at any stage of pregnancy and thereby create a head-on collision with *Roe v Wade*. Supporters especially focused on Georgia's Human Life Amendment, H.R. 536, which would need to receive two-thirds or more support in each legislative chamber in order to appear on the statewide ballot for majority ratification.[201]

As absolutists' efforts jelled, albeit with little notice by major news

---

[197] Brian Rohrbough, et al, *An Open Letter to Dr. James Dobson*, May 23, 2007 (available at http://www.coloradorighttolife.org/openletter). See also Alan Cooperman, *Supreme Court Ruling Brings Split in Antiabortion Movement*, Washington Post A3 (June 4, 2007). A few abortion opponents had voiced similar criticisms as early as 1997. See Garrow, *Liberty and Sexuality* at 738 (cited in note 2) (quoting Matt Trewhella and Judie Brown).

[198] Id.

[199] Stephanie Simon, *Absolutists Turn Against Other Foes of Abortion*, Los Angeles Times A1 (June 6, 2007).

[200] Garrow, *Liberty and Sexuality* at 673, 702–14 (cited in note 2); David J. Garrow, *Abortion Before and After Roe v. Wade*, 62 Albany L Rev 833, 842–43, 846–48 (1999). See also David J. Garrow, *A Deadly, Dying Fringe*, New York Times A27 (Jan 6, 1995).

[201] Georgia HR 536 (available at http://www.legis.ga.gov/legis/2007_08/search/hr536.htm). See also Andy Peters, *Ga. Legislators Have Roe in Their Sites*, Fulton County Daily Report (Feb 4, 2008) (available at http://www.dailyreportonline.com/Editorial/News/singleEdit.asp?individual_SQL=2%2F4%2F2008%4021037); Mike Billips, *House Panel Tables Human Life Amendment*, Macon Telegraph (Feb 21, 2008) (available at http://www.macon.com/206/story/273390.html).

outlets, long-time prolife lawyer James Bopp, Jr., a veteran Supreme Court litigator who had submitted an amicus brief in *Gonzales v Carhart*, distributed an erudite and strongly argued warning memo to antiabortion colleagues. Writing in tandem with Richard Coleson, another experienced right-to-life attorney, Bopp reviewed the unhappy history of attempts to reverse *Roe* and prohibit abortion. In the 1970s and '80s, activists had hoped "a federal constitutional amendment or statute" might someday be adopted, but "prospects for doing so now or in the near future are nonexistent," Bopp bluntly stated.[202] At the Supreme Court, only a partial victory could be won, for even *Roe*'s most outspoken foe, Justice Antonin Scalia, "believes that the Constitution requires return of abortion regulation to the states, not that it requires protection of the unborn." Indeed, Bopp emphasized, "[t]he Supreme Court's current makeup assures that a declared federal constitutional right to abortion remains secure for the present. This means that now is not the time to pass *state* constitutional amendments or bills banning abortion," for any such enactments would immediately be struck down by lower federal courts and might not even be granted review by the Supreme Court. The result would be "yet another federal court decision declaring that state law on abortion is superseded by the federal constitution," plus "the pro-abortion attorneys who brought the legal challenge will collect statutory attorneys fees from the state that enacted the provision in the amount of hundreds of thousands of dollars." Any absolutist enactment will thus "have enriched the pro-abortion forces for no gain for the pro-life side."[203]

What's more, Bopp hypothesized, if the Supreme Court did consider an absolutist challenge to *Roe*, "there is the potential danger that the Court might actually make things worse than they presently are." Such a case would result in Justice Kennedy voting with the four *Gonzales* dissenters to strike down a complete prohibition of abortion, and that might allow Justice Ginsburg, author of the *Gonzales* dissent, to write on behalf of a majority or prevailing plurality. If so, Bopp warned, Ginsburg might reprise her *Gonzales* dissent, which Bopp read as silently abandoning *Casey* and *Stenberg*'s reliance upon Fourteenth Amendment substantive due process liberty as the

---

[202] James Bopp, Jr. and Richard E. Coleson, to Whom It May Concern, *Pro-Life Strategy Issues* 2 (Aug 7, 2007) (available at http://www.personhood.net/docs/BoppMemorandum1 .pdf).

[203] Id at 3.

constitutional grounding of the abortion right and instead invoking only the Equal Protection Clause in support of a woman's right to abortion.

Bopp's reading of Ginsburg's dissent was unprecedented—no previous commentator had identified the unacknowledged substitution that he discerned. Bopp highlighted how Ginsburg had stated that "legal challenges to undue restrictions on abortion procedures do not seek to vindicate some generalized notion of privacy; rather, they center on a woman's autonomy to determine her life's course, and thus to enjoy equal citizenship stature."[204] Ginsburg's use of "rather" seemed to dispense rather expressly with any reliance upon any constitutional privacy right, and the ensuing phrase clearly culminated with an emphasis upon "equal citizenship stature." In between "rather" and "equal citizenship," however, Justice Ginsburg had invoked "a woman's autonomy," and her one other, previous usage of "autonomy"—in a quotation from *Planned Parenthood v Casey*—had passingly signaled that "autonomy" indeed had been used multiple times as part of *Casey*'s articulation of a substantive due process liberty basis for the abortion right.[205] *Casey*'s usage of autonomy—"These matters, involving the most intimate and personal choices a person may make in a lifetime, choices central to personal dignity and autonomy, are central to the liberty protected by the Fourteenth Amendment"[206]—left no doubt that Ginsburg's invocation of "a woman's autonomy" did indeed thus place reliance on due process liberty, even if her construction quickly drew a reader's eye toward "equal citizenship" and rapidly past "autonomy."

Bopp's fear of a judicial transposition in abortion's constitutional foundation was nonetheless highly revealing. If an equal protection/gender equality rationale "gained even a plurality in a prevailing case," his memo warned, "this new legal justification for the right to abortion would be a powerful weapon in the hands of pro-abortion lawyers that would jeopardize all current laws on abortion," including measures such as parental involvement and mandatory waiting-period statutes. In addition, "states would likely have to

---

[204] *Gonzales v Carhart*, 127 S Ct at 1641 (Ginsburg, J, dissenting).

[205] Id at 1640 (quoting 505 US at 851).

[206] 505 US at 851. *Casey* also employed "autonomy" in four additional instances, twice speaking of "personal autonomy" and once each invoking "economic autonomy" and "physical autonomy." See 505 US at 857, 860, 861, 884.

fund abortions that they are not currently required to fund in programs for indigent persons."[207]

More broadly, Bopp reiterated, "the pro-life movement must at present avoid fighting on the more difficult terrain of its own position, namely arguing that abortion should not be available in cases of rape, incest, fetal deformity, and harm to the mother." As poll after poll revealed, "public support for the pro-life side drops off dramatically whenever these 'hard' cases are the topic." Instead, "in the current environment, the public debate should be framed so that our opponents have to defend on their 'hardest' terrain, exposing them as unreasonable and outrageous. . . . That has been the genius of the vigorous effort to inform the public about PBA." Bopp explained that "[t]hose who object that the PBA ban leaves in place other means of abortion misunderstand or ignore the strategy and the profoundly favorable change in social attitudes wrought by the effort." He added that "doing the lesser implies no capitulation on the greater."[208]

Bopp also emphasized that the absolutists' public demand that incrementalists "repent for their alleged deception of the public and abandonment of the unborn . . . poses a serious threat to the cohesion necessary for the long-term success of any movement." The absolutists were endangering right-to-life unity while refusing to appreciate that their legislative efforts were fundamentally misdirected since "bans on the core abortion right at the state level are currently both useless and potentially dangerous." Instead, Bopp recommended, they should strive for enactments such as state partial-birth bans and the inclusion of "unborn victims in homicide laws." Interestingly, only at the very bottom of a long, twelve-item list did Bopp include statutes that would *require* "the woman to view ultrasound images of her unborn baby."[209]

Bopp's memo received a hostile and acerbic reception from absolutists. Robert J. Muise, an attorney at the Thomas More Law Center, a major backer of the Georgia Human Life Amendment, issued a lengthy rebuttal to Bopp in late September. Declaring that

---

[207] Bopp and Coleson, *Pro-Life Strategy Issues* at 3, 4 (cited in note 202). See also id at 11 (arguing that if an embryonic personhood case reached the current Supreme Court, a majority is "likely to switch to a more absolutist equal protection rationale for the abortion right, and all current regulations on abortion would be subject to, and likely would be struck down under, this new rationale").

[208] Id at 5, 6.

[209] Id at 6–7, 8, 9.

"after 34 years of abortion on demand through all nine months of pregnancy, it is time to rethink pro-life strategy," Muise stressed that "ending all abortions is the ultimate goal." He avowed that the Georgia measure "should be the pro-life movements' main effort" since it "provides a historic opportunity to educate the general public regarding the harm caused by all abortions, not just late-term, partial-birth abortions, which, in comparison, are far fewer in number." Acknowledging that "[d]emonstrating the humanity of the victim is a key component in social reform," he insisted that "a case must be presented to the United States Supreme Court that challenges the central premise of *Roe*—that the unborn is not a person within the meaning of the law."[210]

Muise maintained that "an amendment to the Georgia Constitution has a very good chance of succeeding," and that after it was challenged in the federal courts, "there is hope that Justice Kennedy will be persuaded to do the right thing when the opportunity presents itself once again." Muise explicitly premised that hope on religious affiliation: "there is good reason to believe (and to pray) that Chief Justice Roberts and fellow Justices Alito, Scalia, and Thomas (all fellow Catholics) could influence Kennedy in a similar fashion. It is certainly worth the effort to try." More realistically, Muise added that "given the political landscape"—that is, who as president might be nominating new Justices from 2009 forward—"we may have to wait another generation to have as good a chance as we have at the moment."[211]

But the absolutists' anger at the incrementalists' partial-birth political strategy was profound. "[I]f prohibiting a rare and seldom used procedure by means of a ban that will not save one life is the great success of framing the abortion debate, then the pro-life movement has settled for failure," Muise complained. Indeed, he rather oddly went on, "one could argue that the *supporters* [emphasis added] of abortion succeeded in focusing the abortion debate on a relatively rare, late-term abortion procedure, leaving untouched the ground where the battle truly takes place—early term abortions." Adopting—or mocking—Bopp's use of the word "terrain," Muise added that "[t]he abortion debate over the past decade has thus focused

---

[210] Robert J. Muise, to All Concerned Pro-Life Supporters, *Response to Bopp & Coleson Memo of August 7, 2007 re: Pro-Life Strategy Issues* (Sept 24, 2007), 1, 2, 3 (available at http://www.personhood.net/docs/MuiseResponse.pdf).

[211] Id at 3, 4.

not on the 'terrain' where over 90% of all abortions are performed
. . . but on the 'terrain' that will not prevent the killing of one
unborn child." At bottom, "the incremental approach has had the
effect of making the abortion issue negotiable," whereby people can
easily express opposition to the "partial-birth" procedure while simultaneously having no qualms about what Muise termed "the hor-
rors of early term abortions."[212]

Abortion rights supporters and editorialists who viewed *Gonzales*
as an unprecedented defeat of historical proportions ought to have
reconsidered the insistent pessimism of their sky-is-falling, *Roe*-is-
dead political mindset had they fully understood just how angrily
divided and despairing their supposedly triumphant opponents actually were. Absolutists were hoping to mount 2008 embryonic
personhood referenda in perhaps four other states in addition to
Georgia—Colorado, Michigan, Mississippi, and Montana—but the
few major news stories that reported their efforts all highlighted
how "little support or funding from big national antiabortion
groups" they were receiving.[213] The executive director of the National Right to Life Committee, David O'Steen, stated simply that
NRLC was "not involved" with any such referenda.[214]

While the medical aftermath and impact of the *Gonzales* decision
suggested that PBABA's upholding would have only a minimal impact upon the provision and availability of second-trimester abortions, the political fallout and effects of the ruling indicated that
abortion opponents were unprepared or unwilling to take any significant advantage from what was widely heralded as an unparal-
leled, landmark victory. Experienced national antiabortion leaders
like Douglas Johnson and James Bopp readily understood how well
their incrementalist strategy of gradual rollback meshed with public
opinion's complexities and ambivalences concerning abortion. But
although a major new right-to-life focus on enacting fetal ultrasound statutes might well triumph in state after state while painting
abortion rights adversaries as know-nothings who sought to deny
women access to a truthful—and perhaps disturbing—scientific im-

---

[212] Id at 9, 10, 11.

[213] Nicholas Riccardi, *Foes of Abortion Shift to States*, Los Angeles Times A1 (Nov 23, 2007).

[214] Judith Graham and Judy Peres, *Rights for Embryos Proposed*, Chicago Tribune (Dec 3, 2007) (available at http://www.chicagotribune.com/news/nationworld/chi-eggsdec03,1,3297674.story?).

age, many of the movement's most zealous and energetic grassroots activists viewed *Gonzales* as a meaningless culmination of an illegitimate strategy and were instead intensely committed to championing an absolutist strategy destined for unquestionably certain defeat.

VIII

If the actual medical and political impacts of *Gonzales* confounded most commentators' expectations, the same unexpected truth—that the ruling appeared unlikely to have any major direct effects whatsoever—gradually seemed to also come true on the legal front as well. Soon after the decision came down, the Supreme Court vacated and remanded two cases it had been holding for *Gonzales*, one from Virginia and one from Missouri,[215] and shortly thereafter the Second Circuit Court of Appeals vacated its own previous ruling against PBABA, which the Solicitor General had not petitioned to the Supreme Court.[216] In late May a federal district court dissolved its earlier injunction against a state partial-birth ban law Utah adopted in 2004 that almost identically mirrored PBABA,[217] but in Wisconsin, state Attorney General J. B. Van Hollen refused requests to revive a state ban which echoed the Nebraska statute struck down in *Stenberg* and which had been enjoined in 2001.[218] In an impressive formal opinion delivered to state legislative leaders, Van Hollen explained that a request to lift the injunction "would have to demonstrate that the Wisconsin statute does not impose an undue burden on a woman's right to choose a D&E abortion." However, "both the Nebraska statute and Wis. Stat. § 940.16 criminalize D&E abortions by banning the vaginal delivery of a fetal part, such as an arm or leg," in contrast to the narrower and more precise definition of "delivery" used in PBABA and upheld in *Gonzales*.[219]

---

[215] See *Herring v Richmond Medical Center for Women*, 127 S Ct 2094 (2007), and *Nixon v Reproductive Health Services of Planned Parenthood of the St. Louis Region*, 127 S Ct 2120 (2007). See also Jerry Markon, *Va. Law to Be Reconsidered in Wake of High Court Ruling*, Washington Post B6 (April 24, 2007).

[216] See *National Abortion Federation v Gonzales*, 224 Fed Appx 88 (2d Cir 2007).

[217] See *Utah Women's Clinic v Walker*, No 2:04CV00408 PGC, May 31, 2007 (D Utah); see also *Court Lifts Partial-Birth Injunction*, Salt Lake Tribune (June 1, 2007).

[218] See *Christensen v Doyle*, 249 F3d 603 (7th Cir 2001). See also *Christensen v Doyle*, 530 US 1271 (2000).

[219] J. B. Van Hollen to Scott Fitzgerald and Michael Huebsch, May 31, 2007, at 7

The Sixth Circuit Court of Appeals reached a similar conclusion in early June in affirming a district court decision holding Michigan's 2004 Legal Birth Definition Act unconstitutional. The unique law, avidly supported by the Thomas More Law Center, sought to prohibit "partial-birth" abortions by means of statutory language different from both Nebraska and PBABA. Concluding that "*Gonzales* left undisturbed the holding from *Stenberg* that a prohibition on D&E amounts to an undue burden," the Sixth Circuit held that "the Michigan statute, which applies when 'any anatomical part' of the fetus passes the vaginal introitus, is easily the most sweeping and the most burdensome of the three."[220] Thus it "would prohibit D&E" and "impose an unconstitutional undue burden" pursuant to both *Stenberg* and *Gonzales*.[221]

In mid-July, Louisiana became the first state to adopt a new, post-*Gonzales* partial-birth ban law that mirrored PBABA.[222] In contrast to the federal statute's maximum penalty of two years' imprisonment, the Louisiana measure specified up to ten years' punishment for physicians who violated it, but the enactment received almost no national press attention whatsoever.[223] Yet the balance of 2007 saw not a single other state follow Louisiana's lead, and the lack of activity prompted *Legal Times*' Tony Mauro to contrast that quiescence with the histrionic initial reactions to *Gonzales*. "[T]hose fears have not come true, with no prosecutions on the federal or state level, little legislative action, and quiet adjustments in abortion

(available at http://www.doj.state.wi.us/ag/opinions/2007_05_31Huebsch-Fitzgerald.pdf). See also Patrick Marley and Stacy Forster, *Abortion Ban Unenforceable, Van Hollen Says*, Milwaukee Journal Sentinel (May 31, 2007) (available at http://www.jsonline.com/story/index.aspx?id=613359).

[220] *Northland Family Planning Clinic v Cox*, 487 F3d 323, 336 (6th Cir 2007). See also *Planned Parenthood of Kansas and Mid-Missouri v Drummond*, No 07-4164-CV-C-ODS (WD Mo), 2007 WL 2463208 (Order Granting Temporary Restraining Order), and 2007 WL 2811407 (Order Granting Preliminary Injunction) (applying the undue burden test to abortion regulations and citing *Gonzales v Carhart*, 127 S Ct at 1626–27, as authority).

[221] *Northland Family Planning Clinic*, 487 F3d at 337. The Sixth Circuit also observed that "the Supreme Court's holding in *Stenberg* pertaining to the need for a health exception to otherwise valid D&X prohibitions was *modified somewhat* in *Gonzales*." Id at 340 (emphasis added). Early in 2008 the Supreme Court denied both Michigan's and the Thomas More Law Center's petitions for certiorari in the case without reported dissent. See *Cox v Northland Family Planning* and *Standing Together to Oppose Partial-Birth Abortion v Northland Family Planning Clinic*, 2008 WL 59327 and 59328.

[222] See Louisiana Acts 2007, No 473, § 1 (Louisiana RS 14 § 32.10–11 and 40 § 1299.35.17).

[223] Doug Simpson, *La. Becomes First State to Outlaw Late-Term Abortion Procedure*, Associated Press (July 13, 2007) (available in LexisNexis Newswires File).

procedures that have so far kept doctors on the safe side of the law," Mauro wrote.[224]

Perhaps the most significant and striking characterization of *Gonzales*'s significance, however, came in some remarkable off-the-bench statements by Justice John Paul Stevens, one of the decision's four dissenters. Asked by Jeffrey Rosen in a late June interview for the *New York Times Magazine* about the Court's upholding of PBABA, Justice Stevens responded that "[t]he statute is a *silly* statute." Repeating himself—"[i]t's a silly statute"—Stevens went on to say that "[i]t's just a distressing exhibition by Congress, but what we decided isn't all that important."[225] That latter statement was a truly memorable comment by the Court's senior Justice, and when Rosen then asked whether federal constitutional protection for abortion would survive, Stevens answered, "Well, it's up to Justice Kennedy." He added that "I don't know about the two new justices"—a reference to Chief Justice Roberts and Justice Alito's views on *Roe* and *Casey*—"but I kind of assume it may well be up to him." Yet Stevens also went on to say that Justice Kennedy indeed saw his stance in *Gonzales* as entirely congruent with *Casey*: "I don't think he thinks this requires him to change his views at all."[226]

IX

Gonzales v Carhart has changed the law, politics, and medicine of abortion far less than most early observers hastily thought. It has decisively confirmed *Ayotte*'s clear message from early 2006 that pre-enforcement facial challenges to statutes regulating abortion are now strongly disfavored, a shift that marks a very decisive change from previous federal judicial procedure. In state and lower

---

[224] Tony Mauro, *Abortion Ban Back at 4th Circuit*, Legal Times (Oct 29, 2007) (available at http://www.law.com/jsp/article.jsp?id=1193389426200). As Mauro and other journalists also noted, at oral argument a majority of the Fourth Circuit Court of Appeals panel hearing *Richmond Medical Center for Women v Herring* on remand from the Supreme Court (see note 215 above) sounded unpersuaded by Virginia's effort to revive its previously enjoined state partial-birth ban statute in light of *Gonzales*. See also Robert Barnes, *Judges Appear Hesitant on Virginia "Partial Birth" Abortion Ban*, Washington Post A10 (Nov 2, 2007).

[225] Jeffrey Rosen, *The Dissenter*, New York Times Magazine 50 (Sept 23, 2007).

[226] Id. Justice Stevens also volunteered a critical opinion of Justice Harry A. Blackmun's opinion for the Court in *Roe v Wade*. "In all candor, I think Harry could have written a better opinion. I think if the opinion had said what Potter Stewart said very briefly [in an additional concurrence], it might have been much more acceptable, instead of trying to create a new doctrine that really didn't make sense." Stevens added that "a better opinion might have avoided some of the criticism."

federal courts, both the pro-life[227] and pro-choice[228] sides will continue to register small, little-noticed successes, and, in the very, very long run, the hypothesis that federal constitutional protection will eventually recede toward an end-of-the-first-trimester benchmark, after which any legal abortion will require case-by-case medical review and approval, remains the historical best guess as to how the controversy will reach stasis, notwithstanding the chorus of cynical pessimists who believe that the only remaining question about *Roe v Wade* is the date of its final, formal interment.[229] They would do well to acknowledge that even Justice Kennedy's opinion in *Gonzales* fails to provide any avenue by which abortion opponents can move toward the prohibition of other second-trimester abortion methods, the most ostensible next step in any incremental rollback of the basic abortion right, and indeed may instead represent an additional new obstacle to any such effort.

No matter how little, or how much, the U.S. Supreme Court ever substantively further limits or vitiates *Roe* and *Casey*, judicial self-image and institutional self-interest continue to be the highest possible hurdles to any explicit overruling of *Roe v Wade* or even *Planned Parenthood v Casey* and its much-mocked undue burden test. Pro-choice critics of *Gonzales v Carhart* would do well to recognize, and acknowledge, that Justice Kennedy's majority opinion once

---

[227] See *Lawrence v State*, No PD-0236–07, Texas Court of Criminal Appeals, Nov 21, 2007 (available at http://www.cca.courts.state.tx.us/opinions/HTMLopinionInfo.asp?Opin ionID=16213 and at 2007 WL 4146386). The Court upheld the application of Texas's murder statute, which allows capital punishment for anyone who knowingly and intentionally murders more than one individual, to a man who killed his girlfriend whom he knew was pregnant with a four- to six-week-old embryo. The court held that the Texas Penal Code's definition of an individual as "a human being who is alive, including an unborn child at every stage of gestation from fertilization" does not conflict with federal constitutional protection of abortion, for the federal case law "has no application to a case that does not involve the pregnant woman's liberty interest in choosing to have an abortion."

[228] See *Keisler v Dunkle*, CA No 07-3577, ED Pa, Nov 8, 2007 (permanently enjoining abortion opponent John D. Dunkle, pursuant to the FACE statute, from publishing the names and personal data of abortion clinic staffers or patients, and ordering the federal government to "monitor the Defendant's website and weblog to ensure that Defendant is in compliance with the terms of this Order"); and Doron Taussig, *The Terrorist and the Baby-Killer*, Philadelphia City Paper (Jan 31, 2008) (available at http://www.citypaper.net/ articles/2008/01/31/the-terrorist-and-the-babykiller). See also Lisa Wangsness, *New Law Expands Abortion Buffer Zone*, Boston Globe B1 (Nov 14, 2007), and John C. Drake, *Buffer Zone Law Passes Its First Test*, Boston Globe B1 (Dec 9, 2007) (detailing Massachusetts's enactment and enforcement of a statute that expands to 35 feet from clinic entrances a buffer zone that previously had required abortion opponents to remain at least 6 feet away from clinic patrons within 18 feet of clinic entrances).

[229] See David J. Garrow, *Roe v Wade Revisited*, 9 Green Bag 2d 71, 79, 81 (2005).

again adopts and applies that standard. No matter how patronizing some readers may insist upon seeing Kennedy's opinion to be, the substantive truth remains that it upheld PBABA only in the narrowest and most carefully circumscribed manner. *Gonzales* will not significantly alter the medical practice of abortion, even for "late-term" procedures, nor has *Gonzales* brought about any measurable change in the basic dynamics of U.S. abortion politics.

Legally, however, *Gonzales v Carhart* does indirectly open a door to one category of very significant risks indeed. While there is little prospect of U.S. Attorneys or the U.S. Department of Justice using PBABA to institute criminal investigations or prosecutions of prudent and careful abortion providers, the likelihood that further states in addition to Louisiana and Utah will adopt "partial-birth" ban laws modeled on PBABA that can pass facial constitutional muster in the lower federal courts will increasingly give a far larger population of state and local prosecutors the statutory authority to prosecute, or persecute, reputable physicians who perform second-trimester abortions. Prosecutorial integrity may be a safe assumption at the federal level, but recent efforts in Kansas, instigated by former state Attorney General Phill Kline, who after his loss of that office in 2007 became district attorney for Johnson County, illustrate the dire danger that state PBABAs could pose to doctors in the hands of unscrupulous, politically motivated prosecutors.

While state Attorney General, Kline unsuccessfully attempted to pursue multiple charges against Dr. George Tiller of Wichita, one of the country's best-known providers of late-term abortions. A state judge dismissed Kline's charges, although Kline's successor subsequently filed different and far narrower accusations alleging that the required second opinions Tiller obtained attesting to the medical necessity of abortions on viable fetuses did not come from totally independent physicians, as Kansas law specifies.[230] Far more seriously, Kansans for Life, using an unusual provision of state law that allows for citizens to petition for the empanelment of a grand jury,

---

[230] *Abortion Charges Dismissed*, New York Times A15 (Dec 23, 2006); *Charges Against Doctor Aren't Reinstated*, New York Times A28 (Dec 28, 2006); *Concern Over Abortion Records*, New York Times A13 (Jan 9, 2007); and *Doctor Faces Abortion Charges from New Attorney General*, New York Times A20 (June 29, 2007). See also *Alpha Medical Clinic v Anderson*, 128 P3d 364 (Kan 2006), and, for further background, Miriam E. C. Bailey, *The Alpha Subpoena Controversy: Kansas Fires First Shot in Nationwide Battle Over Child Rape, Abortion and Prosecutorial Access to Medical Records*, 74 UMKC L Rev 1021 (2006).

gathered almost eight thousand signatures calling for a special Sedgwick County grand jury to criminally target that one particular
physician. Tiller unsuccessfully sought to block that interest group
hijacking of the criminal system, first in federal court and then
before the Kansas Supreme Court,[231] and in early 2008 the grand
jury will convene, shortly before Tiller's scheduled trial on the
earlier misdemeanor charges.[232]

While Kline's new district attorney post gives him no jurisdiction
over Dr. Tiller, Johnson County does include the Overland Park
headquarters of Planned Parenthood of Kansas and Mid-Missouri.
In mid-October 2007 Kline filed a 107-count criminal complaint
against the Planned Parenthood affiliate, alleging that the organization had repeatedly violated state laws regulating late-term procedures and the documentation required for such abortions.[233] A
state district judge found probable cause to proceed, and Planned
Parenthood faces fines totaling up to $2.5 million should the al-
legations be sustained at trial and after appeal.[234] Right-to-life cham-
pions heralded the charges as showing a new way to target abortion
providers,[235] and within weeks Kansas abortion opponents mounted
yet another citizens' petition drive, this one in Johnson County,
which quickly garnered enough signatures to empanel a grand jury

---

[231] See *Tiller v Gale*, No 07-1269-JTM, D Kansas, Oct 11, 2007 (available at 2007 WL
2990558), and *Tiller v Corrigan*, No 99,434, Kansas Supreme Court, Nov 29, 2007 (available at http://www.kscourts.org/Kansas-Courts/Supreme-Court/Orders/99434_Tiller2
.pdf).

[232] Stephanie Simon, *Pressure Rises for Abortion Provider*, Los Angeles Times A10 (Sept
17, 2007); Stephanie Simon, *Kansas GOP Tells Candidates to Forsake Abortion Focus*, Los
Angeles Times A10 (Dec 1, 2007); Stephanie Simon, *Abortion Provider Must Turn Over
Files*, Los Angeles Times A12 (Jan 31, 2008); *Tiller v Corrigan*, No 99,951, Kansas Supreme
Court, Feb 5, 2008 (available at http://www.kscourts.org/Kansas-Courts/Supreme-Court/
Orders/99,951-Tiller.pdf); Ron Sylvester, *High Court Postpones Subpoena on Tiller*, Wichita
Eagle (Feb 6, 2008) (available at http://www.kansas.com/213/story/303361.html); Judy
Peres, *Abortion Foes Put Grand Jury on Case*, Chicago Tribune (Feb 11, 2008) (available at
http://www.chicagotribune.com/news/chi-abortion_peres_11feb11,0,1654594.story).

[233] See *State v Comprehensive Health of Planned Parenthood of Kansas and Mid-Missouri*,
No 07 CR 0271, Johnson County District Court, Oct 15, 2007 (available at http://www
.mainstreamcoalition.com/blog/Planned%20Parenthood%20Complaint.pdf).

[234] Initiation of Action, *State v Comprehensive Health of Planned Parenthood of Kansas and
Mid-Missouri*, No 07 CR 0271, Johnson County District Court, Oct 17, 2007 (available
at http://www.mainstreamcoalition.com/blog/Planned%20Parenthood%20Complaint.pdf).
See also Laura Baker, *Planned Parenthood Says That Charges Are All About Politics*, Kansas City
Star (Oct 18, 2007) (available at http://primebuzz.kstar.com/?q=node/7643).

[235] See Robert D. Novak, *A New Front in the Abortion Wars*, Washington Post A25 (Oct
25, 2007).

tasked with pursuing a further criminal probe aimed at Planned Parenthood.[236]

In the end, perhaps all of the Kansas criminal charges and investigations targeting Dr. Tiller and Planned Parenthood will come to naught, but the litigation costs imposed by defending against such politically motivated use of the criminal justice process will no doubt total many hundred thousands of dollars. While no such special interest hijacking of the prosecutorial function is likely to ever trouble abortion providers in Manhattan, San Francisco, or Chicago, the post-*Gonzales* events in Kansas highlight in an unusually stark fashion the significant risks that the upholding of PBABA could come to pose for physicians who practice in states where parallel statutes can win enactment *and* where state or local prosecutors decide to seek partisan advantage or personal benefit by means of an unscrupulous pursuit of wholly reputable medical entities like Planned Parenthood. With scholarly studies showing abortion services "increasingly concentrated among a small number of very large providers,"[237] the years ahead could well witness the increasing disappearance of providers, or particularly providers who offer services beyond first-trimester terminations, from states in which both the political culture and prosecutorial incentives are so openly hostile to abortion doctors as is already true in Kansas.[238] There is no imaginable end to federal constitution protection for abortion yet in sight, but *Gonzales v Carhart*'s upholding of PBABA indirectly creates the likelihood of significant risks indeed for phy-

---

[236] Cheryl Wetzstein, *Grand Jury to Probe Abortion-Clinic Practices*, Washington Times A10 (Dec 5, 2007); Diane Carroll, *Grand Jury Is Selected for Planned Parenthood Investigation*, Kansas City Star (Dec 11, 2007) (available at http://www.kansascity.com/news/local/story/398274.html); Diane Carroll, *Johnson County Grand Jury Hires Special Counsel*, Kansas City Star (Dec 21, 2007) (available at http://www.kansascity.com/news/local/story/412766.html); Diane Carroll, *Johnson County Grand Jury Seeks Abortion Recipients' Medical Records*, Kansas City Star (Jan 31, 2008) (available at http://www.kansascity.com/news/local/story/468741.html); Diane Carroll, *Grand Jury Won't Indict Planned Parenthood*, Kansas City Star (March 4, 2008) (available at http://www.kansascity.com/105/story/515892.html).

[237] Finer and Henshaw, 35 Perspectives on Sexual and Reproductive Health at 12 (cited in note 164). See also id at 13 (noting "the continuing consolidation of abortion provision at clinics, particularly specialized clinics"), and Finer, et al, 37 Perspectives on Sexual and Reproductive Health at 111 (cited in note 166) (reporting that "providers that perform 2,000 or more abortions per year . . . performed 56% of all abortions in the United States in 2000").

[238] See Joffe, *The Abortion Procedure Ban* at 59 (cited in note 186) (arguing that "[i]n the long run, the major impact of [*Gonzales*] on abortion access will likely be a chilling effect on young physicians who contemplate entering this field").

sicians who provide abortions in locales where prosecutors are willing, and perhaps eager, to abuse the criminal process for political ends.

JODY FREEMAN and ADRIAN VERMEULE

MASSACHUSETTS v EPA: FROM POLITICS TO EXPERTISE

I. INTRODUCTION

On one view, *Massachusetts v EPA*[1] was a rather narrow administrative law decision. A 5–4 majority of the Supreme Court held that the Environmental Protection Agency (EPA) had failed to justify adequately its denial of a petition for rulemaking filed by a coalition of states and private plaintiffs. This sort of case is the routine fare of the District of Columbia Circuit, rather than the stuff of which headlines are made. Yet *MA v EPA* garnered massive public and professional attention.

Much of this attention resulted, of course, from the substantive question at issue in the rulemaking petition: whether EPA has authority to regulate, and (under certain conditions) must decide whether to regulate, greenhouse gas emissions from tailpipes in the United States' new automobile fleet. This was a case about global warming, the newspapers said, and the immediate symbolism of the case was that the Court had nudged the federal government into

Jody Freeman is Professor of Law, Harvard Law School. Adrian Vermeule is Professor of Law, Harvard Law School.

AUTHORS' NOTE: Thanks to Alexander A. Boni-Saenz, Michael Kolber, and Noah Purcell for excellent research assistance. For insightful comments, we are indebted to Michael Asimow, David Barron, Jack Beermann, Eric Biber, Lisa Bressman, Jake Gersen, Lisa Heinzerling, Richard Lazarus, Peter Strauss, and Cass Sunstein. The article also benefited from discussion at the Harvard Law School Faculty Workshop. Special thanks to David Strauss for detailed comments and editorial assistance.

[1] 127 S Ct 1438 (2007).

action on the most consequential regulatory question of the day.

From a broader perspective, however, we will argue that the regulatory controversies surrounding global warming illustrate a larger theme: the Court majority's increasing worries about the politicization of administrative expertise, particularly under the Bush administration. On this view, *MA v EPA* is best understood not so much as an environmental law case, not primarily anyway; rather it is a companion case to *Gonzales v Oregon,*[2] *Hamdan v Rumsfeld,*[3] and other episodes in which Justice Stevens and Justice Kennedy have joined forces to override executive positions that they found untrustworthy, in the sense that executive expertise had been subordinated to politics.

If the problem is the politicization of expertise, the majority's solution in *MA v EPA* was a kind of *expertise-forcing,* or so we will claim. Expertise-forcing is the attempt by courts to ensure that agencies exercise expert judgment free from outside political pressures, even or especially political pressures emanating from the White House or political appointees in the agencies.[4] Expertise-forcing is in tension with one leading rationale of the *Chevron* doctrine,[5] a rationale that emphasizes the executive's democratic accountability and that sees nothing wrong with politically inflected presidential administration of executive-branch agencies. Whereas the *Chevron* worldview sees democratic politics and expertise as complementary, expertise-forcing has its roots in an older vision of administrative law, one in which politics and expertise are fundamentally antagonistic.[6]

---

[2] 546 US 243 (2006).

[3] 126 S Ct 2749 (2006).

[4] From here on, we will use "White House" to include political appointees in the agencies; nothing in our thesis depends upon whether political pressures that distort agencies' expert judgments emanate from officials in the Executive Office of the President, or instead from appointees who take their cues from the White House.

[5] *Chevron USA, Inc. v Natural Resources Defense Council, Inc.*, 467 US 837 (1984).

[6] There is an older tradition of environmental law cases in the D.C. Circuit in which Judge Skelly Wright evinces frustration with executive "footdragging" in the implementation of statutory requirements. *Calvert Cliffs' Coordinating Committee, Inc. v United States Atomic Energy Commission,* 449 F2d 1109 (DC Cir 1971). See also *Sierra Club v Morton,* 514 F2d 856, 873–74 (DC Cir 1975) (citing the "action-forcing" elements of NEPA to justify potential judicial oversight of agency inaction); *Scientists' Institute for Public Information, Inc. v Atomic Energy Commission,* 481 F2d 1079, 1092 (DC Cir 1973) (requiring an environmental impact statement from the Atomic Energy Commission and claiming that "we must reject any attempt by agencies to shirk their responsibilities under NEPA by labeling any and all discussion of future environmental effects as 'crystal ball inquiry'"). Judge Leventhal wrote opinions in some notable cases adhering to this tradition as well.

Part II describes the problem of politicized expertise. Part III explains how the Court in *MA v EPA* embraced expertise-forcing as the solution to that problem in its two holdings on the merits. First, the Court's interpretation of the Clean Air Act (CAA) shows that it has retreated from the *Chevron* worldview just described, as well as from the idea, most prominent in *FDA v Brown & Williamson*,[7] that statutes should be interpreted in light of a "nondelegation canon"—meaning that courts should force Congress to speak clearly if it intends to delegate regulatory authority over major political and economic questions. In *MA v EPA*, the Court did the opposite of what it did in *Brown & Williamson*: it interpreted statutory ambiguity to find that the agency already possessed the requisite legal authority to regulate in an important area, and declined to call on Congress for a fresh statement. This divergence is put in its best light by understanding the Court's project in *MA v EPA* as one of expertise-forcing. Second, the Court's careful scrutiny and close cabining of the EPA's discretion to decline to regulate by "deciding not to decide" is also best understood as a component of the Court's expertise-forcing project.

Part IV considers the implications of the expertise-forcing approach adopted by the Court, in both legal and political terms. Aside from its immediate impact on pending litigation and proposed legislation related to climate change, the case has longer-term doctrinal implications, particularly for an agency's traditionally capacious flexibility to defer discretionary decisions—"to decide not to decide." In constraining EPA's discretion and subjecting the agency's deferral of a decision to hard look review, the Court seems to adopt a kind of anticircumvention principle: agencies cannot perpetually defer the threshold decisions necessary to trigger regulation if doing so would undermine the main purposes of the statute. Before *MA v EPA*, it was unclear whether discretionary decisions not to promulgate regulations were even reviewable, let alone subject to "hard look" review. In this regard, *MA v EPA* could

---

See, for example, *Ethyl Corp. v EPA*, 541 F2d 1, 68 (DC Cir 1976) (Leventhal concurring) (noting that judges must ensure that agencies exercise their expertise rationally). See also *Consumer Federation of America v Federal Power Commission*, 515 F2d 347 (DC Cir 1975) (finding that the Federal Power Commission had neglected its rate-control responsibilities, pursuing instead a deregulatory agenda). Justice Stevens could be seen, according to Professor Richard J. Lazarus, as the new Skelly Wright. Richard J. Lazarus (remarks at the Environmental Law Panel, Harvard Law School Worldwide Alumni Congress, June 2007).

[7] 529 US 120 (2000).

be *State Farm*[8] for a new generation: just as *State Farm* held deregulatory decisions reviewable, in order to allow a judicial hard look at a decision that allegedly injected politics into an expert judgment, so too *MA v EPA* held the denial of a petition requesting regulation to be reviewable, and for similar reasons.[9] Alternatively, the Court's expertise-forcing enterprise may be limited, either because *MA v EPA* is a unique decision about global warming or because expertise-forcing, which necessarily relies on judicial predictions about political events, is an unpredictable business.

In a broader perspective, *MA v EPA* can be seen, along with *Gonzales* and *Hamdan*, as one in a series of rebukes to the administration, an expression of the Court's growing concern about potential executive overreaching. Viewed in this light, political interference with agency decision making is a species of a larger problem. Our main suggestion for administrative law, then, is that *MA v EPA* is part of a trend in which the Court has at least temporarily become disenchanted with executive power and the idea of political accountability and is now concerned to protect administrative expertise from political intrusion.[10]

II. The Problem: Political Interference with Agency Expertise

Every administration exerts some degree of political influence over agency decision making. After all, it is the prerogative of the democratically elected chief executive to shape agency policy within the bounds of often vague and incomplete statutes. And some administrations are more aggressive in this regard than others.[11] Yet

---

[8] *Motor Vehicles Manufacturers' Association v State Farm Mutual Automobile Insurance Co.*, 463 US 29 (1983).

[9] The Chief Justice, dissenting on the Court's standing holding, suggested that *MA v EPA* was *SCRAP* for a new generation, which may also be true. See *MA v EPA*, 127 S Ct at 1471 (Roberts dissenting).

[10] For a broadly compatible account of recent cases, not focused on *MA v EPA*, see Peter L. Strauss, *The Overseer, or "The Decider"? The President in Administrative Law*, 75 Geo Wash L Rev 696 (2007). For an argument that the Court has at least occasionally been suspicious of presidential interference with agency expertise throughout the post-*Chevron* era, see Lisa Schultz Bressman, *Deference and Democracy*, 75 Geo Wash L Rev 761 (2007).

[11] See Elena Kagan, *Presidential Administration*, 114 Harv L Rev 2245, 2247 (2001) (showing that President Clinton expanded upon President Reagan's initial attempts at exerting more presidential control over administration). For a contrary view about whether this is a desirable development, see Peter L. Strauss, *Presidential Rulemaking*, 72 Chi Kent L Rev 965, 984 (1997).

the accounts circulating about the Bush administration as *MA v EPA* moved through the courts were of a different scope and scale than in the past: the administration had been altering scientific reports, silencing its own experts, and suppressing scientific information that was politically inconvenient. And this was being done so systematically, critics said, as to leave no doubt that it was authorized by the White House.

Most relevant to *MA v EPA*, there were suggestions of widespread tampering by the Bush administration with the global warming data reported by numerous federal agencies, including EPA. In September 2002, under Administrator Christine Whitman, EPA staff chose to delete a section on global warming from an annual report on the state of air pollution rather than accept major revisions demanded by the White House.[12] White House officials, it was said, had objected to the discussion of scientific research in the report indicating a significant rise in global temperatures and linking the rise to human activity, and referring to a National Academy of Sciences Report that the White House had earlier endorsed. White House officials replaced these sections with reference to a study funded by the American Petroleum Institute that questioned climate change science. After considering its options, EPA staff concluded in an internal memorandum that the edited section "no longer accurately represents the scientific consensus on climate change" and dropped it entirely. To publish the changes, the memorandum speculated, would expose the agency to "severe criticism from the science and environmental communities for poorly representing the science."[13] Episodes such as this apparently created significant tension between career agency staff and political appointees.

During 2002 and 2003, Philip Cooney, the Chief of Staff to President Bush's Council on Environmental Quality (and a former lobbyist for the American Petroleum Institute with no scientific training), rewrote or altered reports by federal agencies on various aspects of climate change, with the effect of introducing greater doubt and uncertainty into these reports than the science war-

[12] See Jeremy Symons, *How Bush and Co. Obscure the Science*, Wash Post B04 (July 13, 2003); Andrew C. Revkin and Katharine Q. Seeyle, *Report by E.P.A. Leaves Out Data on Climate Change*, NY Times A1 (June 19, 2003).

[13] Environmental Protection Agency, *Issue Paper: White House Edits to Climate Change Section of EPA's Report on the Environment* (Apr 29, 2003), in Union of Concerned Scientists, *Scientific Integrity in Policymaking* 34–38 (March 2004).

ranted.[14] Scores of scientists in agencies such as the National Oceanic and Atmospheric Administration (NOAA) and EPA reported being pressured to delete references to climate change and global warming from official documents, including their communications with Congress.[15] James Hansen, the top climate scientist at the National Aeronautics and Space Administration (NASA), reported that the administration had tried to stop him from publicly calling for prompt reductions in greenhouse gases linked to global warming, and that officials from NASA headquarters had ordered the agency's public affairs staff to review his upcoming lectures, web postings, and interviews out of concern for "coordination."[16]

While we express no view as to their accuracy, it is clear that accusations of political interference with expert agency decisions were being made frequently during this time, and attracted significant media attention. Reports of such manipulation were not limited to climate change but extended to scientific judgments concerning environmental, health, and safety regulation more generally. A report by the Union of Concerned Scientists alleges a wide variety of examples of administration interference with the science produced by federal agencies, including an attempt to bar a Department of Agriculture employee from discussing his findings about antibiotic-resistant bacteria in the air around hog farms, and directives made by political appointees to botanists, biologists, and ecologists in the U.S. Fish and Wildlife Service (USFWS) to refrain "for nonscientific reasons . . . from making . . . findings that are protective of [endangered] species."[17] Numerous other books and articles like-

---

[14] See Andrew C. Revkin, *Bush Aide Edited Climate Reports*, NY Times A2 (June 8, 2005). Following these revelations, Mr. Cooney resigned and was hired three days later by Exxon Mobil. See Andrew C. Revkin, *Former Bush Aide Who Edited Reports Is Hired by Exxon*, NY Times A1 (June 15, 2005).

[15] As the decision in *MA v EPA* was pending, the nonprofit Government Accountability Project (the self-declared "nation's leading whistleblower organization") released a report detailing numerous instances of administration interference with expert scientists in numerous agencies. Tarek Maassarani, *Redacting the Science of Climate Change: An Investigative and Synthesis Report* (Government Accountability Project 2007), online at http://www .whistleblower.org/doc/2007/Final%203.28%20Redacting%20Climate%20Science%20 Report.pdf.

[16] Andrew C. Revkin, *Climate Expert Says NASA Tried to Silence Him*, NY Times 1–6 (Jan 29, 2006).

[17] Union of Concerned Scientists, *U.S. Fish and Wildlife Survey Summary* 1 (Feb 2005) ("One in five agency scientists revealed they have been 'directed to inappropriately exclude or alter technical information from a USFWS scientific document,' such as a biological opinion."). Accusations of political interference of this kind have arisen before—Reagan administration officials were reported to have pressured FWS staff to alter their findings

wise have alleged an unprecedented degree of politicization of agency expertise under the George W. Bush administration.[18] We are not concerned with the merits of these claims; our point is simply that these accusations were well known, and certainly no secret to the Supreme Court Justices.[19]

The administration had taken other steps that fueled similar concerns about political interference with agency decisions generally, and manipulation of agency science in particular. For example, the Office of Information and Regulatory Affairs (OIRA) in the Office of Management and Budget (OMB) had in 2003 published a draft peer review bulletin that was widely criticized as an effort to politicize agency science.[20] The proposal required agencies to rigorously peer review all "significant regulatory information" intended for public dissemination, and for "especially significant regulatory information" follow a strict process of "formal, independent, external peer review" prescribed by OIRA. The proposal barred agency scientists, or any scientist funded by the agency (no matter how indirectly), from participating in the peer review process, with no such bar applying to industry scientists—even where the scientific information under review was produced by the regulated

---

regarding the status of the spotted owl, and the Bush I administration was found to have improperly interfered in an adjudicative decision by the Endangered Species Act Committee over whether to exempt western forests from the requirements of the Act. But in the past such shenanigans were considered exceptions to the rule.

[18] See, for example, Rena Steinzor and Wendy Wagner, eds, *Rescuing Science from Politics* (Cambridge, 2007). In 2004, twenty Nobel Prize winners released a statement criticizing the administration's handling of scientific information, saying in part, "When scientific knowledge has been found to be in conflict with its political goals, the administration has often manipulated the process through which science enters into its decisions. This has been done by placing people who are professionally unqualified or who have clear conflicts of interest in official posts and on scientific advisory committees; by disbanding existing advisory committees; by censoring and suppressing reports by the government's own scientists; and by simply not seeking independent scientific advice." Guy Gugliotta and Rick Weiss, *President's Science Policy Questioned; Scientists Worry That Any Politics Will Compromise Their Credibility*, Wash Post § 856(a)(2) (Feb 19, 2004).

[19] See, for example, Brief of Former EPA Administrators Carol M. Browner et al as Amici Curiae in Support of Petitioners, *MA v EPA*, No 05-1120, *3 (filed Aug 31, 2006) (available on Westlaw at 2006 WL 2569575) (charging that the EPA "subordinate[d] science-based regulatory decisionmaking to non-statutory policy considerations").

[20] Office of Management and Budget, Proposed Bulletin on Peer Review and Information Quality, 68 Fed Reg 54023-02 (2003). The proposal was roundly criticized by the American Public Health Association, the Association of American Medical Colleges, and the Federation of American Societies for Experimental Biology, among other leading scientific organizations. See letter from Dr. George C. Benjamin, Executive Director of the APHA, to Dr. Margo Schwab, OIRA (Dec 11, 2003); letter from Dr. Jordan J. Cohen, President of the AAMC, and Dr. Robert J. Wells, President of the FASEB, to Dr. Margo Schwab, OIRA (Dec 4, 2003).

industry.[21] Perhaps slightly less visible, but well known to Washington insiders, the President twice tried to nominate Susan Dudley to be Director of the Office of Information and Regulatory Affairs in the Office of Management and Budget.[22] The Dudley nomination was widely perceived not only as a White House effort to exert more centralized political control over agency staff[23] but also as an effort to rein in environmental, health, and safety agencies, which tend to support their rulemakings with public health and other scientific data. Democrats in the Senate had blocked the confirmation out of concern that science-driven regulatory policy would be subordinated to political ideology.[24] This was fueled to some extent by historical allegations that OIRA interfered with agency science in its effort to cut back on regulation,[25] and by Dudley's own background and public statements—she had worked since 1998

[21] See 68 Fed Reg at 54023-02 (cited in note 20). OMB drafted the bulletin pursuant to the Information Quality Act, in which Congress directed OMB to develop guidelines to ensure the "quality, objectivity, utility, and integrity of information" distributed by federal agencies. Information Quality Act, Pub L No 106-554, § 515(a), 114 Stat 2763, 2763A-153 (1995), codified in 44 USC § 3516 (2000). After widespread criticism of the proposed bulletin, including a workshop on the bulletin at the National Academy of Sciences attended by several hundred people, OMB issued a revised draft bulletin on Apr 28, 2004. See Office of Management and Budget, Revised Information Quality Bulletin on Peer Review, 69 Fed Reg 23230-02 (2004). OMB adopted this revised proposal as its final bulletin. Office of Management and Budget, Final Information Quality Bulletin for Peer Review, 70 Fed Reg 2664-02 (2005). The final bulletin explicitly permitted government employees to serve as peer reviewers, as long as they "comply with applicable Federal ethics requirements" and as long as they did not contribute to the information being reviewed. The bulletin also permits outside scientists who receive funding from a federal agency to review that agency's work, as long as the funding they receive is based on "investigator-initiated, competitive, peer-reviewed proposals." Id at 2675.

[22] Since the Reagan administration, OIRA has overseen agency rulemaking on behalf of the White House. During recent Republican administrations it has been accused of using cost-benefit analysis as a one-way ratchet to discourage what in its view is overzealous and insufficiently justified regulation by proregulatory agency staff. See Nicholas Bagley and Richard L. Revesz, *Centralized Oversight of the Regulatory State*, 106 Colum L Rev 1260, 1263–70 (2006) (detailing OIRA's use of cost-benefit analysis).

[23] For an argument that this perception of OIRA's as a centralizing force is inaccurate and that it has primarily played an antiregulatory role in the administrative state, see id at 1264.

[24] See Rebecca Adams, *Groups Mobilize Effort to Block Regulatory Czar*, CQ Weekly (Oct 27, 2006).

[25] OIRA has in the past been accused of politicizing agency science in addition to exerting a deregulatory effect through the use of cost-benefit analysis. See, for example, Lisa Heinzerling and Rena I. Steinzor, *A Perfect Storm: Mercury and the Bush Administration: Part II*, 34 Envir L Rep, 10485, 10490–91 (2004). On the politicization of science in regulatory policy, see Sidney A. Shapiro, *OMB and the Politicization of Risk Assessment*, 37 Envir L 1083 (2007). See generally Wendy E. Wagner, *The "Bad Science" Fiction: Reclaiming the Debate over the Role of Science in Public Health and Environmental Regulation*, 66 L & Contemp Probs 63 (2003).

at the Mercatus Center, an antiregulation thinktank that the *Wall Street Journal* once called "[t]he most important thinktank you've never heard of."[26] (The President finally made her a recess appointment on April 4, 2007.)

In addition, in early 2007, after the Court had heard oral argument in *MA v EPA*, but while the decision was still pending, the President signed Executive Order 13422 (EO 13422). The new Executive Order amends Executive Order 12866 (which requires agencies to do a cost-benefit analysis for "major" rules) by mandating that each agency establish a "regulatory policy office," run by a political appointee, to supervise the development of agency rules and guidance documents. Executive Order 13422 also instructs that agencies must identify "a specific market failure" to justify regulating,[27] and requires staff to submit not only proposed rules but proposed guidance documents—which had not previously been subject to OMB scrutiny under Executive Order 12866—to OMB for review.

The Congressional Research Service, an arm of the Library of Congress that provides nonpartisan research to members of Congress, summarized the impact of the new executive order this way: "The changes made by this executive order represent a clear expansion of presidential authority over rulemaking agencies. In that regard, E.O. 13422 can be viewed as part of a broader statement of presidential authority presented throughout the Bush Administration."[28] Scholars and members of Congress opposed to EO 13422 were more pointed, calling it an executive power grab, and expressing concern that its purpose is to enable White House political

---

[26] Mercatus is funded primarily by industry, especially the Koch family, an oil and gas company from Kansas that donates heavily to Republican causes. Democrats cited a variety of positions Dudley has taken on regulatory issues as worrisome, pointing to her arguments that the EPA should value the lives of older people less than the lives of younger people when doing cost-benefit analyses and that the benefits as well as the costs of ozone pollution should be taken into account when setting new ozone standards. See Judy Pasternak, *Bush Backed Shunned Nominees: His Three Choices for Jobs Dealing with the Environment Were Previously Blocked as Pro-Industry*, LA Times A1 (Apr 1, 2007).

[27] Exec Order 13422, 72 Fed Reg 2703 (2007) ("Each agency shall identify in writing the specific market failure (such as externalities, market power, lack of information) or other specific problem that it intends to address (including, where applicable, the failures of public institutions) that warrant new agency action, as well as assess the significance of that problem, to enable assessment of whether any new regulation is warranted.").

[28] Curtis W. Copeland, *Changes to the OMB Regulatory Review Process by Executive Order 13422* 14 (Congressional Research Service, Feb 2007), online at http://www.fas.org/sgp/crs/misc/RL33862.pdf.

staff to override agency scientists and experts.[29] Whatever its ultimate impact, and regardless of its merits, the new executive order added to a growing sense that the administration was interested in greater control over agencies, in particular those that imposed expensive regulations in the name of public health and safety. This only intensified concern about the potential for politicization of expertise. Even if the Supreme Court Justices were unaware of the particulars of either the President's efforts to appoint Dudley, or the new executive order, by the time *MA v EPA* reached the Court the general picture of which they are a part, including allegations of interference with climate-related science, had clearly taken shape, and concerns about politicization were widely known.[30]

Against this backdrop, a scientific consensus that had solidified over the last decade was gelling in the public's mind: global temperatures were in fact rising and contributing, among other things, to elevated sea levels and more intense hurricanes, and the rising temperatures were linked to human activity, specifically, the emissions of greenhouse gases from the burning of fossil fuels. In the few years before *MA v EPA* reached the Supreme Court, the rate of publication of articles on global warming in major U.S. newspapers and journals had increased dramatically.[31] Scientists both within and outside government were becoming more vocal in calling for a policy response, including federal regulation of greenhouse gas emissions. Indeed, as the Court considered *MA v EPA*, the Intergovernmental Panel on Climate Change (IPCC) was preparing to release its fourth assessment report, which would state the scientific consensus on the warming trend and outline the potential

---

[29] See Robert Pear, *Bush Directive Increases Sway on Regulation*, NY Times A1 (Jan 30, 2007). In an e-mail to the administrative law list about the new Executive Order, Professor Peter Strauss wrote: "The important thing about the new Regulatory Policy Officer provision is that it is to be a PRESIDENTIAL appointee—that is, one the President can fire and replace without having to get senatorial confirmation. This remarkably tightens White House control over agency business . . . what this does—in the week House and Senate have shown some signs of cleaning out the stables—is further to arm the political potentials of White House controls." Posting of Peter Strauss, Professor, Columbia Law School, to adminlaw@chicagokent.kentlaw.edu.

[30] See, for example, Juliet Eilperin, *U.S. Pressure Weakens G-8 Climate Plan; Global-Warming Science Assailed*, Wash Post A1 (June 17, 2005).

[31] A simple Lexis-Nexis search of the keywords "climate change" or "global warming" in major U.S. newspapers' headlines returned 2,189 hits for the three years prior to the *MA v EPA* decision (Apr 1, 2004 through March 31, 2007), compared with only 1,125 hits for the three years before that (Apr 1, 2001 through March 31, 2004).

risks of unmitigated greenhouse gas emissions more forcefully than ever before.[32]

At the same time, states and environmentalists, frustrated with EPA's refusal to regulate greenhouse gases at the federal level, had launched public nuisance suits against major power plants and the automobile industry seeking injunctive relief or damages for their contributions to the harms caused by global warming.[33] In response to a listing petition by environmental groups, the U.S. Fish and Wildlife Service, after much delay, agreed in late 2006 to determine whether to list the polar bear as "threatened" under the Endangered Species Act because of loss of habitat due in part to melting arctic sea ice caused by global warming.[34] And Al Gore's movie, *An Inconvenient Truth*, hit theaters nationwide.

This was the political, cultural, and legal context in which the Supreme Court decided *MA v EPA*. Whatever their personal views, it would have been impossible for the Justices not to know of the growing scientific consensus on climate change, or to be unaware of accusations that the administration was trying to suppress and manipulate agency science.[35]

The EPA actions that prompted the litigation in *MA v EPA* arguably fit the pattern of political interference described above, or at least plausibly raised suspicions. First, the agency's General Counsel[36] had reversed course from two previous General Counsels

---

[32] The "Summary for Policymakers" of the fourth IPCC report was published in February 2007, so its major findings were well known and publicized prior to the Court's decision in *MA v EPA*. The IPCC was established in 1988 by the World Meteorological Organization and the United Nations Environment Programme. See Intergovernmental Panel on Climate Change, *About IPCC*, online at http://www.ipcc.ch/about/index.htm ("The [IPCC's] role is to assess on a comprehensive, objective, open and transparent basis the scientific, technical and socio-economic literature produced worldwide relevant to the understanding of the risk of human-induced climate change, its observed and projected impacts and options for adaptation and mitigation. IPCC reports should be neutral with respect to policy, although they need to deal objectively with policy relevant to scientific, technical and socio economic factors. They should be of high scientific and technical standards, and aim to reflect a range of views, expertise and wide geographical coverage."). All three working groups of the IPCC have issued their sections for the Fourth Assessment Report, titled "Climate Change 2007." See id (providing three Working Group hyperlinks for separate contributions to the report).

[33] See *California v General Motors*, 2007 WL 2726871 (ND Cal); *Connecticut v American Electric Power*, 406 F Supp 2d 265 (SDNY 2005).

[34] Department of the Interior, Endangered and Threatened Wildlife and Plants; 12-Month Petition Finding and Proposed Rule to List the Polar Bear (Ursus Maritimus) as Threatened Throughout Its Range, 72 Fed Reg 1064 (Jan 9, 2007).

[35] See note 19 and accompanying text.

[36] Memorandum from Robert E. Fabricant, EPA General Counsel, to Marianne L. Hor-

in deciding that carbon dioxide and other greenhouse gases were not "pollutants" regulable under the Act.[37] This determination had implications beyond the matter of EPA's own discretion to regulate greenhouse gases, which added to its political import: if upheld, it would effectively derail California's attempt to regulate tailpipe emissions under CAA § 209, which authorizes California, alone among the states, to independently establish emissions standards under certain conditions, subject to waiver by the EPA. If carbon dioxide were not a pollutant in the first place, as EPA claimed, the state would have no authority to regulate it under the auspices of the Act, and its tailpipe emissions regulations, which ten other states had adopted pending the waiver grant by EPA, would be invalid.[38]

Based in part on its determination that carbon dioxide and other greenhouse gases were not pollutants, the agency in 2003 denied a rulemaking petition filed by the International Center for Technology Assessment and other parties seeking regulation under § 202(a)(1) of the CAA. This section provides that the Administrator of EPA "shall by regulation prescribe . . . standards applicable to the emission of any air pollutant" from any class of motor vehicles "which in his judgment cause, or contribute to, air pollution which may reasonably be anticipated to endanger public health or welfare."[39] In the petition denial, EPA cited its legal opinion that greenhouse gases are not pollutants, and then explained that even if they were, the agency would decline to regulate them. This was because EPA "disagreed with the regulatory approach urged by the petitioners [via § 202]" and preferred a different policy approach for several reasons, including that "the science of climate change is extraordinarily complex and still evolving," that regulation under § 202 would be an inefficient and piecemeal approach to the climate change issue, and that unilateral EPA regulation could "weaken U.S. efforts to persuade key developing countries to reduce the GHG intensity of their econo-

---

inko, EPA Acting Administrator, *EPA's Authority to Impose Mandatory Controls to Address Global Climate Change Under the Clean Air Act* (Aug 28, 2003).

[37] Prior general counsels had consistently deemed greenhouse gases to be pollutants, but nevertheless declined to regulate them.

[38] See *Central Valley Chrysler-Jeep, Inc. v Witherspoon*, 2007 WL 135688 (ED Cal) (staying proceedings pending the outcome in *MA v EPA*). California ultimately prevailed in this case, *Central Valley Chrysler-Jeep, Inc. v Goldstene*, No CV F 04-6663 (ED Cal, Dec 11, 2007), but was afterward denied a waiver by the EPA, letter from Stephen L. Johnson, Administrator, U.S. Environmental Protection Administration, to Arnold Schwarzenegger, Governor, State of California (Dec 19, 2007). See also note 130 and accompanying text.

[39] 42 USC § 7521(a)(1) (2000).

mies."[40] The denial referred to the President's "comprehensive" global climate change policy, which consisted of encouraging voluntary reductions of greenhouse gases and promoting technology development, along with further scientific research to reduce remaining uncertainties.[41] In support of its conclusion that the science was too uncertain to warrant regulation, the agency relied on selective and somewhat misleading excerpts from a 2001 report by the National Research Council,[42] which emphasized uncertainty while downplaying many statements of certainty or near-certainty that cut against EPA's position.[43]

The agency thus declined to make the threshold judgment necessary to trigger regulation of vehicle emissions under § 202. Indeed, in its petition denial EPA emphasized that the exercise of the statutory authority to regulate greenhouse gases turns on a judgment to be made by the Administrator, that the "requisite endangerment finding" has not been made,[44] and that "the CAA provision authorizing regulation of motor vehicle emissions does not impose a mandatory duty on the Administrator to exercise her judgment."[45] EPA simply exercised its discretion not to assess whether greenhouse gases "cause or contribute to, air pollution which may reasonably be anticipated to endanger public welfare."[46] It decided not to decide. As we will detail below, the Court recognized this and explicitly framed its holding in the same way: EPA, the Court held, "has offered no reasoned explanation *for its refusal to decide* whether

---

[40] Environmental Protection Agency, Control of Emissions from New Highway Vehicles and Engines, 68 Fed Reg 52922, 52931 (Sept 8, 2003).

[41] Id.

[42] National Research Council, *Climate Change Science: An Analysis of Some Key Questions* (2001), online at http://www.nap.edu/html/climatechange/.

[43] Notably, critics pointed out, the agency omitted the opening line of the report, which reads: "Greenhouse gases are accumulating in Earth's atmosphere as a result of human activities, causing surface air temperatures and subsurface ocean temperatures to rise." Id at 1. Brief of Amici Curiae Climate Scientists David Battisti et al in Support of Petitioner, *MA v EPA*, No 05-1120, *3 (filed May 15, 2006) (pointing out EPA's mishandling of NAS Report and disregard of weight of evidence: "EPA and the appeals court stated that they considered the NAS/NRC report *Climate Change Science* to be the scientific authority for the decision to deny the petition to regulate. We feel an obligation to inform this Court that they misunderstood or misrepresented the science contained in the report [and] to correct the public record as to what Climate Change Science and subsequent NAS reports say about climate change . . . .").

[44] 68 Fed Reg at 52929 (cited in note 40).

[45] Id.

[46] 42 USC § 7521(a)(1) (2000).

greenhouse gases cause or contribute to climate change."[47]

Although EPA had cited a number of policy reasons for declining to regulate, its claims about lingering and pervasive scientific uncertainty were a linchpin of the petition denial. Given the charged context in which EPA arrived at this position, it was not surprising that questions arose about whether the petition denial was in fact the product of expertise—a decision supported by the scientific evidence—or whether it was an instance of politics overriding scientific judgment.

III. The Solution: Expertise-Forcing

On this picture, EPA found itself in an exceedingly uncomfortable position—pressed on the one hand by an administration that opposed regulating greenhouse gases, and on the other by experts, both within and outside the agency, who believed global warming required a regulatory response. Making the statutory judgment that greenhouse gas emissions "cause, or contribute to, air pollution that may reasonably be anticipated to endanger public health or welfare" would trigger a statutory obligation to regulate new vehicle emissions in some manner, might trigger regulation of stationary sources under the Act, and would keep alive California's bid to independently regulate tailpipe emissions. That course of action would infuriate the White House, which had taken the position that more study was needed and that unilateral domestic regulation of greenhouse gases was both premature and undesirable. At the same time, a statutory judgment that greenhouse gases did not endanger health and welfare would outrage many scientists, environmentalists, and other constituencies important to the agency, damaging the agency's scientific credibility.

As a result, the cross-cutting political constraints had forced EPA to indefinitely put off a decision, making no first-order judgment at all, or so one might reasonably conclude. That course of action had the collateral benefit of leaving in place the nonregulatory status quo, thus satisfying the White House's major concern. Deciding not to decide guaranteed objections from scientists and environmentalists, but it was at least less damaging to EPA than a substantive first-order judgment that greenhouse gases have no adverse public health and welfare effects—a judgment that would be hard

---

[47] *MA v EPA*, 127 S Ct at 1463 (emphasis added).

to make with a straight face, given the burgeoning scientific consensus. And although EPA could in theory agree with the scientific consensus on warming and find that greenhouse gases have adverse public health and welfare effects, *and nevertheless* conclude that it is not "sensible" to regulate emissions from new motor vehicles,[48] that conclusion could be very difficult to defend—at least more difficult than declining to make the threshold judgment in the first place.

On this account, the majority's worry in *MA v EPA* was that politics had disabled the EPA's expert judgment about the crucial regulatory questions.[49] The majority's basic problem, then, was to liberate the EPA from these cross-cutting and paralyzing political pressures, both enabling it to bring expertise to bear on the regulatory problems and prodding it to do so. How could this be accomplished?

The solution was two-fold. In the first place, the majority took a flexible and capacious view of standing law, allowing states and (perhaps) private landowners to trigger vigorous judicial review of executive action. The Court's standing holding was of course necessary to proceed to the merits. In one sense, it represents nothing very new—the Court's holding only reinforces its return to more liberalized standing in cases like *Laidlaw*[50] and *Akins*,[51] and backs away from Justice Scalia's opinion in *Lujan*,[52] which sought to tighten the injury-in-fact test.

Yet on our account, the practical effect of granting standing in *MA v EPA* may be somewhat different than in these other cases. On the facts of *MA v EPA*, capacious standing affects the allocation of authority *within* the executive branch, allowing states and (per-

---

[48] The petition denial suggests as much, noting that the motor vehicle fleet is one of "many sources" of greenhouse gas emissions and a "sensible regulatory scheme would require that all significant sources of emissions be considered." 68 Fed Reg at 52931. For this and other policy reasons, EPA concluded that it would decline to regulate motor vehicle emissions even if it had the authority to do so.

[49] The Court's decision merely to grant certiorari in *MA v EPA* (and in *Environmental Defense v Duke Energy*, 127 S Ct 1423 (2007), another environmental case decided the same day) was striking on its own—only rarely have environmental plaintiffs been granted certiorari as petitioners. One needs to go back thirty-five years to *Sierra Club v Morton*, 405 US 727 (1972), to find a successful certiorari petition by environmentalists granted over the opposition of the government. And, of course, the petitioners lost that case on the merits. We thank Richard Lazarus for making this point.

[50] *Friends of the Earth, Inc. v Laidlaw Environmental Services (TOC), Inc.*, 528 US 167 (2000).

[51] *Federal Election Commission v Akins*, 524 US 11 (1998).

[52] *Lujan v Defenders of Wildlife*, 504 US 555 (1992).

haps) similarly situated private parties to disable strong "presidential administration"[53] of line agencies, even agencies that are not legally independent.[54] In affording the states standing, the Court signaled its dissatisfaction with the political accountability on which strong presidential administration relies for its legitimacy. At a minimum, allowing access to judicial review was a necessary first step in the Court's expertise-forcing project.

In the second place, the majority's holdings on the merits made it extremely difficult for the agency to maintain its posture of refusing to make a first-order decision. By interpreting the relevant statutory provisions with no deference to the EPA's disclaimer of authority, and by narrowly cabining the grounds on which EPA might decline to make a first-order statutory judgment one way or another, the Court makes it virtually unavoidable for EPA to make such a judgment, with a consequent pressure to regulate if its judgment is that greenhouse gas emissions from new tailpipes can reasonably be anticipated to contribute to the endangerment of public health and welfare. At a minimum, the Court significantly raises the costs to the agency of declining to regulate. And by ruling out as impermissible all nonscientific considerations, the Court makes it much more difficult for the President to dictate the outcome on other policy grounds. The Court's two merits holdings are thus best understood as components of its expertise-forcing project.

Below, we examine each major aspect of the Court's decision in *MA v EPA*—its holdings on standing, statutory authority, and administrative discretion to "decide not to decide." After some brief remarks on standing, we make two principal claims: first, that the Court's refusal to grant *Chevron* deference to EPA's view of its statutory authority, especially in light of the *Brown & Williamson*[55] precedent, suggests that for the current Court insulating expertise from politics is a greater imperative than forcing democratic accountability, and, second, that narrowing the permissible grounds on which an agency can make a second-order decision to defer a discretionary first-order decision—something the Court has never

---

[53] Kagan, 114 Harv L Rev 2245 (cited in note 11). See also Lawrence Lessig and Cass Sunstein, *The President and the Administration*, 94 Colum L Rev 1 (1994).

[54] When we refer to "presidential control" we include the political appointees within the agency who likely reflect the administration's policy priorities; when we refer to "line" agencies, we refer to career staff.

[55] *FDA v Brown & Williamson Tobacco Corp.*, 529 US 120 (2000).

done before—represents an effort to guard against politically motivated agency circumvention of broad statutory purposes.

A. STANDING

We begin with a short summary of the Court's standing analysis.
Our main interest is in what the Court held on the merits; the
precise grounds on which the Court found standing, and the relationship between the standing analysis in *MA v EPA* and in
earlier decisions, are not critical for our thesis. All that matters,
for our purposes, is that the Court allowed the suit to proceed in
order to resolve it on the merits on expertise-forcing grounds.

The Court's analysis had at least three strands. First, and receiving most of the attention, was the Court's suggestion that
federal standing law embodies some form of "special solicitude"
for states that bring lawsuits as plaintiffs to vindicate their sovereign interests. Second was a brief but pregnant suggestion, based
on a significant concurrence by Justice Kennedy in *Lujan v Defenders of Wildlife*,[56] that statutes can create "procedural rights,"
the vindication of which does not require "meeting all the normal
standards for redressability and immediacy."[57] Third—and distinct
from the "special solicitude" holding—was an ordinary standing
analysis that focused on Massachusetts qua large landowner rather
than qua sovereign, which found that Massachusetts's own coastal
property was threatened by rising sea levels traceable to the effects
of greenhouse gases.

It seems obvious that the first two strands of this analysis were,
at least in part, a by-product of intra-Court coalition building. To
garner a crucial fifth vote, Justice Stevens needed to write an opinion that Justice Kennedy, the Court's likely swing voter, would

---

[56] 504 US 555 (1992). Justice Kennedy's *Lujan* concurrence referred to Congress's power
to create legal rights of action for which there is no analogue in the common law:

> We must be sensitive to the articulation of new rights of action that do not have
> clear analogs in our common-law tradition. . . . In my view, Congress has the
> power to define injuries and articulate chains of causation that will give rise to
> a case or controversy where none existed before, and I do not read the Court's
> opinion to suggest a contrary view.

Lujan, 504 US at 580 (Kennedy concurring).

[57] *MA v EPA*, 127 S Ct at 1453, quoting *Lujan*, 504 US at 572 n 7. The majority opinion
in *MA v EPA* refers more narrowly than did Justice Kennedy's *Lujan* concurrence to
Congress's ability to create "procedural rights" to challenge agency action; it is for such
rights that the normal requirements of immediacy and redressability do not apply.

join. The idea that states as sovereigns enjoy special judicial solicitude resonates with Justice Kennedy's views about constitutional federalism—both judicial protection for tacit principles of
state sovereign immunity, and judicial enforcement of limited federal authority, especially under the Commerce Clause. And emphasizing Congress's role in creating procedural rights, as Justice
Stevens's opinion does, elevates Justice Kennedy's *Lujan* concurrence into binding law.

It is hardly clear, however, that a special law of standing for
states is consistent with the prior views of Justice Souter, who—
in opinions joined by Justice Stevens—emphasized in both the
sovereign immunity cases[58] and the Commerce Clause[59] cases that
there are "political safeguards of federalism." Presumably, if those
political safeguards are robust, states need no special solicitude in
Article III litigation. Indeed, perhaps states should be especially
disfavored as plaintiffs because they have substitute political remedies. In the case of greenhouse gas regulation, surely the states
can spur legislative oversight of a recalcitrant EPA by enlisting
sympathetic members of their congressional delegations to hold
hearings or otherwise make life difficult for the agency. As a general matter, states surely have more opportunities to hold agencies
accountable than do most private parties, and the availability of
these remedies could militate against granting them standing.

On the other hand, we might understand the states in *MA v
EPA* as claiming that they had *already* used the national political
process, and won.[60] On this view, the CAA itself supported their

---

[58] See, for example, *Seminole Tribe v Florida*, 517 US 44, 183 (1996) (Souter dissenting)
(describing how the "plain statement rule, which 'assures that the legislature has in fact
faced, and intended to bring into issue, the critical matters involved in the judicial decision,'
is particularly appropriate in light of our primary reliance on 'the effectiveness of the
federal political process in preserving the States' interests") (citations omitted).

[59] See, for example, *United States v Morrison*, 529 US 598, 647 (2000) (Souter dissenting)
(criticizing the revival of the "state spheres of action" consideration in Commerce Clause
analysis: "The defect, in essence, is the majority's rejection of the Founders' considered
judgment that politics, not judicial review, should mediate between state and national
interests . . . ."); *United States v Lopez*, 514 US 549, 604 (1995) (Souter dissenting) (val-
orizing deference to "rationally based legislative judgments '[as] a paradigm of judicial
restraint,'" because "[i]n judicial review under the Commerce Clause, it reflects our respect
for the institutional competence of the Congress on a subject expressly assigned to it by
the Constitution and our appreciation of the legitimacy that comes from Congress's political accountability in dealing with matters open to a wide range of possible choices")
(citation omitted).

[60] State and local officials, not environmental groups, were responsible for pressing for
national air regulation. See Christopher J. Bailey, *Congress and Air Pollution* 104–5, 109

position, and they were merely turning to the courts to enforce their political victory. Our suggestion is just that, whatever the merits of the "political safeguards" argument for limited state standing, it appears that the majority Justices who might have subscribed to that position at least temporarily set it aside and accepted a possible inconsistency with their broader federalism jurisprudence in order to obtain Justice Kennedy's indispensable fifth vote.

The second thread in the majority's standing analysis, the idea that Congress can by statute create procedural rights whose vindication is an adequate basis for standing, is more deeply threatening to the views of standing held by the four Justices in dissent, especially Justice Scalia, who believes that Congress's power to create statutory rights is ultimately limited by Article III requirements. In *Lujan*, Justice Kennedy's concurrence parted ways with Justice Scalia's opinion by suggesting that statutes might create injuries and articulate chains of causation, which would be adequate for Article III purposes, providing the injury is sufficiently concrete,[61] even if those injuries were not "injuries in fact" in some independent sense. And a majority of the Court, in *FEC v Akins*, had adopted a similar view in the setting of informational injuries.[62] By reviving Justice Kennedy's concurrence, the *MA v EPA* majority extends the analysis of *Akins* to a new setting, and pushes the Court further toward a model of standing in which the relevant question is whether there is a legal right to sue, a right created by statutes or other sources of law.[63] It is not surprising, then, that Chief Justice Roberts's dissent on the standing issue argued that under the restrictive *Lujan* framework, the state's injuries should be

(Manchester, 1998) (citing the role of groups of local officials, including the U.S. Conference of Mayors, the American Municipal Association, and the National Association of Counties, which felt pressure from voters to act but lacked resources to act themselves and remained concerned about disadvantages to their jurisdictions caused by a race to the bottom).

[61] Justice Kennedy's concurrence does seem to require that a litigant show he has suffered whatever injury Congress has defined in a *concrete and personal way*. See *Lujan*, 504 US at 581 (Kennedy concurring) (requiring that the congressionally defined injury be "concrete").

[62] 524 US 11 (1998) (holding that FECA creates a right of action for voters to challenge an FEC decision not to undertake an enforcement action, and that petitioners met the prudential standing test that allows Congress to create standing beyond common law rights of action, as well as the Article III test for injury, having suffered a concrete injury by being denied information that they sought).

[63] See generally Cass R. Sunstein, *What's Standing After Lujan? Of Citizen Suits, "Injuries," and Article III*, 91 Mich L Rev 163 (1992).

counted as highly speculative, depending upon long and uncertain causal chains, themselves incorporating uncertain predictions about the behavior of other nations and actors. In this way, Chief Justice Roberts emphasized (perhaps unintentionally) that *MA v EPA* seems in part to undercut the *Lujan* framework substantially.

The third prong of the majority's standing analysis, which is independent of the "special solicitude" afforded to states, argues entirely *within* the *Lujan* framework that the state's injuries as a landowner were sufficiently concrete and were redressable by the requested relief, in the simple sense that obtaining relief might make things better for the state and could not make things any worse. Here, *MA v EPA* clearly pulls against Justice Scalia's narrow interpretation of injury and redressability in *Lujan*. Even putting aside the Court's ambiguous gesture toward a different model of standing, this more generous version of the *Lujan* approach may have a large effect on cases where litigants, who are potential beneficiaries of the regulation, attempt to persuade judges to order or encourage administrative regulation of third parties—a common feature of environmental cases, and precisely the situation in *MA v EPA*.

The multiple bases for standing identified in the Court's opinion produce a great deal of uncertainty. It is not clear which if any components of the Court's standing analysis will generalize beyond this case. There is reason to think that "special solicitude" in particular will be limited and short-lived, its invention made necessary by the unique facts and judicial lineup in *MA v EPA*. Yet it is open to a future Court—and to lower courts in the interim—to emphasize any one of the Court's standing rationales, especially the third and most ordinary strand. To the extent that it can be separated from "special solicitude," the revival of the *Lujan* concurrence may make standing easier to achieve in future cases.

For our purposes, however, the differences among these three rationales are interesting but tangential. Common to all is that an expansive view of standing—whether for states because they are special, for statutory rights generally, or even through the generous application of the *Lujan* framework—increases the scope for judges to oversee the legality of executive action.[64] This runs directly

---

[64] Although the Court declined to extend this expansive view of standing to private taxpayers this term, see *Hein v Freedom from Religion Foundation, Inc.*, 127 S Ct 2553, 2559

counter to the earlier trend of narrowed standing; restricting judicial oversight of executive action is an explicit purpose of the
Lujan framework, according to Justice Scalia, its author.[65] The
Court in *MA v EPA* must obviously grant standing in order to
assess whether the EPA, in denying the petition to regulate, acted
lawfully. Yet standing here has a more specific effect as well: instead
of using standing to engage in judicial oversight of an undiffer-
entiated executive (the kind of oversight that Justice Scalia wished
to prevent in *Lujan*), the Court can be understood, in the particular
circumstances of the case, as granting standing in order to review
the allocation of authority *within* the executive, specifically between the White House and its political appointees in the agency,
on the one hand, and career staff at EPA on the other. On a view
that emphasizes the democratic accountability of the executive as
a source of legitimacy, this approach is hard to justify or even
understand; pressure from the White House to exercise discretionary authority in one way or another is a good, not a bad, and
shows that the system of presidential administration is functioning
properly. As we will explain below, however, the Court has seemingly turned away from this benign view of presidential administration toward an older model of administrative law that emphasizes the tension between democratic politics—and in
particular presidential political control over line agencies—and
technocratic expertise.

B. STATUTORY AUTHORITY

We now turn to the first merits question in *MA v EPA*: whether
EPA has statutory authority to regulate greenhouse gases as "pollutants." The relevant provision of the CAA, § 302(g), defines air
pollutants as "any air pollution agent or combination of such
agents, including any . . . physical [or] chemical . . . substance
or matter which is emitted into or otherwise enters the ambient
air."[66] At a minimum, EPA argued, the definition of "pollutant"

(2007), the case can be distinguished from *MA v EPA* because it was not brought under
a statutory grant of authority.

[65] See Antonin Scalia, *The Doctrine of Standing as an Essential Element of the Separation
of Powers*, 17 Suffolk U L Rev 991, 991 (1983) ("My thesis is that the judicial doctrine of
standing is a crucial and inseparable element of [the separation of powers], whose disregard
will inevitably produce—as it has in the past few decades—an overjudicialization of the
processes of self-governance.").

[66] 42 USC § 7602(g) (2000).

contains sufficient ambiguity that the Court should defer to EPA's reasonable reading that it lacks such authority. The Court rejected EPA's definitional argument, emphasizing the literal breadth of the definition and holding that greenhouse gases were clearly covered. Justice Scalia's dissent, joined by three other Justices, focused in part on this issue, arguing that the definition was at least ambiguous.

EPA also argued, more broadly, that the overall statutory scheme, the history of congressional action in this and related areas, and possible conflicts between EPA regulation of new vehicle emissions under the CAA and the regulation of fuel efficiency by the Department of Transportation (DOT) under the Energy Policy and Conservation Act, all suggested that the EPA lacked authority or could reasonably interpret the statutes in that fashion, even if the immediately relevant statutory sections at first glance seemed clear. As for the statutory scheme, EPA emphasized that several of its most prominent features, such as the system of National Ambient Air Quality Standards (NAAQS), seemed implicitly geared to coping with localized pollutants rather than greenhouse gases, which have the same incremental effect on global warming regardless of the location in which they are emitted. The NAAQS system does not seem workable for greenhouse gases in part because states could never ensure compliance with federally established concentration limits; those gases are emitted from many worldwide sources not under their control.

Similar arguments had carried the day in *Brown & Williamson*,[67] in which the Court held that the FDA lacked authority to regulate nicotine as a drug under a similarly broad statutory definition. The Food, Drug and Cosmetic Act (FDCA) defined a "drug" as "articles (other than food) intended to affect the structure or any function of the body,"[68] and, at least facially, nicotine surely met that definition. The *Brown & Williamson* majority overrode this clear text, however, through a grab-bag of interpretive techniques, including an appeal to the specific or counterfactually reconstructed intentions of the enacting Congress of 1938 (whose median member probably did not intend to ban tobacco or authorize an agency to do so, or at least would not have so intended if asked

---

[67] 529 US 120 (2000).

[68] 21 USC § 321(g)(1) (2000).

the question), and a claim that later "tobacco-specific" labeling legislation was inconsistent with regulatory prohibition of tobacco, and thus should be understood as an implied partial repeal of the broad statutory definition of "drug." Finally, the FDA had made many representations that it lacked the relevant authority, before changing its view during the Clinton administration, and many bills designed to give the FDA express regulatory authority had died in Congress.[69]

Most important of all was an interpretive canon emphasized (though arguably not invented) by the Court in *Brown & Williamson*:[70] statutes should not be construed to give agencies authority over questions of great "economic and political" significance unless Congress has spoken clearly. Given the strong argument that Congress had spoken clearly in the FDCA, this "major questions" canon was widely thought to be quite powerful; perhaps it meant that Congress had to speak not only clearly but also specifically in order to confer authority on agencies. Other cases had implicitly followed a similar approach. In *Gonzales v Oregon*, for example, the Court had interpreted federal laws regulating controlled substances to deny the Attorney General the authority to regulate the prescription of controlled substances to patients lawfully committing suicide under Oregon's assisted suicide statute.[71]

In *MA v EPA*, however, it is plausible to think that EPA was in a far stronger position than either the FDA or the Attorney General had been in their cases. In *Brown & Williamson*, the nondelegation canon for major questions pulled against *Chevron* deference; the FDA would not win if the relevant statutes were ambiguous, but only if they clearly conferred the authority the agency claimed. In *MA v EPA*, however, *Chevron* and the major questions canon pulled in the same direction. The agency could lose only if the Court found that the relevant statutes clearly mandated rejecting the agency's view. The interpretive techniques of

---

[69] See *Brown & Williamson*, 529 US at 146–56.

[70] See, for example, *MCI Telecommunications Corp. v AT&T Co.*, 512 US 218, 228–31 (1994).

[71] 546 US 243, 259 (2006) ("The [Controlled Substances Act] gives the Attorney General limited powers, to be exercised in specific ways. . . . Congress did not delegate to the Attorney General authority to carry out or effect all provisions of the CSA. Rather, he can promulgate rules relating only to 'registration' and 'control,' and 'for the efficient execution of his functions' under the statute.").

Brown & Williamson, in other words, needed only to generate sufficient ambiguity for the EPA to win under *Chevron*. Doubtless for these reasons, the Solicitor General's brief devoted a great deal of space and emphasis to the *Brown & Williamson* arguments.

Surprisingly, however, there was little discussion of either the definitional question generally, or *Brown & Williamson* in particular, at oral argument. When petitioners' counsel began his argument on the definition of "pollutant," he was shut down by the Justices in a way that strongly suggested that the issue would pose no difficulty for the Court, and would likely come out his way.[72] And although the Justices obviously disagreed in the end about the definition of "pollutant," neither the majority opinion nor Justice Scalia's dissent said much about *Brown & Williamson*. Perhaps this was because all concerned thought the two cases could be easily distinguished. For one thing, the remedial implications of granting the FDA authority to regulate tobacco in *Brown & Williamson* were potentially far more serious than granting the EPA statutory authority to regulate greenhouse gases in *MA v EPA*—the FDA arguably would have had to ban tobacco under the terms of the FDCA; at a minimum it would have been authorized to do so.[73] For another thing there was a great deal of postenactment legislation in *Brown & Williamson* indicating that Congress did not intend to ban tobacco products; such "postenactment legislative history" did not exist in *MA v EPA*.[74]

Whether for these or other reasons, the majority dispensed with the issue of statutory authority with celerity. What did it matter, the Court said in a footnote, whether Congress had dealt with the only other nonlocalized emission problem, stratospheric ozone, in a separate statutory section?[75] What's the problem, the Court said in a

---

[72] See Transcript of Oral Argument, *MA v EPA*, No 05-1120, *17–18 (Nov 29, 2006). Given the lack of attention to the authority issue at oral argument, it is particularly striking that four Justices dissented on the issue.

[73] See *Brown & Williamson*, 529 US at 161–92 (Breyer dissenting). By contrast, in *MA v EPA*, the result of finding agency authority was not so dire. Section 202(a) gives EPA considerable discretion to tailor the timing and stringency of tailpipe emissions regulation of the new vehicle fleet, including allowing for considerations of economic and technological feasibility.

[74] *MA v EPA*, 127 S Ct at 1461–62.

[75] Id at 1461 n 29 ("We are moreover puzzled by EPA's roundabout argument that because later Congresses chose to address stratospheric ozone pollution in a specific legislative provision, it somehow follows that greenhouse gases cannot be air pollutants within the meaning of the Clean Air Act.").

brisk paragraph, if EPA must regulate motor vehicle mileage standards to control emissions? There might be conflict with the DOT, "but there is no reason to think the two agencies cannot both administer their obligations and yet avoid inconsistency."[76] After all, EPA is charged with protecting public health and welfare, whereas DOT is charged with promoting fuel economy. Finally, as to the specific or imaginatively reconstructed intentions of the enacting Congress—a prominent argument for limiting agency authority in *Brown & Williamson*—Justice Stevens wrote that "[w]hile the Congresses that drafted [§ 202(a)] might not have appreciated the possibility that burning fossil fuels could lead to global warming, they did understand that without regulatory flexibility, changing circumstances and scientific developments would soon render the CAA obsolete."[77]

Is *MA* v *EPA* consistent with *Brown & Williamson*?[78] Viewed from one angle the answer is no, from another yes. The argument that they are inconsistent runs as follows. Under the conventional understanding of *Brown & Williamson*, the major questions canon means that if an agency is to exercise jurisdiction over a major question, Congress must confer that jurisdiction clearly. Surely the regulation of greenhouses gases is an economic and political issue of major significance; if *Brown & Williamson* were followed, the Solicitor General argued, the Court could find statutory authority to regulate greenhouse gas emissions only by finding the relevant statutes entirely clear.

In *MA v EPA*, the arguments against agency authority seem, at least arguably, as strong as the equivalent arguments in *Brown & Williamson*. Setting to the side Justice Scalia's objections for the moment, there is a decent (though not ironclad) argument that the immediately relevant text of §§ 202(a) and 302(g) was clear. But of course the immediate text in *Brown & Williamson* was in this sense also quite clear, arguably even more so than in *MA v EPA*. It is

---

[76] Id at 1461.

[77] Id at 1462.

[78] Justice Scalia in dissent said not a word about *Brown & Williamson*. Perhaps his vote with the majority in that case was inconsistent with his textualist jurisprudence, which generally disparages drawing inferences about implicit congressional intentions, especially from rejected bills and the like. On the other hand, Justice Scalia may have thought, very simply, that any *Brown & Williamson*-style discussion of the broader statutory scheme and its history was unnecessary, given his argument that the immediate text of the provisions at issue was facially ambiguous.

hard to deny, on any view of what counts as plain meaning, that nicotine plainly fits within the definition, "articles (other than food) intended to affect the structure or any function of the body." No Justice in *Brown & Williamson* suggested that the immediately relevant texts were ambiguous, and there is no opinion in *Brown & Williamson* closely analogous to the Scalia dissent in *MA v EPA*.

The guiding assumption of *Brown & Williamson* is that what counts as clear for purposes of *Chevron* cannot be judged solely in light of the statutory sections immediately at hand; rather it must be judged in light of the whole statutory scheme and other statutes. And the arguments from the overall statutory scheme that the Solicitor General emphasized in *MA v EPA* were at least as strong as in *Brown & Williamson*. What is striking is just that the *MA v EPA* majority seems to afford much less weight to those arguments than did the *Brown & Williamson* majority. In this sense, where *Brown & Williamson* denied an agency authority because Congress had not clearly granted it, *Massachusetts v EPA* thrusts authority upon the agency, even though Congress had not clearly granted it.

The possible inconsistency goes deeper, however. The major questions canon has been explained as a nondelegation canon, one that aims to prod Congress, rather than agencies, into shouldering political responsibility for large policy choices.[79] In *MA v EPA*, by contrast, the consequence of not affording *Chevron* deference to EPA on the major questions surrounding greenhouse gases was precisely the opposite: Congress need take no further action, because EPA already (the Court ruled) has the authority to make a first-order judgment about whether greenhouses gases should be regulated. *MA v EPA* is in this sense an anti-nondelegation case, one that extends agency authority over a controversial regulatory domain in the face of the agency's own disavowals, where the overall statutory landscape did not clearly grant authority, and where Congress had not expressed a recent and clearly focused judgment on the relevant questions.

How, if at all, can the two cases be made legally consistent? The simplest argument is that in *MA v EPA*, unlike in *Brown & Williamson*, the relevant sections of the Clear Air Act were sufficiently clear to override even the combined effect of *Chevron* and the major-questions canon. If statutes are clear, there can be no inconsistency

---

[79] See Cass R. Sunstein, *Chevron Step Zero*, 92 Va L Rev 187 (2006); John F. Manning, *The Nondelegation Doctrine as a Canon of Avoidance*, 2000 Supreme Court Review 223 (2000).

with the statutory default rules, whatever they are; it is just that the default presumptions have been overcome. Now suppose, on the other hand, that one does not think the relevant statutes entirely clear about EPA's authority. There is still a sense in which the two cases are perfectly consistent: they both suggest that no *Chevron* deference will be afforded to agencies on interpretive questions of major economic and political significance, whether the agency is attempting to expand its jurisdiction (*Brown & Williamson*) or to exclude from its jurisdiction a politically touchy subject (*MA v EPA*). On this view, even if the CAA did not clearly give EPA authority to regulate greenhouse gases, still the Court took that to be the better reading of the statutes, all things considered; here the effect of the major-questions canon is to eliminate the *Chevron* default that would ordinarily entitle the agency to win unless the statute clearly runs against the agency's view.

There are other differences as well, which could explain the two outcomes. The most obvious is that *Brown & Williamson*, like *Gonzales*, involved an instance of putative agency *overreach*, whereas *MA v EPA* involved a case of putative agency *underreach*. Whereas the FDA had always said it *lacked* authority to regulate tobacco prior to changing its mind in the Clinton administration, the EPA had always said it *possessed* the authority to regulate greenhouse gases until changing *its* mind in the George W. Bush administration. Perhaps the Court reserves the nondelegation approach—in the sense of forcing Congress to clarify its intent to grant regulatory authority—for the former situation, and resorts to expertise-forcing in the latter; we return to this possibility shortly.[80]

In our view, however, the most convincing reconstruction is simply that the *MA v EPA* majority seems to be engaged in a different enterprise than the *Brown & Williamson* majority. Whereas the latter was pursuing a nondelegation approach, one that required a clear statement from Congress in order to bring major issues within the scope of the agency's jurisdiction, the former does not seem interested in getting a clear statement, from a current Congress, about the bounds of EPA's authority. Consider that the statutory provi-

---

[80] Of course underreach can be converted into overreach simply by an agency choosing to act where it has not before, as occurred with the FDA in *Brown & Williamson*. The analogous question in this setting would be: if EPA had chosen to regulate greenhouse gases under Section 202(a), and had been challenged, would a reviewing court have determined that it overreached, and sent the matter to Congress for a clearer expression of authority?

sions that (the Court argued) clearly gave EPA authority over greenhouse gas emissions were enacted in the 1960s and 1970s, before greenhouse gases and global warming moved to the top of scientific and public agendas. A nondelegation approach would prod Congress to reconsider the subject, today, in explicit terms. *MA v EPA* shows no interest in that project.

If a nondelegation approach does not explain *MA v EPA*, then what is the majority's enterprise? Our basic suggestion is that the enterprise is not at all to force politically accountable policy choices, either by Congress or (least of all) the president. Rather, the enterprise is expertise-forcing: the majority's enterprise is to clear away legal obstacles and political pressures in order to encourage or force EPA to make an expert first-order judgment about greenhouse gases, a judgment constrained by the statutory factors of health and welfare set out in § 202(a). To explain this claim, we must set it in its legal context: the Court's holding that EPA had supplied no valid reason for deciding not to make a first-order judgment at all.

C. DECIDING NOT TO DECIDE: "HOW ABOUT NEVER? IS NEVER GOOD FOR YOU?"[81]

We now turn to the Court's holding on the second merits question. Here the issue was whether EPA had discretion to defer making the threshold finding necessary to trigger regulation for the variety of policy reasons it offered—whether EPA could simply decide not to decide. No prior Supreme Court case had raised precisely this question about the extent of an agency's discretionary rulemaking authority.

On what grounds may an administrative agency reject a petition for rulemaking? On what grounds, if any, may a reviewing court overturn that decision? Is a rejection of a rulemaking petition reviewable at all? Before *MA v EPA*, the law on these questions was surprisingly unclear, especially at the level of the Supreme Court. *Heckler v Chaney*[82] had announced a limited presumption of unreviewability, at least for enforcement discretion; it was thus clear that agencies had broad discretion, unless statutes clearly dictated otherwise, to decide whether or not to initiate enforcement proceedings. It was not so clear whether the same discretion extended, with equal

---

[81] Robert Mankoff, *Businessman Talking into Telephone Cartoon*, New Yorker (May 3, 1993).
[82] 470 US 821 (1985).

force at least, to denials of petitions for rulemaking. On the one hand, the basic logic of *Heckler v Chaney*—that agencies have limited budgets and limited time, and so must be given discretion to set priorities and allocate resources—carries over to the rulemaking setting; rulemaking proceedings are not on average any less costly or time consuming than enforcement proceedings, and may often be more so.[83] Thus the Court has seemed reluctant to compel agency action when agencies with discretionary grants of authority prefer not to act, except in very narrow circumstances, such as when Congress has prescribed a specific legal duty the agency refuses to undertake, or when the agency has unreasonably delayed legally required action that it has initiated but failed to complete.[84]

In *Norton v Southern Utah Wilderness Alliance*,[85] decided in 2004, Justice Scalia wrote for the Court that "a claim [to compel agency action unlawfully withheld under § 706(1) of the APA] can proceed only where a plaintiff asserts that an agency failed to take a discrete action that it is required to take."[86] The Court declined to require the Bureau of Land Management (BLM) to regulate environmentally damaging off-road vehicle (ORV) use on public lands eligible for wilderness designation, even though the agency had a statutory obligation to manage the lands "so as not to impair their suitability for preservation as wilderness."[87] That managerial mandate required nothing so specific as regulating off-road vehicles. *SUWA* did not actually involve the denial of a petition for rulemaking, and the decision does not announce or confirm a presumption of "unreviewability" for anything. But it does indicate that the relevant question for courts reviewing agency inaction is just whether, on

---

[83] Eric Biber, *Two Sides of the Same Coin: Judicial Review under APA Sections 706(1) and 706(2)* 11–19 (Vill Envir L J article, forthcoming spring 2008) (discussing the importance of the resource allocation rationale in administrative law).

[84] Circuit courts have sometimes provided remedies against delaying agencies. See *Public Citizen Health Research Group v Chao*, 314 F3d 143, 146 (3d Cir 2002) (finding unreasonable delay in OSHA's development of hexavalent chromium rules and ordering the parties to set a timetable for the rulemaking through mediation or else have one set by the court); *In re International Chemical Workers Union*, 958 F2d 1144, 1150 (DC Cir 1992) (imposing a deadline on OSHA for completion of a cadmium rulemaking); *American Horse Protection Association v Lyng*, 812 F2d 1, 7–8 (1987) (reversing the district court's grant of summary judgment to the Secretary of Agriculture in an animal advocates' action against the secretary's refusal to institute rulemaking proceedings in light of the inadequacy of regulations to prevent neglect of show horses).

[85] 542 US 55 (2004) ("*SUWA*").

[86] Id at 64.

[87] Id at 65, citing 43 USC § 1782(c) (2000).

the merits of the relevant statutes, the agency is failing to do something it is legally obliged to do.[88]

MA v EPA establishes that agency denials of rulemaking petitions are in fact reviewable, and that an agency may decline to make rules only on the basis of factors the statute makes relevant.[89] In the specific context of § 202, the Court determined that the relevant statutory factors are whether the air pollutant "cause[s], or contribute[s] to, air pollution which may reasonably be anticipated to endanger public health or welfare." These factors are scientific and causal; they do not include broader considerations of foreign affairs and public policy. Further, if EPA does make a threshold finding of endangerment, it has no choice but to regulate motor vehicle emissions, although within the terms of § 202(a) itself it would have considerable latitude to determine the timing and content of the ensuing regulation. In addition, the Court's holding presumably leaves EPA some residual discretion to "decide not to decide"; that is, to again decline to make the endangerment judgment. However, this residual discretion is highly constrained: such decisions must be "reasoned judgments" reviewable under the arbitrary and capricious standard. Crucially, *the same statutory factors that govern the agency's decision about whether or not a pollutant meets the endangerment standard also govern its decision about whether or not to make that judgment in the first place.* That is, roughly speaking, EPA may decline to make a statutory judgment only on technocratic and scientific grounds, not political ones.[90]

To understand the significance of these holdings, we must begin

---

[88] In *SUWA*, the relevant statutory provision required the Bureau of Land Management to "manage [lands under its jurisdiction] so as not to impair the suitability of such areas for preservation as wilderness" and "in accordance with a land use plan." *SUWA*, 542 US at 59, citing 43 USC § 1782(c). The plaintiffs argued that the agency violated this duty by failing to protect public lands from environmental damage caused by ORVs. The Court unanimously held, per Justice Scalia, that this failure was not remediable under the APA. BLM had a general nonimpairment mandate but discretion to decide how to achieve it, and there was no specific discrete mandate to ban or regulate ORVs. *SUWA*, 542 US at 65–72.

[89] See Biber, *Two Sides of the Same Coin: Judicial Review under APA Sections 706(1) and 706(2)* at 24–25 (cited in note 83) (explaining why it may be appropriate to treat decisions not to issue rules differently from decisions not to enforce).

[90] Arguably, the Court still leaves room for the agency to cite considerations such as time and resource constraints, or other priorities, as reasons why it declines to regulate, but even if that might be helpful to the agency in some contexts, that is unlikely to leave the EPA much flexibility here. It is hard to imagine the agency defending the view that other issues are more important at the moment than addressing climate change.

with some general points about decision making.[91] Why might an agency decide not to decide, and why might courts worry about such second-order decisions? Begin by imagining an agency that only considers social welfare, not its own political position. There are a number of reasons such well-motivated agencies might wish to defer decisions: they believe they will make a better decision later, after collecting more information; they have more important things to do with limited resources; or, most generally, because the agency believes that the "option value" of postponing a decision—the value of making it later and not now—is greater than the net benefit of deciding now, even with appropriate discounting of future value.

A major source of option value is that more information will often be available in the future, enabling a better decision.[92] Under some circumstances this will surely be normatively desirable. On the other hand, making a slightly worse-informed decision now can be better than waiting if there are opportunity costs or interim losses from a nondecision. In theory, holding other factors constant, agencies should postpone their decisions just until the costs of further delay exceed the expected gain in new information.[93] Of course, both the cost of delay and the benefits of waiting are affected by the stakes of the decision, in terms of the magnitude and probability of the risks involved. When stakes are high (as when a nondecision might lead to significant irreversible negative consequences), the cost of delaying a decision could be substantial. At the same time, high stakes raise the cost of an erroneous decision as well, and thus increase the benefit of collecting more information. Depending on which risk is perceived to be greater—the potentially irreversible costs of deciding too soon versus the potentially irreversible costs of delaying too long—it can be sensible to wait for additional or better information.

So far we have imagined well-motivated agencies deciding whether to decide on the basis of social welfare. However, political

---

[91] As we have said, the EPA here effectively declined to regulate greenhouse gases, but the actual choice it made—and the choice it had to defend to the Court—was not to make the threshold endangerment finding at all.

[92] See generally Avinash Dixit and Robert S. Pindyck, *Investment Under Uncertainty* (Princeton, 1994).

[93] We bracket the problem that "[t]o maximize subject to the constraint of information costs one would have to know the expected value of information, but this is not in general possible." Jon Elster, *Introduction*, in *Rational Choice* 1, 25 (1986).

incentives may also come into play. The private costs to the agency of deciding now might exceed the social costs, if the agency's decision will cause it to be punished by the White House, or excoriated by scientists, or targeted by regulated constituencies. In this revised calculus, from the agency's standpoint, it should decide not to decide when the expected private costs of making a decision now, either way, are greater than the private benefits.

Some issues are so politically fraught, however, that no matter how an agency decides (in a first-order sense), a large constituency will be angered; indeed, this is our picture of EPA's position with respect to greenhouse gases. The agency may be loath to make a first-order expert judgment because it fears that the judgment will have to be made in some particular direction, a direction that will produce further problems or demand politically hazardous regulatory action. Or the agency may realize that a judgment in any direction will result in political punishment.

In our view, the Court's holding on the second merits issue can best be understood in just these terms: it rested on the worry that EPA decided not to decide because of a divergence between political costs to the agency and social costs. On this account, the majority believed that EPA was postponing the statutory judgment not because of the social benefits of waiting for more information, or as a result of a careful calibration by the agency of the costs and benefits of further delay given its resource constraints in light of other pressing priorities, or for other valid reasons. Indeed, it would be implausible to attribute to the agency the desire to defer regulation in order to gather more information; EPA's alternative legal position was that it lacked authority to regulate and could not revisit the issue. Rather, EPA was postponing its decision in order to duck cross-cutting political pressures from the White House and business-friendly interest groups, on the one hand, and from green interest groups, scientists, and many states, on the other.

It is important for this account that an agency decision not to decide is not neutral; it leaves the regulatory status quo ante in place.[94] Because of how the status quo was set, deciding not to make the first-order decision in *MA v EPA* (that is, declining to decide whether the statutory endangerment test is met) appeased the White House by leaving greenhouse gases unregulated, and had the major

---

[94] See *MA v EPA*, 127 S Ct at 1473 n 1 (Scalia dissenting).

advantage (from EPA's perspective) of not forcing EPA to make implausible scientific and technical claims that would have incurred widespread condemnation from climate scientists, environmentalists, and the public at large. Better to lapse into passivity, on this view, than to be seen actively cooperating with an effort to politicize science. To be sure, even to decide not to decide required EPA to write an opinion that overstated the uncertainty of the climate science, and thus caused it to be condemned by expert scientists, environmentalists, and other informed observers. However, EPA's nondecision did not require a substantive claim that greenhouse gases have no adverse health and welfare effects; plausibly, it thus produced a lesser backlash than a first-order judgment against regulation would have.

D. THE ANTICIRCUMVENTION PRINCIPLE

On this account, the majority's basic response was to narrow the bases on which EPA could decide not to decide. By excluding the most obviously political factors, such as a concern that regulation might interfere with the administration's foreign policy objectives, the majority forced EPA to defend its second-order decision solely by reference to narrower technocratic factors, above all the value of waiting for further information. If second-order agency discretion to postpone the exercise of technocratic first-order judgment is open-ended, then in a highly politicized environment, decisions not to decide will—at least if sustained indefinitely—undermine the enterprise of technocratic decision making. Conversely, in such an environment, cabining second-order decision making is an indirect means of ensuring that expert judgments—regardless of how they come out—are at least made. This cabining of the discretion to decide not to decide is, in our view, the heart of expertise-forcing.[95] Unbounded discretion to decide not to decide circumvents, and thus threatens to fatally undermine, the complex statutory scheme; if agencies can eternally make no decision, the expert judgment contemplated by § 202(a) will never take place.

As previously mentioned, the majority cabined EPA's discretion

---

[95] Compare *In re International Chemical Workers' Union*, 958 F2d 1144, 1149 (DC Cir 1992) ("[T]he benefits of agency expertise and creation of a record will not be realized if the agency never takes action.").

to decide not to decide by holding that EPA must make its second-order decision by reference to the same constrained set of statutory factors—scientific and technical considerations—that constrain the first-order judgment required by § 202(a). As the majority said:

> [EPA] has offered a laundry list of reasons not to regulate [centering on other executive branch programs, the President's foreign-policy stance, and the reactions of other nations]. Although we have neither the expertise nor the authority to evaluate these policy judgments, it is evident that they have nothing to do with whether greenhouse gas emissions contribute to climate change. *Still less do they amount to a reasoned justification for declining to form a scientific judgment.* . . . If the scientific uncertainty is so profound that it precludes EPA from making a reasoned judgment as to whether greenhouse gases contribute to global warming, EPA must say so. . . . In short, EPA has offered no reasoned explanation for its refusal to decide whether greenhouse gases cause or contribute to climate change.[96]

Now, this is not obviously correct at all. Why exactly do the statutory factors that constrain the making of a judgment also constrain the second-order decision not to make such a judgment in the first place? Justice Scalia, in dissent, excoriated the majority for collapsing these two very different questions, arguing that under § 202(a) and the larger statutory scheme, the statutory factors that constrain the EPA's first-order judgments do not at all constrain its second-order judgments to decide not to make a first-order judgment. If that is so, then under *SUWA*, not to mention *Chevron*, there is no clear statutory command that the EPA's inaction has violated—not even in the limited sense that the EPA's nondecision has taken statutorily irrelevant factors into account. As Justice Scalia put it:

> When the Administrator *makes* a judgment whether to regulate greenhouse gases, that judgment must relate to whether they are air pollutants that "cause, or contribute to, air pollution which may reasonably be anticipated to endanger public health or welfare." But the statute says *nothing at all* about the reasons for which the Administrator may *defer* making a judgment— the permissible reasons for deciding not to grapple with the

---

[96] *MA v EPA*, 127 S Ct at 1462–63 (emphasis added).

issue at the present time. . . . [T]he statutory text is silent, as
texts are often silent about permissible reasons for the exercise
of agency discretion. The reasons the EPA gave are surely considerations executive agencies *regularly* take into account (and
ought to take into account) when deciding whether to consider
entering a new field: the impact such entry would have on other
Executive Branch programs and on foreign policy.[97]

The majority does not respond clearly to this important point.
Justice Stevens's exposition tends to collapse the two different
levels of judgment into one another, often skipping back and forth
in the same sentence. There is a conclusory assertion that EPA's
nonscientific "policy judgments" do not "amount to a reasoned
justification for declining to form a scientific judgment"[98]—but
why not? There is also something of a suggestion that EPA did
not label its decision as a nondecision of the sort Scalia refers to,
but rather as a decision not to regulate. It is true that EPA used
some unfortunate language, quoted by the Court, blurring the
distinction between the first- and second-order decisions.[99] But as
we have seen, where the status quo is nonregulatory, a decision
not to decide is also a decision not to regulate; in this sense EPA
stated things accurately. In any event the thrust of EPA's approach
was quite clear, regardless of the label; it seems uncharitable to
conclude that the Court's disposition of the case really rests on
this sort of gotcha.

The more charitable reconstruction of the majority's argument
is that *courts should interpret statutes so as not to allow circumvention
of a statute's main provisions.* This anticircumvention principle is a
necessary corollary to the majority's expertise-forcing project.
Suppose that EPA could, on policy grounds, perpetually decide
not to decide, thereby declining indefinitely to make the first-
order judgment contemplated by § 202(a). (In a famous *New Yorker*
cartoon, a man is pictured holding a phone and staring at a calendar; the caption says, "How about never? Is never good for
you?") Such a situation might well be taken to undermine the
purposes of the statutory scheme, perhaps irreparably. In the
Court's view, the basic purpose of § 202(a), and of the broader
statutory scheme in which it is nested, is to ensure that EPA applies

---

[97] Id at 1473 (Scalia dissenting) (citation omitted) (emphases in original).

[98] Id at 1463 (majority opinion).

[99] Id.

its expertise to make judgments about the health and welfare effects of pollutants. Fulfilling this mission necessarily requires the agency to assess scientific information on an ongoing basis, to estimate risks in the context of degrees of uncertainty, and to calibrate when and to what extent to regulate exposure to harmful substances. It is hard to see how that purpose could be fulfilled if EPA also enjoys unbounded discretion to perpetually duck the relevant questions for whatever reasons it chooses.

Of course what counts as a circumvention is itself a legal question. On Justice Scalia's view, if the relevant statutes do not clearly (or at all) constrain EPA's discretion to decide not to decide, there is simply no circumvention in the first place; deciding not to decide is something the EPA has statutory authority to do. Justice Scalia would presumably agree that this discretion cannot be boundless. The agency could not decline to make a threshold judgment under § 202(a), because, say, the agency thinks it will disproportionately benefit Democratic voters who live in urban areas. But Justice Scalia and the other dissenting Justices would give the EPA much greater latitude than the majority to consider a broader range of factors at the second-order decision stage, including presidential priorities, the agency's preference for alternative regulatory and nonregulatory strategies, remaining scientific uncertainties, and the potential implications for foreign policy, all of which the agency cited to support its petition denial.

In our view, what best explains the difference between this view and the majority's implicit approach is that strong anticircumvention principles are best understood as a form of interpretive purposivism.[100] On the majority's account of the statutory purposes, it would seem absurd for the statute to require strong, and tightly constrained, first-order judgment about pollution's effects on health and welfare while conferring unbounded discretion on EPA to decide never to make such judgments; from a purposivist perspective, the latter discretion looks like a kind of loophole. This account fits the lineup of the decision: Justices Stevens and Breyer, the Court's most committed purposivists, implicitly rely

---

[100] This is a familiar theme in the debate over textualism and purposivism, or "form" and "substance," in the interpretation of the tax code; where taxpayers comply with the literal terms of the code but circumvent its intent or purposes in a manner that reduces their tax burdens, purposivist courts will invoke anticircumvention principles. See, for example, *Helvering v Gregory*, 69 F2d 809 (2d Cir 1934), affd, 293 US 465 (1935); Joseph Isenbergh, *Musings on Form and Substance in Taxation*, 49 U Chi L Rev 859 (1982).

upon a strong anticircumvention principle, while Justices Scalia and Thomas, the Court's most committed textualists, dissent on a textualist ground—that the statute's text itself places no constraints on the agency's discretion to decide not to decide.

Another reading, compatible with though different from the anticircumvention idea, is that the majority was implicitly invoking a kind of prophylactic principle, one intended to bar bad-faith decisions not to decide by EPA.[101] Suppose that agencies do, in theory, have discretion to decide not to decide on the basis of the sorts of factors Justice Scalia emphasized. Suppose also, however, that the majority saw EPA as using those legitimate factors to cover up ideological disagreement with the statute's basic policy choices and feared that the subterfuge could not be smoked out through ordinary arbitrary and capricious review. On this reading, rather than invoking an anticircumvention principle, the Court constrained the agency's initial decision-making discretion in order to ensure EPA would not use legitimate factors in bad faith. It is hard to rule this idea in, or out, on the basis of the Court's limited discussion; both the prophylactic principle and the anticircumvention principle can plausibly be read into the opinion. But some such principle there must be, if the opinion is to make sense.

In making these points, we are assuming a certain picture of the relationship between politics and expertise: politics is a threat to expertise rather than its complement. One might, of course, have a different picture. Perhaps agency judgments should be, above all, politically accountable; perhaps "political pressure from the White House" is just accountability to the Chief Executive. The majority never spells out its view of this relationship, nor does it explicitly discuss circumstances under which it believes it would consider it normatively desirable for agencies not to decide. Yet we think our account of the dangers of nondecision plausibly explains the Court's approach in *MA v EPA*. This approach hearkens back to an older, pre-*Chevron* vision of administrative law in which independence and expertise are seen as opposed to, rather than defined by, political accountability, and in which political influence over agencies by the White House is seen as a problem rather than a solution.[102]

---

[101] Thanks to David Strauss for advancing the idea in this paragraph.

[102] We do not wish to overstate how much "older" this tradition is than the *Chevron*

Chief among these pre-*Chevron* cases, and decided just a year before *Chevron*, is *Motor Vehicles Manufacturers' Association v State Farm Mutual Automobile Insurance Co.*,[103] the famous administrative law case in which the Court used "hard look review" to invalidate the National Highway Traffic Safety Administration's (NHTSA) repeal of the passive restraint rule. In scrutinizing the agency's proffered explanations, and in finding them insufficient as a rationale for repeal, the majority implicitly rejected the agency's real motivation. In fact, NHTSA was simply responding to a shift in administration priorities: between the rule's promulgation and its repeal, Ronald Reagan had been elected on a deregulatory agenda. (Indeed, the dissent explicitly acknowledges this rationale, and treats it as sufficient to justify the agency's turnabout.) *State Farm* is expertise-forcing in the sense that the Court expects the agency to make discretionary policy decisions that can be justified by the relevant statutory factors, and not politics. The inference is that political influence is a source of danger rather than of accountability. The Court's role is to ensure that political interference does not undermine the agency's pursuit of its statutory duty, in this case to enhance automobile safety.

Industrial Union Department, AFL-CIO v American Petroleum Institute (the "*Benzene*" case)[104] can be viewed in this light as well. In *Benzene*, the Supreme Court invalidated a rigorous workplace exposure standard, finding both that the Occupational Safety and Health Administration (OSHA) had misinterpreted its statutory authority, and that the agency's reasoning in support of the stricter benzene exposure standard was not supported by substantial evidence. In interpreting the Occupational Safety and Health Act, a plurality of the Court effectively read into the statute a requirement that the agency make a threshold finding of "significant risk" before it could set a safety standard for toxics, although Congress had not explicitly required this. The case can be understood as an

---

tradition that we believe superseded it. Indeed, *State Farm*, which we cite as a plausible example of expertise-forcing, was roughly contemporaneous with *Chevron*. These different "models" of administrative law usually coexist; what changes is emphasis. Our point is simply that the era of hard look gave way to the era of *Chevron* deference, not that the tradition of expertise-forcing ever disappeared entirely. See Kagan, 114 Harv L Rev at 2245 (cited in note 11) (suggesting that most models of administrative law persist in some form).

[103] 463 US 29 (1983). See also Cass R. Sunstein, *Reviewing Agency Inaction After Heckler v Chaney*, 52 U Chi L Rev 653 (1985).

[104] 448 US 607 (1980).

effort by the Court to pull back on the reins of an overzealous agency, which perhaps it saw as responding to the prolabor political priorities of the Carter administration. On this view, the Court sees its role as ensuring that politically motivated agencies do not overreach, just as the Court in *State Farm* was concerned that politics not produce regulatory underreach.[105]

MA v EPA hearkens back, as well, to a number of action-forcing decisions authored primarily by Judge Skelly Wright in the D.C. Circuit concerning the implementation of the National Environmental Policy Act (NEPA). In *Calvert Cliffs' Coordinating Committee, Inc. v United States Atomic Energy Commission*,[106] the best known of these cases, the court held that the commission's rules governing consideration of environmental issues were insufficient. The statutory language required disclosure of environmental impacts "to the fullest extent possible." But this language, wrote Judge Skelly Wright,

> does not provide an escape hatch for footdragging agencies; it does not make NEPA's procedural requirements somehow "discretionary." . . . They must be complied with to the fullest extent, unless there is a clear conflict of *statutory* authority. Considerations of administrative difficulty, delay or economic cost will not suffice to strip the section of its fundamental importance.[107]

---

[105] Of course, the *Benzene* case may alternatively be viewed as an instance of judicial *interference* with agency expertise if one believes that the agency was trying to use the best available science to comply with statutory commands. After all, the Supreme Court essentially insisted that the agency produce scientific evidence ("substantial evidence") to support the claim that benzene was sufficiently dangerous at levels below ten-parts-per-million to justify the stricter one-part-per-million standard, something the agency claimed it could not do given the available epidemiological data and the limitations on doing human exposure studies. We thank Lisa Heinzerling for pointing out this alternative reading.

[106] 449 F2d 1109 (DC Cir 1971).

[107] Id at 1114–15. It was the courts' responsibility to oversee the implementation of new environmental legislation:

> [I]t remains to be seen whether the promise of this legislation will become a reality. Therein lies the judicial role. In these cases, we must for the first time interpret the broadest and perhaps most important of the recent statutes: [NEPA]. We must assess claims that one of the agencies charged with its administration has failed to live up to the congressional mandate. Our duty, in short, is to see that important legislative purposes, heralded in the halls of Congress, are not lost or misdirected in the vast hallways of the federal bureaucracy.

Id at 1111. Other circuits followed the lead set by Skelly Wright in the D.C. Circuit by enforcing agency compliance with NEPA. See, for example, *Davis v Coleman*, 521 F2d

Finally, there are two important CAA cases that embody the expertise-forcing view that we see revived in *MA v EPA*. In *NRDC v Train*,[108] the D.C. Circuit required EPA to list lead as a criteria pollutant under § 108 of the Act (the first step toward setting a national air quality standard), despite the agency's claim that it had near-absolute discretion not to do so. Section 108 requires the administrator to list each air pollutant that "in his judgment has an adverse effect on public health and welfare . . . the presence of which in the ambient air results from numerous sources; and . . . for which he plans to issue air quality criteria."[109] The Court rejected the agency's view that it could simply decline to issue air quality criteria, and therefore never trigger the obligation to set a standard. Acceding to this interpretation would render the mandatory language in the section "mere surplusage," said the Court. Once the first two conditions are met, the agency must list the pollutant. Although there may be political reasons why the agency is reluctant to list lead (notably, it would trigger a NAAQS for lead, which would mean high compliance costs for fuel producers), the Court sees its role as forcing the agency to act in conformance with the purpose of the statute: "The structure of the Clean Air Act . . . its legislative history, and the judicial gloss placed upon the Act leave no room for an interpretation which makes the issuance of air quality standards for lead under section 108 discretionary. The Congress sought to eliminate, not perpetuate, opportunity for administrative footdragging."[110]

It goes too far to say that all of these cases are specifically concerned with expertise-forcing as a rebuke to "strong presidential administration," though some of them are. More generally, in this line of cases, the courts force expertise as a way to check a number of bureaucratic pathologies, including vulnerability to interest group pressure or institutional resistance to a new statutory mission. Yet it is fair to say that in all of these decisions, the reviewing court performs an expertise-forcing role: courts must ensure that agencies make rational decisions based on relevant statutory factors. This view is perhaps best articulated in Judge

---

661 (9th Cir 1975); *Save Our Ten Acres v Kreger*, 472 F2d 463, 467 (5th Cir 1973); *Scherr v Volpe*, 466 F2d 1027, 1033 (7th Cir 1972).

[108] 545 F2d 320 (2d Cir 1976).

[109] Id at 322.

[110] Id at 328.

Leventhal's "statement" in support of the D.C. Circuit's decision in *Ethyl Corp. v EPA*,[111] which upheld EPA's controversial regulation of lead emissions from motor vehicles. In *Ethyl Corp.*, the relevant provision authorized EPA to regulate emissions that "will endanger" the public health or welfare, and the court deferred to the agency's interpretation that this authorized regulation where the agency found a "significant risk" of harm. Noting that the CAA is "precautionary" and that the agency must operate at the frontiers of scientific knowledge, the court held that the statute does not require proof of actual harm.[112]

In his statement, Judge Leventhal sought to counter the views of Chief Judge Bazelon, who had also concurred in the decision but for very different reasons—because he believed courts were ill-equipped to review the substantive rationality of technical agency decisions:[113]

> Taking [Judge Bazelon's] opinion in its fair implication, as a signal to judges to abstain from any substantive review, it is my view that while giving up is the easier course, it is not legitimately open to us at present. . . . In the case of agency decision-making the courts have an additional responsibility set by Congress. Congress has been willing to delegate its legislative powers broadly and courts have upheld such delegation because there is court review to assure that the agency exercises its delegated power within statutory limits, and that it fleshes out objectives within those limits by an administration that is not irrational or discriminatory. . . . The substantive review of administrative action is modest, but it cannot be carried out in a vacuum of understanding. Better no judicial review at all than a charade that gives the imprimatur without the substance of judicial confirmation that the agency is not acting unreasonably. Once the presumption of regularity in agency action is challenged . . . the agency's record and reasoning has to be looked at. . . . Restraint, yes, abdication, no.[114]

---

[111] 541 F2d 1, 68–69 (DC Cir 1976). This was not a concurrence but a "statement."

[112] Id at 13 (majority opinion).

[113] Id at 66–68 (Bazelon concurring). This exchange was part of a long-standing debate between the two judges about the extent to which courts were capable of, and obligated to, "engage in meaningful review of the substantive rationality of agency decisions raising complex scientific and technological issues." Samuel Estricher, *Pragmatic Justice: The Contributions of Judge Harold Leventhal to Administrative Law*, 80 Colum L Rev 894, 906 (1980). Leventhal explained his approach, with special reference to environmental cases, in Harold Leventhal, *Environmental Decisionmaking and the Role of the Courts*, 122 U Pa L Rev 509 (1974).

[114] *Ethyl Corp.*, 541 F2d at 68–69 (Leventhal concurring statement).

The implicit suspicion of politics that we detect in the majority opinion in *MA v EPA* fits within this older understanding of the court's role. And it stands in notable contrast to the more sanguine view of politics represented by both *Chevron* (also authored by Justice Stevens) and *Brown & Williamson* (in which four of the five members of the *MA v EPA* majority—all but Kennedy—dissented). In *Chevron*, the majority endorsed the notion that political considerations could lawfully influence agency policy decisions (in that case deciding whether the term "stationary source" included multiple units operating under a fictional bubble even if the approach arguably led to more lenient enforcement of air regulation). That EPA changed its mind about this definition over the years was a sign of political responsiveness to a democratically accountable executive; it did not represent unwanted political interference. In *MA v EPA*, however, the Court rejected this kind of political accountability, refusing to defer to the agency's claim of discretion to decide not to decide.

IV. Trends and Implications

A. REALISM AND GLOBAL WARMING

The simplest approach to *MA v EPA* is to say that it is really just a global warming case, produced by a confluence of political and regulatory circumstances that may or may not generalize to other areas. Most of the Justices voted on the most basic ideological lines (on this account): left-of-center Justices voted to make EPA do something about global warming, right-of-center Justices voted to the contrary, and as usual Justice Kennedy was the median and decisive voter. The left-of-center Justices won because they happened to obtain, or were tactically clever enough to obtain, Justice Kennedy's support in the context of global warming; but each policy area is a new battle.

Even as realism, this account is too crude, in part because it focuses too closely on the immediate case and not enough on the context of the Court's decision making in recent years. We mean to offer a larger view of this context, in which *MA v EPA* is part and parcel of a larger trend toward increasing suspicion, on the part of many of the Justices, that the Bush administration has politicized administrative and professional expertise in a number of domains—not just global warming. If those trends either affect or reflect Justice Kennedy's thinking, that makes them all the more important, given the Court's current configuration.

In any event, we also wish to put *MA v EPA* in the best possible light from an internal legal point of view. The Court did not, of course, write an opinion explicitly limited to global warming; it wrote an opinion in general administrative law terms, and the lower courts will have to deal with the opinion on those terms. The expertise-forcing approach we have imputed to the Court helps to make sense of some otherwise puzzling features of the opinion, such as the implicit assumption that the statutorily relevant factors constrain both the EPA's first-order judgments and its second-order decisions to decide. Absent an expertise-forcing rationale, the Court's opinion is vulnerable to Justice Scalia's criticisms on this score;[115] with the expertise-forcing rationale, the opinion makes a great deal of sense. From an internal legal point of view, whether such a rationale crossed Justice Stevens's mind, or Justice Kennedy's, is irrelevant; what matters is that it helps fit *MA v EPA* into the larger fabric of administrative law in an intelligible way. Others are free to analyze *MA v EPA* from the external standpoint of ideology, or legal realism, but that is not our main interest here.

B. PUTTING MA V EPA IN CONTEXT

We see the Court's decision in *MA v EPA* as of a piece with other cases, decided in the last few terms, which similarly involve executive override of expert judgments by professionals or agencies. For example, in *Gonzales*, the Court rejected the Attorney General's determination that it was not "legitimate medical practice" under the federal Controlled Substances Act (CSA) for a physician to prescribe controlled substances to patients lawfully committing suicide under Oregon's assisted suicide statute—a ruling that would leave prescribing physicians vulnerable to criminal prosecution. Although the case was strongly inflected with federalism concerns, the majority's rationale also turned on the Attorney General's lack of expertise to make determinations about standards of medical care. Congress assigned such expert medical judgments to the Department of Health and Human Services (HHS), Justice Kennedy's majority opinion explains, rather than

---

[115] See notes 97–98 and accompanying text.

the Department of Justice; the Attorney General is authorized under the CSA only to prevent "illicit drug dealing and trafficking as conventionally understood." The Attorney General's interpretive rule thus not only failed to attract *Chevron* deference (owed to agency interpretations of their own ambiguous regulations under the Court's ruling in *Auer v Robbins*[116]) because discretion to make such judgments was not delegated to him by Congress; it failed to garner even *Skidmore* deference[117] because it lacked the traditional indicia of expertise. On this point, Justice Kennedy noted that the Attorney General brought neither experience nor expertise to bear in making his interpretive ruling—he failed, for example, to consult expert agencies such as HHS. Although *Gonzales* is less centrally concerned with scientific judgments than *MA v EPA*, the majority opinion is tinged with underlying suspicion about politically motivated executive usurpation of judgments normally left to experts.

This concern appears even in seemingly unrelated terrorism cases that have reached the Court in recent years. The principal issues in *Hamdan* were the President's authority to establish military tribunals and Congress's power to limit federal court jurisdiction, neither of which raised the questions of scientific or medical judgment at issue in *MA v EPA* or *Gonzales*. Yet this decision too can be seen through the "politics versus expertise" lens. Justices Stevens and Kennedy again teamed up to rein in executive assertions of authority that appear to disregard established professional or bureaucratic practices and procedures. The Court held that the President's military commissions violate the Uniform Code of Military Justice (UCMJ)—what the Court refers to as "an integrated system of military courts and review procedures."[118] Invocations of political exigency alone cannot justify departing from the long-established rules and procedures that normally govern courts-martial, wrote Justice Stevens for the majority. Such departures may be permissible where the normal procedures are shown to be "impracticable," the Court allowed, but the President

---

[116] 519 US 452 (1997).

[117] See *United States v Mead Corp.*, 533 US 218; *Skidmore v Swift & Co.*, 323 US 134 (1944).

[118] Id at 2770, quoting *Schlesinger v Councilman*, 420 US 738, 758 (1975).

had failed to articulate a reason, or place anything in the record, to show why that is so.[119]

We do not mean to suggest that the outcomes in *Gonzales* and *Hamdan* can be entirely explained, or ought to be primarily viewed, in terms of the Court's desire to insulate expert decision making from political interference. Other concerns—federalism in *Gonzales*, say, or separation of powers and due process in *Hamdan*—may better account for the outcomes. Still, these cases are all to a greater or lesser extent inflected with a worry about executive willingness to cast aside expertise and professional methodologies and procedures in the name of political expedience. The EPA's determination that greenhouse gases are not air pollutants, and that even if they were, the agency would decline to regulate them under the CAA, can be seen as a species of the same problem.

At the same time, and more broadly, *MA v EPA* can be seen as one in a series of rebukes to the Bush administration's generous vision of executive power. In the cases discussed above, crucial Justices such as Kennedy and Stevens perceived overreaching by the administration. On this view—whether right or wrong—the administration implausibly asserted in *Hamdan* the power to establish military tribunals that would try enemy combatants without standard court-martial procedures; in *Gonzales*, it implausibly claimed that the power to regulate controlled substances conferred an implicit power to establish medical practice standards, with the effect of criminalizing otherwise legal assisted suicide. In *MA v EPA*, the alleged agency failing was underreach rather than overreach, but the same Justices may have seen the same unbounded vision of executive power at work in the form of political interference with agency expertise.

The Court's rebuke of the administration is perhaps most evident in a passage toward the end of the *MA v EPA* decision, where the majority went out of its way to chastise EPA's invocation of foreign policy considerations, among other reasons, for refusing to regulate greenhouse gas emissions. As Justice Stevens wrote, "In particular, while the President has broad authority in foreign affairs, that authority does not extend to the refusal to execute

---

[119] *Hamdan*, 126 S Ct at 2792 ("The absence of any showing of impracticability is particularly disturbing when considered in light of the clear and admitted failure to apply one of the most fundamental protections afforded not just by the Manual for Courts-Martial but also by the UCMJ itself: the right to be present.").

domestic laws."[120] This passage bites hard on a line cast in an amicus brief, filed on behalf of former Secretary of State Madeleine Albright, which aimed to raise the Court's ire about the potential for just such executive overreach by warning that the foreign affairs rationale could be used more generally as an executive trump card.[121]

C. HARD LOOK REVIEW OF RULEMAKING DENIALS: STATE FARM FOR A NEW GENERATION

On the view we attribute to the *MA v EPA* majority, courts have a role to play not only through ex post judicial review of agency decisions, but also through expertise-forcing when agencies are deciding not to decide because of political pressures. If agencies refuse to exercise their first-order expertise, in any direction, because issues are politically too controversial, or because they fear that an expert judgment would point in the direction of politically costly action—a plausible description of what occurred when EPA considered whether to regulate greenhouse gases—courts can review the reasons agencies give for postponing their first-order decisions in order to flush out these socially harmful motivations. Where agencies have no valid reason for further delay, courts will indirectly force them to make the first-order expert judgment they have been avoiding.

MA v EPA seems to adopt this perspective when it makes two important findings. The first is that *rulemaking denials are reviewable.*[122] The Court distinguished rulemaking denials from decisions not to enforce on the grounds that the former are less frequent and more likely to involve issues of law rather than fact—both

---

[120] *MA v EPA*, 127 S Ct at 1458.

[121] Brief for Amicus Curiae Madeleine K. Albright in Support of Petitioners, *MA v EPA*, No 05-1120, *16–19 (filed Aug 31, 2006) (available on Westlaw at 2006 WL 2570988). The amicus brief argued that the administration's reliance on the foreign policy rationale for declining to regulate, if generalized beyond this context, could lead to a significant expansion of executive power. Since so many domestic regulatory issues now overlap with foreign policy questions, the Court should be wary of approving of a foreign affairs "trump" over domestic statutory obligations. See also Mark Moller, *Blame Bush for Massachusetts v. EPA?* (SCOTUSblog, Apr 3, 2007), online at http://www.scotusblog.com/movabletype/archives/2007/04/blame_bush_for.html (remarking that the Court seems increasingly distrustful of executive claims of inherent authority to ignore Congress in domestic affairs).

[122] 127 S Ct at 1459 (adopting the language from a D.C. Circuit case, the Court confirmed that "[r]efusals to promulgate rules are thus susceptible to judicial review, though such review is 'extremely limited' and 'highly deferential'").

implicit responses to the worry that agencies must have discretion to allocate resources on cost-benefit grounds, as they do with respect to nonenforcement. Consistently with *SUWA*, the Court focused on whether the relevant statutory provisions were best understood to allow EPA to do what it did. This doctrinal development is far more adventurous, and potentially consequential, than anything the Court did in its standing analysis. The result is that a category of agency decision making that once enjoyed all the benefits of "inaction" is treated as if it were "action" and subjected to review.[123]

The second crucial point is that *agency decisions not to decide are (presumptively) subject to "hard look" review.* At least absent a clear statutory command to the contrary, the reviewing court will require the agency to offer a nonarbitrary reason for the decision not to decide. One type of arbitrariness is legal error: agencies must consider only those factors made relevant by the particular statute at hand. In other words, hard look review applies *both* to the agency's decision about whether to make a threshold determination in the first place, *and* to the agency's decision about whether the threshold has been crossed. When making both the first-order judgment under § 202 and the second-order decision about whether to decide, EPA may not consider extraneous nonstatutory factors such as foreign policy, or its preference for other regulatory or nonregulatory approaches that might fit better with the President's priorities. Rather, the agency is to focus primarily on information, scientific uncertainty, and the costs and benefits of acquiring further information. Does the state of the science enable the EPA to make a rational judgment now, in either direction, about the health and welfare effects of a given pollutant? What are the costs of deciding not to decide, as against the informational advantages that would arise from postponing the first-order judgment until the science is solidified?

---

[123] Lisa Schultz Bressman, *Judicial Review of Agency Inaction: An Arbitrariness Approach*, 79 NYU L Rev 1657 (2004). Bressman argues for a revision to the nonreviewability doctrine applied to agency inaction cases because "an agency is susceptible to corrosive influences when it refuses to act, just as when it decides to act. These influences may produce administrative decisionmaking that is arbitrary from a democratic perspective, no matter how rational or accountable it may be from a political standpoint." Id at 1661. Presidential control, Bressman argues, may be inadequate to prevent arbitrariness: "The President exercises control in a manner that is too corrupting and sporadic to reduce the potential for faction. Like Congress, he may pressure agencies to depart from broad statutory purposes in favor of personal priorities." Id at 1690.

Of course the case does not answer all questions. Crucial to the holding is the point that § 202(a) excludes nonscientific and non-technical factors from the agency's initial decision-making cal-culus. Some statutes can plausibly be read to share that feature; others presumably cannot. All organic statutes are different; in some settings statutes will be read to give agencies more or less discretion to decide not to decide. The main contribution of the decision, however, is to clarify that there is nothing magic about such initial decisions. They are reviewable on the ordinary terms of administrative law. Properly understood, *MA v EPA* is not—as the Chief Justice noted disdainfully in his dissent—*SCRAP* for a new generation; it is *State Farm* for a new generation.

D. THE LIMITS OF EXPERTISE-FORCING

Expertise-forcing is never a complete solution to the problem of political interference, just a first step. It is always possible that the same political distortions that cause the agency to avoid a decision will also cause it to skew the first-order decision that the court forces it to make. But for various reasons, an agency whose preference might be to duck an issue altogether might also want to exercise its expert judgment accurately, or at least in an unbiased fashion, on issues that it is forced to confront.

For one thing, agency officials might be sufficiently concerned for the agency's reputation as an expert that it will not openly distort its first-order opinions, incurring mockery and outrage from scientific and technocratic experts, even if the agency would be quite happy to avoid making a first-order judgment altogether. A person who is willing to refrain from pointing out that the emperor is wearing no clothes may balk at saying out loud that the clothes exist. For another thing, if the agency realizes that any first-order judgment it makes will alienate some constituency or other—either the White House or environmental constituencies will be outraged, whatever the agency does—then it may decide to let the scientific chips fall where they may, on the principle that one might as well be honest if dishonesty will not pay. Finally, of course, judicial review can also take a hard look at the reasons the agency gives for its first-order decision making, and may be able to control political distortions at that stage as well.[124]

---

[124] There have been extended disputes over the usefulness of hard look review and its

It is also true that the Court in *MA v EPA* did not quite force a first-order judgment, although it went a long way in that direction. It remains notionally possible for EPA on remand to say that the scientific uncertainty is indeed "so profound" that it cannot sensibly make the statutory judgment, one way or another, and so must still wait. And the door is at least arguably still open, however narrowly, for the EPA to say that resource constraints and other priorities weigh in favor of nondecision. That is, even while ruling out a host of considerations as irrelevant to the decision not to decide, the Court left open the possibility that the agency might still decline to decide because of resource constraints, or other policy priorities, or reasons *other than* those forbidden political or policy judgments that are extraneous to the statutory factors. It is even conceivable, though unlikely, that such a renewed nondecision might be upheld after another round of arbitrary and capricious review. If that second round of judicial review works well, then there should be nothing troubling about this scenario; it means that EPA does indeed have valid reasons to continue postponing its first-order judgment. At a minimum, in this scenario *MA v EPA* would have achieved its expertise-forcing aims at the second decision-making level, even if not at the first; although the EPA would not have been forced to make an expert first-order decision, it would have been constrained to make its second-order decision not to decide on expert or technocratic grounds, rather than political ones.

We may further conjecture—although there is no direct evidence for this in the opinion—that Justice Stevens, Justice Kennedy, and perhaps others in the majority are implicitly betting that EPA will not be able to say, with a straight face, that the scientific uncertainty is indeed "so profound" that no present judgment is possible.[125] Given the scientific consensus, solidifying daily, that anthropogenic global warming is not only a real phenomenon but due in significant part to human-controlled emissions of greenhouse gases, the residual uncertainties are diminishing rapidly.

---

associated procedural requirements. Compare William F. Pedersen, Jr., *Formal Records and Informal Rulemaking*, 85 Yale L J 38 (1975) (claiming that more demanding procedures enhance the flow of information and promote democratic values), with Thomas O. McGarity, *Some Thoughts on "Deossifying" the Rulemaking Process*, 41 Duke L J 1385 (1992) (detailing the difficulties of "ossification" in the rulemaking process). We are bracketing these debates.

[125] Especially as the *only* basis for nondecision, without the benefit of covering fire from other political factors in a multifactor opinion.

EPA will, on this conjecture, be unable to maintain that the level of uncertainty is still so high as to disable any first-order judgment at all. If this is so, then a kind of politics—EPA's concern for its scientific reputation, and for the reaction of experts who will condemn an EPA claim that black is white—will enforce the majority's attempt to prod EPA to make an expert judgment independent of politics.

The expertise-forcing logic that ultimately underpins *MA v EPA*, and the corollary anticircumvention principle, are plausible but, we concede, not obviously correct. It is not at all clear that even absent the Court's ruling, EPA would or could indefinitely postpone the making of a statutory judgment; perhaps it would embark on that course anyway, precisely for political reasons. If a Democratic president were to come to power in 2008, or a Republican president more concerned about global warming, the political calculus would shift. Indeed, it may already have shifted with the election of a Democratic Congress in 2006; legislators have considerable power to prod agencies in desired directions, even where there is a president of the other party in office—in this case, a weakened president. Perhaps the Court took an incomplete view of the political landscape, and a broader view would have shown that there is no problem, or that the problem will soon be cured. Given the currently swelling consensus that global warming is a serious problem, it is hard to imagine that the EPA could really have postponed a first-order judgment indefinitely.

These points can be taken further, to suggest that the Court's expertise-forcing approach may have been affirmatively perverse. As we have noted, the logic of expertise-forcing supposes that the agency's initial preference is to make no decision either way, but that, if forced to decide, it will exercise its expert judgment on the merits, or at least that the prospect of a second round of ex post judicial review can provide the agency with sufficient incentive to make its first-order judgment in a rationally defensible fashion. This is only one possibility; another is that the political pressure from the White House is sufficiently great, and the incentives provided by the prospect of judicial review sufficiently weak, that an agency that can no longer refuse to decide will just decide in a slanted way. To the extent that the majority is worried about the politicization of EPA's scientific and technocratic judgments under the Bush administration, perhaps the Court should be encouraging the EPA to decide not to make a judgment until that administration has left office, at least if the Court believes that the politicization will be reduced in the next administration.

All this just shows, however, that expertise-forcing is an approach that rests on uncertain judicial judgments about the likely course of politics, and about the likely costs and benefits of alternative approaches.[126] But this is not a unique problem for expertise-forcing; other strategies of judicial review also rest on uncertain predictions. The question is under what conditions might expertise-forcing amount to a useful strategy for courts worried about the politicization of administrative expertise. Where agencies are postponing a first-order judgment in order to deflect political pressure, from the executive or elsewhere, but would render an unbiased first-order judgment if forced to do so, courts committed to a certain vision of the centrality of expertise in the administrative state can prod agencies into revealing their true expert judgments. It is plausible, although by no means clear, that *MA v EPA* presented such conditions. Whether or not it did, the expertise-forcing rationale puts the majority's opinion in its best light, providing answers to the otherwise troubling legal points raised in Justice Scalia's dissent.

E. IMPLICATIONS FOR CLIMATE CHANGE REGULATION

Whether or not *MA v EPA* is the new *State Farm*, and regardless of whether the Court's expertise-forcing project has staying power, the decision has a number of important short-term implications for environmental law and policy, particularly as it relates to climate change. First, the Court's holding that EPA has authority to regulate greenhouse gases under the CAA kept alive California's legal claim that it is entitled to regulate tailpipe emissions of carbon dioxide under § 209(b) of the Act, which confers on California a special authority to go beyond federally established emissions standards, and § 177, which allows other states to adopt California's standards so long as they are "identical." In 2003, the California legislature passed AB 1493, which requires the state's

---

[126] For concerns that *MA v EPA*'s expertise-forcing approach has proven ineffective so far, and the suggestion that state regulation is a useful alternative to politicized EPA decision making, see David J. Barron, *From Takeover to Merger: Reforming Administrative Law in an Age of Agency Politicization* (George Washington forthcoming article on file with authors).

Air Resources Board (ARB) to set standards for greenhouse gas emissions from new vehicles, and to implement the regulations over a phase-in period. After promulgating the regulations, the ARB was promptly sued by the automobile industry, which argued, first, that EPA lacked the authority to regulate greenhouse gases under the CAA (that is, that California enjoys no "special status" under § 209 to regulate a substance the Act does not cover). Second, the industry argued that, in any event, California's tailpipe regulations are preempted by the EPCA,[127] which reserves the right to establish fuel efficiency standards to the Department of Transportation; this latter point turns on an argument that there is no way to regulate carbon dioxide emissions without tightening fuel efficiency standards. When *MA v EPA* was decided, litigation challenging California's legal authority to set tailpipe standards was pending in both Vermont and California.[128]

The decision in *MA v EPA* that greenhouse gases meet the definition of "pollutant" and are thus regulable under the Act eliminated the auto industry's first argument above. The Court also lent some help to California on the second argument by suggesting that any ensuing EPA regulation of new vehicle emissions under § 202(a) could live compatibly with DOT regulation of fuel efficiency. This language was thought at the time to supply a hint to the district courts in Vermont and California about the Court's view of the preemption argument. Although it is hard to know how strong a role the Supreme Court's language on preemption played, the states certainly briefed the issue, and the district court judgments both cited it in their decisions in favor of California on the preemption challenge.[129] Also, at the time *MA v EPA* was handed down, California was still hoping to secure EPA approval for its tailpipe regulations in the form of an EPA waiver under § 209 of the CAA (an application the agency had left pending until the Court decided *MA v EPA*). Such a waiver was necessary, quite apart from prevailing on the preemption challenges, before any of the states could implement the California standards. Although EPA ultimately

---

[127] Energy Policy and Conservation Act, Pub L No 94-163 § 301, 89 Stat 871 (1975), amending 15 USC § 1901 et seq (2000).

[128] See *Central Valley Chrysler-Jeep, Inc. v Witherspoon*, 2007 WL 135688 (ED Cal); *Green Mountain Chrysler Plymouth Dodge Jeep v Crombie*, 508 F Supp 2d 295 (D Vt 2007).

[129] See *Central Valley Chrysler-Jeep, Inc. v Goldstene*, 2007 WL 4372878 (ED Cal); *Green Mountain*, 508 F Supp 2d at 351.

decided against granting the waiver,[130] the decision in *MA v EPA*
seemed at the time to add political, if not legal, pressure on the
agency to grant it, thus fueling the states' momentum.

MA v EPA has larger implications for global warming regulation
generally than might appear at first glance. First, if California's
emissions standards survive appellate review, and if the state suc-
ceeds in its appeal of EPA's waiver denial (an uphill battle in the
final year of the Bush II administration, but arguably less difficult
to imagine in a new administration), the standards will go into effect
not only in California but in the twelve other states that have
adopted them under the "identicality" requirement in CAA § 177.[131]
This means that the auto industry will be facing, for the first time,
multistate regulation of greenhouse gases even if the federal government ultimately takes no action either to regulate these emissions
directly via EPA implementation of § 202(a)(1), or to further increase fuel efficiency standards via NHTSA regulation of CAFE
(corporate average fuel economy) standards pursuant to the EPCA.
The practical result is that the auto manufacturers will, in all likelihood, need to increase fuel efficiency or take other steps in order
to achieve compliance with the California standards. More broadly,
this would force the transportation sector to shoulder at least some
of the burden of achieving greenhouse gas reductions nationwide,
regardless of whether Congress wishes in new climate legislation
to spare the transportation sector and burden other sectors, such

---

[130] Section 209 establishes certain criteria that California must satisfy to obtain the
waiver, including that the state show that it faces "compelling and extraordinary" circumstances that justify its setting higher tailpipe emissions standards than EPA sets nationally.
See 42 USC § 7543(b)(1)(B) (2000). These criteria have not proved an obstacle to past
waivers, which California has routinely been granted, because the substances being regulated under these waivers were localized pollutants that contribute to California's severe
ozone problem, one that has historically been unmatched anywhere in the nation as a
result of California's concentration of automobiles and its unique topography. Although
the statute places the burden on those opposing the waiver, meeting the same standard
when carbon dioxide is the "pollutant" being regulated is somewhat more complicated.
California must show that it is in "compelling and extraordinary circumstances" when it
comes to the impacts of global warming. On one view, California clearly faces unique
challenges: given its long coastline and its significant dependence on mountain snowmelt
for water, global warming could do more damage to California than other states. On
another view, many states will suffer as a result of global warming, and California's situation
is not any more compelling or extraordinary than, say, Florida's. EPA rejected California's
arguments in the waiver denial. See letter from Stephen L. Johnson, Dec 19, 2007, cited
in note 18.

[131] The Pew Charitable Trusts, *U.S. State and Regional Action on Global Warming* (Dec 6,
2007), online at http://www.pewtrusts.org/uploadedFiles/wwwpewtrustsorg/Fact_Sheets/
Global_warming/state%20actions.pdf.

as electric utilities, to a greater extent. Had *MA v EPA* come out the other way on the definition of "pollutant," this would have been much harder to achieve.

A second major implication of *MA v EPA* was that the Court's grant of standing breathed life into other global warming lawsuits pending around the country, including two federal common law public nuisance suits brought by a coalition of states against, in one suit, the major power plants, and in another, the automobile industry. Both suits sought relief for the defendants' contributions to the harms caused by global warming.[132] The plaintiffs in these cases ultimately failed because of threshold justiciability issues,[133] but at the time, the majority's "three strands" approach to standing seemed to provide lower courts ample flexibility to grant standing when they otherwise might have declined to do so under *Lujan*.[134] In the wake of these decisions, which reveal a judicial reluctance to entertain nuisance suits of this kind, a potentially larger implication of the Court's opinion in *MA v EPA* for any future nuisance cases is that the courts will find that the CAA preempts common law nuisance claims.[135]

A third implication is somewhat more technical, and relates to the ability of EPA to use the existing CAA to regulate greenhouse gases quite broadly, even if Congress passes no new climate legislation. If EPA makes the first-order finding of endangerment necessary to trigger regulation under § 202(a)(1) (the mobile source provision at issue in the case) the fact that greenhouse gases are now "pollutants" under the Act may mean that EPA must regulate them under provisions of the Act designed to target stationary sources as well, including the "new source review" (NSR) program, which requires new or "modified" stationary sources to meet stringent technology-based permit limits. NSR defines "regulated pol-

---

[132] See *Connecticut v American Electric Power Co.*, 406 F Supp 2d 265 (SDNY 2005). The suit was filed by eight states, including California and New York, as well as New York City and three land trusts, against the five largest carbon dioxide emitters in the United States. *California v General Motors*, 2007 WL 2726871 (ND Cal), was filed by the state of California against six manufacturers of motor vehicles for contributing to global warming. The New York suit seeks injunctive relief while the California suit seeks damages.

[133] See *American Electric*, 406 F Supp 2d at 274; *General Motors*, 2007 WL at *16.

[134] See note 52.

[135] See *City of Milwaukee v Illinois*, 451 US 304 (1981). We thank Lisa Heinzerling for this point.

lutant" as "any pollutant subject to regulation under the Act."[136] The question is, what would make greenhouse gases "regulated pollutants"? An endangerment determination alone would not be sufficient to trigger regulation under NSR because a pollutant must be the focus of a *promulgated* national ambient air quality or emission standard in order to be considered a "regulated NSR pollutant." But a promulgation of tailpipe standards for carbon dioxide following an endangerment finding under § 202(a)—a rulemaking EPA promised to undertake in the wake of *MA v EPA*[137]—could trigger carbon dioxide into being an NSR regulated pollutant automatically, even if EPA has not set a *de minimis* threshold.[138]

In addition to this, in the wake of *MA v EPA*, EPA has lost its principal explanation for why it has not set standards for greenhouse gases in yet another CAA program known as the New Source Performance Standards program, something for which it is under attack in pending litigation.[139] This is all to say that the full implications of the Court's decision for the potential use of the CAA as an instrument for regulating greenhouse gas emissions are still unknown, but they are potentially far-reaching.

Fourth, *MA v EPA* will have repercussions for the implementation

---

[136] Regarding NSR for stationary sources governed by the "Prevention of Significant Deterioration" provisions of the Act, see 42 USC § 7475(a)(4) (2000) (providing that "the proposed facility is subject to the best available control technology for each pollutant *subject to regulation* under this Act emitted from, or which results from, such facility") (emphasis added); 40 CFR § 52.21(b)(50) (2006) ("Regulated NSR pollutant, for purposes of this section, means the following: (i) Any pollutant for which a national ambient air quality standard has been promulgated and any constituents or precursors for such pollutants identified by the Administrator . . . (ii) Any pollutant that is subject to any standard promulgated under section 111 of the Act; (iii) Any Class I or II substance subject to a standard promulgated under or established by title VI of the Act; or (iv) Any pollutant that otherwise is subject to regulation under the Act . . . .").

[137] EPA announced in its December 2007 priority list that it planned to issue a notice of proposed rulemaking regarding automobile greenhouse gas emissions by the end of 2007 and issue a final rule by October 2008. Environmental Protection Agency, Statement of Priorities, 72 Fed Reg 69922-01, 69934 (Dec 10, 2007). As of April 2008, EPA still had not published the proposed rule.

[138] See 40 CFR 52.21(b)(23)(ii) (2006) (defining significance as a "rate of emissions that would equal or exceed" a set list of emissions rates for different pollutants). We thank Peter Wyckoff, Senior Counsel at Pillsbury Winthrop Shaw Pittman, for pointing this prospect out in an exchange. See e-mail from Peter Wyckoff to Jody Freeman (July 11, 2007).

[139] In a case pending before the D.C. Circuit, a coalition of states, cities, and environmental groups have challenged EPA's 2006 New Source Performance Standards for utility and industrial power plants for failing to establish a standard for greenhouse gases. EPA had declined to do so on the basis that it had no authority under the CAA, a position that the Supreme Court in *MA v EPA* has now overruled. See *Coke Oven Environmental Task Force v EPA*, No 06-1131 (DC Cir, filed Apr 7, 2006).

of *other* environmental statutes as well, including the National Environmental Policy Act (NEPA)[140] and the Endangered Species Act (ESA).[141] For example, a number of lawsuits have been filed in recent years alleging federal agency violations of NEPA's environmental impact disclosure requirements because of a failure to consider greenhouse gas impacts for proposed federal projects.[142] And similar lawsuits have been filed against states, and sometimes private parties, under state environmental disclosure and mitigation statutes.[143] Although the Court's decision in *MA v EPA* does not engage the NEPA issue, the finding that greenhouse gases are "pollutants" adds weight to the argument that their environmental impact must be disclosed. This will greatly complicate and presumably slow NEPA compliance because, as yet, there are no established protocols for how to assess the environmental impacts of greenhouse gases, which may be emitted (or reduced) depending on the nature of the proposed development project.

Moreover, as J. B. Ruhl has argued, after *MA v EPA*, it is possible to claim that "it is incumbent on *all* federal regulatory agencies to assess how global climate change is to be integrated into their respective regulatory programs."[144] There are a variety of ways in which the provisions of the ESA could be used to reduce greenhouse gas emissions. For example, § 7's "jeopardy" consultation provision requires federal agencies to consult with either the Fish and Wildlife Service or the National Marine Fisheries Service (the two agencies with responsibility to implement the ESA) in order to ensure that

---

[140] 42 USC § 4321 et seq (2000).

[141] 16 USC § 1531 et seq (2000).

[142] See, for example, *Center for Biological Diversity v National Highway Traffic Safety Administration*, 2007 WL 3378240 (9th Cir) (holding that the National Highway Traffic Safety Administration's failure to take climate change effects into account when promulgating fuel economy standards for light trucks and SUVs violates NEPA impact disclosure requirement).

[143] See *Center for Biological Diversity v National Highway Traffic Safety Administration*, No 06-71891 (9th Cir, filed Apr 12, 2006) (challenging the failure to consider impacts of 2006 CAFE standards on global warming under NEPA). See also Tim Reiterman, *State Sues San Bernardino County to Nullify Its Blueprint for Growth*, LA Times B3 (Apr 13, 2007) (describing a recent case by California Attorney General Jerry Brown against San Bernardino County for failing to comply with the California Environmental Quality Act in its General Plan).

[144] See J. B. Ruhl, *Climate Change and the Endangered Species Act, Building Bridges to the No-Analog Future* 30 (Boston University Law Review article forthcoming spring 2008) ("Like the EPA after *Massachusetts v EPA*, the [Fish and Wildlife Service] surely will find itself effectively barred from taking the position that climate change is not occurring or, if it is occurring, that it has no anthropogenic causal component.").

actions they authorize, fund, or carry out do not "jeopardize" the continued existence of listed species or "adversely modify" their critical habitat.[145] Presumably, § 7 could be used by the Services to leverage greenhouse gas reductions from the consulting agencies as a condition of the "no jeopardy" findings necessary for the projects to go forward.[146] ESA § 9, which requires public and private persons to ensure they do not "take" endangered species (broadly defined by regulation to include both direct harm and indirect harm via habitat modification), could be used to impose greenhouse gas reductions on private parties as well. Whether or not the services choose to exercise their discretion and use the ESA this way,[147] and whether or not citizen suits will seek to force them to do so, remains to be seen.[148] But in the wake of *MA v EPA*, these agencies, like the EPA, will be under increasing pressure to mitigate global climate change through the findings and decisions they make regarding species endangerment and conservation.[149]

More broadly, the decision in *MA v EPA* helped to shift the momentum in the political and legal struggle to force the incumbent administration to respond to the global warming problem with measures that go beyond voluntarism.[150] Within the organized environmental community, and among the proregulatory states seeking federal action, the case is considered to be a huge victory, even though the "victory" amounted to sending the threshold endangerment decision back to EPA. At a political level, the case has

---

[145] 16 USC § 1536(a)(2) (2000).

[146] Now that the FWS have announced their intent to list the polar bear as threatened because of global warming, this possibility is all the more real. See note 34.

[147] See Ruhl, *Climate Change and the Endangered Species Act* (cited in note 144) (proposing that the ESA should not be used to regulate greenhouse gas emissions, but instead should focus on establishing protective measures for species that have a chance of surviving the climate change transition and establishing a viable population in the future climate regime).

> Unlike where the Clean Air Act takes the EPA, however, accepting that human-induced climate change is occurring does not lead inevitably to particular administrative duties or findings under the ESA. No provision of the ESA addresses pollutants, emissions, or climate in any specific regulatory sense. Rather, the statute operates on fairly holistic levels, requiring the FWS to consider what constitutes endangerment, take, jeopardy, and recovery of species.

Id at 30.

[148] See id (noting that some environmental groups have announced their intention to use litigation under the ESA to seek protection of climate-threatened species).

[149] Id.

[150] See J. DeShazo and Jody Freeman, *Timing and Form of Federal Regulation: The Case of Climate Change*, 155 U Pa L Rev 1499, 1517–18 n 54 (2007).

enormous symbolic value. From the perspective of the groups demanding federal regulation, it communicated to the public something on the order of: *even the Supreme Court thinks something must
be done*.

The decision also added fuel to the legislative fire in Congress.
Numerous climate-change bills were proposed in the 110th Congress after the Democratic takeover in 2006, building on earlier
proposals in the 109th Congress that went nowhere. Even if passage
must await a new administration, all of this activity has helped to
build momentum and political support for federal climate legislation
sooner rather than later. Interestingly, the Court's remand to EPA
did not quell this legislative activity, as our expertise-forcing perspective might predict. Instead, the decision seems only to have
added to a sense of urgency that a federal law to cut greenhouse
gas emissions is necessary because the problem of climate change
is so serious, and because the CAA, as currently written, is a less-
than-ideal vehicle for addressing it. In this sense, one might argue,
MA v EPA has a democracy-forcing aspect because, by airing out
the issues, it reinforced the need for a comprehensive new legislative
approach.[151]

V. Conclusion

For all of these reasons, *MA v EPA* is a highly consequential
environmental law case. And it is indisputably a major political
event. But it is also, in our view, an important administrative law
case, not primarily because of the standing holding but above all
because of the Court's willingness to restrict and carefully scrutinize
agency discretion to "decide not to decide." If our expertise-forcing
theory is right, the Court is concerned at the moment to insulate
expert agencies from political influence. This is not, on our account,
because the Court believes that expert decisions should be completely separated from politics or because the Court naively views
presidential influence as something new that must be nipped in the
bud. Neither is the case. All administrations exert political pressure
on their executive agencies, and many have been accused of "interference," something we suspect the Court knows well. In our

---

[151] Among other limitations, the CAA's major tool for setting air pollution standards—
the NAAQS process—is unsuitable for greenhouse gas emissions. States cannot ensure
compliance with "national standards" for carbon dioxide and other greenhouse gases.

view—and we expect this is the Court's view—it is inevitable that political considerations will come into play in executive agencies headed by political appointees who are accountable to the President.[152] Our suggestion is simply that the pendulum may have swung too far, at least in the view of the majority Justices, in the direction of strong presidential administration, and that they wished to nudge it in the other direction.

After *MA v EPA* was decided, new accusations emerged about attempts by the Bush administration to manipulate "expert" decisions by public health agencies.[153] Dr. Richard H. Carmona, the former Surgeon General, who served from 2002 to 2006, claimed that he was told "not to speak or issue reports about stem cells, emergency contraception, sex education, or prison, mental and global health issues," that his speeches and reports were altered by political appointees without his consent, and that "on issue after issue the administration made decisions about important public health issues based solely on political considerations, not scientific

---

[152] Courts have never tried, for example, to ban ex parte communications among executive branch officials, or between agency officials and the White House, in the context of rulemaking. See, for example, *Sierra Club v Costle*, 657 F2d 298, 405–06 (DC Cir 1981) ("The court recognizes the basic need of the President and his White House staff to monitor the consistency of executive agency regulations with Administration policy. He and his White House advisers surely must be briefed fully and frequently about rules in the making, and their contributions to policymaking considered. . . . The authority of the President to control and supervise executive policymaking is derived from the Constitution; the desirability of such control is demonstrable from the practical realities of administrative rulemaking. Regulations such as those involved here demand a careful weighing of cost, environmental, and energy considerations. They also have broad implications for national economic policy. Our form of government simply could not function effectively or rationally if key executive policymakers were isolated from each other and from the Chief Executive. Single mission agencies do not always have the answers to complex regulatory problems. An overworked administrator exposed on a 24-hour basis to a dedicated but zealous staff needs to know the arguments and ideas of policymakers in other agencies as well as in the White House."). Such ex parte contacts are only unlawful when an agency is engaged in an on-the-record adjudication. See, for example, *Portland Audubon Society v Environmental Species Committee*, 984 F2d 1534, 1537 (9th Cir 1993) (finding that the President is an "interested party" within the meaning of section 557(d) of the APA for purposes of formal adjudications).

[153] Gardiner Harris, *Surgeon General Sees 4-Year Term as Compromised*, NY Times A1 (July 11, 2007). Former EPA Administrator Christine Todd Whitman has also recently admitted that she resigned because she refused to sign off on a rule about the CAA's New Source Review program, 40 CFR § 52.21(c) (2005), that was being pushed by Vice President Cheney, see Jo Becker and Barton Gelman, *Leaving No Tracks*, Wash Post A1 (June 27, 2007). The rule was later struck down by the D.C. Circuit, which used particularly harsh language in doing so. See *New York v EPA*, 443 F3d 880, 887 (DC Cir 2006) (criticizing the EPA, stating that "[o]nly in a Humpty Dumpty world would Congress be required to use superfluous words while an agency could ignore an expansive word that Congress did use," and "declin[ing] to adopt such a world-view").

ones."[154] Two things are striking about this episode. First, it was accompanied by statements by two other former Surgeon Generals from two prior administrations (one Democratic and one Republican) who also claimed to have weathered political interference, though to a lesser degree, which reveals that the problem is to some extent endemic. Second, the occasion for these statements was a hearing before the House Oversight and Government Reform Committee, which suggests that political remedies are in fact available when political interference with agency expertise goes too far. Perhaps a judicial response to strong presidential administration is unnecessary because the legislative branch can fend for itself. To be sure, this can be more difficult when the presidency and the Congress are both in the hands of the same party,[155] as was the case during the events that led to *MA v EPA*. But such dominance rarely lasts long. Given this is the case, the Court may soon retreat from its current project and return to a *Chevron* worldview premised on strong presidential administration. For now though, the Court seems to have rediscovered an old problem, and returned to an older judicial role.

---

[154] Harris, NY Times A1 (cited in note 153).

[155] See generally Daryl Levinson and Richard H. Pildes, *Separation of Parties, Not Powers*, 119 Harv L Rev 2311 (2006).

ROBERT V. PERCIVAL

MASSACHUSETTS v EPA: ESCAPING THE COMMON LAW'S GROWING SHADOW

In its first full Term with its newest member, the U.S. Supreme Court marched decidedly to the right with decisions narrowing abortion rights, striking down affirmative action programs, invalidating campaign finance regulations, and making it more difficult for victims of employment discrimination to seek redress. In the face of this rightward shift the most surprising decision of the Term was the Court's embrace of claims that the U.S. Environmental Protection Agency (EPA) had acted unlawfully by refusing to use the Clean Air Act to combat climate change. In *Massachusetts v EPA*,[1] the Court held that EPA had the authority to regulate emissions of greenhouse gases from motor vehicles under the Clean Air Act, and it ordered the agency to reconsider its refusal to do so.

The Court's decision vividly illustrates important features of its approach to regulatory issues today. The Court decided the case by a 5–4 margin, with Justices in the majority and dissent sharply

Robert V. Percival is the Robert F. Stanton Professor of Law and the Director of the Environmental Law Program at the University of Maryland School of Law.

AUTHOR'S NOTE: I would like to thank the members of the Georgetown Environmental Research Workshop, including Lisa Heinzerling, E. Donald Elliott, Richard Lazarus, and John Echeverria, for valuable comments on a previous draft of this article. I also would like to thank Maryland law students Gaddiel Baah, Julie Grufferman, and Elaine Lutz for research assistance.

[1] 127 S Ct 1438 (2007).

disagreeing with each other on issues of constitutional law, statutory interpretation, and administrative law. As in each of the other twenty-three cases the Court decided by a single vote during this Term, Justice Kennedy cast the deciding vote. The ultimate lineup of the other eight Justices was entirely predictable. Justices Stevens, Souter, Ginsburg, and Breyer joined Kennedy in siding with the environmental plaintiffs, while Justices Scalia, Thomas, Chief Justice Roberts, and Justice Alito voted to uphold the agency's refusal to act.

At first glance *Massachusetts v EPA* may seem to be a surprising green turn by the Court (one scholar called it "as close as we will come" to a "*Brown v. Board of Education* for the environment"[2]). Environmental advocates hope it will spawn regulatory action to combat climate change; some anticipate a new flood of lawsuits against major sources of greenhouse gas emissions. While the decision *is* a profoundly important victory for environmentalists, lurking beneath its surface is a harsh reality: the decision confirms that the Justices are even more sharply split over foundational principles of the regulatory state than they were before the addition of the Court's two newest members.

Four Justices highly skeptical of environmental regulation narrowly construe regulatory statutes and seek to restrict citizen access to the courts to implement and enforce federal regulatory programs. Four other Justices are decidedly more sympathetic to the broad purposes of the environmental laws and the citizen suit provisions incorporated into them. Justice Kennedy is the man in the middle—skeptical of regulation, but open to accommodating the orderly evolution of the modern regulatory state.

The struggle between these two camps echoes centuries-old tensions between the common law's skepticism of regulatory interventions by government and the civil law's greater tolerance for them. These tensions were most evident when U.S. courts heard early challenges to the New Deal's regulatory programs. Despite the rise of the modern regulatory state, these tensions frequently resurface as courts review regulatory decisions by administrative agencies. After describing this emerging pattern, this article examines how it is reflected in the sharp divisions between the majority and dissenting opinions in *Massachusetts v EPA*. It then discusses

---

[2] Jonathan Z. Cannon, *The Significance of Massachusetts v. EPA*, Va L Rev In Brief 53 (May 21, 2007), online at http://www.virginialawreview.org/inbrief/2007/05/21/cannon.pdf.

the implications of this decision for the struggle to overcome barriers to global, collective action to respond to climate change.

I. The Growing Shadow of the Common Law on Judicial Review of Regulatory Decisions

Before examining the Court's decision in *Massachusetts v EPA*, it is important first to consider how the Court has evolved in its treatment of challenges to regulatory decisions. Prior to the enactment of comprehensive federal regulatory statutes, the common law of nuisance was the first line of legal defense for the environment. In the early decades of the twentieth century, the Supreme Court itself heard many prominent disputes between states over transboundary air and water pollution.[3] When massive pollution from large sources, such as copper smelters, caused visible environmental harm, it was possible for plaintiffs to satisfy the common law's demands for individualized proof of causal injury. The U.S. Supreme Court issued injunctions to control pollution in several cases, though it did not relish performing the role of a national regulatory agency. The common law helped encourage noxious activities to locate away from populated areas, and it spurred the development of new technology to control pollution.

During the 1970s Congress enacted comprehensive regulatory legislation to protect the environment. The regulatory programs these new laws erected were designed to overcome the inadequacies of the common law in combating chronic, multisource pollution problems by giving expert administrative agencies the authority to adopt preventive regulations. Emphasizing the comprehensive nature of the regulatory scheme established by the Clean Water Act, the U.S. Supreme Court interpreted this law to supplant the federal common law of interstate nuisance.[4]

Courts reviewing the first generation of regulations implementing these programs confronted claims by regulated entities that agencies had adopted excessively burdensome regulations that would do little to protect human health and the environment. Responding to such claims, a plurality of the Supreme Court in 1980 invalidated an Occupational Safety and Health Administration

---

[3] See Robert V. Percival, *The Clean Water Act and the Demise of the Federal Common Law of Interstate Nuisance*, 55 Ala L Rev 717, 717 n 4 (2004).

[4] *City of Milwaukee v Illinois*, 451 US 304 (1981).

(OSHA) regulation to protect workers against exposure to benzene.[5] By creative interpretation of a definitional provision in the Occupational Safety and Health (OSH) Act, the plurality imposed new preconditions on agency issuance of regulations. OSHA was directed to perform a risk assessment to determine if current levels of workplace exposure to benzene posed a "significant risk" and to ascertain that such a risk could be appreciably reduced by regulation. For a plurality decision interpreting a single statute, *Benzene* had a surprisingly large impact as agencies operating under a plethora of regulatory authorities routinely began to conduct risk assessments. However, the Court quickly signaled that it would not hamstring preventive regulation when it rejected industry efforts to write a cost-benefit analysis requirement into the OSH Act.[6]

Despite *Benzene*, reviewing courts generally were not hostile to the first generation of federal environmental, health, and safety regulations. Three years after *Benzene*, the Court's *Chevron* decision[7] directed reviewing courts to give greater deference to reasonable agency interpretations of ambiguous statutory provisions. While *Chevron* (and *Vermont Yankee*[8]—a decision giving agencies more procedural freedom) reversed victories by environmental groups in the Courts of Appeals, the Supreme Court was not on a mission to tilt judicial review in an antiregulatory direction. This was confirmed by its *State Farm* decision[9] where the Court required the National Highway Transportation Safety Administration (NHTSA) to reconsider its decision to rescind a regulation requiring motor vehicles to employ passive restraints to reduce deaths in auto accidents.

A key feature of the new regulatory legislation was its authorization for citizen suits to enforce regulations and to require agencies to perform nondiscretionary duties. The courts facilitated such actions by recognizing that aesthetic injury could give rise to standing to sue by environmental interests. While disappointing environmentalists by rejecting the Sierra Club's efforts to establish auto-

---

[5] *Industrial Union Department, AFL-CIO v American Petroleum Institute*, 448 US 607 (1980) ("*Benzene*").

[6] *American Textile Manufacturers Institute v Donovan*, 452 US 490 (1981).

[7] *Chevron, USA v Natural Resources Defense Council*, 467 US 837 (1984).

[8] In *Vermont Yankee Nuclear Power Corp. v Natural Resources Defense Council*, 435 US 519 (1978), the Court directed lower courts not to impose additional procedural requirements on agencies that go beyond requirements contained in the underlying regulatory statute.

[9] *Motor Vehicle Manufacturers Ass'n v State Farm Mutual Auto. Insur. Co.*, 463 US 29 (1983).

matic standing, the Supreme Court's decision in *Sierra Club v Morton*[10] established that allegations of aesthetic injury could give rise to standing and that "the fact that particular environmental interests are shared by the many rather than the few does not make them less deserving of legal protection through the judicial process."[11] The following year the Court upheld the standing of a student group to challenge a railroad tariff that allegedly would reduce the market for recycled materials in *United States v Students Challenging Regulatory Agency Procedures (SCRAP)*.[12] The Court reiterated not only that aesthetic and environmental harm could give rise to standing, but also that "standing is not to be denied simply because many people suffer the same injury."[13] As Justice Stewart explained in his opinion for the Court: "To deny standing to persons who are in fact injured simply because many others are also injured, would mean that the most injurious and widespread Government actions could be questioned by nobody. We cannot accept that conclusion."[14]

While the Supreme Court generally was not viewed as a champion of environmental interests when it was under the leadership of Chief Justice Burger, in a number of decisions it did not hesitate to read the new federal regulatory statutes broadly. This is illustrated by the Court's landmark 1978 "snail darter" decision interpreting the Endangered Species Act[15] and its unanimous 1985 decision upholding regulations applying the Clean Water Act to wetlands adjacent to navigable waters.[16] In addition to broadly interpreting the scope of federal regulatory authority to achieve the ambitious goals of the Acts, the Court emphasized the importance of deferring to agency expertise. Thus in *Riverside Bayview*, Justice White writing for a unanimous Court stated:

> In view of the breadth of federal regulatory authority contemplated by the Act itself and the inherent difficulties of defining precise bounds to regulable waters, the Corps' ecological judg-

---

[10] 405 US 727 (1972).

[11] Id at 734.

[12] 412 US 669 (1973).

[13] Id at 687.

[14] Id at 688.

[15] *Tennessee Valley Authority v Hill*, 437 US 153 (1978).

[16] *United States v Riverside Bayview Homes, Inc.*, 474 US 121 (1985).

ment about the relationship between waters and their adjacent wetlands provides an adequate basis for a legal judgment that adjacent wetlands may be defined as waters under the Act.[17]

The Court today is sharply split on its approach to review of environmental regulations. After William Rehnquist became Chief Justice and Antonin Scalia joined the Court in 1986, the Court became more solicitous of private property rights and more skeptical about environmental standing. In each area of law, the Justices championing this shift reimported common law principles to judicial review of regulatory decisions. In a law review article written three years before he joined the Court,[18] Justice Scalia boldly revealed his antipathy to environmental standing based on his ideological distaste for strict implementation of the environmental laws. In 1992, he authored both the Court's most restrictive environmental standing decision (*Lujan*)[19] and a landmark property rights decision (*Lucas*).[20] In the former Justice Scalia questioned the constitutional authority of Congress to authorize certain citizen suits, while in the latter he dismissed state legislative findings concerning what activities pose a danger to public health and the environment. Elevating common law principles to constitutional status, he declared in *Lucas* that regulations that deprive real property of all economically viable use require payment of just compensation unless they proscribe only activities that would be nuisances prohibited at common law. Justice Scalia insisted in *Lucas* that legislative findings that regulation is necessary to prevent environmental harm are insufficient in themselves to preclude takings liability. Instead the Court held that only regulations forbidding activities that were common law nuisances at the time the Constitution was adopted could qualify for the nuisance exception to takings liability. Signaling his openness to a more flexible approach to applying common law notions, Justice Kennedy in a concurring opinion expressed his discomfort with Justice Scalia's approach. Justice Kennedy concluded that "nuisance prevention" is not the "sole source of state authority to impose severe restrictions" given the state's interest in

[17] Id at 134.

[18] Antonin Scalia, *The Doctrine of Standing as an Essential Element of the Separation of Powers*, 17 Suffolk U L Rev 881 (1983).

[19] *Lujan v Defenders of Wildlife*, 504 US 555 (1992).

[20] *Lucas v South Carolina Coastal Council*, 505 US 1003 (1992).

"enacting new regulatory initiatives in response to changing conditions . . . ."[21]

In another property rights case decided two years later, the Court limited the ability of government authorities to seek regulatory exactions from developers. It required that the government demonstrate not only an "essential nexus" between the state interest and nature of the exaction,[22] but also that the magnitude of the exaction is "roughly proportional" to the impact of the development.[23] In similar fashion, the Court in *City of Boerne v Flores*[24] considerably limited the remedial powers Congress may exercise under Section 5 of the Fourteenth Amendment by requiring that it show "congruence and proportionality" between its legislative goals and the prevention of actual violations of Fourteenth Amendment rights. In each of these cases, the Court constructed its own type of common law demonstration of injury that the government must satisfy before its regulatory action can be upheld.

While the Burger Court's environmental decisions did not feature ideologically predictable coalitions of Justices on either side, the Rehnquist Court's decisions were a different matter, particularly after the Court embarked on its campaigns to revive constitutional limits on federal power, to vindicate state sovereignty, and to strengthen constitutional protection for property rights. Most of these cases were decided by a stable coalition of five Justices over strident dissents by the other four members of the Court. Prominent features of these decisions included the majority's profound distrust of legislative findings of harm and its insistence on more demanding demonstrations of causal connections between regulated activities and the harm the regulation seeks to prevent.

For example, in *United States v Lopez*[25] the Court held by a 5–4 majority that the Commerce Clause did not give Congress the authority to prohibit the possession of firearms in the vicinity of schools because the statute at issue regulated an activity that did not "substantially affect" interstate commerce. The five-Justice majority in *Lopez* emphasized that Congress had not made factual

---

[21] Id at 1035 (Kennedy concurring).

[22] This requirement was first established in *Nollan v California Coastal Commission*, 483 US 825 (1987).

[23] *Dolan v City of Tigard*, 512 US 374 (1994).

[24] 521 US 507 (1997).

[25] 514 US 549 (1995).

findings concerning the impact of firearm possession near schools on interstate commerce. However, five years later in *United States v Morrison*[26] it invalidated legislation creating a federal civil cause of action for victims of gender-motivated violence, despite the fact that Congress had made extensive findings concerning the substantial impact of such violence on interstate commerce.

Even when the Rehnquist Court rebuffed efforts to narrow the scope of the environmental laws through judicial interpretation, some Justices sought to fashion implied common law limits on their application. In *Babbitt v Sweet Home Chapter of Communities for a Great Oregon*[27] the Court reversed a lower court's interpretation of the Endangered Species Act that limited its prohibition on "taking" endangered species to embrace only the direct physical application of force. The Court upheld regulations that also barred the destruction of the species' critical habitat if it caused harm to their members. Justice O'Connor wrote a separate concurring opinion arguing that common law principles of proximate cause necessarily limit application of this provision.[28]

Both Justice O'Connor and Chief Justice Rehnquist abandoned Justice Scalia's campaign to restrict environmental standing in 2000 when they joined five other Justices in upholding the standing of citizens living near a company that repeatedly violated the Clean Water Act to sue to enforce permit limits.[29] The decision emphasized that plaintiffs need not demonstrate that the permit violations had caused actual harm to the environment, but rather only that they caused the plaintiffs to have reasonable concerns about the impact of the violations. The following year the Court unanimously upheld the constitutionality of the Clean Air Act, rejecting an industry challenge premised on the long dormant nondelegation doctrine.[30]

While rebuffing most constitutional challenges to environmental regulation, the Rehnquist Court cited constitutional concerns in construing the scope of the environmental laws more narrowly. In 2001, the Court in *Solid Waste Agency of Northern Cook County v U.S. Army Corps of Engineers (SWANCC)* held that the Clean Water

---

[26] 529 US 598 (2000).

[27] 515 US 687 (1995).

[28] Id at 708–09.

[29] *Friends of the Earth v Laidlaw Environmental Services*, 528 US 167 (2000).

[30] *Whitman v American Trucking Associations*, 531 US 457 (2001).

Act did not authorize the regulation of dredge and fill activities in isolated wetlands.[31] The Court's 5–4 majority declined to reach the constitutional issue because it found that Congress had not intended to allow the Corps to regulate isolated wetlands. Stating that it expected a clear statement of Congressional intent to support "an administrative interpretation of a statute [that] invokes the outer limits of Congress' power,"[32] the Court majority concluded that regulation of isolated wetlands exceeded the Corps' authority under the Act.[33]

The sharp division in the Court concerning the scope of the Clean Water Act was further illustrated the next year when the Court split 4–4 in a wetlands case in which Justice Kennedy had recused himself.[34] But it was only after Chief Justice Rehnquist's death and the confirmation of Chief Justice Roberts that the full dimensions of the Court's divisions became most apparent. In 2006 the Court split 4–1–4 in deciding whether the Clean Water Act could be applied to wetlands adjacent to nonnavigable tributaries of navigable waters.[35]

In an opinion authored by Justice Scalia, a plurality of four Justices (including Chief Justice Roberts, Justice Thomas, and Justice Alito) endorsed a radically restrictive interpretation of "waters of the United States" that would have significantly narrowed the scope of federal jurisdiction under the Clean Water Act had it commanded a majority of the Court.[36] While rejecting the petitioners' argument that the Act applies only to waters navigable in fact or susceptible of being so rendered, the plurality relied on a 1954 dictionary definition of "waters" to conclude that it includes "only relatively permanent, standing or flowing bodies of water."[37] Addressing the difficulty of squaring this conclusion with the Court's unanimous holding in *Riverside Bayview*, the plurality creatively explained *"Riverside Bayview* rested upon the inherent ambiguity in

---

[31] *Solid Waste Agency of N. Cook County v U.S. Army Corps of Engineers*, 531 US 159 (2001).

[32] Id at 172.

[33] Id at 174.

[34] *Borden Ranch Partnership v U.S. Army Corps of Engineers*, 261 F3d 810 (9th Cir 2001), aff'd by an equally divided Court, 537 US 99 (2002).

[35] *Rapanos v United States*, 126 S Ct 2208 (2006).

[36] Id.

[37] Id at 2220–21.

defining where water ends and abutting ('adjacent') wetlands begin, permitting the Corps' reliance on ecological considerations *only to resolve that ambiguity* in favor of treating all abutting wetlands as waters."[38]

In an opinion authored by Justice Stevens, four dissenting Justices (including Justices Souter, Ginsburg, and Breyer) argued that federal Clean Water Act jurisdiction extends to wetlands adjacent to nonnavigable tributaries of navigable waters. They argued that the case was squarely controlled by the Court's unanimous decision in *Riverside Bayview* and that contrary interpretations were inconsistent with the legislative history and purposes of the Clean Water Act.

> The Army Corps has determined that wetlands adjacent to tributaries of traditionally navigable waters preserve the quality of our Nation's waters by, among other things, providing habitat for aquatic animals, keeping excessive sediment and toxic pollutants out of adjacent waters, and reducing downstream flooding by absorbing water at times of high flow. The Corps' resulting decision to treat these wetlands as encompassed within the term "waters of the United States" is a quintessential example of the Executive's reasonable interpretation of a statutory provision.[39]

Neither of these opinions commanded a majority of the Court because the decisive ninth vote was cast by Justice Kennedy who wrote an opinion concurring only in the judgment that the decision below should be reversed and the case remanded to the lower court. Justice Kennedy sharply rejected the radical narrowing of the Act advocated in the Scalia plurality opinion, and he acknowledged the importance of broadly protecting wetlands. While he agreed with much of the dissent, he supported a remand because he wanted the court below to apply a new standard he articulated in his concurrence. Justice Kennedy concluded that "to constitute 'navigable waters' under the Act, a water or wetland must possess a 'significant nexus' to waters that are or were navigable in fact or that could reasonably be so made."[40] Thus, in Justice Kennedy's view, to successfully assert federal jurisdiction under the Act the government must show that "the wetlands, either alone or in combination with similarly situated lands in the region, significantly affect the chem-

---

[38] Id at 2226 (emphasis in original).

[39] Id at 2252 (Stevens dissenting).

[40] Id at 2236 (Kennedy concurring in the judgment).

ical, physical, and biological integrity of other covered waters more readily understood as 'navigable.'"[41] He noted that if the effects are only "speculative or insubstantial" the wetlands will not be subject to federal jurisdiction, but he concluded that a "reasonable inference of ecologic interconnection" can be drawn for wetlands adjacent to navigable waters.

Because he cast the decisive vote in the case, Justice Kennedy's view of the applicable law now appears to be controlling even though it was rejected by all eight of the other Justices. Justice Kennedy himself emphatically rejected the view of the four-Justice plurality opinion authored by Justice Scalia. He argued that the limitations it seeks to impose on federal jurisdiction "are without support in the language and purposes of the Act or in our cases interpreting it."[42] He explained that the "plurality's first require-ment—permanent standing water or continuous flow, at least for a period of 'some months'—makes little practical sense in a statute concerned with downstream water quality"[43] and has no support in the statutory text even when dictionary definitions of "waters" are applied. Justice Kennedy argued that "exclusion of wetlands lacking a continuous surface connection to other jurisdictional waters—is also unpersuasive" because wetlands are not "*indistinguishable*' from waters to which they bear a surface connection."[44] Thus, he con-cluded that "the plurality's opinion is inconsistent with the Act's text, structure, and purpose."[45]

Justice Kennedy and the four dissenting Justices also rejected the plurality's notion that federal jurisdiction should be interpreted nar-rowly to avoid constitutional concerns. Justice Kennedy noted that thirty-three states and the District of Columbia filed an amicus brief supporting a broad interpretation of federal jurisdiction be-cause it "protects downstream States from out-of-state pollution that they cannot themselves regulate."[46]

Addressing the administrative difficulties of applying his "sub-stantial nexus" approach to defining federal jurisdiction, Justice Kennedy suggested that:

---

[41] Id at 2248.

[42] Id at 2242.

[43] Id (citation omitted).

[44] Id at 2244.

[45] Id at 2246.

[46] Id.

[t]hrough regulations or adjudication, the Corps may choose to identify categories of tributaries that, due to their volume of flow (either annually or on average), their proximity to navigable waters, or other relevant considerations, are significant enough that wetlands adjacent to them are likely, in the majority of cases, to perform important functions for an aquatic system incorporating navigable waters.[47]

For wetlands adjacent to navigable-in-fact waters, Justice Kennedy concluded that adjacency can be sufficient for the Corps to establish jurisdiction. "Absent more specific regulations, however, the Corps must establish a significant nexus on a case-by-case basis when it seeks to regulate wetlands based on adjacency to nonnavigable tributaries."[48] Justice Kennedy states that "[w]here an adequate nexus is established for a particular wetland, it may be permissible, as a matter of administrative convenience or necessity, to presume covered status for other comparable wetlands in the region."[49]

For now, the end product of *Rapanos* is that the scope of federal jurisdiction under the Clean Water Act is hopelessly confused. In an unusual concurring opinion, Chief Justice Roberts described the result of the 4–1–4 split as "unfortunate" because "no opinion commands a majority of the Court on precisely how to read Congress' limits on the reach of the Clean Water Act."[50] As a result, he noted, "Lower courts and regulated entities will now have to feel their way on a case-by-case basis."[51] Surprisingly, he suggested that the situation "readily . . . could have been avoided" if the Army Corps of Engineers had issued new regulations after *SWANCC* clarifying the limits of its jurisdictional reach. Citing *Chevron*, the Chief Justice noted "Given the broad, somewhat ambiguous, but nonetheless clearly limiting terms Congress employed in the Clean Water Act, the Corps and the EPA would have enjoyed plenty of room to operate in developing *some* notion of an outer bound to the reach of their authority."[52] Yet because the Chief Justice joined in full Justice Scalia's plurality opinion, which rejected any deference to a broader definition of "waters of the United States" than the one

---

[47] Id at 2248.

[48] Id at 2249.

[49] Id.

[50] Id at 2236 (Roberts concurring).

[51] Id.

[52] Id.

articulated by Justice Scalia, the Chief Justice's concurrence contributes further to the confusion.

While purporting to interpret Congressional intent, the opinions
of the Justices in *Rapanos* reflect the more fundamental split that
permeates much of the Court's jurisprudence in reviewing regulatory decisions by administrative agencies.[53] Four Justices (Justices
Scalia, Thomas, Chief Justice Roberts, and Justice Alito) join an
opinion expressing extreme hostility to a long-standing regulatory
interpretation (referring to it as a thirty-year-old "entrenched executive error" and stating that it "would authorize the Corps to
function as a *de facto* regulator of immense stretches of intrastate
land—an authority the agency has shown its willingness to exercise
with the scope of discretion that would befit a local zoning board").[54]
Four other Justices (Justices Stevens, Souter, Ginsburg, and Breyer)
vote to uphold the regulation because they are willing to defer to
the judgment of a federal agency that it is essential to achieving
the Congressional purpose. The Justice in the middle—Justice Kennedy—acknowledges the importance of the regulatory goal while
seeking to impose new procedural requirements on the agency to
avoid overreaching.

Justice Scalia's group of Justices made highly exaggerated claims
that § 404 imposes high costs on landowners while appearing dismissive of the ecological costs of filling wetlands. Justice Kennedy
correctly calls Scalia's opinion "unduly dismissive" of the
"[i]mportant public interests . . . served by the Clean Water Act
in general and by the protection of wetlands in particular."[55] In a
footnote Justice Stevens criticizes the plurality's "antagonism to
environmentalism" and its claim that his dissent is "policy-laden"
by observing that "[t]he policy considerations that have influenced
my thinking are Congress' rather than my own."[56] This debate
illustrates the sharply contrasting views concerning the value of
federal regulatory programs to protect the environment among the
Justices currently on the Court.

While four Justices readily accept the importance of legislation

---

[53] For a more detailed discussion contrasting the precautionary and reactive approaches
to environmental regulation embraced by different members of the judiciary, see Robert
V. Percival, *Environmental Law in the Twenty-First Century*, 25 Va Envir L J 1, 9–18 (2007).

[54] *Rapanos*, 126 S Ct at 2232, 2224 (Scalia plurality opinion).

[55] Id at 2246 (Kennedy concurring in the judgment).

[56] Id at 2259 n 8 (Stevens dissenting).

authorizing precautionary regulation, four others are reluctant to accept legislative findings to justify regulation and narrowly construe the scope and purposes of federal regulatory programs to protect the environment, even though the comprehensiveness of these programs was the Court's initial rationale for supplanting the federal common law of nuisance. Four Justices (Chief Justice Roberts and Justices Scalia, Thomas, and Alito) insist on more demanding, and more individualized, factual showings of causal connections before federal regulations are upheld or enforced, while four other Justices (Stevens, Souter, Ginsburg, and Breyer) are more tolerant of regulatory decisions founded on assessments of risk at the wholesale level.

This split reflects fundamental differences in the Justices' attitudes toward precautionary regulation. One group of Justices (Stevens, Souter, Ginsburg, and Breyer) is inclined to interpret the environmental statutes to facilitate achievement of their precautionary purposes by upholding regulation of activities believed to contribute to environmental harm. Another group of Justices (Scalia, Thomas, C. J. Roberts, and Alito) is profoundly skeptical of precautionary regulation and concerned about its cost and fairness. Even though regulatory legislation was adopted in response to the perceived inadequacies of the common law (particularly its demand for individualized proof of causal injury), these Justices insist on a kind of common law standard of proof connecting activities to be regulated with demonstrated environmental harm. This split permeates a wide range of decisions concerning who has standing to sue in environmental cases, the scope of federal regulatory authority, and even what constitutes a regulatory taking.

Justice Kennedy straddles both camps. He demands a greater showing of causal injury to justify regulation than the more precautionary group of Justices, but he also recognizes that "[t]he common law of nuisance is too narrow a confine for the exercise of regulatory power in a complex and interdependent society."[57] While Justices Scalia and Thomas seek to keep environmental plaintiffs out of court on constitutional grounds, questioning whether citizen suits violate separation of powers principles, Justice Kennedy opines that the purchase of a plane ticket to visit foreign endangered species would have been enough to give an environmental group standing

---

[57] *Lucas v South Carolina Coastal Commission*, 505 US 1003, 1035 (1992) (Kennedy concurring in the judgment).

in *Lujan v Defenders of Wildlife*.[58] While rejecting Justice Scalia's disdainfully narrow interpretation of the scope of the Clean Water Act in *Rapanos v United States*,[59] Justice Kennedy still insists on the government showing a "significant nexus" between wetlands it seeks to regulate and navigable waters. This produced the 4–1–4 split in *Rapanos* that has caused enormous confusion concerning the scope of federal authority under the Clean Water Act because Justice Kennedy's view of the applicable law now appears to be controlling even though it was rejected by all eight of the other Justices.

The *Rapanos* decision starkly highlights the differences between a precautionary approach to regulatory policy and a reactive one. The four Justices who voted to uphold federal regulation in the case were willing to defer to the judgment of a federal agency that it is essential to regulate wetlands adjacent to tributaries of navigable waters in order to prevent degradation of water quality. The four Justices who voted against the government were skeptical that such regulation would prevent ecological harm, but also fearful that this approach would allow federal agencies to regulate virtually anything. The influence of common law notions of causation is apparent in Justice Kennedy's approach, which acknowledges the importance of precautionary regulation, while insisting on some factual demonstration that regulated activities are connected to substantial environmental harm. No decision highlights so sharply the differences between the Justices in their approaches to judicial review of environmental regulations than *Rapanos*.

The sharp split between the Justices in their attitudes toward regulatory policy is strikingly similar to centuries-old debates between common law and civil law approaches to protection of public health, as Professor Noga Morag-Levine has demonstrated.[60] Her research traces the evolution of judicial hostility in England toward continental Europe's "civil law model" that "relied on centralized, agency-based, state administration aimed at the implementation of regulatory standards through expert legislators and bureaucrats."[61] By contrast, the "common law model fundamentally distrusted bu-

---

[58] 504 US 555, 579 (1992) (Kennedy concurring in part and concurring in the judgment).

[59] 126 S Ct 2208, 2248 (2006).

[60] Noga Morag-Levine, *Common Law, Civil Law, and the Administrative State: Early-Modern England to the Lochner Era*, Const Comm (forthcoming), online at http://ssrn.com/abstract=1031229.

[61] Id (manuscript at 4).

reaucratic administration, and as a consequence, identified courts as the proper locus of administrative governance."[62] This controversy persisted throughout nineteenth-century U.S. debates over exercise of the police power. Proponents of the common law approach favored it because it "gave precedence to the communal norms and lay knowledge that juries could bring to regulatory decisions and the specialized knowledge of legally-trained judges."[63] Nineteenth-century English nuisance cases were tried before juries who expressed the sense of the community concerning what enterprises caused too much environmental harm to be located near populated areas.[64] With the shift away from the common law toward the administrative state as a vehicle for protecting public health and the environment, it no longer appears obvious that the common law is more protective of communal norms than precautionary regulation.

II. The Massachusetts v EPA Decision

Massachusetts v EPA came before the Court the Term after it split so badly in *Rapanos*. The case originated in October 1999 when a group of public interest organizations filed a petition asking EPA to regulate emissions of greenhouse gases from new motor vehicles under § 202 of the Clean Air Act. When the petition was filed, no one would have predicted that it ultimately would spawn a monumental Supreme Court decision. Petitions for rulemaking often languish unanswered, and it was only after a lawsuit filed in December 2002 to compel a response was settled by EPA agreeing to respond to the petition that the agency denied it in September 2003.[65] EPA argued that it did not have the authority to regulate greenhouse gas emissions under the Clean Air Act and that even if it had such authority it would choose not to exercise it.

EPA's denial of the petition was challenged in the U.S. Court of Appeals for the D.C. Circuit by the public interest groups joined

---

[62] Id.

[63] Id.

[64] An illustration of this is the prosecution in April 1838 of James Muspratt for maintaining an alkali works in Liverpool. The case was tried before a special jury of twelve merchants who, following a three-day trial, found the defendant guilty of creating and maintaining a nuisance within the borough. A copy of the original trial transcript is available in the rare book collection of the Harvard Law School Library.

[65] 68 Fed Reg 52922 (Sept 8, 2003).

by twelve states, the territory of American Samoa, and the cities of Baltimore and New York City. A three-judge panel of that court split sharply in upholding EPA's decision by a 2–1 vote.[66] Judge Sentelle concluded that because the harm alleged from global warming was so widespread it did not constitute the kind of "particularized injuries" that could give the petitioners standing to challenge EPA's decision. Without specifically deciding the questions of standing and statutory authority, Judge Randolph concluded that EPA had acted properly in denying the petition. Judge Tatel dissented, concluding that the petitioners had standing, that EPA had the authority to regulate emissions of greenhouse gases under the Clean Air Act, and that EPA had not adequately justified its denial of the petition.

While the inability of the D.C. Circuit panel to muster a majority on any particular rationale for upholding EPA's denial of the petition left its decision a confused muddle, few expected the Supreme Court to agree to review it. Not only was there no circuit conflict, but there was no possibility of one developing in the future because the Clean Air Act gives the D.C. Circuit exclusive venue to review EPA decisions of national applicability.[67] Nevertheless, the Supreme Court agreed to review the D.C. Circuit's decision.

When the Court issued its decision in April 2007, no one was surprised that the case was decided by a 5–4 vote of the Justices, though the ultimate outcome was surprising to many. In the course of deciding to reverse EPA's decision not to regulate emissions of greenhouse gases under the Clean Air Act, the Court addressed constitutional principles of standing to sue, interpreted the Clean Air Act, and applied principles of administrative law to reject EPA's rationale for failing to act as arbitrary and capricious. The Court held: (1) that the harm projected from global warming and climate change gives Massachusetts standing to sue even if the harm is widely shared and EPA can do little to alleviate most of it, (2) that the Clean Air Act gives EPA the authority to regulate greenhouse gas emissions, and (3) that EPA is required to regulate such emissions unless it determines that they do not contribute to climate change or the agency provides a reasonable explanation of why it cannot or will not determine whether they do.

---

[66] *Massachusetts v EPA*, 415 F3d 50 (DC Cir 2005).

[67] 42 USC § 7607(b)(1) (2000).

At a most basic level the result in *Massachusetts v EPA* is easy to understand: Justice Kennedy, the only "swing" Justice now on the Court, sided with the four liberal/moderate Justices (Stevens, Souter, Ginsburg, and Breyer) instead of the four conservatives (Scalia, Thomas, C. J. Roberts, and Alito).[68] More than one-third of all the Court's decisions in its 2006 Term were the product of 5–4 votes and Justice Kennedy was in the majority in all twenty-four of those cases. Justice Stevens's majority opinion in the case shows signs of an attempt to court Justice Kennedy by extensively quoting from Justice Kennedy's concurring opinion in *Lujan v Defenders of Wildlife*.

In his majority opinion Justice Stevens concluded that states have a special interest in protecting their land and citizens from environmental harm and that it is not necessary for EPA regulations to redress most of the harm for a state to have standing. He concluded that the Clean Air Act was meant to be a comprehensive regulatory scheme that requires EPA to control air pollutants that pose significant risks to the environment.

Justice Stevens's majority opinion spawned passionate dissents from Chief Justice Roberts and Justice Scalia. The Chief Justice argued that the effects of global warming are too generalized, too uncertain, and too unlikely to be effectively redressed by domestic regulation to provide any plaintiff with standing to sue. Justice Scalia argued for deference to EPA's decisions that it has no authority to regulate greenhouse gases and that it would not exercise such authority even if it had it. He endorsed the notion that greenhouse gases are not covered by the text of the Clean Air Act because "pollutants" are only substances that foul the air near the surface of the earth.

A. STANDING TO SUE

One surprise in *Massachusetts v EPA* is the ease with which the majority dispatched concern about the states' standing to sue. The Court upheld the states' standing by reaching back to a century-old precedent not cited by any of the parties to the case—*Georgia v Tennessee Copper Company*.[69] At oral argument Justice Kennedy had surprised counsel for Massachusetts by mentioning the case

---

[68] 127 S Ct at 1446.

[69] Id at 1454, quoting *Georgia v Tennessee Copper Co.*, 206 US 230, 237 (1907).

and describing it as "your best case" for establishing standing.[70] Decided at a time when the Court itself served as an original forum for resolving environmental disputes between states, the *Tennessee Copper* decision upheld a state's right to an injunction to stop harm caused by pollution originating in another state.

Despite vigorous objections from Chief Justice Roberts joined by the other three dissenters, the holding on standing may prove to be the most significant aspect of the Court's decision. Building on previous warnings from Justice Kennedy that standing to enforce regulatory statutes should not require proof of common law injury, Justice Stevens's majority opinion firmly rejects the notion that litigants should only have access to court when the harm they assert is neither too small nor too large, but rather "just right"— a kind of "Goldilocks" theory of standing. It also rejects the idea that standing is defeated if success enforcing a regulatory statute is unlikely to resolve more than a small portion of the problem the statute seeks to address. This represents a welcome appreciation of the realities of the modern administrative state and the purposes of precautionary regulation.

On closer analysis, Justice Kennedy's decision to join in full Justice Stevens's majority opinion on the issue of standing should not be that surprising. Justice Kennedy previously had been careful to indicate that his views on standing were not as extreme as Justice Scalia's. In *Lujan v Defenders of Wildlife* Justice Kennedy authored an important concurring opinion, joined by Justice Souter, that significantly tempered the result because the two concurring Justices were part of a six-Justice majority. Justices Kennedy and Souter indicated that the purchase of a plane ticket or the announcement of a specific date on which members of the plaintiff group would visit sites affected by the challenged regulation would be sufficient to establish standing. Justice Kennedy also expressed greater receptivity to the plaintiff's "ecosystem nexus," "animal nexus," and "vocational nexus" theories of standing,[71] which Justice Scalia had rejected with great disdain. He also clearly rejected the notion that standing should be limited by common law principles. "As Government programs and policies become more complex

---

[70] Transcript of Oral Argument, *Massachusetts v EPA*, No 05-1120, *15 (argued Nov 29, 2006), online at http://www.supremecourtus.gov/oral_arguments/argument_transcripts/05-1120.pdf.

[71] 504 US at 579 (Kennedy concurring in part and concurring in judgment).

and far-reaching, we must be sensitive to the articulation of new rights of action that do not have clear analogs in our common-law tradition."[72] Justice Kennedy observed that "Congress has the power to define injuries and articulate chains of causation that will give rise to a case or controversy where none existed before . . . ."[73] In its discussion of standing, Justice Stevens's majority opinion in *Massachusetts v EPA* quotes this language and emphasizes that Congress has authorized the very type of challenge to EPA action that the petitioners brought in the case.

The papers of the late Justice Harry A. Blackmun shed further light on Justice Kennedy's differences with Justice Scalia's efforts to restrict environmental standing. They reveal that Justice Kennedy stated that he was "not comfortable" in 1990 when voting with Justice Scalia at conference to restrict environmental standing in *Lujan v National Wildlife Federation*.[74] In *Lujan v Defenders of Wildlife*, Justices Kennedy and Souter refused for months to join Justice Scalia's initial draft opinion because it sought to convert the prudential notion that courts should decline to hear generalized grievances into a constitutional one that would bar environmental plaintiffs from seeking redress for widely shared injuries.[75] In a memo to Justice Scalia, Justice Souter wrote:

> Despite ambiguous dicta in some of our cases, I doubt anyone would lack standing to sue on the basis of a concrete injury that everyone else has suffered; Congress might for instance, grant everyone standing to challenge government action that would rip open the ozone layer and expose all Americans to unhealthy doses of radiation. Yet the repeated references to a particularity requirement, which might be taken as conceptually independent of a concreteness requirement, draw that conclusion into doubt.[76]

After Justice Kennedy expressed agreement with Justice Souter and informed Justice Scalia that he would not join his majority opinion unless he deleted the references to "particularity," Justice Scalia

---

[72] Id at 580.

[73] Id at 580.

[74] 497 US 871 (1990).

[75] This is described in more detail in Robert V. Percival, *Environmental Law in the Supreme Court: Highlights from the Blackmun Papers*, 35 Envir L Rptr 10637, 10658–59 (2005).

[76] Letter from Justice David H. Souter to Justice Antonin Scalia (May 8, 1992), Harry A. Blackmun Papers, Manuscript Division, U.S. Library of Congress.

made the requested changes.[77] A law clerk later reported to Justice Blackmun that word had spread throughout the building that Justice Scalia was "irate at [Justice Kennedy] for submitting his concurrence and felt that it 'scuttled' his majority opinion."[78]

Justice Scalia's campaign to restrict environmental standing suffered its worst setback eight years after *Lujan*, when all the Justices except for Scalia and Thomas joined Justice Ginsburg's majority opinion in *Friends of the Earth v Laidlaw Environmental Services*.[79] This decision rejected the notion that citizen plaintiffs must prove significant harm to the environment in order to establish standing to bring enforcement actions against polluters who violated their Clean Water Act permits. Traditional common law notions of standing initially would have barred the beneficiaries of regulation from having standing while providing regulated entities access to the courts. The Supreme Court halted this trend in *Laidlaw*, declaring that to insist that plaintiffs demonstrate "injury to the environment" would "raise the standing hurdle higher than the necessary showing for success on the merits in an action alleging noncompliance with [a Clean Water Act] permit."[80] The Court instead endorsed standing for plaintiffs with reasonable concerns about the effects of environmental violations on the environment in areas where they live or recreate.[81] The majority's broad view of environmental standing in *Massachusetts v EPA* confirms the continued vitality of *Laidlaw*, though by a margin (5–4) substantially narrower than the 7–2 result in *Laidlaw*.

In its discussion of standing in *Massachusetts v EPA*, Justice Stevens's majority opinion emphasizes the century-old precedent not cited in any of the briefs, but mentioned at oral argument by Justice Kennedy: *Georgia v Tennessee Copper Company*.[82] This case was a landmark in the development of the federal common law of interstate nuisance and the first case in which the U.S. Supreme Court issued an injunction to limit interstate pollution. In 1904 the state of Georgia invoked the Court's original jurisdiction over disputes between states to sue two companies that owned copper smelters

---

[77] Percival, *Highlights from the Blackmun Papers* at 10659 (cited in note 75).

[78] Id.

[79] 528 US 167 (2000).

[80] Id at 181.

[81] Id at 181–89.

[82] 206 US 230 (1907).

in the extreme southeast corner of Tennessee. Sulfur emissions from the smelters had destroyed vegetation over vast swaths of land extending into northern Georgia. Private nuisance suits against the companies operating the smelters—the Tennessee Copper Company and the Ducktown Sulphur, Copper & Iron Company—had resulted in damages awards, but the Tennessee Supreme Court had refused to issue an injunction to limit the pollution because of the importance of the smelters to the local economy.[83] The governor of Georgia had personally appealed to the governor of Tennessee to take action to stop the pollution, but the Tennessee governor responded that he had no authority to do so.

In October 1905 the U.S. Supreme Court agreed to hear Georgia's public nuisance claim, citing *Missouri v Illinois*,[84] where it had heard an original action involving interstate water pollution. In the *Missouri* case the Court had declared that "if the health and comfort of the inhabitants of a State are threatened, the State is the proper party to represent and defend them."[85]

Georgia litigated the case on the assumption that it would have to show damage to state property in order to be entitled to relief. Thus, it compiled evidence of erosion of public roads caused by the destruction of all vegetation in the vicinity of the smelters. More than two thousand affidavits ultimately were submitted to the record as well as the report of a commission appointed by the governor of Georgia to investigate the extent of harm caused by the smelter emissions. Georgia's conclusions were supported by testimony from three chemists, eight foresters, four entomologists, and a geologist. It submitted photographs to document the effects of the pollution, including the destruction of vegetation and attendant soil erosion. Affidavits were presented to document the destruction of crops, gardens, orchards, forests, and farms and injuries to roads and highways. More than fifteen hundred witnesses stated that the emissions had caused them some damage, including harm to their vocations and means of livelihood.

In the Court's decision, issued in May 1907, Justice Oliver Wendell Holmes deemed it unnecessary for Georgia to prove injury to state property. He noted:

---

[83] *Madison v Ducktown Sulphur, Copper & Iron Co.*, 83 SW 658, 659 (Tenn 1904).

[84] 180 US 208 (1901).

[85] Id at 241.

The case has been argued largely as if it were one between two
private parties; but it is not. The very elements that would be
relied upon in a suit between fellow-citizens as a ground for
equitable relief are wanting here. The State owns very little of
the territory alleged to be affected, and the damage to it capable
of estimate in money, possibly, at least, is small. . . . The alleged
damage to the state as a private owner is merely a makeweight,
and we may lay on one side the dispute as to whether the destruction of forests has led to the gullying of its roads.[86]

Because Georgia was suing "for an injury to it in its capacity of
quasi-sovereign," Holmes declared that it "has an interest independent of and behind the titles of its citizens, in all the earth and air
within its domain."[87] Thus, he concluded that the state's quasi-
sovereign interest should give it "the last word as to whether its
mountains shall be stripped of their forests and its inhabitants shall
breathe pure air."[88] Because the Court found that the evidence
clearly established that sulfur emissions from the smelters caused
significant damage in Georgia, it declared that the state was entitled
to an injunction to limit the emissions. Relying on this precedent
a century later, the *Massachusetts v EPA* Court concluded that the
Commonwealth of Massachusetts "is entitled to special solicitude
in our standing analysis."[89]

In his dissent, Chief Justice Roberts argues that the majority has
created a new relaxed standard of standing for cases brought by
states. He maintains that the discussion of quasi-sovereign state
interests in *Tennessee Copper* was not relevant to the question of
standing, but rather to a state's greater entitlement to equitable
relief when it sues in the capacity of *parens patriae*. To be sure,
Tennessee Copper predated by several decades the appearance of
standing as a distinct analytical concept in the Court's jurisprudence.[90] But the logic behind the Court's willingness to entertain
an action by a state to protect its citizens from environmental harm
caused by sources outside its jurisdiction—that the state's entry into
the union ceded to the federal government (as represented by the
Supreme Court) the state's ability to defend its sovereign interests

---

[86] *Georgia v Tennessee Copper Co.*, 206 US at 237.

[87] Id.

[88] Id.

[89] 127 S Ct at 1454–55.

[90] *Stark v Wickard*, 321 US 288, 310 (1944).

against pollution originating outside its boundaries—is entirely un-affected by the development of standing doctrines.

Moreover, Justice Stevens's majority opinion then goes on to explain in completely conventional terms why Massachusetts meets every element of traditional standing doctrine: injury, causation, and redressability. He states that the standing affidavits submitted by the Commonwealth "have satisfied the most demanding standards of the adversarial process."[91] Thus, while the majority's discussion of standing plausibly can be interpreted as relying on a special rule of standing for states, it is better understood as holding that the state would have standing without the need for any special rule, contrary to the assertions of the Chief Justice. Contrary to the Chief Justice's surmise, the failure of any litigant to cite *Tennessee Copper* is probably more of a commentary on the litigants' neglect of legal history than on the decision's precedential value.

This is not meant to suggest that it necessarily would be a bad idea to establish special standing rules for cases involving challenges to decisions by administrative agencies. The traditional private law model of litigation involving plaintiffs alleging harm caused by the actions of a specific defendant seems ill-suited to litigation chal-lenging decisions by administrative agencies. Agencies were created to establish precautionary regulations preventing harm before it occurs. Actions to require agency fidelity to laws authorizing pre-cautionary regulation should not require plaintiffs to demonstrate the kind of injury that would give rise to redress under the common law. The Court already has recognized this, at least implicitly, by establishing special standing rules for cases involving allegation of procedural injury. A wholesale rethinking of standing doctrine ap-plicable to challenges to agency action would be a most welcome development.

Perhaps the most significant portion of the majority opinion is its discussion of the conventional elements of standing. Gone is the "code-pleading formalism" of Justice Scalia's *Lujan* opinion[92] that sought to use standing doctrine expressly to disadvantage environ-mental interests. The Court's approach instead is reminiscent of *Sierra Club v Morton* where it described the purpose of standing as "a rough attempt to put the decision as to whether review will be

[91] 127 S Ct at 1455.

[92] *Lujan v Defenders of Wildlife*, 504 US 555, 593 (1992) (Blackmun dissenting).

sought in the hands of those who have a direct stake in the outcome" that will neither "insulate executive action from judicial review" nor "prevent any public interests from being protected through the judicial process."[93] Addressing the injury prong of standing doctrine, the majority forcefully rejects the notion advocated by Justice Scalia in *Lujan* that injuries that are widely shared cannot give rise to standing.[94] The Court concludes that the harms caused by climate change—sea level rise destroying coastal property, irreversible harm to natural ecosystems, reduction of water storage in snowpack, and an increase in the ferocity of storms and the spread of disease—can give rise to standing even though they will affect vast areas and large populations.[95] Thus, the Court expressly rejects the "Goldilocks" approach to standing—the notion that the injury alleged by plaintiffs has to be neither too small nor too large, but "just right."

Equally important is the Court's treatment of the causation and redressability prongs of standing doctrine. The Court rejects the notion that because auto emissions are only a small portion of total global greenhouse gas emissions they cannot give rise to standing. Justice Stevens notes that regulatory agencies "do not generally resolve massive problems in one fell regulatory swoop."[96] He deems "erroneous" the "assumption that a small incremental step, because it is incremental, can never be attacked in a federal judicial forum."[97] This is enormously important because a contrary rule "would doom most challenges to regulatory action."[98] Likewise the plaintiffs need not demonstrate that success in court in itself will solve the climate change problem, only that it will help slow or reduce it. Even if developing countries increase their emissions of greenhouse gases, a reduction in domestic emissions will help slow the pace of climate change, which is sufficient for meeting the redressability requirement.[99]

The Court summarizes why it finds plaintiffs to have standing in the following manner:

---

[93] *Sierra Club v Morton*, 405 US 727, 740 (1972).

[94] 127 S Ct at 1456.

[95] Id at 1456–57.

[96] Id at 1457.

[97] Id.

[98] Id.

[99] Id at 1458.

[T]he rise in sea levels associated with global warming has already harmed and will continue to harm Massachusetts. The risk of catastrophic harm, though remote, is nevertheless real. That risk would be reduced to some extent if petitioners received the relief they seek. We therefore hold that petitioners have standing to challenge the EPA's denial of their rulemaking petition.[100]

In a strident dissent, Chief Justice Roberts maintains that even if global warming is a "crisis" and "the most pressing environmental problem of our time," the Court should not hear this case because it is a problem best addressed by Congress and the President.[101] Dismissing the forty-three unchallenged declarations submitted by petitioners about the adverse impact of climate change as "pure conjecture," he argues that global warming is too widespread, occurring over too long a time span, and affected by too many other complexities for the contribution from emissions of U.S. motor vehicles to give rise to standing. Even though this source represents 6 percent of global carbon dioxide emissions and 4 percent of global greenhouse gas emissions, the Chief Justice deems it to be playing only a "bit part" in the climate change problem. He does not state precisely how large, how concentrated, how fast, or how free of other complexities a source category's contribution to the problem would have to be to give rise to standing.

The Chief Justice's dissent illustrates the inappropriateness of applying private law models of adversary litigation when determining who should be able to seek judicial review of decisions by administrative agencies. Unlike the traditional model of private law litigation where one party seeks redress for harm caused by another, public law litigation seeks to require agencies to conform to law when exercising their regulatory authorities to prevent diffuse harm to the general public. If plaintiffs must demonstrate the same level of individualized proof of causal injury that could give rise to liability at common law before they can access courts to compel agencies to obey the law, the law's precautionary purposes will be severely undermined. Moreover, courts reviewing public law challenges to agency action are not well equipped to make the kind of factual determinations of causal injury that the private law model requires.

Chief Justice Roberts suggests in his dissent that no matter how

---

[100] Id.

[101] Id at 1463 (Roberts dissenting).

serious an environmental problem may be, no one should be able to enforce an agency's legal obligation to respond to it unless they can demonstrate something akin to the kind of causal injury that would be redressable in a common law action. This ignores the fact that the very laws Congress authorized citizens to enforce were adopted in reaction to the inadequacies of the common law for preventing chronic and diffuse environmental harm. Reimporting stringent common law causation requirements into standing analysis would make it impossible for anyone to enforce these laws, frustrating achievement of the congressional purpose.

The Chief Justice's dissent echoes the arguments made by dissenters in a crucial, early D.C. Circuit decision upholding EPA's first regulations limiting the amount of lead additives in gasoline.[102] Standing was not at issue in that case because it involved a challenge made by the lead industry, which maintained that the regulations should be invalidated because EPA could not prove specific harm to public health caused by lead emissions from gasoline. EPA argued that the harmful effects of lead were well known, that gasoline lead additives significantly contributed to levels of lead in the ambient air, and that this added significantly to the total body burden of lead, harming public health. However, a panel of the court initially invalidated the regulations, finding by a 2–1 vote that the case against gasoline additives was "speculative and inconclusive [ ] at best" because the agency could not prove that specific instances of harm to public health had been caused by gasoline lead additives.[103]

The D.C. Circuit then reviewed the case en banc, parsing a record that ran for more than ten thousand pages. It ultimately reversed the panel by a 5–4 vote, upholding the EPA regulations. In his dissent, Judge Wilkey argued that EPA had not adequately demonstrated a causal connection between lead emissions and harm to public health. "[O]nly if the Administrator can say that an identifiable measurable increment of lead in the human body is derived from auto fuel additives and that this measurable increment of lead itself (taking into consideration all other sources of lead) causes a significant health hazard, can the Administrator claim that controlling or prohibiting lead would reduce significantly such health

---

[102] *Ethyl Corp. v EPA*, 541 F2d 1 (DC Cir 1976) (en banc).

[103] *Ethyl Corp. v EPA*, 5 Envir L Rptr 20096, 20097 (DC Cir, Jan 28, 1975).

hazard."[104] Writing for the majority, Judge J. Skelly Wright rejected this approach:

> Where a statute is precautionary in nature, the evidence difficult to come by, uncertain, or conflicting because it is on the frontiers of scientific knowledge, the regulations designed to protect the public health, and the decision that of an expert administrator, we will not demand rigorous step-by-step proof of cause and effect. Such proof may be impossible to obtain if the precautionary purpose of the statute is to be served.[105]

The court held that EPA's reasoning was sound and adequately supported by the evidence, rejecting the notion that the agency should be required to produce a definitive study quantifying the harm from gasoline lead additives.

Writing for the dissenters, Judge Wilkey noted that many other sources of lead exposure existed (e.g., diet, drinking water, peeling lead-based paint) and that EPA could not quantify the precise increment contributed by emissions from gasoline lead additives. He argued that only convincing proof of actual harm would suffice and he decried the "amazing lengths" the majority will go "to produce a decision for some uncertain, ill-defined, supposed environmental benefit."[106] Judge Wright responded that it made no sense to employ "tunnel-like reasoning"[107] that would foreclose regulation of gasoline lead additives simply because other sources of lead exposure contributed to the lead poisoning problem, particularly when "lead automobile emissions were, far and away, the most readily reduced significant source of environmental lead."[108]

Chief Justice Roberts's arguments that there is insufficient proof of harm from climate change to establish standing mirror the arguments of the *Ethyl* dissenters. In addition to deeming the harm to be too uncertain and insufficiently documented, the Chief Justice argues that because other sources contribute to the harm, standing

---

[104] 541 F2d 1, 95 (Wilkey dissenting).

[105] Id at 28 (Wright majority opinion) (footnote omitted). In a footnote to his majority opinion in *Massachusetts v EPA* Justice Stevens quotes from the *Ethyl* majority's statement that the Clean Air Act and "common sense . . . demand regulatory action to prevent harm, even if the regulator is less than certain that harm is otherwise inevitable." 127 S Ct 1438, 1447 n 7.

[106] 541 F2d at 104 (Wilkey dissenting).

[107] Id at 30 (Wright majority opinion).

[108] 541 F2d 1, 31 (Wright majority opinion).

is foreclosed. He opines that Massachusetts fails to meet the redressability prong of standing doctrine because future increases in
greenhouse gas emissions from China and India may wipe out any
benefit from controlling U.S. vehicle emissions. Yet, as Justice Stevens notes, any reductions in greenhouse gas emissions achieved by
EPA regulation will contribute to some reduction in the harmful
effects of climate change, an argument the Chief Justice charac-
terizes as: "Every little bit helps, so Massachusetts can sue over any
little bit."[109] Justice Stevens responds that accepting the premise
"that a small incremental step, because it is incremental, can never
be attacked in a federal judicial forum . . . would doom most challenges to regulatory action."[110] The history of EPA's regulation of
gasoline lead additives amply demonstrates this. The regulation
upheld in *Ethyl* was a crucial initial step in the total phaseout of
gasoline lead additives, a measure now generally considered to be
among the most beneficial EPA ever has adopted and one now
widely emulated throughout the world.

To be sure, *Ethyl* was not a case about standing, but as the Court
indicated in *Laidlaw* the factual showing necessary to establish standing should not be more onerous than that needed to establish success on the merits.[111] Yet Chief Justice Roberts's dissent in *Massachusetts v EPA* seems to advocate a return to such an approach.
Because the Chief Justice's opinion is joined by the three other
dissenters, it confirms that the Court is now even more sharply
divided in its approach to standing than it was in *Laidlaw*, where
only Justices Scalia and Thomas embraced extraordinarily restrictive
requirements for environmental plaintiffs.

The Chief Justice concludes by arguing that the majority has
"made standing seem a lawyer's game" by adopting "utterly ma-
nipulable" standards reminiscent of the Court's approach in
SCRAP.[112] One can fairly question whose approach to standing—
the majority's or the dissent's—is more prone to manipulation and
more likely to be used systematically to bar certain types of plaintiffs
from access to the courts. The majority's approach to standing
clearly is more compatible with lawsuits by the beneficiaries of
environmental regulation who are more numerous and more widely

---

[109] 127 S Ct at 1470 (Roberts dissenting).

[110] Id at 1457 (Stevens majority opinion).

[111] *Friends of the Earth v Laidlaw Environmental Services, Inc.*, 528 US 167, 181 (2000).

[112] 127 S Ct at 1471 (Roberts dissenting).

dispersed than business interests regulated under the environmental statutes.

B. SCOPE OF REGULATORY AUTHORITY UNDER THE CLEAN AIR ACT

As illustrated by its decision in the *Rapanos* case, the Roberts Court has been sharply divided on issues involving the scope of federal regulatory authority under the environmental laws. Some observers of the Court believed that this split would not reemerge in *Massachusetts v EPA* because—assuming the Court reached the issue, instead of deciding the case on grounds of standing or of the EPA's discretion not to decide—the language of the Clean Air Act was so sweeping that the question of the EPA's authority to regulate emissions of greenhouse gases that contribute to climate change was not a close one. However, the Court ultimately split 5–4 on the question of EPA's authority.

Section 202(a)(1) of the Clean Air Act empowers EPA to prescribe by regulation "standards applicable to the emission of any air pollutant from any class or classes of new motor vehicles or new motor vehicle engines, which in [the EPA Administrator's] judgment cause, or contribute to, air pollution which may reasonably be anticipated to endanger public health or welfare."[113] In 1998 EPA's general counsel issued a legal opinion finding that carbon dioxide, a greenhouse gas, could be regulated under the Clean Air Act, a position endorsed by his successor in 1999. When EPA denied the petition to regulate greenhouse gas emissions from motor vehicles, its new general counsel revoked the prior legal opinion and replaced it with his own. The new opinion concluded that carbon dioxide is not an "air pollutant" regulable under the Act and thus EPA did not have the authority to grant the relief requested in the petition.

To justify this conclusion, EPA relied heavily on the Court's decision in *FDA v Brown & Williamson Tobacco Corp.*[114] In that case a 5–4 majority reversed efforts by the U.S. Food and Drug Administration (FDA) to regulate tobacco products under the federal Food, Drug & Cosmetic Act (FDCA). While the FDA had long believed that it did not have the authority to regulate tobacco products under the FDCA, it changed its mind after concluding

---

[113] 42 USC § 7521(a)(1) (2000).

[114] 529 US 120 (2000).

that tobacco products were used primarily to deliver nicotine to smokers, bringing them within the definition of "drug delivery devices" subject to regulation under the FDCA.

Rather than deferring to the agency's interpretation of its regulatory authorities pursuant to *Chevron*, the majority in *Brown & Williamson* concluded that Congress clearly did not intend to give FDA the authority to regulate tobacco products because the agency might be required to ban them entirely to achieve the goals of the Act. Writing for the majority, Justice O'Connor described the thousands of premature deaths from smoking-related diseases to be "one of the most troubling public health problems facing our Nation today."[115] But she concluded that no matter how serious the problem the agency seeks to address, it could not go beyond the bounds of the authority given it by Congress.[116]

In similar fashion, EPA argued in *Massachusetts v EPA* that because Congress was aware of the importance of the problem of climate change, but had not expressly given the agency a directive to regulate emissions that cause it, the agency lacked the authority to do so under the Clean Air Act. Thus, it concluded that greenhouse gases could not be considered to be "air pollutants" subject to regulation under the Act.

Despite the agency's *Brown & Williamson* argument, EPA's refusal to regulate greenhouse gas emissions bore all the earmarks of a politically dictated decision for which the agency had to manufacture a supporting legal rationale. The clear text of the Act seems to contradict the agency's position. The Clean Air Act broadly defines "air pollution" to include "any air pollution agent or combination of such agents, including any physical, chemical, biological, radioactive . . . substance or matter which is emitted into or otherwise enters the ambient air."[117] On its face, it is difficult to see how greenhouse gases could fail to be covered by such a broad definition. EPA has a legal obligation under the Clean Air Act to regulate air pollutants from motor vehicles that "cause, or contribute to, air pollution which may reasonably be anticipated to endanger public health or welfare . . ."[118] and "welfare" is

---

[115] Id at 125.

[116] Id.

[117] 42 USC § 7602(g) (2000).

[118] 42 USC § 7521(a)(1) (2000).

broadly defined to include "effects on . . . weather . . . and climate."[119]

In his majority opinion, Justice Stevens concluded that the statutory text of the Clean Air Act unambiguously includes carbon dioxide and other greenhouse gases within the definition of "air pollutant": "On its face, the definition embraces all airborne compounds of whatever stripe, and underscores that intent through the repeated use of the word 'any.'"[120] He rejected any notion that Congress had implicitly directed EPA not to regulate greenhouse gases as not remotely plausible and found no conflict between congressional funding for climate change research and any pre-existing mandate to regulate harmful air pollutants.

Perhaps the most significant portion of the Court's discussion of statutory interpretation is its treatment of *Brown & Williamson*. Justice Stevens distinguished the decision on several grounds. First he notes that, unlike tobacco products regulated as "drugs," EPA would not be required to ban all emissions of greenhouse gases, but rather only to regulate them. (To be sure, FDA had disclaimed any intent to ban tobacco in *Brown & Williamson*, but the Court majority nonetheless expressed the view that the Food, Drug & Cosmetic Act would require such radical action.) Second, unlike the FDA, EPA had not long disclaimed authority to regulate greenhouse gas emissions and Congress had not enacted legislation confirming the lack of such authority. Finally, the Court rejected the notion that regulation of greenhouse gas emissions from motor vehicles necessarily would conflict with the Department of Transportation's (DOT's) duty to set fuel efficiency standards, an argument made by auto manufacturers seeking to preempt state controls on emissions from their products. The Court concluded that the fact "that DOT sets mileage standards in no way licenses EPA to shirk its environmental responsibilities. . . . The two obligations may overlap, but there is no reason to think the two agencies cannot both administer their obligations and yet avoid inconsistency."[121]

The Court majority concluded by noting that Congress designed the Clean Air Act to provide comprehensive protection

---

[119] 42 USC § 7602(h) (2000).

[120] 127 S Ct at 1460 (Stevens majority).

[121] Id at 1462.

against air pollution and to be capable of responding to changed circumstances and new scientific understandings. "While the Congresses that drafted § 202(a)(1) might not have appreciated the possibility that burning fossil fuels could lead to global warming, they did understand that without regulatory flexibility, changing circumstances and scientific developments would soon render the Clean Air Act obsolete."[122] This is reflected in the broad language used by Congress in "an intentional effort to confer the flexibility necessary to forestall" the Act from becoming obsolete. The Court concluded that "[b]ecause greenhouse gases fit well within the Clean Air Act's capacious definition of 'air pollutant' . . . EPA has the statutory authority to regulate the emission of such gases from new motor vehicles."[123]

In dissent Justice Scalia argues that greenhouse gases are not "agent[s] of air pollution"[124] because substances that pollute the air do so primarily only at ground level or near the surface of the earth. According to Scalia, EPA's conception of what constitutes air pollution properly focuses on impurities in the ambient air at ground level or near the surface of the earth and not on substances in the upper atmosphere like greenhouse gases. He derives this conclusion—which seems dubious, in view of the expansive language of the statute—by focusing on dictionary definitions of the words "pollute" ("[t]o make or render impure or unclean") and "air" that focus more on air at ground level.[125]

Four of the Justices in the majority in *Massachusetts v EPA*—Justices Breyer, Stevens, Souter, and Ginsburg—were the four dissenters in *Brown & Williamson*. Justice Kennedy is the lone defector from the majority in *Brown & Williamson*. The two newest members of the Court—Chief Justice Roberts and Justice Alito—join Justices Scalia and Thomas, who were in the majority in *Brown & Williamson*, in adopting its approach to statutory interpretation. This may not herald a long-term shift away from *Brown & Williamson* because it is unclear how durable Justice Kennedy's defection will be. Two months after *Massachusetts v EPA* was decided, Justice Kennedy rejoined the four dissenters from that case to form a five-Justice majority in *National Association of Homebuilders*

---

[122] Id.

[123] Id.

[124] Id at 1476 (Scalia dissenting) (alteration in original).

[125] Id at 1477.

v Defenders of Wildlife.[126] In that case the Court refused to read important requirements of the Endangered Species Act (ESA) as compatible with the Clean Water Act (CWA). The Court held that the crucial consultation and no-jeopardy provisions of Section 7 of the ESA are not applicable when EPA delegates administration of the CWA's national permit program to states because those provisions apply only when a federal agency is engaged in discretionary action. This stands in sharp contrast with the *Massachusetts v EPA* majority's conclusion that the Clean Air Act should be read flexibly to avoid conflict with the Energy Policy and Conservation Act.

C. EXERCISE OF AGENCY DISCRETION

To justify its denial of the petition to regulate greenhouse gas emissions from motor vehicles, EPA concluded that even if it had the authority to regulate such emissions, it would decline to do so. But the majority in *Massachusetts v EPA* rejected this conclusion on the ground that it was founded on "reasoning divorced from the statutory text."[127] The Court conceded that EPA "has significant latitude as to the manner, timing, content, and coordination of its regulations with those of other agencies."[128] But it stated that this was "not a roving license to ignore the statutory text," but rather "a direction to exercise discretion within defined statutory limits."[129] Thus, it held that:

> Under the clear terms of the Clean Air Act, EPA can avoid taking further action only if it determines that greenhouse gases do not contribute to climate change or if it provides some reasonable explanation as to why it cannot or will not exercise its discretion to determine whether they do.[130]

Because climate change is a global problem that will be solved only if addressed globally, EPA had sought to defend its refusal to regulate greenhouse gas emissions on the ground that it might interfere with the President's ability to negotiate a global solution.

---

[126] 127 S Ct 2518 (2007).

[127] 127 S Ct at 1462.

[128] Id.

[129] Id.

[130] Id.

The Court brushed aside these concerns. While noting that it had "neither the expertise nor the authority to evaluate these policy judgments," it concluded that they did not "amount to a reasoned justification for declining to form a scientific judgment" about the impact of greenhouse gas emissions from motor vehicles on climate change.[131]

The Court expressly rejected the notion that the President's foreign policy powers could trump domestic environmental mandates. It recognized that "the President has broad authority in foreign affairs," but it declared that such "authority does not extend to the refusal to execute domestic laws."[132] An amicus brief filed on behalf of former Secretary of State Madeleine Albright argued that there is no tension between domestic regulation of greenhouse gas emissions and the ability of the United States to conduct foreign policy on climate change, particularly since the U.S. policy has been to encourage other nations to take voluntary action to reduce such emissions.[133] The brief also warned of the danger of allowing foreign policy concerns to trump domestic legal requirements.

Finally, the Court rejected the notion that uncertainty surrounding various aspects of climate change justified EPA's refusal to act. "If the scientific uncertainty is so profound that it precludes EPA from making a reasoned judgment as to whether greenhouse gases contribute to global warming, EPA must say so."[134] The Court declared that the agency's expressed policy preference not to regulate greenhouse gas emissions "because of some residual uncertainty" is "irrelevant" to the statutory question of "whether sufficient information exists to make an endangerment finding."[135] The Court thus found that EPA had acted arbitrarily and capriciously because it had not offered a "reasoned explanation for its refusal to decide whether greenhouse gases cause or contribute to climate change."[136]

In his dissent, Justice Scalia argued that EPA had no obligation

---

[131] Id at 1463.

[132] Id.

[133] Brief for Amicus Curiae Madeleine K. Albright in Support of Petitioners, *Massachusetts v EPA*, No 05-1120 (filed Aug 31, 2006) (available on Westlaw at 2006 WL 2570988).

[134] 127 S Ct at 1463.

[135] Id.

[136] Id.

to decide whether greenhouse gas emissions contribute to climate change because it had sufficient reasons to defer making such a judgment. Justice Scalia stated that he is "willing to assume" *arguendo* "that the Administrator's discretion in this regard is not entirely unbounded—that if he has no reasonable basis for deferring judgment he must grasp the nettle at once."[137] But he concluded that the reasons offered by EPA were "perfectly valid reasons" for deferring judgment. Justice Scalia argued that the Clean Air Act "says *nothing at all* about the reasons for which the Administrator may *defer* making a judgment . . . ."[138] Thus, he concluded that there is no warrant for the majority's claim that the reasons proffered by the Administrator are divorced from the statutory text. In fact he maintained that EPA has indeed "said precisely" that scientific uncertainty is so profound that it precludes the agency from making a reasoned judgment whether greenhouse gases contribute to global warming.[139] Justice Scalia and the other three dissenters thus are willing to wrap EPA in the mantle of global warming skeptics to defend the agency's refusal to act. The fact that a view so divorced from the scientific mainstream would command deference from four Justices of the U.S. Supreme Court is disheartening.

There is nothing truly exceptional about the Court's decision from the standpoint of administrative law. The Court did confirm that agency denials of rulemaking petitions are subject to judicial review, distinguishing them from refusals to initiate enforcement actions,[140] but this was consistent with the prior conclusions of the courts of appeals. While it may be true that the U.S. Supreme Court itself had never before reversed an agency's denial of a rulemaking petition, this may be a product of the fact that most such petitions languish unanswered by agencies. The Administrative Procedure Act provides for judicial review of "agency action," which is defined to include "the whole or a part of an agency rule . . . or denial thereof, or failure to act."[141] As the Court notes,[142] the Clean Air Act's judicial review provisions provide for review

---

[137] Id at 1472 (Scalia dissenting).

[138] Id at 1473 (emphasis in original).

[139] Id at 1474.

[140] Id at 1459 (Stevens majority opinion).

[141] 5 USC § 702 (2000); 5 USC § 551(13) (2000).

[142] 127 S Ct at 1451 n 16.

of decisions promulgating standards under § 202 of the Act and of "final action" taken under the Act, which would seem to include denial of the petition at issue in the case. There was no controversy over the reviewability of EPA's action and the Court's decision simply confirms what already was widely understood. In this sense it is akin to the Court's *State Farm* decision where the Court itself confirmed for the first time that arbitrary and capricious review was not toothless even as applied to an agency's decision to rescind previously issued regulations.[143] Thus, the *Massachusetts v EPA* decision breaks no new ground from the standpoint of judicial review of an agency's refusal to act.

However, the majority's willingness to push EPA toward grasping the regulatory "nettle" does stand in sharp contrast to the approach the judiciary embraced during the 1980s when environmentalists sought to force the agency to take action to control the nation's acid rain problem. Even though the Clean Air Act had provisions giving EPA authority to force upwind sources of pollution to reduce emissions to prevent harm to downwind states, EPA refused to exercise such authority. Despite mounting evidence of the damage caused by acid rain, in case after case brought by environmental interests, the courts refused to force EPA to act. In one case, then Circuit Judge Ruth Bader Ginsburg was remarkably candid in explaining why the judiciary was unwilling to require EPA to act:

> As counsel for the EPA acknowledged at oral argument, the EPA has taken *no* action against sources of interstate air pollution under either § 126(b) or § 110(a)(2)(E) in the decade-plus since those provisions were enacted. Congress, when it is so minded, is fully capable of instructing the EPA to address particular matters promptly. . . . Congress did not supply such direction in this instance; instead, it allowed and has left unchecked the EPA's current approach to interstate air pollution. The judiciary, therefore, is not the proper place in which to urge alteration of the Agency's course.[144]

In *Massachusetts v EPA* it is the Supreme Court, and not the D.C. Circuit, that is requiring the agency to reconsider its refusal to decide whether to regulate. Perhaps because climate change is

---

[143] *Motor Vehicle Mfrs. Ass'n v State Farm Mutual Auto. Insur. Co.*, 463 US 29 (1983).

[144] *New York v EPA*, 852 F2d 574, 581 (DC Cir 1988) (R. Ginsburg, concurring).

now considered a global environmental crisis far more serious than the problem of acid rain, the Court is unwilling to tolerate continued executive inaction. It also rejects what in this age of globalization could become a nearly universally applicable excuse for agency inaction—that domestic regulation might interfere with the President's ability to negotiate a global approach to a problem.

Professor Ronald Cass opines that "the Justices stretch, twist, and torture administrative law doctrines to avoid the inconvenient truth that this is not a matter in which judges have any real role to play."[145] But in fact the Court is resuming precisely the role it played in the early twentieth century in responding to states' concerns about environmental problems originating outside their borders. When activities causing significant, foreseeable environmental harm had not been controlled by other government entities, the judiciary for centuries was the vehicle for providing redress. Now this role has been largely delegated to administrative agencies by the enactment of comprehensive regulatory programs to protect the environment. In *Massachusetts v EPA* the Court acts to require EPA to reconsider using these authorities to address a critical global problem, a far more modest step than those the Court took in the days when it wrote its own pollution control injunctions.

III. The Implications of Massachusetts v EPA

The states' effort to force EPA to regulate greenhouse gas emissions from motor vehicles is only one of many legal initiatives that respond to the climate change problem.[146] Yet the Court's decision in *Massachusetts v EPA* is likely to have effects that extend far beyond the issues addressed in the case. First, the Court's decision appears to confirm that standing doctrine is still comfortably in the mold of the *Laidlaw* and *Sierra Club v Morton* model that does not employ it as a vehicle to disadvantage environmental interests. While Chief Justice Roberts's dissent attempts to confine the Court's holding on standing to a special rule only applicable

---

[145] Ronald A. Cass, *Massachusetts v. EPA: The Inconvenient Truth About Precedent*, Va L Rev In Brief 75 (May 21, 2007), online at http://www.virginialawreview.org/inbrief/2007/05/21/cass.pdf.

[146] See, e.g., Justin R. Pidot, Georgetown Environmental Law & Policy Institute, *Global Warming in the Courts: An Overview of Current Litigation and Common Legal Issues* (Georgetown Univ, 2006), online at http://www.law.georgetown.edu/gelpi/current_research/documents/GWL_Report.pdf.

to states, the Court's discussion of each element of traditional standing doctrine suggests that the decision is not so confined. Yet because both the Chief Justice and Justice Alito embraced the restrictive vision of standing Justice Scalia has long championed, *Massachusetts v EPA* clarifies that the Court is now more closely divided on this issue than it was in 2000 when *Laidlaw* was decided.

It is highly important that the Court majority expressly rejected the notion that standing cannot be premised on harm that is widely shared, burying the "Goldilocks" approach to standing. The Court also clearly rejected the claim that standing is unavailable on re-dressability grounds unless the relief sought by litigants is likely to solve most of a problem. Following the Court's decision, a federal district court rejected a challenge to state regulations to control greenhouse gas emissions and noted:

> The fact that global warming will not be solved by changes in any one industry or by regulation of any one source of emissions in no way undercuts the vital nature of the problem or the validity of partial responses; rather, it points to the necessity of responses, however incomplete when viewed individually, on any number of fronts. ("Agencies, like legislatures, do not generally resolve massive problems in one fell regulatory swoop. They instead whittle away at them over time.").[147]

Second, the Court's decision that the Clean Air Act gives EPA the authority to regulate emissions of greenhouse gases raises the question whether the Act now preempts common law nuisance litigation premised on climate change. As noted above, more than a quarter century ago the Supreme Court held that the federal Clean Water Act preempted the federal common law of nuisance for interstate water pollution.[148] In *Connecticut v American Electric Power Company*[149] eight states and the City of New York are pursuing a federal and state common law nuisance action against six of the largest electric utilities in the United States, which together account for 10 percent of U.S. emissions of carbon dioxide. The plaintiffs in this case are asking the court to order the defendants

---

[147] *Green Mountain Chrysler Plymouth Dodge Jeep v Crombie*, 508 F Supp 2d 295, 320 (D Vt 2007), quoting *Massachusetts v EPA*, 127 S Ct at 1457.

[148] *City of Milwaukee v Illinois*, 451 US 304 (1981).

[149] 406 F Supp 2d 265 (SDNY 2005), on appeal to the U.S. Court of Appeals for the Second Circuit.

to make modest annual reductions in their emissions of greenhouse gases. So long as EPA took the position that it had no authority under the Clean Air Act to regulate emissions of greenhouse gases, no one could credibly argue that the Act preempted the federal common law of nuisance. Now that the U.S. Supreme Court has ruled to the contrary, it is possible the Clean Air Act will be found to have such preemptive effect.

Two years ago a federal district judge in New York dismissed *Connecticut v American Electric Power* on political question grounds and the case is now before the U.S. Court of Appeals for the Second Circuit on appeal. Shortly after *Massachusetts v EPA* was decided, the Second Circuit asked the parties in this appeal to express their views on the impact of the decision on the appeal. Plaintiffs responded by arguing that although the Court clarified that the Clean Air Act gives EPA authority to regulate emissions of greenhouse gases, the Act cannot preempt a federal common law nuisance action until EPA actually issues such regulations. Defendants maintained that the mere fact that the Act provides EPA with authority to address climate change gives it preemptive effect even if EPA has chosen not to exercise such authority.

Plaintiffs would seem to have the better of the argument. The Court's decision in *City of Milwaukee v Illinois*, which held the Clean Water Act preempts the federal common law of nuisance, was premised on the comprehensive nature of the regulatory scheme enacted by Congress. The Clean Water Act itself prohibits all discharges of pollutants to surface waters unless they are authorized by a permit issued pursuant to the Act. Following the enactment of the 1990 Clean Air Act Amendments, the Clean Air Act now provides for a national permit program, but it does not include any direct regulation of emissions of greenhouse gases. Thus, until EPA acts either to establish such regulations or expressly to preempt other control of them, the federal common law in this area would not appear to be preempted.[150] However, the political question ground for upholding dismissal of the action is still available. In September 2007 a federal district court in San Francisco dismissed a climate change nuisance suit brought by the

---

[150] But see Shi-Ling Hsu, *A Realistic Evaluation of Climate Change Litigation Through the Lens of a Hypothetical Lawsuit*, 78 U Colo L Rev (forthcoming 2008) (available online at http://works.bepress.com/cgi/viewcontent.cgi?article=1005&context=shi_ling_hsu), for a discussion of the formidable obstacles to such lawsuits being successful.

California Attorney General against six large automobile manufacturers on political question grounds.[151] The decision generally
followed the reasoning of *Connecticut v American Electric Power*. In
August 2007 a Mississippi federal district court also cited the political question doctrine as an alternative ground for rejecting a
private tort suit against oil, chemical, and coal companies alleging
that global warming exacerbated the damage caused by Hurricane
Katrina.[152]

One preemption issue that may be resolved by the *Massachusetts
v EPA* decision is the question whether state regulation of greenhouse gas emissions is preempted by the federal Energy Policy
and Conservation Act (EPCA). This argument has been the central
element of the auto industry's challenge to California legislation
requiring the first reductions in greenhouse gas emissions from
motor vehicles.[153] In 2002 the California Legislature adopted legislation requiring the California Air Resources Board (CARB) to
issue "regulations that achieve the maximum feasible and cost-
effective reduction of greenhouse gas emissions from motor vehicles."[154] In 2004 CARB issued regulations limiting emissions of
greenhouse gases from motor vehicles beginning with the 2009
model year. The regulations set limits on emissions per mile traveled and require substantial reductions in such emissions by the
2016 vehicle year. The companies argue that because the only
practicable way to reduce emissions of greenhouse gases from motor vehicles is to improve their fuel economy, California's regulations should be preempted by EPCA's mandate that the Department of Transportation establish national fuel economy
standards. This argument seems a bit of a stretch since the two
programs were adopted for entirely different purposes—California's to combat climate change and EPCA's to reduce U.S. dependence on imported oil. In 1983 the U.S. Supreme Court held
that California's moratorium on the construction of new nuclear
power plants was not preempted by the federal Atomic Energy
Act because it was an economic measure rather than a safety reg-

---

[151] *California v General Motors Corp.*, 2007 WL 2726871 (ND Cal 2007).

[152] *Comer v Murphy Oil USA, Inc.*, No. 05-CV-436LG (SD Miss, Aug 30, 2007) (the
court also dismissed the case for lack of standing).

[153] *Central Valley Chrysler-Jeep v Witherspoon*, 2006 WL 2734359 (ED Cal 2006).

[154] Cal Health & Safety Code § 43018.5 (West 2006).

ulation.[155] Though it is true that improving fuel economy is currently the most viable option for reducing greenhouse gas emissions from motor vehicles—in fact carbon dioxide emissions from vehicles usually are calculated by reference to vehicles' fuel economy—the different purposes of the California and federal programs should be sufficient to insulate the California regulations from preemption.

In *Massachusetts v EPA* the Court rejected EPA's argument that EPCA's mandate that DOT establish national fuel economy standards indicates that Congress could not have intended to give EPA the authority under the Clean Air Act to regulate greenhouse gas emissions. "The two obligations may overlap, but there is no reason to think the two agencies cannot both administer their obligations and yet avoid inconsistency."[156] While not legally controlling on the *state* preemption question, the Court's decision already has lent strong support to the argument that Congress did not intend to preempt states from regulating greenhouse gas emissions when it adopted the EPCA. Indeed, two federal district courts already have relied on it in rejecting challenges to state adoption of California's regulations on greenhouse gas emissions from motor vehicles.[157]

The Court's decision that EPA acted arbitrarily and capriciously in denying the petition to regulate greenhouse gas emissions confirms the availability of judicial review for agency action refusing to initiate rulemaking. Given that the Clean Air Act specifically provides for such review, there is nothing exceptional about this aspect of the decision. By highlighting the legal risk an agency incurs when it formally denies a petition for rulemaking, the decision may give agencies even more incentive to let such petitions languish unanswered, particularly since courts generally tolerate lengthy delays when litigation is brought to compel a response.

While decisions not to initiate rulemaking generally are treated with great deference by reviewing courts, as the majority recognized, if the Court had accepted EPA's rationale for refusing to act it would be exceedingly easy for any agency in the future to

---

[155] *Pacific Gas & Electric v State Energy Resources Conservation and Development Commission*, 461 US 190 (1983).

[156] 127 S Ct 1438, 1462 (2007).

[157] *Green Mountain Chrysler Plymouth Dodge Jeep v Crombie*, 508 F Supp 2d 295 (D Vt 2007); *Central Valley Chrysler-Jeep, Inc. v Goldstone*, 2007 WL 4372878 (ED Cal 2007).

justify such a refusal. By requiring EPA to base its decision only on statutorily relevant factors, the Court denies the agency the option of manufacturing virtually universally applicable excuses for inaction. Faced with an undoubtedly serious problem and a comprehensive statutory scheme capable of responding to it, the Court refused to allow the agency an easy escape valve to excuse its inaction.

The Supreme Court's decision in *Massachusetts v EPA* profoundly surprised both EPA and the White House. After believing that the agency had successfully extricated itself from the need to develop regulations to control greenhouse gas emissions, EPA staff now are scrambling to develop expertise on the issue. But it is far from clear that the decision will spur any fundamental change in the Bush administration's approach to climate change. Six weeks after the Supreme Court's decision was released, President Bush issued Executive Order 13,432 directing EPA to cooperate with DOT and the Department of Energy before taking any action to address the problem of greenhouse gas emissions from motor vehicles.[158]

The climate change problem is a classic "tragedy of the commons"[159] that can only be addressed effectively through global collective action. The challenge facing the nations of the world has been how to fashion an effective global response to this problem. Following the model of the successful Montreal Protocol on Substances that Deplete the Ozone Layer, 154 nations at the Rio "Earth Summit" in 1992 signed the United Nations Framework Convention on Climate Change (UNFCCC). The UNFCCC endorsed the principle of controlling emissions of greenhouse gases to prevent harm to the global environment, but it did not establish specific numeric limits or timetables for reducing emissions. This treaty was signed by President George H. W. Bush and ratified unanimously by the U.S. Senate on October 15, 1992. At the time it ratified the treaty, the United States was the fourth nation in the world to ratify the treaty, following action by three island nations.[160] Today 192 nations—virtually every nation in the

---

[158] Executive Order 13,342, 72 Fed Reg 27,717 (May 14, 2007).

[159] Garrett Hardin, *The Tragedy of the Commons*, 162 Science 1243 (1968).

[160] Mauritius, the Seychelles, and the Marshall Islands were the first to ratify the UNFCCC. United Nations Framework Convention on Climate Change, Status of Ratification, online at http://unfccc.int/files/essential_background/convention/status_of_ratification/application/pdf/unfccc_conv_rat.pdf.

world—have ratified this treaty, which entered into force on March 21, 1994.[161]

While the UNFCCC did not establish binding limits on emissions of greenhouse gases, it spawned a process of negotiations that culminated in the Kyoto Protocol in December 1997. The Protocol requires developed nations to reduce their emissions of greenhouse gases between 2008 and 2012 to achieve an overall 5 percent reduction below 1990 levels. The United States played a major role in negotiation of the Kyoto Protocol, which was signed by President Clinton, but never submitted to the U.S. Senate for ratification. Four months before the Protocol was adopted, the U.S. Senate had passed a resolution insisting that any global scheme for controlling emissions of greenhouse gases should require developing countries to limit their emissions during the same time frame as developed countries.[162] But this was rejected during the Kyoto negotiations as fundamentally unfair to the developing world because developed countries had contributed the vast majority of emissions that created the climate change problem. The ultimate understanding reached in Kyoto was that as a simple matter of fairness developed countries should take the first steps to reduce emissions of greenhouse gases and that the question of controls on emissions from developing countries would be addressed in subsequent negotiations.

During the 2000 presidential campaign George W. Bush had promised to support mandatory controls on emissions of carbon dioxide as a means for controlling climate change. But shortly after he assumed office, President Bush repudiated this campaign promise and expressly rejected the Kyoto Protocol. He did so in March 2001 immediately after his new EPA administrator, Christie Todd Whitman, had returned from her first international conference where she had assured her counterparts from other countries of the new administration's commitment to mandatory controls on carbon dioxide emissions. Five years later President Bush reportedly confided to a group of historians that he regrets the "in your face" manner in which he repudiated the Kyoto Protocol as "too abrupt, too defiant and too negative without offering an al-

---

[161] Id.

[162] S Res 98, 105th Cong, 1st Sess (July 25, 1997).

ternative."[163] But his administration has consistently taken the position that the Kyoto Protocol is fatally flawed because it does not require developing countries to control their emissions.

While the Bush administration initially believed that it could block the Kyoto Protocol from entering into force, virtually every country other than the United States and Australia ratified it. As a result, the Protocol entered into force on February 16, 2005. At the time of its entry into force, many U.S. business leaders were quoted as saying that it was inevitable that the United States ultimately would have to adopt mandatory controls on greenhouse gas emissions. But the Bush administration has continued to oppose all proposals for regulating greenhouse gas emissions. Because the United States has been the largest emitter of greenhouse gases in the world, its continued refusal to agree to such controls has provided convenient cover for developing countries to refuse to adopt such controls. While China is now poised to pass the United States as the largest emitter of greenhouse gases, it has contributed a much smaller cumulative share of historical emissions and its per capita emissions are still only about one-fifth those of the United States.

As scientific evidence continues to mount that climate change is occurring at an even more alarming rate than previously anticipated, U.S. opposition to mandatory controls on greenhouse gas emissions has become an increasingly isolated position. In November 2007 Australian voters elected a new Prime Minister who made ratification of the Kyoto Protocol his first priority. As a result, at the most recent Conference of the Parties to the UNFCCC, held in Bali in December 2007, the United States was the only developed country that continued to oppose mandatory controls on greenhouse gas emissions. U.S. environmentalists assured representatives from other countries that the U.S. position would change after the presidential election of 2008, and they noted that states containing more than 40 percent of the U.S. population were adopting their own controls on greenhouse gas emissions. The Supreme Court's *Massachusetts v EPA* decision also was cited as increasing the prospects for federal regulation in the United States. The United States ultimately joined the other nations of the world in adopting the "Bali Action Plan," which

---

[163] Peter Baker, *In Bush's Final Year, the Agenda Gets Greener*, Wash Post A1, A10 (Dec 29, 2007).

recognizes "that deep cuts in global emissions will be required to achieve the ultimate objective of the [UNFCCC]" and establishes a process for negotiating a post-Kyoto control plan.[164]

Following the conclusion of the Bali conference, the U.S. Congress enacted compromise energy legislation that requires new motor vehicles sold in the United States to achieve an average of thirty miles per gallon by the year 2020, a 40 percent improvement over current fuel economy standards.[165] President Bush agreed to sign the legislation, noting that he had endorsed a goal of reducing U.S. gasoline consumption by 20 percent over the next decade during his January 2007 State of the Union message.[166] Hours after President Bush signed the legislation on December 21, 2007, EPA Administrator Steve Johnson stunned the states and the environmental community by announcing that he was denying California's request for permission to put its controls on greenhouse gas emissions from motor vehicles in effect, effectively vetoing control schemes adopted by seventeen states.[167] His action represented the first time in the history of the Clean Air Act that California had been denied approval to adopt an air pollution control standard more stringent than the federal government. California's fifty previous waiver requests had been routinely granted.

Administrator Johnson argued that the new energy legislation represented a "national approach to addressing the problem of climate change" that would be preferable to a "patchwork" of state standards. But the new energy legislation was never intended to represent a national response to climate change. Its requirements are not as stringent as the California plan, the adoption of which could not create any "patchwork" because the Clean Air Act requires states other than California either to follow the national standard or standards identical to the California plan. Johnson argued that because of "the global nature of the problem of climate change" California did not have a "need to meet compelling and

---

[164] Conference of Parties to the UNFCCC, COP 13, *Bali Action Plan*, online at http://unfccc.int/files/meetings/cop_13/application/pdf/cp_bali_action.pdf.

[165] *President Bush Signs H.R. 6, the Energy Independence and Security Act of 2007* (Dec 19, 2007), online at http://www.whitehouse.gov/news/releases/2007/12/20071219-6.html.

[166] See *2007 State of the Union Policy Initiatives* (Jan 23, 2007), online at http://www.whitehouse.gov/stateoftheunion/2007/initiatives/sotu2007.pdf.

[167] EPA Newsroom, *America Receives a National Solution for Vehicle Greenhouse Gas Emissions* (Dec 19, 2007), online at http://yosemite.epa.gov/opa/admpress.nsf/d0cf6618525a9efb85257359003fb69d/41b4663d8d3807c5852573b6008141e5!OpenDocument.

extraordinary conditions,"[168] quoting the statutory standard governing California waiver requests in § 209 of the Clean Air Act.

EPA's action was widely denounced as arbitrary and capricious and contrary to law. California Governor Arnold Schwarzenegger vowed to sue to overturn it.[169] An editorial writer deemed it particularly hypocritical since EPA previously had praised California's program to control greenhouse gas emissions when reporting to the international community on the nation's progress in responding to climate change.[170] It quickly leaked that EPA staff had opposed the decision and advised Administrator Johnson that it would be overturned in court. The hasty announcement of the decision and EPA's tortured attempt to link it to the just-signed energy legislation suggests that its rationale rests largely on political, rather than carefully considered legal grounds.

Through its decision in *Massachusetts v EPA*, the U.S. Supreme Court briefly joined the mounting global forces pushing for regulatory action to control emissions of greenhouse gases. While the Bush administration's policy has seriously jeopardized the difficult quest for a collective global response to this critical problem, actions by U.S. states to fill the gap left by federal inaction have provided some hope to the rest of the world. EPA's decision to veto state controls on emissions from motor vehicles represents a severe setback, but one that may be quickly overturned in court.

IV. Conclusion

A century ago, the U.S. Supreme Court recognized that it had a duty to respond to states seeking relief from serious harm caused by pollution originating outside their borders. In a series of cases spanning several decades, the Court used the common law of nuisance to issue injunctions limiting air pollution from smelters and requiring cities to construct sewage treatment plants and garbage incinerators and to stop practices that caused visible environmental harm to neighboring states.[171] The Court even-

---

[168] Letter from EPA Administrator Stephen Johnson to California Gov. Arnold Schwarzenegger (Dec 19, 2007), online at http://www.epa.gov/otaq/climate/20071219-slj.pdf.

[169] Press Release, *Governor Schwarzenegger Issues Statement After U.S. EPA Rejects California's Tailpipe Emissions Waiver Request* (Dec 19, 2007), online at http://gov.ca.gov/index.php?/press-release/8353/.

[170] *Arrogance and Warming*, NY Times A38, Dec 21, 2007.

[171] *Georgia v Tennessee Copper Co.*, 237 US 474 (1915); *Wisconsin v Illinois*, 281 US 696 (1930); *New Jersey v City of New York*, 284 US 585 (1931).

tually abandoned this role after Congress adopted comprehensive regulatory programs to protect the environment. A key element of nearly all these programs are citizen suit provisions designed to ensure that the agencies charged with protecting public health and the environment perform their duties in implementing and enforcing the law.

Today the Court is badly split in its approach toward these regulatory programs and the role of the judiciary in ensuring their implementation. Four Justices recognize the importance of these programs and the need for them to be able to adapt to newly discovered environmental problems not fully anticipated when the underlying regulatory legislation was adopted. Four other Justices are openly hostile toward these programs and seek to limit their reach by approaching them through the traditional paradigm of private law litigation. The latter advocate narrow constructions of the scope of federal regulatory authority and they seek to limit the ability of citizens to enlist the judiciary in ensuring that agencies act in conformity to law. The man in the middle—Justice Kennedy—straddles both camps. In *Massachusetts v EPA* he joined the four Justices sympathetic to precautionary regulation to hold that the Clean Air Act authorizes EPA to regulate greenhouse gas emissions and to recognize the standing of states to force EPA to reconsider its refusal to adopt such regulations. As a result, the Court has now stepped in to nudge the executive to use its regulatory authority to respond to the most serious environmental issue of our time.

While this decision is a landmark victory for environmentalists, it also confirms just how sharply divided the Court is on virtually all aspects of its approach to regulatory policy. The Justices hostile toward federal regulatory programs appear to be influenced by common law notions that judicial intervention is unwarranted in the absence of individualized proof of causal injury. Yet the inadequacies of the common law in protecting the environment were a major reason why Congress adopted regulatory programs and the comprehensiveness of these programs is the reason why the Court found them to preempt federal common law.

Due to the enactment of comprehensive regulatory legislation, the common law no longer serves as the first line of defense for public health and the environment. Instead, it functions largely as a backstop to respond to problems not adequately dealt with by precautionary regulation. The petition seeking EPA regulation of greenhouse gases that was the focal point of the litigation in *Massachusetts v EPA* is only one of a series of legal initiatives to respond to climate change. Because the United States has refused to regulate emissions of greenhouse gases, nuisance litigation has resurfaced as a vehicle for responding to this problem.

While the Court's decision may help plaintiffs establish standing premised on the harms caused by climate change, it is still unlikely that nuisance litigation directed at this problem will be successful. Unlike the harm caused by the copper smelters in *Georgia v Tennessee Copper*, the century-old precedent on which the *Massachusetts v EPA* Court relied for its standing analysis, the causes and consequences of climate change are truly global in scope. *Massachusetts v EPA* confirms that it is not necessary to tackle the entire problem at once in order to seek judicial redress. Its "every little bit helps" approach is consistent with what the plaintiffs in *Connecticut v American Electric Power* are seeking—modest reductions in emissions of greenhouse gases from the defendant utilities. Indeed, this is essentially what the Supreme Court ultimately mandated in *Tennessee Copper*—modest emissions reductions that did not threaten the economic viability of the enterprises, but which helped spur the development of new pollution control technology.[172] Although the U.S. Supreme Court's decision in *Tennessee Copper* ultimately resulted in an injunction that limited emissions from a copper smelter, the initial emissions limits were set at a level that did not threaten the economic viability of the company. But the threat of future liability and particularly the uncertainty concerning the ultimate remedy to be applied by courts in abating nuisances helped encourage the companies to develop new technology.

Like the litigation in *Georgia v Tennessee Copper* a century ago, *Massachusetts v EPA* should spawn renewed efforts to confront a widely acknowledged environmental problem that no court could possibly hope to solve by itself. In the face of what many believe to be the most widespread and serious environmental problem humans face, the Court has taken a modest step to enter the

---

[172] See Robert V. Percival, *Resolución de Conflictos Ambientales: Lecciones Aprendidas de la Historia de la Contaminación de las Fundiciones de Minerales*, in Alejandra Quezada Apablaza, ed, *Prevención y Solución de Conflictos Ambientales: Vias Administrativas, Jurisdiccionales y Alternativas* 399, 407–17 (LexisNexis, 2004).

vacuum left by executive inaction. Like its decision a century ago in *Tennessee Copper*, the Court's *Massachusetts v EPA* decision is a victory for states seeking federal help to begin the long process of combating a problem that extends beyond their jurisdiction. With its decision in *Massachusetts v EPA* the Court returns in part to the role it played in the early twentieth century by forcing action, at the behest of a state, when no other federal institution was responding to a serious environmental problem.

Massachusetts v EPA does not herald a new age of judicial activism to protect the environment. The sharp dissents on standing and the merits joined by the four dissenting Justices are a reminder that the Supreme Court remains as sharply divided as humanly possible on crucial issues of environmental law. By joining the dissenting Justices in *Massachusetts v EPA* and the plurality in *Rapanos* the two newest members of the Court—Chief Justice Roberts and Justice Alito—confirm that they, along with Justices Scalia and Thomas, are highly skeptical of federal environmental regulation. Their views on standing to sue in environmental cases clearly represent a shift in a more restrictive direction away from the views of the *Laidlaw* majority that included both of their predecessors, Chief Justice Rehnquist and Justice O'Connor. Thus, for now, the shadow cast by the common law approach to judicial review of regulatory decisions has grown and the fate of most environmental litigants before the Court remains firmly in the hands of a single Justice—Justice Kennedy.

In *Massachusetts v EPA* the Court emerged from the growing shadow of the common law paradigm to produce a truly remarkable decision. The decision, and the unusual efforts by U.S. states to address a global problem, have rekindled hopes for the ultimate development of a global consensus approach for responding to climate change, despite the Bush administration's continuing opposition. EPA's decision to deny California's request for approval of its program of state controls indicates that careful judicial scrutiny of agency action must continue to ensure that the environmental laws are used appropriately in addressing the most serious environmental problem of our time.

RANDAL C. PICKER

TWOMBLY, LEEGIN, AND THE RESHAPING OF ANTITRUST

The Court's 2006 Term was an unusually active one for antitrust as the Court decided four substantial antitrust cases. Each of the cases will undoubtedly attract substantial academic attention.[1] The overall direction of the four cases is reasonably clear: plaintiffs face greater regulatory obstacles to reaching the court system (*Credit Suisse*), are more likely to get tossed from court without reaching a jury once they get there (*Twombly*), and will have to work harder to make out substantive antitrust liability (*Weyerhaeuser* and *Leegin*). Taken as a group, the cases represent a substantial raising of the hurdles that antitrust plaintiffs face, even if each case represents a simple one-step extension of current Supreme Court doctrine.

The Court's antitrust Term started with *Weyerhaeuser*,[2] in which a unanimous Court extended its analysis of predatory pricing in *Brooke Group*[3] to predatory bidding. The standard predatory pricing case concerns investing in losses through below-cost sales to achieve

Randal C. Picker is Paul and Theo Leffmann Professor of Commercial Law, the University of Chicago Law School and Senior Fellow, the Computation Institute of the University of Chicago and Argonne National Laboratory.

AUTHOR'S NOTE: I thank the Paul H. Leffmann Fund and the Sarah Scaife Foundation for their generous research support.

[1] And like this article, some will address all four of the cases together. See Joshua D. Wright, *The Roberts Court and the Chicago School of Antitrust: The 2006 Term and Beyond*, 3 Competition Policy Intl 24 (Aut 2007).

[2] *Weyerhaeuser Co. v Ross-Simmons Hardwood Lumber Co., Inc.*, 127 S Ct 1069 (2007).

[3] *Brooke Group Ltd. v Brown & Williamson Tobacco Corp.*, 509 US 209 (1993).

monopoly power. One competitor is alleged to sell at a price below an appropriate measure of cost in an effort to drive other competitors from the market, so that once monopoly has been achieved, the first seller can jack up its prices and more than cover its early losses. Predatory pricing is the Loch Ness monster of antitrust: occasional sightings that on further investigation turn out to be something else. Predatory pricing has received substantial attention from economists who can, as with much of game theory, spin out intricate stories in which predatory pricing is sensible but find it hard to articulate which real-world conditions will actually sustain it.[4] Given that difficulty, it is hardly surprising how mixed the case-law is on predatory pricing.[5]

But compared to predatory buying, predatory pricing is the easy case, the fastball down the middle. The much more unusual situation alleged in *Weyerhaeuser* is predatory buying: a producer buys more of an input than it needs in order to push input prices up, sufficiently to cause competing producers also buying the input to exit from the market. Going forward, that eliminates competition to buy the input, and the successful predator is left as the only input buyer (predating to achieve *monopsony*, as opposed to predatory pricing's push to *monopoly*). In *Weyerhaeuser*, the Court rejected the much more expansive approach formulated by the Ninth Circuit and instead applied its 1993 *Brooke Group* approach for predatory pricing to predatory buying.

In *Twombly*,[6] in a 7–2 decision authored by Justice Souter, the Court transplanted its prior decision in *Matsushita*[7] regarding summary judgment standards to a motion to dismiss for failure to state a claim (Rule 12(b)(6)). The Court concluded that an antitrust complaint could not merely allege conspiracy but instead must set forth a factual context that would allow illegal conspiracy to be distinguished from legal parallel independent action. *Matsushita* had implemented this rule for summary judgment motions, and *Twombly* extends that rule much earlier in the case to Rule 12(b)(6) motions. Justice Stevens dissented, joined, except in one part of his opinion, by Justice Ginsberg.

[4] Patrick Bolton, Joseph F. Brodley, and Michael H. Riordan, *Predatory Pricing: Strategic Theory and Legal Policy*, 88 Georgetown L J 2239 (1999–2000).

[5] *United States v AMR Corp.*, 335 F3d 1109 (10th Cir 2003).

[6] *Bell Atlantic Corp. v Twombly*, 127 S Ct 1955 (2007).

[7] *Matsushita Elec. Industrial Co. v Zenith Radio Corp.*, 475 US 574 (1986).

In *Credit Suisse*,[8] five Justices joined an opinion for the Court by Justice Breyer in concluding that federal securities law "implicitly" precluded claims asserting antitrust violations in the sale of new securities. That result tracked the Court's prior decision in *Gordon*,[9] which addressed another securities/antitrust intersection, as well as the Court's more recent preference for regulatory schemes over antitrust as seen in *Trinko*.[10] Justice Stevens wrote a separate opinion concurring in the judgment, while Justice Thomas dissented and Justice Kennedy recused himself.

Finally, on the last day of the Term, after announcing its hotly contested decision in *Seattle School District No. 1* on promoting racial integration in lower schools, the Court announced its 5–4 result in *Leegin*.[11] In an opinion by Justice Kennedy, the Court overruled its nearly century old decision in *Dr. Miles*[12] and held that contractual minimum resale price maintenance must be judged under the rule of reason and is no longer per se illegal. In contractual minimum RPM, a manufacturer—Sony—requires a retailer—Best Buy—to agree to sell a Sony HD TV set for a price at least as great as a floor-price set by Sony. In overturning *Dr. Miles*, the Court continued its trend of killing off old Supreme Court precedents treating a variety of practices as per se illegal. In addition, *Dr. Miles* was hard to square both with the Court's rule for nonprice vertical restraints adopted in *Sylvania* and with its rule for unilateral price restrictions established in *Colgate*.[13]

So all four cases are comfortably situated as natural steps in the case-by-case evolution that is the common law of the Sherman Act as created by the Supreme Court. Filling in the gaps in the caselaw, or doctrinal tuckpointing as it were. But this minimalist description of these cases captures poorly the overall sense of these cases and misses substantial disagreement within the Court. As a group, these cases impose meaningful limits on where antitrust will operate. For better or worse—more on that below—each of these cases reduces the role of private antitrust lawsuits, including the role of private

---

[8] *Credit Suisse Securities (USA) LLC v Billing*, 127 S Ct 2383 (2007).

[9] *Gordon v New York Stock Exchange, Inc.*, 422 US 659 (1975).

[10] *Verizon Communications, Inc. v Law Offices of Curtis V. Trinko, LLP*, 540 US 398 (2004).

[11] *Leegin Creative Leather Products, Inc. v PSKS, Inc.*, 127 S Ct 2705 (2007).

[12] *Dr. Miles Medical Co. v John D. Park & Sons Co.*, 220 US 373 (1911).

[13] *Continental T.V., Inc. v GTE Sylvania Inc.*, 433 US 36 (1977); *United States v Colgate*, 250 US 300 (1919).

antitrust plaintiffs in initiating cases and the role of the courts in deciding those cases.

Twombly will shrink substantially the ability of antitrust plaintiffs to file a complaint and find conspiracies through discovery. Indeed, the Court's precise point was to eliminate what it saw as fishing expeditions in discovery. In our joint system of public and private enforcement of antitrust laws, this tilts the balance considerably toward public enforcers (the Antitrust Division of the Department of Justice, the Federal Trade Commission, and state attorneys general). *Credit Suisse* explicitly looks to other governmental actors—most directly, the Securities and Exchange Commission—as it substitutes agency definition and enforcement of competition policy in securities markets for private antitrust lawsuits in lower courts. Both *Credit Suisse* and *Twombly* thus centralize antitrust enforcement, while *Leegin* and *Weyerhaeuser* reduce the scope of the substance of antitrust law itself. And while *Weyerhaeuser* was decided unanimously, *Leegin* was 5–4, with Justice Kennedy writing for this Term's usual majority and Justice Breyer writing for the expected dissenters. In a Term filled with disputes over the role that precedent should play, *Leegin* ended the Term with a full-out fight over the rule of stare decisis in antitrust cases.

We should dispense with *Weyerhaeuser* and *Credit Suisse* quickly. *Weyerhaeuser* is a one-off: a unanimous decision on an issue—predatory bidding—that the Supreme Court hadn't confronted before and isn't likely to see again soon. *Credit Suisse* is oddly situated procedurally—that accounts for the dissent—and the result flows naturally from the Court's prior cases in the area. This isn't to say that there aren't deep issues about the interaction of general competition policy and more specific industry regulation—an important topic worthy of a separate paper (hint)[14]—but *Credit Suisse* doesn't raise that topic directly. So I will offer brief discussions of *Weyerhaeuser* and *Credit Suisse* before turning to more extended discussions of *Twombly* and *Leegin*.

Twombly raises some basic questions about the mechanics of an adversarial court system. Plaintiffs will often have much less information about possible liability than defendants. To situate that in antitrust, plaintiffs are rarely invited to the proverbial smoke-filled

---

[14] Dennis Carlton and I address many of these issues—though not the specifics of *Credit Suisse*—in our forthcoming paper *Antitrust and Regulation*, in Nancy Rose, ed, *Economic Regulation and Its Reform: What Have We Learned?* (Chicago, 2008).

rooms in which price-fixing conspiracies are hatched. The best price-fixing conspiracies will be those in which the least is known publicly. This information asymmetry poses a dilemma if we intend to rely on private enforcement of antitrust statutes. Will we let private plaintiffs make bald assertions of conspiracy with few if any facts to substantiate their claims? If so, we can be sure that antitrust plaintiffs will delight in rifling the files of defendants hoping to discover something—*anything*—that will make out a claim. But the alternative to these fishing expeditions seems to be to allow some defendants to get away with antitrust violations or to hope that the government will target these conspiracies.

Leegin raises two important issues. One is a mixed question of economics and institutional design: what is accomplished when a manufacturer and a retailer agree on a minimum retail price? This is a long-standing question, and *Leegin* recognizes that our best understanding of contractual minimum RPM makes it difficult to conclude that it is almost always pernicious. Given that, as a matter of first impression, we wouldn't treat contractual minimum RPM as per se illegal. But *Leegin* isn't a case of first impression—far from it—and that takes us to the second issue in *Leegin*.

The Court has bobbed and weaved with contractual minimum RPM since its 1911 decision in *Dr. Miles* condemning the practice as per se illegal, but it had always chosen to duck rather than revisit *Dr. Miles*. *Leegin* forced the Court to confront its approach to stare decisis, at least in antitrust, if not more broadly. For the Court, stare decisis turns, in part, on the textual context. When the Court interprets the Constitution, Congress can't overturn the Court's interpretation. If a prior constitutional ruling of the Court is to be overturned, the Court must do it itself. But for statutes, if the Court chooses one interpretation rather than another, Congress can always jump in and revise the statute to impose its preferred interpretation. Hence, says the Court, it should tread more lightly in overturning its own interpretations of statutes. I think that that is wrong in important ways and that the Court should move toward applying its approach to stare decisis in constitutional cases to statutory situations as well.

All of this takes us to the Court's tools in antitrust. One of those tools is specifying who the decision maker will be in the first instance, and *Credit Suisse* reflects a preference for specialized industry consideration and the possibility of trading off competition concerns against other values. In *Twombly*, the Court has its hand on every possible lever of policy: direct control over the discovery rules and hierarchical control over the district courts implementing them, and yet the Court eschews sharp, refined approaches for the much more blunt instrument of early-case dismissal. Finally, in *Leegin*, it isn't clear that the Court fully appreciates the tools in its hand, or if it does so, it certainly doesn't seem to want to acknowledge that. The decisions of the Court interpreting the Sherman Act define the default point for any subsequent congressional action. Setting that point is a critical tool for establishing antitrust policy, and the sharpness of that tool in turn is set by how the Court itself approaches stare decisis in antitrust.

I. Weyerhaeuser: Doctrinal Simplicity and the Engines of Competition

The claim in *Weyerhaeuser* is predation to monopsony. In English, Weyerhaeuser was said to be paying too much for the red alder sawlogs that it needed to produce lumber and was doing so to drive its competitors for those sawlogs from the market so that it could become the only purchaser of those logs. With those firms gone, Weyerhaeuser would have a monopsony over the red alder sawlogs—it would be the only *buyer* of those logs—and it could then reduce the price that it would pay for those logs. This is predatory bidding—predation to monopsony—the flip side of the much more familiar, if still elusive in reality, predatory pricing, which is dropping sale prices initially to drive competing sellers from the market so as to emerge as the sole *seller* of a product.

Consider the facts of *Weyerhaeuser* itself. Ross-Simmons operated a hardwood-lumber sawmill in Washington. Sawmills turn logs into lumber, and indeed raw logs account for 75 percent of a sawmill's total cost. Ross-Simmons processed red alder sawlogs at its mill. Roughly two decades after Ross-Simmons commenced operations, Weyerhaeuser entered the northwestern hardwood-lumber market. Over time, Weyerhaeuser expanded its operations, and by 2001, it was purchasing roughly 65 percent of the alder logs available for sale in the Pacific Northwest.[15]

Ross-Simmons saw a nefarious intent in this pattern and filed an antitrust action alleging that Weyerhaeuser had used "its dominant

---

[15] *Weyerhaeuser*, 127 S Ct at 1072.

position in the alder solid market to drive up the prices for alder sawlogs to levels that severely reduced or eliminated the profit margins of Weyerhaeuser's alder sawmill competition."[16] We now see where we are. Ross-Simmons is not alleging that Weyerhaeuser was seeking market power in the lumber market, that is, the market for finished goods produced by sawmills.[17] Instead, the claim is that Weyerhaeuser was trying to limit competition in the purchasing of alder sawlogs. With Ross-Simmons and other firms like it gone, Weyerhaeuser would be able to dictate prices that it would pay to purchase alder sawlogs. With its newly acquired monopsony power, it would push those prices down, and depending on how price sensitive the alder sawlogs producers were, alder sawlogs sales would drop, as would Weyerhaeuser's production of finished lumber. But Weyerhaeuser would make sufficient profits from reducing its input prices that dropping sales of lumber would be profitable for it.

Competition over inputs is a critical way in which we organize production in the most efficient possible fashion. At the market price, a firm that wishes to purchase more of the input needs to offer a higher price. Doing so will lead to greater supply of that input, but also may cause a less efficient user of the input to reduce its use if it can't make money facing higher input prices. Input prices therefore serve as the medium we use to allocate production away from less efficient firms toward more efficient ones. This also means that we will see a standard pattern in these cases, where less efficient firms will have strong incentives to complain about the tactics being used by more efficient competitors.

The District Court presented the jury with the following instruction. Weyerhaeuser behaved anticompetitively if it "purchased more logs than it needed, or paid a higher price for logs than necessary, in order to prevent [Ross-Simmons] from obtaining the logs they needed at a fair price."[18] The appearance of the f-word should almost always make us nervous, but here we can probably offer an interpretation more congenial to economics. Presumably the notion

---

[16] Id at 1073.

[17] Although the Court recognized that predatory bidding could lead to market power in both the input market and the output market, id at 1076 n 2, the case appears to have been litigated on the premise that Weyerhaeuser was not seeking market power in the finished lumber market.

[18] Id at 1073.

of a "fair" price was intended to capture a price unaffected by the alleged predatory behavior.

Focus on how the jury instruction operates in practice. Weyerhaeuser buys more sawlogs. What does it do with them? Weyerhaeuser either sticks them in its inventory or processes them and converts them into finished lumber. If it inventories a sawlog, it incurs a cost but no revenue. If it processes it, it then sells the finished lumber, and we can calculate profits or losses. "Purchase more logs than it needed" sounds like Weyerhaeuser was stockpiling sawlogs. Weyerhaeuser presumably has some inventory of sawlogs, but under Ross-Simmons's theory Weyerhaeuser's inventory should have been growing as it was trying to cut off Ross-Simmons's supply of logs by cornering the market. Attempts to corner the market are highly dependent on the elasticity of supply, as the Hunt brothers were dismayed to learn in their 1980s attempt to corner the silver market, though everyone agrees that the supply of red alder sawlogs—which take many years to grow—is relatively inelastic in the short run.

Confronted with this situation, the Court did exactly what we should have anticipated. In its predatory pricing cases, the Court has made clear that we should be particularly concerned about antitrust doctrine that interferes with the key levers of competition that routinely produce benefits for consumers.[19] Lowering prices is almost always good for consumers, and we should be nervous about the possibility that the fear of antitrust liability will cause even a moment's hesitation about lowering a price. *Brooke Group* established a two-part test for predatory pricing. First, prices must be shown to be below cost. What cost? The Supreme Court won't tell us—"we again decline to resolve the conflict among the lower courts over the appropriate measure of cost"[20]—but presumably we are talking about marginal cost, or, perhaps more accessibly as in *Brooke Group* itself, average variable cost. With below-cost pricing made out, we turn to the second prong, which requires "a demonstration that the competitor has a reasonable prospect, or, under § 2 of the Sherman Act, a dangerous probability, of recouping its investment in below-cost prices."[21]

---

[19] *Brooke Group*, 509 US at 223.

[20] Id at 222 n 1.

[21] Id at 224.

In the predatory bidding context at stake in *Weyerhaeuser*, consumers benefit from the competition among efficient and less efficient producers. Inefficient producers lead to higher prices, and consumers should want those producers driven from the market by more efficient producers. Consumers want competition and want that output produced by the most efficient producers. The jury instruction in *Weyerhaeuser* threatened to interfere with that process by punting a question about fairness to the jury, and it is hard to imagine an instruction that would strike more fear into the heart of a producer competing for inputs. The Court recognized that and moved to simplify antitrust doctrine by synchronizing the tests for predatory pricing and predatory bidding by applying the *Brooke Group* test to both cases.[22]

II. CREDIT SUISSE: MOVING COMPETITION POLICY TO AGENCIES

Two federal statutes might apply to the conduct in question: how are we to determine which applies? In some cases, Congress may address this directly by including an antitrust "savings" clause, as it did in the Telecommunications Act of 1996.[23] That doesn't mean, of course, that there won't be messy cases,[24] but at least Congress, as author of both federal statutes, will have made clear its plan for how the statutes should work together. But if Congress hasn't addressed this directly, what should we do? This isn't a question specific to antitrust, nor is it a new question for antitrust—we faced this question in trying to mesh together the Interstate Com-

---

[22] For additional commentary on *Weyerhaeuser*, see John B. Kirkwood, *Controlling Above-Cost Predation: An Alternative to Weyerhaeuser and Brooke Group* (unpublished manuscript, 2007), online at http://papers.ssrn.com/sol3/papers.cfm?abstract_id=1027261; Keith N. Hylton, *Weyerhaeuser, Predatory Bidding and Error Costs* (Boston University School of Law Working Paper No 08-03, 2008), online at http://papers.ssrn.com/sol3/papers.cfm?abstract_id=1084106 (arguing that there are distinctions between predatory bidding and predatory pricing but that concerns about court mistakes justify applying the *Brooke Group* doctrine to cover both); Thomas A. Lambert, *Weyerhaeuser and the Search for Antitrust's Holy Grail*, 2006–2007 Cato S Ct Rev 277 (arguing that *Weyerhaeuser* implicitly addresses the circumstances under which a more efficient rival can be excluded consistent with Section 2 of the Sherman Act); Gregory J. Werden, *Monopsony and the Sherman Act: Consumer Welfare in a New Light* (unpublished manuscript, 2007), online at http://papers.ssrn.com/sol3/papers.cfm?abstract_id=975992).

[23] The note following 47 USC § 152 provides that "[n]othing in this Act or the amendments made by this Act shall be construed to modify, impair, or supersede the applicability of any of the antitrust laws."

[24] See *Verizon Communications, Inc. v Law Offices of Curtis V. Trinko, LLP*, 540 US 398 (2004).

merce Act, passed in 1887, and the Sherman Act (passed in 1890)[25]—
but it is the issue in *Credit Suisse*.

In January 2002, a group of investors sued ten investment banks,
alleging that their sales practices for initial public offerings (IPOs)
violated the antitrust laws. The complaint stated that the commissions earned by the investment banks were being established non-
competitively, that investors were being forced to buy less attractive
IPOs to get access to the really good ones—a tying claim—and that
investors were being forced to promise to place bids in the after-
market after the IPO at prices higher than the IPO price (so-called
laddering). The investment banks moved to dismiss the complaint
on the ground that the federal securities laws barred the antitrust
claims. The district court did so, but the Second Circuit reversed,
and that took the case to the Supreme Court.

Justice Breyer, along with five other Justices, concluded that the
securities laws were "clearly incompatible" with the antitrust laws
in these circumstances. Justice Kennedy didn't participate; Justice
Stevens wrote a separate opinion concurring in the judgment; and
Justice Thomas dissented. We might start with Justice Thomas's
dissent. He noted that the Court had framed *Credit Suisse* as a case
of whether the securities laws "implicitly" precluded application of
the antitrust laws. Of course, implicit preclusion arises only if the
federal statute doesn't address the matter explicitly. What do the
securities laws say?

The 1933 and 1934 securities laws provided rights that were to
be "in addition to any and all other rights and remedies that [might]
exist in law or in equity"[26] and therefore presumably in addition to
the Sherman Act (1890), the Clayton Act (1914), and the Federal
Trade Commission Act (1914). So the core antitrust principles continue to apply, and the Second Circuit was right to allow the IPO
antitrust lawsuit to move forward. Next case. But Justice Thomas's
position faced two hurdles. The Court majority believed that Justice
Thomas's argument hadn't been presented below. Moreover, the
argument was inconsistent with how the Court had approached the
question of implicit preclusion in its prior cases in the area, in
particular in *Gordon* and *NASD*.[27] All of that allowed the Court to

[25] *United States v Trans-Missouri Freight Association*, 166 US 290 (1897); Carlton and
Picker, *Antitrust and Regulation* (cited in note 14).

[26] 15 USC §§ 77p(a), 78bb(a).

[27] *Gordon v New York Stock Exchange, Inc.*, 422 US 659 (1975), and *United States v National
Association of Securities Dealers, Inc.*, 422 US 694 (1975).

move forward with its analysis of implicit preclusion, but also suggests that these issues will be argued differently the next time the Court confronts a possible conflict between the securities laws and antitrust.

Justice Breyer synthesized *Gordon* and *NASD* as turning on four considerations. He focused on "(1) the existence of regulatory authority under the securities law to supervise the activities in question; (2) evidence that responsible regulatory entities exercise that authority; and (3) a resulting risk that the securities and antitrust laws, if both applicable, would produce conflicting guidance, requirements, duties, privileges, or standards of conduct." He added that the analysis should also consider whether the practices in question "lie squarely within an area of financial market activity that the securities laws seek to regulate."[28]

With this test in hand, the Court set off on relatively brief and unremarkable examination of the regulations that control initial public offerings. This is an area of extensive oversight by the Securities and Exchange Commission. Indeed, a central purpose in passing the 1933 and 1934 securities acts and creating the SEC was to create a substantial regulatory apparatus to control IPOs. The SEC has broad regulatory authority over IPOs and exercises it extensively. That is true generally but also true with regard to the IPO underwriting syndicates challenged in the original complaint in this case. As the Court emphasized, the SEC draws exceedingly fine lines between the allowed and the forbidden, which in turn created a severe risk that courts acting on antitrust lawsuits will interfere with the authority of the SEC.

In its two most recent cases at the intersection of antitrust and regulation—*Trinko* and *Credit Suisse*—the Court has shown a high level of deference in favor of the regulatory scheme and in limiting the application of the antitrust laws. With regulations generally receiving a high level of deference under the *Chevron* doctrine, *Trinko* and *Credit Suisse* represent push toward entrusting competition policy to specialized regulators. At a minimum, that shifts control over chunks of competition policy from courts to agencies, but it is probably a shift in emphasis as well. Specialized regulators will typically weigh competition policy as just one factor among many and, compared against a baseline of court-enforced antitrust

---

[28] *Credit Suisse*, 127 S Ct at 2392.

law, this almost certainly represents a step back for the role of competition policy in these regulated industries.[29]

III. Twombly: How Do You Plead What You Don't Know?

In *Bell Atlantic Corp. v Twombly*, a 7–2 decision, the Court ruled that the mere assertion in a complaint of an underlying agreement violating Section 1 of the Sherman Act was insufficient to withstand a motion to dismiss when the parallel behavior in question could just as easily be explained as independent behavior. The majority opinion, authored by Justice Souter, emphasized the high costs associated with antitrust discovery. In reaching its conclusion, the Court "retired"—as it put it—its 1957 decision in *Conley v Gibson*, which had embraced "the accepted rule that a complaint should not be dismissed for failure to state a claim unless it appears beyond doubt that the plaintiff can prove no set of facts in support of his claim which would entitle him to relief."[30] *Twombly* will be asserted routinely in efforts to dismiss antitrust complaints, and it may have broad effects outside of antitrust as well.[31]

Twombly focuses on the pleading requirements established by the Federal Rules of Civil Procedure and, in particular, that staple of first-year civil procedure, Rule 8 of the FCRP. That rule requires that a pleading set forth "a short and plain statement of the claim showing that the pleader is entitled to relief."[32] What might that look like? Generations of students have considered Form 9 and especially its second sentence: "On June 1, 1936, in a public highway called Boylston Street in Boston, Massachusetts, defendant negligently drove a motor vehicle against plaintiff who was then crossing said highway."[33] That is all it says. Nothing about how the car was being driven—too fast? swerving?—just where and when and only one more word—"negligently."

What does all of that tell us about the complaint in *Twombly*?

[29] For additional commentary on *Credit Suisse*, see Keith Sharfman, *Credit Suisse, Regulatory Immunity, and the Shrinking Scope of Antitrust* (unpublished manuscript, 2007), online at http://papers.ssrn.com/sol3/papers.cfm?abstract_id=997405.

[30] *Bell Atlantic Corp.*, 127 S Ct at 1968.

[31] For additional commentary on *Twombly*, see Scott Dodson, *Pleading Standards after Bell Atlantic v. Twombly*, 93 Va L Rev in Brief 121 (2007) (online at http://www.virginialawreview.org/inbrief/2007/07/09/dodson.pdf).

[32] FRCP 8.

[33] FRCP Form 9.

The oral argument focused on Paragraph 51 of the complaint.[34] That paragraph alleged:

> In the absence of any meaningful competition between the RBOCs in one another's markets, and in light of the parallel course of conduct that each engaged in to prevent competition from CLECs within their respective local telephone and/or high speed internet services markets and the other facts and market circumstances alleged above, Plaintiffs allege upon information and belief that Defendants have entered into a contract, combination or conspiracy to prevent entry in their respective local telephone and/or high speed internet service markets and have agreed not to compete with one another and otherwise allocated customers and markets to one another.[35]

If you don't speak telephonese, "RBOCs" are the Regional Bell Operating Companies, meaning, to again search for English, the local phone companies that emerged from the breakup of the original AT&T, while a "CLEC" is a competitive local exchange carrier, meaning a new entrant into the landline phone market. The core allegation is one of market division: you take the East, I'll take the West, and we won't compete with each other. Market division is one of the dwindling number of per se violations of Section 1 of the Sherman Act.[36]

Of course, a plaintiff actually has to *prove* that Section 1 of the Sherman Act was violated, that is, that there actually was a contract, combination, or conspiracy in restraint of trade. Independent parallel behavior isn't enough—even if the defendants are watching each other quite carefully. Paragraph 51 of the complaint alleges parallel behavior—the RBOCs have not entered each other's markets—and then—giant puff of smoke and POOF—agreement. We are given no facts of the agreement—where and when and what brands of cigars were being smoked in the proverbial smoke-filled room?—but just a bald assertion that an agreement exists. Other parts of the complaint try to make out why the RBOCs should have entered and why not entering was against their own interests, but there is ultimately little more than an allegation of parallel behavior and then a claim of agreement.

---

[34] Oral Argument Transcript, *Bell Atlantic Corp. v Twombly*, No 05-1126, *3, 22, 41 (Nov 27, 2006).

[35] *Bell Atlantic Corp.*, 127 S Ct at 1970 n 10.

[36] *United States v Topco Associates, Inc.*, 405 US 596 (1972).

Even prior to *Twombly*, it was clear that more than that would be required at trial to win an antitrust case. The Supreme Court's 1976 decision in *Matsushita* requires that "[t]o survive a motion for summary judgment or for a directed verdict, a plaintiff seeking damages for a violation of § 1 must present evidence 'that tends to exclude the possibility' that the alleged conspirators acted independently."[37] We will not just let juries flip coins: if the plaintiff can't do more than just assert agreement, if the plaintiff can't *with evidence* exclude the possibility that the defendants were acting independently, the plaintiff loses, and indeed, the judge must not let the case go to the jury.

But *Matsushita*'s standard was announced in the context of summary judgment, after the plaintiff had had the opportunity to conduct discovery. What should we insist upon at the time that the complaint is filed? Return to Form 9 and focus on who knows what and what Form 9 tells us about the role of information asymmetry—what I know that you don't know—in pleading. Many of the core facts of the accident are known equally to both parties: the date, the location, the fact that a car struck a pedestrian. Presumably, both the plaintiff and the defendant have equal access to that information, and Form 9 seems to require that the plaintiff plead the facts known to her so as to give notice of the claim alleged.

But one set of facts isn't well known to the plaintiff, that is, exactly how the car was driven. Was the driver yakking away on his cell phone and not paying sufficient attention? Did the driver have a child in the back seat and turn at just the wrong moment to hand back a sippy cup? We don't know and neither does the plaintiff. That is the key point. Form 9 tells the plaintiff to plead the facts that she can know before she undertakes discovery. She does exactly that in Form 9. But she can't know the underlying facts that would give rise to a finding of negligence, and, as to that, Form 9 lets the plaintiff assert—in just one word—that the car was driven "negligently." Justifying that at trial will require more facts, facts that the plaintiff does not have access to when the complaint is filed, facts that will have to emerge through the process of discovery and trial.

Discovery lets the plaintiff get at the underlying facts that are not available to her when the complaint is drafted and lets her move beyond an uninformative assertion of legal liability—"negligently,"

---

[37] *Matsushita Elec. Industrial Co.*, 475 US at 588 (quoting *Monsanto Co. v Spray-Rite Service Corp.*, 465 US 752 (1984)).

as Form 9 puts it—to proof of the underlying facts that demonstrate liability—that the driver was reaching for a sippy cup when the accident occurred. That evidence is initially available only to the defendant, and the lesson of Form 9 is that while we make plaintiffs plead the facts that are available to them without discovery, we don't make plaintiffs plead facts that are available only to the defendant.

The majority opinion in *Twombly* makes very little of this. Form 9 is discussed in footnote 10 of the majority opinion:

> Apart from identifying a seven-year span in which the §1 violations were supposed to have occurred . . . , the pleadings mentioned no specific time, place, or person involved in the alleged conspiracies. This lack of notice contrasts sharply with the model form for pleading negligence, Form 9, which the dissent says exemplifies the kind of "bare allegation" that survives a motion to dismiss. . . . Whereas the model form alleges that the defendant struck the plaintiff with his car while plaintiff was crossing a particular highway at a specified date and time, the complaint here furnishes no clue as to which of the four ILECs (much less which of their employees) supposedly agreed, or when and where the illicit agreement took place. A defendant wishing to prepare an answer in the simple fact pattern laid out in Form 9 would know what to answer; a defendant seeking to respond to plaintiffs' conclusory allegations in the §1 context would have little idea where to begin.

This discussion misses a number of crucial points. We should first put the "answer" problem to one side. As a look at any recently filed answer makes clear, we know how the defendant is going to answer: the defendant is simply going to deny the allegation. Focus instead on what Form 9 says. As Justice Stevens notes in his dissenting opinion, the bare allegation of negligence in Form 9 would have been a conclusion of law under old-school pleading.[38] But it is exactly what Form 9 contemplates, and nothing in the word "negligence" gives the defendant any specific sense of the negligence alleged. It is asserted, with nothing more. Footnote 10 of the majority opinion skips over this entirely in emphasizing that the plaintiff in the Form 9 exemplar lists many facts. Yes, indeed; probably all of the facts known to the plaintiff, but nothing about how the car was driven—something unknown to the plaintiff—other than that it was driven "negligently."

---

[38] *Bell Atlantic Corp.*, 127 S Ct at 1977.

If we turn back to antitrust, the assertion of negligence in Form 9 is no less bare than the standard assertion of the existence of a conspiracy in an antitrust complaint. The problem, of course, is the one-sidedness of the information available on the existence (or non-existence) of a conspiracy, a point that Justice Stevens emphasizes in his dissent.[39] Often the plaintiffs won't be able to get at the facts of conspiracy—the who, what, when, and where contemplated by footnote 10 of the majority opinion—without discovery.

Of course in both cases—in Form 9 and the complaint in *Twombly*—the plaintiffs make a critical assertion—negligence in Form 9 and a contract, combination, or conspiracy in paragraph 51 of the *Twombly* complaint—and it isn't obvious on what basis the assertion is made. Paragraph 51 does little more than parrot the language of Section 1 of the Sherman Act. Does Rule 8 require no more than a simple assertion that Section 1 has been violated ("On information and belief, Plaintiff asserts that Defendant has violated Section 1 of the Sherman Act")? In the world of Form 9, the accident itself allegedly has taken place and perhaps that alone is enough, if we assume that most accidents arise from some sort of wrong. In contrast, paragraph 51 focuses on the *absence* of entry into markets, and that absence might arise from illegal agreement or from countless other causes. The *Twombly* complaint offers little more than the plaintiff's belief that such an agreement exists and will be confirmed only if discovery is permitted.

And remember that FRCP 11 provides that the attorney's signature on the complaint acts as a representation to the court that to the best of the attorney's information and belief the assertion of an agreement "will likely have evidentiary support after a reasonable opportunity for further investigation or discovery." If the attorney can't specify any of that evidentiary support in drafting the complaint, how can she sign the pleading and comply with Rule 11? For the experienced attorney, the likely existence of agreement might be just as self-evident as the likely existence of negligence in the accident in Form 9.

So we face something of a conundrum, almost certainly wanting a pleading system that demands more than just "they violated Section 1" and yet recognizing that the relevant information about liability will be systematically more available to one side than the

---

[39] Id at 1983.

other. A central point of the Federal Rules of Civil Procedure—rules controlled by the Supreme Court—is to figure out exactly how to manage that one-sidedness. The critical question isn't how to frame the answer—those rules will track the leniency or severity of our rules for framing the complaint—but rather how to frame discovery and, more generally, how to manage the one-sidedness of information. It is the fear of discovery run amok that drives the majority opinion,[40] but the Court offers no guidance as to how matters might be improved.

It is hard to imagine an area that the Court controls more completely. Under the Rules Enabling Act, the rules of civil procedure are squarely in the Supreme Court's hands.[41] If the current discovery rules don't work—in antitrust cases or other cases—the Court should fix them. This is a problem of institutional design entrusted to the Court by Congress. The opinion in *Twombly* acts as if the discovery rules come from Mars rather than from the Supreme Court itself. The Court majority is correctly concerned that vague complaints can be used as fishing expeditions, though note that the plaintiff proposed phased discovery starting with whether an agreement existed. If the Court believes that district court judges can't be trusted to manage discovery or that sensible rules cannot be crafted, it should say so. Maybe, in fact, that is effectively what *Twombly* says.

Note where that puts us. Antitrust laws are enforced through a mix of private and public efforts. *Twombly* limits the efficacy of private lawsuits. The Court majority does not seem to recognize the fundamental problem that the critical information regarding the existence or nonexistence of a possible conspiracy resides in the hands of potential defendants. Private litigation substitutes, at least in part, for public enforcement or regulation. The federal government has broad, but not unlimited, authority to serve civil investigative demands (CIDs) prior to bringing an antitrust action.[42] *Twombly* shrinks the domain of private plaintiffs and it does so without even a passing thought about what that will do to the overall level of antitrust enforcement.

---

[40] Id at 1967–68 n 6.

[41] 28 USC § 2072(a).

[42] 15 USC § 1312.

IV. Leegin: Statutory Stare Decisis for Strategic Judges

The decision in *Leegin* was announced on June 28, 2007, the last day of the 2006 Term. *Leegin* brings to a close a nearly 100-year saga of minimum resale price maintenance. That story is worth telling on its own, but the case also reveals sharp fault lines over the role of stare decisis in antitrust.[43]

A. MINIMUM RPM: FROM DR. MILES AND COLGATE TO LEEGIN

The antitrust statutes say very little on their own. Sections 1 and 2 of the Sherman Act set out only the most basic framework, and thus much of the actual practice under the statute arises through judge-made interpretations of the broad phrases of those sections. Section 1 applies to joint activity—"every contract, combination in the form of trust or otherwise, or conspiracy, in restraint of trade"—while Section 2 applies to single-firm activity—monopolization. Antitrust law is common law, that is, judge-made law in which courts revisit recurring fact patterns. In that framework, the job of the Supreme Court is to establish rules that can be implemented by lower courts and which in turn can guide economic activity. And, for the joint activities reached by Section 1, the heart of that analysis over the last century has been the division of particular practices into those that are per se illegal—known to be illegal without extensive consideration or fact-finding in a particular case—and those that must receive more considered attention under the rule of reason.

Section 1 always has been and remains most concerned about horizontal practices, meaning those among firms that are direct competitors. And within that group, horizontal price-fixing has

---

[43] For additional commentary on *Leegin*, see Mark D. Bauer, *Whither Dr. Miles?* (unpublished manuscript, 2007), online at http://papers.ssrn.com/sol3/papers.cfm?abstract_id= 1009972); Shubha Ghosh, *Vertical Restraints, Competition and the Rule of Reason* (unpublished manuscript, 2007), online at http://papers.ssrn.com/sol3/papers.cfm?abstract_id=1005380); Lino A. Graglia, *Leegin Creative Leather Products, Inc. v. PSKS, Inc.: The Strange Career of the Law of Resale Price Maintenance* (University of Texas Law and Economics Research Paper No 115, Nov 2007), online at http://papers.ssrn.com/sol3/papers.cfm?abstract_id=1028562 ("*Strange Career*"); Barak Y. Orbach, *Antitrust Vertical Myopia: The Allure of High Prices* (Arizona Legal Studies Discussion Paper No 07-25, Jan 2008), online at http://papers .ssrn.com/sol3/papers.cfm?abstract_id=1033440; Ittai Paldor, *Rethinking RPM: Did the Courts Have It Right All Along?* (unpublished SJD dissertation, University of Toronto, 2007), online at http://papers.ssrn.com/sol3/papers.cfm?abstract_id=994750.

been the most pernicious practice of all.[44] But contracts among competitors are often artificial: the leading retailers of the day don't usually deal directly with each other. But retailers contract with manufacturers all of the time, or, perhaps with wholesalers who in turn have agreements with manufacturers. These sorts of *vertical* contracts will arise perfectly naturally unless manufacturers fully vertically integrate, meaning that Kellogg not only produces cereal in Battle Creek, Michigan, but that it sets up Kellogg stores across the land to sell its cereal directly to consumers. We know that to be quite unusual, which suggests that there are frequently economies of scale and scope in retailing. It is more efficient to bring together Kellogg's many different brands along with those of General Mills and others, and add also milk, sugar, fruit—things that might go into a bowl of cereal—along with thousands of other products in a modern grocery store.

How should Section 1 approach these necessary vertical transactions? In 1911, in *Dr. Miles Medical Co. v John D. Park & Sons Co.*,[45] the Court put in place a rule that would last nearly a century. Dr. Miles sold proprietary medicines through a network of dealers. One level down it entered into what it denominated as "Consignment Contracts—Wholesale." Consignees in turn were expected to deal with retailers who in turn sold to the public. And the retailers themselves entered into direct "Retail Agency Contracts" with Dr. Miles. So as Dr. Miles's potions traveled down the chain of commerce, each transfer prior to sale to the general public was to be made to a party in a direct contract with Dr. Miles.

The consignment contract between Dr. Miles and its wholesalers seemed to contemplate that title in the medicines would remain with Dr. Miles even though possession had been trans-

---

[44] *United States v Socony-Vacuum Oil Co.*, 310 US 150, 224 n 59 (1940) ("Price-fixing agreements may or may not be aimed at complete elimination of price competition. The group making those agreements may or may not have power to control the market. But the fact that the group cannot control the market prices does not necessarily mean that the agreement as to prices has no utility to the members of the combination. The effectiveness of price-fixing agreements is dependent on many factors, such as competitive tactics, position in the industry, the formula underlying price policies. Whatever economic justification particular price-fixing agreements may be thought to have, the law does not permit an inquiry into their reasonableness. They are all banned because of their actual or potential threat to the central nervous system of the economy."); *United States v Trenton Potteries Co.*, 273 US 392 (1927).

[45] 220 US 373 (1911).

ferred to the wholesaler. Put differently, the consignment contract was an agency contract making it possible for Dr. Miles as principal to direct how its agent wholesalers would act. The majority opinion in *Dr. Miles* seems to waffle on this a bit based on some sloppy statements made by the plaintiff to the Court, but Justice Holmes in his dissenting opinion appropriately saw no reason to do anything other than give the consignment contract its most natural reading.[46]

Dr. Miles wanted to use its continuing control over title to allow it to set the prices which the medicines would be sold by wholesalers to retailers. The contract specified minimum sales prices, meaning that wholesalers could sell to retailers on Dr. Miles's behalf for a price not less than the specified contractual price. But Dr. Miles wanted to control not just wholesale prices—the prices paid by retailers to Dr. Miles—just as it would as if it acted without wholesalers, but also retail prices, meaning the prices paid by consumers to retailers. Again, Dr. Miles could have done that had it run only a mail-order business, and it wanted to achieve that same control over prices while operating through intermediaries. Thus, the retail agency contracts specified minimum sales prices as well.

But, and now we get to legal niceties, the retail agency contracts seemed to contemplate that the retailer actually purchased the medicines and then resold them to its customers. So when possession passed from Dr. Miles to its wholesalers, title didn't pass, but when possession passed from a wholesaler to a retailer, title passed as well. In the agency contract and notwithstanding the passing of title, the retailer agreed that it wouldn't sell at less than the full retail price as printed on the packages by Dr. Miles. So we have the passage of title and then a separate promise about the sales prices for the goods then owned by retailers.

When a former wholesaler of Dr. Miles outside the network of contracts bought from current consignee wholesalers and retailers within the contracts and then sold for less than the full retail price, Dr. Miles sued, alleging tortuous interference with contract and fraudulent dealing. That put the above contractual arrangements in front of the Court. The Court saw two problems. First, re-

---

[46] *Dr. Miles*, 220 US at 409–10 ("That they are agents, and not buyers, I understand to be conceded, and I do not see how it can be denied. We have nothing before us but the form and the alleged effect of the written instrument, and they are both express that the title to the goods is to remain in the plaintiff until actual sale is permitted by the contract").

straints on alienation were generally invalid, and the contracts in issue didn't fall within the narrow class of contracts excepted from that general rule.[47] Second, the Court understood Section 1 of the Sherman Act to condemn price fixing and saw that the contractual arrangements prevented price competition just as much as would a purely horizontal agreement among retailers.[48] That a manufacturer could choose not to sell at all or could choose not to sell through others was irrelevant; if the manufacturer chose to sell to retailers who then sold to consumers, the manufacturer had to accept whatever legal burdens came with its distribution choice.

But the Court complicated the analysis in *Dr. Miles* with its 1919 decision in *Colgate*.[49] Colgate had been indicted for forming a combination to fix resale prices by preventing its wholesale and retail dealers from selling below the minimum prices set by Colgate. Put that way, this seems like an easy case under *Dr. Miles*, and so the government argued to the Court. But confronted with a rather tangled district court opinion[50] and, as Lino Graglia has noted, with the guidance of former Justice Charles Hughes, the author of the *Dr. Miles* opinion who had since left the Court and then returned as an advocate (after running for President!),[51] the Court pieced together a different story. On the one hand, Colgate was said to enter into no contracts with its dealers, but on the other, Colgate had combined with them and received their "assurances and promises" regarding the required minimum prices. The Court expressed "serious doubts" about what to make of all of that, but thought that the best understanding of the case was that Colgate had done no more than exercise its recognized right to choose not to deal with anyone, including the right not to deal with any person who had sold at a price below those announced by Colgate. Unilateral action regarding minimum retail prices

---

[47] Id at 404–07.

[48] Id at 408 ("As to this, the complainant can fare no better than could the dealers themselves if they formed a combination and endeavored to establish the same restrictions, and thus to achieve the same result, by agreement with each other").

[49] *United States v Colgate*, 250 US 300 (1919).

[50] Under the Criminal Appeals Act, the United States was allowed to take a direct appeal to the Court from the district court "from a decision or judgment quashing, setting aside, or sustaining a demurrer to, any indictment, or any count thereof, where such decision or judgment is based upon the invalidity, or construction of the statute upon which the indictment is founded." Act of March 2, 1907, 34 Stat 1246.

[51] Graglia, *Strange Career* at 12 (cited in note 43).

didn't violate the joint action requirement of Section 1 of the Sherman Act (*Colgate*), while joint action on the same did (*Dr. Miles*).[52] A manufacturer implementing *Colgate*-style minimum RPM might face liability under Section 2 of the Sherman Act, which reaches unilateral actions, but Section 2 requires monopolization and not just the market power that suffices for a violation of Section 1.

It didn't take long for the Court to confront the difficulties of separating *Dr. Miles* and *Colgate*, with the Court returning to the question repeatedly in *Schrader's Son* (1920), *Frey & Son* (1921), *Beech-Nut* (1922), and *General Electric* (1926).[53] In *Schrader's Son*, the Court quoted extensively from the district court's opinion on the "distinction without a difference" between *Colgate* and *Dr. Miles*, before dismissing that analysis given the "obvious difference" between the situations presented.[54] Justices Holmes and Brandeis dissented without opinion. In *Frey & Son*, a private antitrust action was brought under *Dr. Miles* seeking damages and a jury verdict was returned in favor of the plaintiff. In a 6–3 decision, the Court concluded that the Fourth Circuit had misunderstood *Colgate* and *Schrader's Son* in reversing the district court, but that the district court too had misunderstood *Colgate* in formulating the key jury instruction.

Beech-Nut added a new wrinkle, as the Federal Trade Commission initiated an action against minimum RPM under its authority under Section 5 of the Federal Trade Commission Act to condemn unfair methods of competition. The Second Circuit once again tried to navigate *Dr. Miles* and *Colgate*. It understood *Dr. Miles* to turn on the existence of an agreement in writing, while in *Beech-Nut*, there was no more than a tacit understanding regarding Beech-Nut's desire for minimum resale prices and the likely consequences if dealers failed to meet those prices. The Second Circuit thus un-

---

[52] As the Court put it, "[i]n the absence of any purpose to create or maintain a monopoly, the act does not restrict the long recognized right of trader or manufacturer engaged in an entirely private business, freely to exercise his own independent discretion as to parties with whom he will deal; and, of course, he may announce in advance the circumstances under which he will refuse to sell." As for *Dr. Miles*, "the unlawful combination was effected through contracts which undertook to prevent dealers from freely exercising the right to sell." *Colgate*, 250 US at 307–08.

[53] *United States v A. Schrader's Son, Inc.*, 252 US 85 (1920); *Frey & Son, Inc. v Cudahy Packing Co.*, 256 US 208 (1921); *Federal Trade Commission v Beech-Nut Packing Co.*, 257 US 441 (1922); *United States v General Electric Co.*, 272 US 426 (1926).

[54] *A. Schrader's Son, Inc.*, 252 US at 99.

derstood the Beech-Nut plan to be protected under *Colgate*.[55] Not so, said the Court, in a 5–4 decision, with both Justices Holmes and Brandeis siding with the dissenters. Written contracts of the sort used in *Dr. Miles* were not required, and indeed the FTC had found none in its consideration of Beech-Nut's sales program. Instead, a course of dealing would suffice to show a combination, so long as that dealing established more than just the mere refusal to sell protected under *Colgate*. Of course, *Colgate* itself involved more than just a naked refusal to sell, but the majority didn't dwell on that point. In his dissenting opinion, Justice Holmes noted that whatever one might think generally about permitted vertical arrangements, the Federal Trade Commission faced the greater burden of showing that the practice in question was an "unfair" method of competition, and that it could hardly be unfair for a manufacturer to control the extent to which its own goods competed with themselves.[56]

Finally, in *General Electric*, the Court held that if a manufacturer entered into genuine agency contracts with wholesalers and retailers, the manufacturer could establish final-market sales prices for its goods (incandescent lightbulbs in this case). The government pressed *Dr. Miles*, but the Court found that case to be one of true sales dressed up as agency, whereas General Electric's contracts created genuine agents.

Think of *Dr. Miles* (1911) through *General Electric* (1926) as the first key window for the Court on minimum resale price maintenance. Jump forward to consider a second key window, say one defined by *Parke, Davis* (1960) to *Sylvania* (1977). With the Court's 1960 decision in *Parke, Davis*, *Colgate* hung by a thread, if that.[57] In a delicious irony, the Court had worked its way up from the snake-oil medicines of Dr. Miles to the modern pharmaceuticals of Parke, Davis, once the world's largest drugmaker.[58] Pursuant to what it understood to be its rights under *Colgate*, Parke had used its

---

[55] *Beech-Nut Packing Co.*, 257 US at 451.

[56] Id at 457 ("And to come back to the words of the statute I cannot see how it is unfair competition to say to those to whom the respondent sells and to the world, you can have my goods only on the terms that I propose, when the existence of any competition in dealing with them depends upon the respondent's will. I see no wrong in so doing, and if I did I should not think that it is a wrong within the possible scope of the word unfair").

[57] *United States v Parke, Davis and Co.*, 362 US 29 (1960).

[58] For discussion of Parke, Davis's history, see http://www.pfizer.com/about/history/pfizer_warner_lambert.jsp.

wholesale and resale catalogs to announce a minimum RPM policy. It did so only after consulting counsel who emphasized the need to proceed unilaterally and without agreement, thereby navigating between *Colgate* and *Dr. Miles*.[59] In the Court's view, Parke had overstepped the *Colgate* line when it sent to wholesalers the names of retailers who were no longer to receive Parke's products. But for the three dissenting Justices (Harlan, Frankfurter, and Whittaker), the Court had sent *Colgate* to its "demise," purporting to "profess respect for Colgate and eviscerate it in application."[60]

But if *Parke, Davis* turned *Colgate* into a zombie—condemned to live among the walking dead—it also had the consequence of pushing manufacturers away from vertical price restraints and toward nonprice vertical restraints. That in turn led to the Court's landmark 1977 decision in *Continental T.V., Inc. v GTE Sylvania Inc.*,[61] which ended more than a decade of per se ping-pong and established a new framework for evaluating certain nonprice vertical restraints. And, though it took three decades, the path from *Sylvania* to *Leegin* was reasonably clear, as Justice White's concurring opinion in *Sylvania* recognized in 1977.

We should start with the Court's 1963 decision in *White Motor*.[62] In a 5–3 decision, the Court declined to find that territorial restrictions in vertical arrangements—a truck manufacturer defining territories for its dealers—were per se illegal.[63] The Court distinguished price-fixing agreement—both the horizontal agreements at the heart of the Sherman Act and the vertical agreements condemned by *Dr. Miles*—but believed it had too little information to assess the actual effects of dealer territories. A trial was required to create a richer record for evaluation.

But four years later, the Court took a different path in its decision in *Schwinn*.[64] In a case argued for the government by Richard Posner, the Court once again considered dealer territories imposed by a manufacturer, in this case, the well-known bicycle maker. The Court, reaching back to its analysis in *Dr. Miles* and *General Electric*, turned the analysis of the vertical territorial restrictions on whether

---

[59] *Parke, Davis*, 362 US at 33.

[60] Id at 49, 57.

[61] 433 US 36 (1977).

[62] *White Motor Co. v United States*, 372 US 253 (1963).

[63] Id at 261, 264.

[64] *United States v Arnold, Schwinn & Co.*, 388 US 365 (1967).

the manufacturer had passed title to the good down the chain of distribution. If title was passed, any restraint by the manufacturer was per se illegal.[65] But if the manufacturer retained title, so that its distributors acted as its agents, the restraint would be evaluated under the rule of reason, as *White Motor* contemplated.

Schwinn set a rule for the ages. Actually, *Schwinn* barely made it a decade. In *Sylvania* (1977), the Court overruled *Schwinn* and returned nonprice vertical restraints to the rule-of-reason analysis that had controlled prior to *Schwinn*.[66] Sylvania had reorganized its distributor program for the TV sets it manufactured and had boosted its share of the market from 1 percent to 5 percent, a still-piddling share against then-dominant RCA, which had a 70 percent market share. An unhappy Sylvania distributor had asserted an antitrust claim against Sylvania for the territorial limits it had imposed on its franchisees. The Ninth Circuit struggled to permit the restriction consistent with *Schwinn*, but the Supreme Court wouldn't play that game and instead overturned *Schwinn*. The decision wasn't unanimous: Justices Brennan and Marshall would have adhered to *Schwinn*, while Justice White thought that *Schwinn* could be distinguished. Justice White was particularly concerned that the opinion in *Sylvania* put at risk *Dr. Miles* ("[t]he effect, if not the intention, of the Court's opinion is necessarily to call into question the firmly established *per se* rule against price restraints").[67]

It is important to trace the path here. We spent the better part of four decades—say 1920 to 1960—trying to make *Dr. Miles* and *Colgate* work together. Generations of antitrust lawyers tried to advise their clients on how to remain on the *Colgate* side of the line—unilaterally imposed minimum RPM—without stepping over the line into the RPM via contract or combination condemned as illegal per se by *Dr. Miles*. The Court's 1960 decision in *Parke, Davis* had to make clear to lawyers that they couldn't provide reliable advice to their clients about how to do that. So they switched away from minimum RPM and moved to nonprice vertical restraints of the sort seen in *White Motor*, *Schwinn*, and *Sylvania*. That set off more doctrinal churn, but the Court moved through that with reasonable dispatch—the fourteen years between *White Motor* and *Syl-*

---

[65] Id at 382.

[66] *Continental T.V., Inc. v GTE Sylvania Inc.*, 433 US 36, 58–59 (1977).

[67] Id at 70.

vania—and *Sylvania* then launched the modern analysis of vertical restraints. We see the nature of legal innovation at work: if *Parke, Davis* limited the practical effect of *Colgate*, it also gave birth to *Sylvania* and then *Leegin*, and *Leegin* restored *Colgate*.

We can move quickly through the balance of the pre-*Leegin* cases. The Court's 1984 opinion in *Monsanto* is noteworthy for a number of reasons.[68] The Court declined the Solicitor General's suggestion that *Dr. Miles* be reconsidered. At the same time, the Court saw two key doctrinal framings for considering vertical restraints. The first was the key distinction between unilateral activity and joint activity—citing to *Colgate* and *Parke, Davis* (really?)—while the second was the line between price and nonprice vertical restraints, that is, the line between the per se illegality of contractual minimum RPM in *Dr. Miles* and the rule-of-reason analysis of nonprice restraints in *Sylvania*. *Monsanto* serves as a natural baseline for assessing recent Supreme Court approaches to stare decisis in antitrust. Finally, in 1997, in *State Oil Co. v Kahn*, the Court overturned its 1968 *Albrecht* decision to move maximum retail price maintenance into the rule-of-reason category. *Albrecht* is interesting in its own right for the way it approached the meaning of "combination" in Section 1 of the Sherman Act, but after *State Oil*, maximum RPM would be evaluated under the rule of reason.[69]

Together, *Sylvania*, *Monsanto*, and *State Oil* set the stage for *Leegin*. Nonprice vertical restraints receive rule-of-reason treatment under *Sylvania*. *Monsanto* suggests that *Colgate* still matters, notwithstanding *Parke, Davis*, and that unilateral minimum RPM is free of Section 1 scrutiny. *State Oil* establishes that contractual maximum RPM was to be evaluated under the rule of reason. As we sliced and diced the vertical restraints space, that seemed to leave us only with contractual minimum RPM, which remained per se illegal under *Dr. Miles*. Until *Leegin*.

B. THE OPINIONS IN LEEGIN

Leegin is a small maker of women's leather belts. Leegin's revenues had been flat for most of the 1980s—hovering around $10 million in annual revenues—but then its growth rapidly accelerated from $15 million in 1988 to $20 million in 1989 and then

---

[68] *Monsanto Co. v Spray-Rite Service Corp.*, 465 US 752 (1984).

[69] *State Oil Co. v Kahn*, 522 US 3 (1997).

to $47 million in 1992.[70] The leather belt market is the ultimate old-economy business: it takes little more than a dead cow to enter the business, and the overall market is almost certainly quite competitive.

Leegin sells women's belts under its Brighton brand and does so in more than 5,000 small stores across the country. One of these was Kay's Kloset, a small women's clothing store in the Dallas suburbs, run by Phil Smith and his wife Kay since 1986. Leegin moved to contractual minimum resale price maintenance in 1997 when it started its "Brighton Retail Pricing and Promotion Policy."[71] Leegin's letter to retailers describing the policy emphasized that it was seeking to avoid what it saw as the poor quality of service of "mega stores like Macy's, Bloomingdales, May Co. and others" and instead wanted to partner with small specialty stores offering "great looking stores selling our products in a quality manner."[72]

In December 2002, Leegin learned that Kay's Kloset was discounting the Brighton brand. The opinion doesn't say when that discounting had started, but Phil Smith's account suggests that it started after September 11, 2001. Leegin had started offering discounts to airline and airport employees at a store at the Dallas/Fort Worth airport, and Kay's Kloset matched those prices.[73] But Leegin cut off Kay's Kloset after it refused to sell at the minimum retail prices, and that in turn led to the antitrust lawsuit by Kay's against Leegin.

Leegin is really a two-issue case: (1) as a matter of first consideration, should contractual minimum RPM be treated as per se illegal, or should it instead receive rule-of-reason treatment? and (2) if rule-of-reason treatment is appropriate, should the Court nonetheless adhere to the result of per se illegality established in *Dr. Miles*? On the first issue, the Court returned to 1628, the date of Coke upon Littleton, which *Dr. Miles* cited for the general proposition that restraints on alienation were invalid. The Court seemed skeptical that a nearly 300-year-old analysis should have

[70] See John Case, *A Business Transformed: How One CEO Transformed His Entire Company in Order to Make Its Service Indispensable to Its Customers*, Inc. Magazine (June 1993).

[71] *Leegin Creative Leather Products*, 127 S Ct at 2711.

[72] Id.

[73] Maria Halkias, *Local Antitrust Fight Goes to D.C.*, Dallas Morning News (March 25, 2007).

sufficed in 1911 and saw no basis for that nearly a century later ("[t]he general restraint on alienation . . . tended to evoke policy concerns extraneous to the question that controls here").[74]

With the analysis in *Dr. Miles* itself pushed to the side, the Court then turned to a fresh consideration of the policies at stake in minimum resale price maintenance. That took the Court to the defining feature of modern antitrust analysis, namely, the role of economics in understanding how we should evaluate particular practices. As has been the Court's pattern in other cases moving practices away from per se illegality and toward rule-of-reason analysis, the Court cited the extensive literature arguing that minimum RPM can have procompetitive benefits.[75]

Minimum RPM shapes interbrand competition, meaning, for example, competition between different manufacturers of belts. Minimum RPM is said to, as the Court put it, "encourage[] retailers to invest in tangible or intangible services or promotional efforts that aid the manufacturer's position as against rival manufacturers."[76] Minimum RPM also expands the mix of price/service combinations. With a set minimum resale price, retailers will compete over services instead. Manufacturers who want low prices can have them, while other manufacturers who believe that higher prices and higher service are warranted can sustain that combination as well. As to minimum RPM, Justice Kennedy's conclusion was clear: "[t]hough each side of the debate can find sources to support its position, it suffices to say here that economics literature is replete with procompetitive justifications for a manufacturer's use of resale price maintenance."[77]

But even if the Court majority believed, as it obviously did, that a fresh consideration would result in rule-of-reason treatment for minimum RPM, what about *Dr. Miles*? Should stare decisis cause the Court to stay with the good doctor? Justice Kennedy started with the Court's history in antitrust. The Sherman Act is effectively a common-law statute, and over the last hundred years the Supreme Court has steadily moved away from rules of per se illegality toward the rule of reason. In many cases, it has overturned prior precedent in doing so, just as it did for maximum

---

[74] *Leegin Creative Leather Products*, 127 S Ct at 2714.

[75] Id at 2715.

[76] Id.

[77] Id at 2714.

RPM in 1997 *State Oil* and as it did last Term in *Independent Ink* in overturning the rule that a patent holder would be presumed to have market power in a tying case.[78]

In considering stare decisis, Justice Kennedy noted the difficulties of making sense of a world populated by *Dr. Miles*, *Colgate*, and *Sylvania*: "If we were to decide the procompetitive effects of resale price maintenance were insufficient to overrule *Dr. Miles*, then cases such as *Colgate* and *GTE Sylvania* themselves would be called into question."[79] Of course, this isn't a new point. Justice White had said as much in his concurrence in *Sylvania* in which he tried to hang on to *Schwinn*. But the passing of time may have made more apparent the costs of trying to make these three cases work together. As Justice Kennedy emphasized: "[i]n sum, it is a flawed antitrust doctrine that serves the interests of lawyers—by creating legal distinctions that operate as traps for the unwary—more than the interests of consumers—by requiring manufacturers to choose second-best options to achieve sound business objectives."[80] This is a regime you can like only if you are a hard-line Darwinist—the survival of the competitors with the fittest lawyers.

That left the Court with two other factors to consider in its analysis of stare decisis. The first is congressional intent. Section 1 of the Sherman Act is quite slim, as it was when it was enacted in 1890, but for nearly forty years it was substantially more chunky. In 1937, Congress enacted the Miller-Tydings Fair Trade Act, which added two extensive provisos to Section 1.[81] The first excepted from the reach of Section 1 contracts providing for minimum resale prices so long as underlying state law allowed the transaction, as it might under a so-called fair trade law. The second proviso made clear that the new exception was not intended to allow horizontal price setting. Miller-Tydings was the law of the land until 1975, when it was struck from the statute and Section 1 was returned to its original form.[82] So for forty years, Congress delegated the legality of minimum RPM to the states, only to reclaim federal authority in 1975. What does this tell us about the stare decisis status of *Dr. Miles*?

In the Court's view, this is a lot of woulda, coulda, shoulda, and

---

[78] *Illinois Tool Works Inc. v Independent Ink, Inc.*, 547 US 28 (2006).

[79] *Leegin Creative Leather Products*, 127 S Ct at 2722.

[80] Id at 25.

[81] 50 Stat 693 (1937).

[82] Consumer Goods Pricing Act of 1975, 89 Stat 801 (Dec 12, 1975).

the Court makes very little of it. Yes, in passing the 1937 act, Congress allowed states to jump in and render minimum RPM legal, and yes, in acting in 1975, Congress took away that authority and thereby restored the full reach of *Dr. Miles*. Prior to 1975, *Dr. Miles* had no effect in states which had enacted a fair trade act and its bar was limited to only those states which had not acted. After 1975, *Dr. Miles* again applied everywhere. But at no point did Congress limit the Court's ability to continue to evolve antitrust doctrine, and Congress certainly didn't enact *Dr. Miles* in 1975.

Finally, that leaves the question of the relevance of reliance for stare decisis in antitrust. As to that, said the Court, actual reliance on *Dr. Miles* had to be limited. No one could seriously claim a century's worth of reliance, as it was only with the 1975 amendments to Section 1 that *Dr. Miles* again applied throughout the nation. Moreover, the alternatives to contractual minimum RPM—unilateral minimum RPM and other vertical contracts—necessarily limited the domain of *Dr. Miles*. All of that meant, for the Court, that reliance interests couldn't justify keeping an inefficient rule. And with that, after nearly a hundred years, *Dr. Miles* was gone; contractual minimum RPM would now be evaluated under the rule of reason.

Justice Breyer dissented, joined by Justices Stevens, Souter, and Ginsburg. *Leegin* came down on the last day of what one guesses had been a frustrating Term for these four Justices. When the Court decided *State Oil* in 1997 and overturned *Albrecht* (1968) and thereby moved maximum RPM from per se illegality to rule-of-reason analysis, the opinion was unanimous. None of the *Leegin* dissenters said a peep about the importance of stare decisis in antitrust. One gets the sense that the dissent in *Leegin* may have just been an easy placeholder for a term's worth of frustration.

Justice Breyer's dissenting opinion emphasized that, were he writing on a blank slate, he would have found the question of whether to apply the rule of reason to minimum RPM difficult. This turns much on the genuine difficulties of establishing an administrative rule that meaningfully implements the rule of reason. Economists may be able to get tenure writing articles that conflict about the theoretical consequences of minimum RPM, but a district court judge actually has to make a decision. As Justice Breyer put it: ". . . antitrust law cannot, and should not, precisely replicate economists' (sometimes conflicting) views. That is because law, unlike economics, is an administrative system the effects of which depend upon the content of rules and precedents only as they are applied by judges and juries in courts and by lawyers advising their clients."[83] That led Justice Breyer to his conclusion: "[a]nd, if forced to decide now, at most I might agree that the *per se* rule should be slightly modified to allow an exception for the more easily identifiable and temporary condition of 'new entry.'"[84]

Part of this clearly turns on Justice Breyer's concern that minimum RPM pushes up prices. Of course, that is almost certainly right, as the whole point of minimum RPM is to ensure that prices meet a floor that some retailers would otherwise push beyond. But, as Justice Scalia emphasized at oral argument, consumers clearly care about more than just price.[85] If higher prices come with better services, consumers may be happier. Evidence of higher prices, without more, tells us nothing about how consumers are faring.

Justice Breyer then turned to the question of whether *Dr. Miles* should be overruled. His core point was that nothing had changed recently that would call *Dr. Miles* into question. The administrative difficulties of making *Dr. Miles* and *Colgate* work together arose as soon as *Colgate* was decided in 1919, as the Court's docket over the next few years made clear. The economic understanding of minimum RPM hadn't changed recently either, a point Justice Breyer made in the oral argument by drawing upon a 1966 economics text on minimum RPM.[86]

As to stare decisis itself, Justice Breyer started with what he saw as the most recent learning on the subject, namely, Justice Scalia's then four-day-old opinion in *Wisconsin Right to Life*.[87] Something more than antitrust seemed to be at stake. Justice Breyer went through a laundry list of considerations in implementing stare decisis. Stare decisis applies with greater force (1) in statutory cases than in constitutional cases; (2) to old mistakes rather than more recent mistakes; (3) when the regime created by the original decision is unworkable; (4) when the original decision "unsettled" the law; (5) when property rights or contract rights are at stake; and, finally,

---

[83] *Leegin Creative Leather Products*, 127 S Ct at 2729.

[84] Id at 2731.

[85] Oral Argument Transcript, *Leegin Creative Leather Products, Inc. v PSKS, Inc.*, No 06-480, *15 (March 26, 2007) ("Leegin Transcript").

[86] Id at *12.

[87] *Federal Election Commission v Wisconsin Right to Life, Inc.*, 127 S Ct 2652 (2007).

(6) when the original law becomes "'embedded' in our 'national culture'." For Justice Breyer, each of these factors pointed to preserving *Dr. Miles*.

That left Justice Breyer with the dog that didn't bark, his missing dissent in *State Oil*. *State Oil* was nine zip with our current dissenters—Justices Breyer, Stevens, Souter, and Ginsburg—all silent. If stare decisis was so important in 1997, why didn't we hear something about it then? This point wasn't lost on Justice Breyer, and he attempted to distinguish *State Oil* and *Leegin*—*State Oil* overruled *Albrecht* and only twenty-nine years had passed, while *Leegin* overruled *Dr. Miles* and we are at almost a century—but that is something of an artificial comparison given the fair trade era—1937–75—and so we might focus on 1975 as the date of full restoration of *Dr. Miles*. With that date, the *Leegin/State Oil* comparison is much tougher for Justice Breyer.

C. THE ECONOMICS OF MINIMUM RESALE PRICE MAINTENANCE

We should follow the path that the Court did in *Leegin*, considering first the structure of the economic argument and then the status of stare decisis in antitrust. We should start with the core notion behind minimum RPM. The manufacturer believes that in-person services need to be provided to best sell its goods at retail. Provision of services is costly and the manufacturer fears that some retailers will try to free ride on other retailers, and if each retailer tries that, no one will provide the required services.

So the classic example of free riding might arise in the 1988 case of *Business Electronics*.[88] Calculators were expensive and complicated back then—and, even today, who has actually mastered Reverse Polish Notation?[89]—and needed to be explained in person. The high-end electronics store invests in educating its customers, and they learn all about how the calculator works. That of course costs money, and the price for the calculator should reflect that. But once the consumer understands the calculator, the consumer can buy from the cheaper place next door. That means the first store incurs costs that it can't recover and therefore won't provide

---

[88] *Business Electronics Corp. v Sharp Electronics Corp.*, 485 US 717 (1988).

[89] Hewlett-Packard started selling calculators using RPN in 1972 and continues to do so today. See *RPN, An Introduction to Reverse Polish Notation* (available at http://www.hp.com/calculators/news/rpn.html).

the services. No one provides the services and the product isn't sold.

Minimum RPM changes the nature of competition. By construction, the stores can't compete on price. Minimum RPM allows the manufacturer to create a specified gap between the wholesale price—set directly by the manufacturer in its sales to retailers—and the retail price. Absent minimum RPM, that difference floats and is determined by the competition among retailers. With it fixed, price competition among retailers will go away but they should shift their competitive juices in other directions. Retailers will take other costly actions and in so doing will compete away the bonus that has been offered to them through the fixed retail price.

At least so goes the theory. Put this way, there is a clear clumsiness associated with minimum RPM. Some retailers might continue to free ride and hope to just make more money. Alternatively, retailers might spend the margin—the gap between retail and wholesale prices—but they might take any number of steps to provide superior services. Some of those might be nice showrooms or other investments in ambience. Recall that Leegin's letter announcing its new RPM policy focused on "great looking stores selling our products in a quality manner." Those investments may benefit the manufacturer providing the minimum RPM bonus, but many of these investments actually benefit all manufacturers.

No one manufacturer actually wants to invest in ambience; as a manufacturer, you want all of the other manufacturers to invest in nice stores. This should make clear the second free-riding problem at stake in minimum RPM. The first is about retailer-retailer competition; the second is about how manufacturers interact with each other when they share retailers. Of course, most retailers are shared retailers. There is the occasional Apple store, and the Nike store on Michigan Avenue in Chicago is legendary, but the vast majority of retailers sell multiple brands. Those brands share retailers.

We now see the ham-handedness of minimum RPM. Minimum RPM decentralizes the "extra" service decisions to the retailers. The retailer might invest in more education for HP calculators, and, if so, HP has taken an important step toward solving the problem of Reverse Polish Notation—though even here, that education benefits any calculator maker using that notation, and so we have another version of the free-riding problem—but the retailer might just as well spend the money on nicer fixtures, and HP gets no particular benefit from that.

Consider a natural alternative: a direct contractual provision from the manufacturer requiring that education be provided.[90] As a nonprice vertical restraint, an education provision would be judged under the rule of reason under the rule announced in *Sylvania*. If the manufacturer believes that education is best provided at each place the product is sold, the manufacturer presumably will require such education in each retail contract. If instead the manufacturer believes that it is important that education be available in each market, the manufacturer will have different contracts for each retailer.

Of course, providing education isn't free, and the manufacturer would need to compensate retailers for providing the education. But if direct payments are made, much of the air is gone from the free-riding balloon. Indeed, if the manufacturer "overpays" for education, retailers will fight to provide education. And an education clause, like any other clause in a contract, needs to be enforced to work, and that requires the manufacturer to create some enforcement mechanism.

Nothing in the core service theory of minimum RPM tells us where the push for extra services should come from. Manufacturers may understand from the get-go that their products need special handling, and if so they may initiate minimum RPM. But in other cases, retailers may be closer to customers and may have a better understanding of the need for extra service. These retailers also may see more directly how the free-riding dynamic operates day by day. In those cases, we should expect to see retailers pushing the manufacturer to implement minimum RPM. In the extreme case, the push might be purely horizontal. How should we treat these cases?[91]

The direction of the push shouldn't matter. We would have to be much more confident than I see reason to be about where the information regarding the importance of services is likely to lie. Although there seems to be no logical reason to exclude the possibility that a local horizontal cartel might facilitate interbrand

---

[90] Leegin Transcript at *41.

[91] At oral argument, Justice Stevens addressed the possibility of a purely horizontal cartel designed to promote interbrand competition. Id at *4–5, 20–21.

competition, we might administratively want to use the manufacturer's agreement to that practice as a way to separate out pernicious horizontal agreements from those that actually promote interbrand competition. The manufacturer has a shared interest in seeing the latter and strong interests in opposing the former. Requiring the smart retailers to persuade the manufacturer to implement minimum RPM means we avoid having horizontal cartels spring up in the guise of providing better services.

Leegin also shouldn't be understood as changing our basic rules about the per se illegality of horizontal cartels. Justice Stevens's questions at oral argument suggested that he recognized that the analytical framework of using minimum RPM to produce retail services meant that there could be net benefits from some retailer cartels. These would be cartels limiting intrabrand competition in an effort to induce service provision and doing so in a context where there was extensive interbrand competition. On those facts, the retailers shouldn't have meaningful market power, and the intrabrand cartel would just be making possible a new price/services combination.

But *Leegin* doesn't go this far and, for now at least, we will continue to treat these horizontal cartels as per se illegal. Given that, we shouldn't need the rule in *Dr. Miles* to get at horizontal cartels—good or bad—implemented by retailers. That is, we shouldn't need to condemn *every* instance of minimum RPM to make sure that we have blocked situations in which harmful retailer-led horizontal cartels have been dressed up as minimum RPM.

In *Leegin*, the Court also focused on the transaction costs of *Dr. Miles*. Manufacturers who want to implement minimum RPM can do so as long as they proceed unilaterally and comply with *Colgate*; what they couldn't do was implement minimum RPM through agreements that violated *Dr. Miles*. But even after *Leegin* with *Dr. Miles* gone, some manufacturers will continue to try to meet *Colgate*. A manufacturer who stays on the *Colgate* side of the *Dr. Miles/ Colgate* line avoids the Section 1 rule-of-reason inquiry entirely. For that manufacturer, there is no triggering contract, combination, or conspiracy and hence no possibility of Section 1 liability. Unilateral activity is dealt with under Section 2, but Section 2 requires monopolization, and that is more than just the market power that will trigger liability under Section 1. With *Dr. Miles* gone, some manufacturers will switch to contractual minimum RPM and accept that they may face a possible Section 1 rule-of-reason inquiry. Others may continue to implement the *Colgate* version of RPM if they wish to avoid Section 1 risk entirely.

D. STARE DECISIS AND STATUTES: PRIOR COURT DECISIONS AS
   STARTING POINTS FOR CONGRESS

Now switch to stare decisis. We start by mapping the lay of the land in antitrust. For doing that, almost any starting point would be arbitrary, but given that *Leegin* overturns *Dr. Miles*, we might start our analysis of stare decisis from a point where the Court *didn't* overturn *Dr. Miles*, its 1984 decision in *Monsanto*.[92] *Monsanto* was the first of five antitrust cases decided during the Court's 1983 Term.[93] The Solicitor General had asked the Court to reconsider *Dr. Miles* in *Monsanto*, but in a footnote, the Court declined to do so. Justice Brennan's brief concurring opinion focused exclusively on the status of *Dr. Miles*. He emphasized the opinion's longevity—seventy-three years at that point—and the fact that Congress had never enacted legislation to overrule *Dr. Miles*.[94]

The 1983 Term is also interesting for the different ways that the cases approached stare decisis. In *Jefferson Parish*, the Court considered the law of tying, that is, the circumstances under which a seller forces a purchaser to take one product with a second product.[95] The question of whether or not to abandon the Court's prior rule that tying cases should receive per se treatment divided the Court. The five-member majority believed that it was "far too late in the history of our antitrust jurisprudence to question the proposition that certain tying arrangements pose an unacceptable risk of stifling competition and therefore are unreasonable 'per se'."[96] The Court saw a steady line of support for per se treatment going back to 1947 (*International Salt*), if not earlier.[97] Justice Brennan, joined by Justice Marshall, concurred, briefly pointing to his earlier concurring opinion in *Monsanto* and emphasizing that Congress had

---

[92] *Monsanto Co. v Spray-Rite Service Corp.*, 465 US 752, 761 (1984).

[93] For discussion of those cases, see Diane Wood Hutchinson, *Antitrust 1984: Five Decisions in Search of a Theory*, 1984 Supreme Court Review 69.

[94] *Monsanto Co.*, 465 US at 768.

[95] *Jefferson Parish Hospital District No. 2 v Hyde*, 466 US 2 (1984).

[96] Id at 9.

[97] *International Salt Co. v United States*, 332 US 392 (1947).

left alone the Court's prior per se treatment of tying.[98] But for Justice O'Connor and the other three Justices joining her opinion concurring in the judgment, it was time "to abandon the 'per se' label and refocus the inquiry on the adverse economic effects, and the potential economic benefits, that the tie may have."[99]

But less than three months later, the Court took a different approach to stare decisis in antitrust. In *Copperweld*,[100] the Court considered the question of whether a parent and its wholly-owned subsidiary were legally capable of conspiring under Section 1 of the Sherman Act. Yes, the two were distinct legal entities and hence could contract with each other, but was that what Section 1 was looking for in its focus on "every contract, combination in the form of trust or otherwise, or conspiracy, in restraint of trade"? In a 5–3 decision, the Court concluded that the parent and the sub lacked sufficient separateness for Section 1 purposes. In so doing, the Court "disapproved and overruled" its prior decisions that were inconsistent with the rule announced in *Copperweld*. Which ones exactly was a point of dispute between the majority and the dissenters. In dissent, Justice Stevens counted at least seven decisions of the Court that he believed to be inconsistent with *Copperweld*,[101] going as far back as 1947 (*Yellow Cab*).[102] The majority attempted to recharacterize most of the cases to suggest that they could have been decided on an alternative basis and to suggest that the issue had never been considered in real depth by the Court.[103] Justice Stevens noted that Congress could have revised the Court's prior rulings on capacity to contract for Section 1 purposes but had declined to do so over four decades.[104]

From the 1983 Term through the 2006 Term—twenty-four Terms—the Supreme Court decided fifty-one antitrust cases, or an

---

[98] *Jefferson Parish*, 466 US at 32 ("Whatever merit the policy arguments against this longstanding construction of the Act might have, Congress, presumably aware of our decisions, has never changed the rule by amending the Act. In such circumstances, our practice usually has been to stand by a settled statutory interpretation and leave the task of modifying the statute's reach to Congress").

[99] Id at 35.

[100] *Copperweld Corp. v Independence Tube Corp.*, 467 US 752 (1984).

[101] Id at 779–82.

[102] *United States v Yellow Cab Co.*, 332 US 218 (1947).

[103] *Copperweld*, 467 US at 760 ("Although the Court has expressed approval of the doctrine on a number of occasions, a finding of intra-enterprise conspiracy was in all but perhaps one instance unnecessary to the result").

[104] Id at 784.

average of more than two per Term.[105] We can try a mechanical approach to the role of stare decisis in antitrust. Of these fifty-one decisions, only five used the phrase "stare decisis": *Leegin* (2007), *State Oil* (1997), *Eastman Kodak* (1992), *Square D* (1986), and *Copperweld* (1984). That suggests immediately one of the weaknesses of the "tag cloud" approach to matching text and ideas: both *Jefferson Parish* and *Monsanto* are missing from the list, even though it was precisely the question of stare decisis that separated the Justices in *Jefferson Parish* and even though Justice Brennan's concurring opinion in *Monsanto* is almost exclusively about the importance of not overturning prior decisions of the Court.

We should start with a basic conception of stare decisis and then work up from there. A minimalist approach to stare decisis might focus on almost a physical notion of repeatability: if the same inputs go into the same production system, the same output should result. Treat the Court as a thing unto itself, not something made up of a changing slate of nine individuals but instead as a coherent, integral entity. In that formulation, mere changes in Court personnel shouldn't change case outcomes. If the Court reaches a conclusion, if the same arguments are subsequently presented to a different instantiation of the Court, the same outcome should result. This isn't to say that the Court can't learn and therefore change results. Operating experience under one rule and new arguments should move the Court just as they do individuals, but it is precisely these input changes that should result in different outcomes, not change in the Court itself.

We might think that an odd, sterile, and mechanical conception of what the Court is. Do we really think that a Court comprised of nine male Justices would approach, say, the First Amendment status of pornography in the same fashion as an all-female Court? If you think not, then you probably believe that one of the inputs brought to Court decision making are the individual experiences of the Justices. We can submit the same briefs to one Court and then resubmit them to a new Court and see different results because the individual experiences of the Justices shape outcomes.

We might think of stare decisis then as about the size of a required change necessary to reach a different result, where stare decisis

---

[105] Fifty-one is the number that emerges from the Westlaw search, run on Nov 21, 2007, on the Supreme Court database using the search request "to(29t) and date(after 1983) and sy(antitrust sherman clayton (federal +1 trade +1 commission)."

might address either the non-Court inputs to decision making or the Court process itself. The input version of stare decisis would focus on the required change in inputs that would permit the Court to change outcomes. A thin version might mean that even small changes in inputs would cause the Court to change outcomes. So even weak new arguments or small changes in data would cause the Court to overrule a prior decision. A thick-input version of stare decisis would require much more substantial changes in circumstances before the Court would abandon prior positions.

A personnel version of stare decisis might focus on voting rules for cases, which the Court might implement by adopting a supermajority decision rule for overruling prior cases. Don't overrule if the vote is only 5–4 in favor; instead, require greater unanimity than that.[106] To be mechanical about this, a 6–3 or better rule would mean that a one-member change on the Court wouldn't by itself change results. A 5–4 case in one Term couldn't become a 5–4 decision the other way if one of the original five Justices were replaced by a new Justice who held the opposite view of the question.

The Court hasn't articulated stare decisis in this fashion. Instead, as Justice Breyer's dissent in *Leegin* emphasized, the Court has typically proceeded under a multifactor approach. So the Court believes that stare decisis weighs more heavily when it construes statutes than when it reads the Constitution.[107] This is based on the view that, save for rare amendments to the Constitution, only the Court can change how the Constitution is applied, but Congress can rewrite statutes if the Court has misunderstood statutory text. Congress's knowing inaction then amounts to a type of silent ratification of the Court's interpretation of a particular statute.

That analysis dramatically overstates the ease with which Congress can overturn the Court's statutory interpretations. This isn't about the normal difficulties of getting legislation enacted in the United States—though those hurdles are genuine—but much more about the Court's power to select positions strategically and know that they won't be overturned. Take a simple example. Assume the

---

[106] Compare Jacob E. Gersen and Adrian Vermeule, *Chevron as a Voting Rule*, 116 Yale L J 676 (2007).

[107] In antitrust, see, e.g., *Illinois Brick Co. v Illinois*, 431 US 720, 736 (1977) ("[W]e must bear in mind that considerations of *stare decisis* weigh heavily in the area of statutory construction, where Congress is free to change this Court's interpretation of its legislation").

relevant statute bears two natural interpretations. If the Court chooses one and both the House and the Senate disagree with the Court's choice, we should expect Congress to rewrite the statute. In contrast, if the Court chooses the interpretation favored by both chambers, Congress leaves the statute alone. This seems to be the framework that animates the Court's views on the importance of stare decisis in cases dealing with statutes.

But consider two other possibilities. The Senate and the House have different preferences over the two natural readings of the statute. The Court will choose one or the other, and *whichever* one the Court chooses, we will not see legislation overturning that choice. If the Court chooses the interpretation favored by the Senate, the Senate will block legislation overturning that choice, and both the Senate and the House must approve new legislation for it to go forward. Alternatively, if the Court chose the House's favored interpretation, the House will block new legislation.

In this simple situation—a statute with two natural readings—we have four possibilities. We will see responsive legislation in only one case—when the Court gets it "wrong" and the Senate and the House both disagree with that choice—but in the other three cases, we won't see new legislation. In only one of those situations should the Court infer acquiescence in the Court's read of the statute; in the other two cases, the two chambers don't agree and therefore can't agree to overturn the Court's interpretation. Note also that an especially strategic Congress wanting to send information to the Court might choose to pass confirmatory legislation in the case in which the Congress agrees with the Court's reading of the statute. Given the presumed agreement between the houses, it should be relatively costless to pass the confirming statute. The point of that legislation isn't to change the meaning of the text but to make clear that when the Court interprets statutory text and nothing issues from Congress, Congress disagrees internally over the meaning of the text. Guaranteed action in both cases in which Congress agrees internally would convey information to the Court about the existence of internal disagreement in Congress over the meaning of the relevant text in cases in which Congress *doesn't* act.

Play this out briefly one more time. Imagine a text with three readings, where the House's preferences are $1 > 2 > 3$ and the Senate's are just the opposite, $3 > 2 > 1$. We shouldn't expect Congress to overturn *any* decision of the Court choosing *any* of the readings. If the Court chooses 1, the House is happy and will block new legislation. Ditto for the Senate if the Court chooses 3. And 2 probably represents the compromise position that would be reached by Congress were it required to act. A decision by the Court followed by congressional inaction would tell us nothing about congressional acquiesce in the Court's reading. The Court's approach to stare decisis for statutes and its power to draw inferences from congressional inaction and silence has ignored the way that the Court's prior interpretation of a statute determines the default position in the next round of legislative gamesmanship. As these examples suggest, the default position established by the Court matters enormously for the subsequent legislative path.

What does this mean for the Court's special rules of stare decisis for statutes, taking seriously, of course, that those rules actually exist meaningfully? The Court should kill them off. Return to the simple four-possibility situation. If the Court chooses the wrong interpretation and Congress overturns it, very little harm is done. If the Court reaches the result desired by both houses of Congress, we probably won't see legislation, absent the sort of exquisite legislative signaling that I describe above. But in that case, the Court has adopted the interpretation favored by the current Congress. And, to head toward stare decisis, if the Court flipped its position, in these cases, Congress would respond. The agreed Congress would overturn the contrary interpretation by the Court.

But if the Court chooses an interpretation and Congress is disabled from acting, what should the Court do in reconsidering the issue? For constitutional issues, Congress is disabled from acting by institutional design, as we have assigned the role of constitutional interpreter to the Court. In our two remaining cases, Congress is disabled from acting not by design but because of internal disagreement. By definition, that internal disagreement is just the opposite of acquiescence in the Court's view. One chamber favors one interpretation, the other the second, and that will be true regardless of which interpretation the Court chooses. Under those circumstances, the Court should give no special weight to that disagreement in figuring out whether to reconsider its prior ruling but instead should rely on whatever general framework the Court brings to stare decisis.

What does that mean for *Leegin*? In my view, the Court majority appropriately gave very little weight to Congress's changes to Section 1. Recall that Section 1 expanded in 1937 with the Miller-Tydings fair trade delegation to the states and then contracted in 1975 when Congress reclaimed federal authority under Section 1. But the Court didn't take that to somehow limit its ability to continue to evolve Section 1 antitrust doctrine, and it understood itself to have full authority to overturn *Dr. Miles*. That isn't to say that the Court was right to overturn *Dr. Miles*, as all I have done above is to sketch some general ways to frame stare decisis and I haven't offered a full theory of it, but it is to say that the fact that *Dr. Miles* interprets a statute shouldn't be given real weight in the stare decisis analysis.

V. Conclusion

So there were four antitrust decisions of note in the 2006 Term. *Weyerhaeuser* is a small, modest decision. The Court isn't likely to see another predatory bidding case soon, and the Court chose to minimize doctrinal complexity by bringing predatory bidding analysis in sync with the Court's prior treatment of predatory pricing in *Brooke Group*. *Credit Suisse* too is minimally incremental. In concluding that federal securities law "implicitly" precluded claims asserting antitrust violations in the sale of new securities, the Court followed its prior decision in *Gordon* as well as the Court's more recent preference for regulatory schemes over antitrust as seen in *Trinko*. Pushing antitrust authority toward specialized regulators like the Securities and Exchange Commission broadens the trade-offs that can be made between antitrust concerns and other values and almost certainly expands the circumstances under which industry actors can act collectively. That matters, so *Credit Suisse* covers more of the economic landscape than *Weyerhaeuser*, but the decision itself is a small step from prior doctrine.

Twombly and *Leegin* are each, in their own ways, blockbusters. *Twombly* will appear in case after case, as antitrust defendants try to rely on its new tougher rules for FRCP 12(b)(6) motions. *Twombly* represents a preference for blunt instruments over sharp edges. The central problem confronted by *Twombly* is discovery run amok. The Court has the tools in its hands to control that by rewriting the discovery rules and overturning lower court decisions implementing those rules. *Twombly* suggests that the Court believes that refinement of those rules will fail in controlling discovery, and it is willing to pay the price that private plaintiffs will have no good way to get at the best-hidden antitrust conspiracies.

Finally, *Leegin* brings to a close—for now or forever?—the 100-year saga of contractual minimum resale price maintenance. Since its decision in 1911 in *Dr. Miles*, the Court has confronted this issue again and again in the slightly refined versions that make up the art of institutional design. Over time, the Court has chipped away at *Dr. Miles*, first in not finding a violation of Section 1 of the Sherman Act for the unilateral minimum RPM in *Colgate* in 1919 and in then broadly subjecting nonprice vertical restraints to rule-of-reason treatment in *Sylvania* in 1977. Given that, on what basis would *Dr. Miles* survive?

That is a question of stare decisis and *Leegin* ends up in an all-out fight over stare decisis in antitrust. That is new: the Court has been overturning old decisions in antitrust for some time and has done so with little stare decisis fanfare. That suggests that the dispute over stare decisis in *Leegin* is just a convenient forum for the larger dispute over stare decisis that is percolating through a divided Court. I don't have a full-blown theory of stare decisis, but I do suggest why the Court has been mistaken to treat stare decisis in statutory cases differently from that in constitutional cases. The Court has made too little of one of its critical tools in shaping statutes, namely, the power to set a default point for subsequent congressional action. Once we treat the Court's decisions as inputs in subsequent lawmaking, there is greater reason to think that the Court should have a uniform approach to stare decisis across the Constitution and statutes.

FREDERICK SCHAUER

ABANDONING THE GUIDANCE
FUNCTION: MORSE v FREDERICK

In its 2006 Term the Supreme Court decided a mere seventy-three
cases with full opinions.[1] This total, a slight increase over the 2005
Term's sixty-nine,[2] is roughly the same as it has been for much of
the last decade. But when we look just slightly further back in time,
we see that the situation was previously quite different. In its 1985
Term, for example, the Court decided 159 cases after hearing and
with full opinions,[3] and for most of the 1970s and 1980s its level
of opinion production was similarly in the range of 140 to 160 cases
a year.

One of the remarkable features of the Supreme Court's declining
workload is that during the period when the Court's own decisional
output has dropped to less than half of what it had been in the not-
so-distant past, the caseloads of the state and lower federal courts
have been increasing substantially. In 1986–87, a year in which the
Supreme Court decided 152 cases with full opinions,[4] there were

Frederick Schauer is Frank Stanton Professor of the First Amendment at the John F.
Kennedy School of Government, Harvard University, and George Eastman Visiting Professor
(2007–2008) and Fellow of Balliol College, Oxford University.

AUTHOR'S NOTE: Research support was provided by the Harvard Law School.

[1] *The Supreme Court, 2006 Term—The Statistics*, 121 Harv L Rev 436, 436 (2007).

[2] *The Supreme Court, 2005 Term—The Statistics*, 120 Harv L Rev 372, 372 (2005).

[3] *The Supreme Court, 1985 Term—The Statistics*, 100 Harv L Rev 304 (1986).

[4] *The Supreme Court, 1986 Term—The Statistics*, 101 Harv L Rev 362 (1987).

35,176 appeals filed in the twelve federal courts of appeals.[5] But over the ensuing two decades, while the Court's output declined from 152 to seventy-three cases decided after oral argument and with full opinions, the work of the Courts of Appeals had roughly doubled, the total for the year ending September 30, 2006, being 66,618.[6] In 1986, therefore, the Supreme Court was issuing one full-opinion decision for every 221 (federal) appeals filed, and in 2006–07 the ratio had changed to one full-opinion decision for every 922 appeals filed. And although these ratios are only for the federal courts, the situation is much the same in the state courts, where caseloads are burgeoning at rates roughly equivalent to those in the federal system.[7]

An especially noteworthy dimension of these statistics is the way in which they support the inference that the need for Supreme Court guidance of lower courts has increased substantially over the past several decades. Although one of the principal functions of the Court has always been to tell the lower courts what the law is, and thus to guide the decisions of lower courts,[8] these guidance obligations are much greater now than they have been in even the recent past. For while the Court is issuing significantly fewer opinions, the lower courts are being called upon to decide substantially more cases. Consequently, and in light of these changes, we might suppose that the Supreme Court would now be increasingly attuned to providing guidance to the lower courts about what the law is.

---

[5] *Annual Report of the Director of the Administrative Office of the United States Courts* 1–2 (1987). See also Richard A. Posner, *Coping with the Caseload: A Comment on Magistrates and Masters*, 137 U Pa L Rev 2215, 2215 n 2 (1989).

[6] *Annual Report of the Director of the Administrative Office of the United States Courts* 1–2 (2006).

[7] See National Center for State Courts, *State Court Caseload Statistics 2006* (2006); National Center for State Courts, *Examining the Work of the State Courts* (2006); American Judicature Society, *Underfunding and Workload*, available at http://www.ajs.org/cji/cji_workload.asp (2007).

[8] On the Court's guidance function, see Ashutosh Bhagwat, *Separate But Equal? The Supreme Court, the Lower Federal Courts, and the Nature of the "Judicial Power,"* 80 BU L Rev 967 (2000); Frank H. Easterbrook, *Ways of Criticizing the Court*, 95 Harv L Rev 802, 807–11 (1982); Lisa A. Kloppenberg, *Measured Constitutional Steps*, 71 Ind L J 297 (1996); Frederick Schauer, *Opinions as Rules*, 62 U Chi L Rev 1455 (1995); Frederick Schauer, *Refining the Lawmaking Function of the Supreme Court*, 17 U Mich J L Ref 1 (1983); Cass R. Sunstein, *Problems with Minimalism*, 58 Stan L Rev 1899 (2006). Indeed, the concern I express in this article was expressed even when the Court's output was more than double its current level. Peter L. Strauss, *One Hundred Fifty Cases Per Year: Implications of the Supreme Court's Limited Resources for Judicial Review of Agency Action*, 87 Colum L Rev 1093 (1987).

Yet just the opposite seems to be occurring. Although the Court's guidance obligations have been increasing, its willingness to take on these obligations has been heading in the opposite direction. Not only does there appear to have been an increase over the past several decades in the number of decisions in which there is no simple majority opinion, but even when there is an opinion of the Court, there is a growing tendency on the part of the Court to avoid issuing a clear, general, and subsequently usable statement of the Court's reasoning or the Court's view of the implications of its decision. Gone are the days of *Miranda v Arizona*,[9] for example, when the Court could announce in unqualified terms not only what the rule of law now was, but also exactly what frontline agents such as police officers needed to do in order to comply with it.[10] Instead, we have seen an increase in narrow and fact-specific rulings, rulings that may in theory produce the right outcome for the particular case before the Court, but which in practice gain little if anything in accuracy but nevertheless entail the cost of providing virtually no assistance for lower courts expected to make their decisions in light of what the Supreme Court has said, and for officials and citizens desiring to know what the law is as they plan their actions.

The Court's seeming abdication of the guidance function is not without supporters. Advocates of judicial minimalism—of deciding "one case at a time"[11]—are the unwitting or witting endorsers of

---

[9] 384 US 436 (1966).

[10] Thus, it is worth underscoring that a police officer who reads a boilerplate *Miranda* warning from a printed card is in effect reading from a Supreme Court opinion, not only a useful practice for litigation- or liability-avoidance, but also a strong, even if oblique, statement about the obligations of other officials to follow the guidance of the Court. That officials of other branches (and police officers and teachers are just as much officers of nonjudicial branches of government as are presidents and members of Congress) should follow the Supreme Court is an unfashionable position these days, see, e.g., Larry D. Kramer, *The People Themselves: Popular Constitutionalism and Judicial Review* (Oxford, 2004); Robert C. Post, *Foreword: Fashioning the Legal Constitution: Culture, Courts, and the Law*, 117 Harv L Rev 4 (2003); Michael Stokes Paulsen, *The Most Dangerous Branch: Executive Power to Say What the Law Is*, 83 Georgetown L J 217 (1994), but some of us still adhere to the view that the country works better in the long run when other officials take Supreme Court opinions as binding upon them. See Larry Alexander and Frederick Schauer, *On Extrajudicial Constitutional Interpretation*, 110 Harv L Rev 1359 (1997); Larry Alexander and Lawrence B. Solum, *Popular? Constitutionalism?* 118 Harv L Rev 1594 (2005) (book review).

[11] See Cass R. Sunstein, *One Case at a Time: Judicial Minimalism on the Supreme Court* (Harvard, 1999). See also Michael C. Dorf, *The Supreme Court, 1997 Term—Foreword: The Limits of Socratic Deliberation*, 112 Harv L Rev 4, 60–69 (1998); Richard H. Fallon, Jr., *The Supreme Court, 1996 Term—Foreword: Implementing the Constitution*, 111 Harv L Rev 54, 141–52 (1997); Abner J. Mikva, *Why Judges Should Not Be Advicegivers: A Response to Professor Neal Katyal*, 50 Stan L Rev 1825 (1998); Jonathan T. Molot, *Principled Minimalism:*

nonguidance, for implicit in the very idea of guidance is that the Court will decide not only the case before it, but also at the same time indicate the proper outcome for other cases that vary to a lesser or greater extent from the case the Court actually decided. Guidance and minimalism are thus opposing virtues, if virtues they be, and the Court's increasing abandonment of its guidance obligations might be seen as simply the cost of its increasing minimalism. In acting minimally at the same time that its guidance obligations seem to be increasing, however, the Court may well be imposing on lower courts and on law-constrained officials costs well beyond what many of the proponents of minimalism have imagined, and perhaps the time has come to question the extent to which a Court that decides so few cases can treat its guidance function so casually.

Many of the Court's recent decisions exemplify this disturbing trend, but *Morse v Frederick*,[12] the Court's most recent case involving the free speech rights of students in the primary and secondary schools, is among the most dramatic. In the thirty-eight years since *Tinker v Des Moines Independent Community School District*,[13] there have been only three Supreme Court cases dealing directly with the issue of student speech, of which *Morse* is the third.[14] Yet during this same period there has been immensely more litigation in the lower courts on this subject than on most of the seemingly more familiar items in the free speech canon. As I will document below, cases involving speech in the schools are overwhelmingly more common in the state and federal inferior courts than are cases dealing with obscenity, indecency, incitement to or advocacy of unlawful activity, defamation, commercial advertising, campaign finance, and any of a host of other First Amendment subjects dominating the

---

Restriking the Balance Between Judicial Minimalism and Neutral Principles, 90 Va L Rev 1753 (2004); Cass R. Sunstein, *Second-Order Perfectionism*, 75 Ford L Rev 2867 (2007); Cass R. Sunstein, *The Supreme Court, 1995 Term—Foreword: Leaving Things Undecided*, 110 Harv L Rev 4 (1996); Ernest A. Young, *Judicial Activism and Conservative Politics*, 73 U Colo L Rev 1139 (2002). For critiques, largely on grounds other than what I discuss here, see, e.g., James E. Fleming, *The Incredible Shrinking Constitutional Theory: From the Partial Constitution to the Minimal Constitution*, 75 Fordham L Rev 2885 (2007); Jeffrey Rosen, *Foreword*, 97 Mich L Rev 1323 (1999); Christopher J. Peters, *Assessing the New Judicial Minimalism*, 100 Colum L Rev 1454 (2000).

[12] 127 S Ct 2718 (2007).

[13] 393 US 503 (1969).

[14] The other two, which will be discussed at length below, are *Hazelwood School District v Kuhlmeier*, 484 US 260 (1988), and *Bethel School District No. 403 v Fraser*, 478 US 675 (1986).

casebooks.[15] Unlike decisions on what are essentially nonrepeatable events—*Bush v Gore*[16] obviously comes to mind, and with respect to the First Amendment the *Pentagon Papers* case[17] might be another example—one might suppose that the frequency with which issues involving speech in the schools arise in the lower courts and in the daily practices of school teachers and administrators would suggest to the Court that this is an area in which there is a particular need to give assistance to the courts below, as well as to provide guidance for school administrators, teachers, and students.[18] Yet precisely the opposite has been the case. Not only have there been only four Supreme Court decisions in four decades,[19] but the ones there have been seem surprisingly unconcerned with the guidance function at all. *Morse v Frederick* is not only the most recent of these, but, for reasons I shall explain, it is the most extreme. Faced with an opportunity to say something helpful to and for those in the trenches, the Court not only selected a highly unrepresentative case for its first foray into the area in nineteen years, but it also decided the

---

[15] Much the same could be said about the speech of public employees, where the typically scanty treatment in the casebooks paints a false picture of the extent to which litigation about the topic proliferates in the lower courts.

[16] 531 US 98 (2000).

[17] *New York Times Co. v United States*, 403 US 713 (1971) (per curiam).

[18] Thus, the importance of the guidance function varies directly with the presence of two distinct factors. One is the frequency with which the issue arises. *Bush v Gore* and the *Pentagon Papers Case* are prime examples of infrequency, and the consequent lesser importance of the guidance function, while criminal procedure issues, especially regarding police practices, are excellent examples of frequency, and thus of the value of guidance from above. Issues involving the First Amendment in the schools may be less frequent than issues of constitutional criminal procedure, but are far more frequent than essentially unique events such as those that gave rise to *Bush v Gore*. Second, the importance of guidance also varies with the identity of the actor making the initial decision. Where the issues are ones in which the initial decisions are typically made by courts or institutions with access to careful guidance by counsel—reapportionment is a good example, and perhaps also questions about the constitutionality of state laws that arguably place a burden on interstate commerce—the importance of the guidance function will be less. But when the initial decisions are made by frontline nonlawyer actors with little access to on-the-spot legal advice—police officers stopping suspects, conducting searches, or engaged in interrogation, for example—the importance of clear guidance, even if mediated by lawyer-produced instruction manuals, seems much greater. Because issues involving speech in the schools are frequent, and because the initial decision is one usually made by a teacher or principal immediately after the precipitating event, these cases appear, with respect to the guidance function, to resemble police practice cases far more than reapportionment, Dormant Commerce Clause, presidential election, or national security newspaper injunction cases.

[19] In reality it is more than four decades. Although the modern free speech era opened in 1919 with *Schenck v United States*, 249 US 47 (1919), and although there were substantial numbers of Supreme Court free speech cases in the 1930s, 1940s, 1950s, and 1960s, *Tinker* in 1969 was the Court's first ever case involving free speech in the public schools.

case on narrow grounds, and in doing so focused on those dimensions of the case least likely to be found in the conflicts that bedevil school administrators and lower courts on almost a daily basis. I will leave to others to debate the wisdom or folly of the actual outcome in *Frederick*, but more broadly consequential is the case's abandonment of the guidance function, a function whose importance is growing dramatically, as the statistics show, just as the Court's attention to it appears to be shrinking.

I. Morse v Frederick

Like most other high school speech cases, *Morse v Frederick* commenced with teenagers acting like, well, teenagers. In 2002, the Winter Olympic Games were held in Salt Lake City, Utah. As is the case every four years, the Olympic torch was carried from the site of the previous games—Nagano, Japan, in 1998—to the current site by a succession of runners, and on January 24, 2002, the Olympic Torch Relay passed through Juneau, Alaska, where Joseph Frederick was then a senior at Juneau-Douglas High School.

Because the school officials deemed the Olympic Torch Relay an important civic event, students were allowed, as a school-sponsored class excursion,[20] to leave the school and join the crowd of spectators watching the torch pass by. As is typical at such events, everything was a bit behind schedule, and so the students were required to wait some time before the torch and accompanying camera crews actually arrived. And as is also typical, the students as a result of the delay became "rambunctious, throwing plastic cola bottles and snowballs and scuffling with their classmates."[21] Finally the torchbearers arrived, with camera crews trailing, and at that time Joseph Frederick and a group of his friends unfurled a fourteen-foot banner,

---

[20] The Court describes the event as "an approved social event or class trip," 127 S Ct at 2622, but in fact the torchbearers were running along a street directly in front of the school. Frederick had argued that this was not an in-school speech case at all, but the Court spent little time dismissing the argument, noting not only that Frederick's presence outside the school as the torchbearers passed by was part of an official school event, but also that teachers and administrators were present along with many students, and that both the high school band and cheerleaders had performed. 127 S Ct at 2624. In the Court's eyes, and probably correctly, this event partook far more of an "away" sporting event than of students engaged in their own independent activities outside the school. And the location of the event in close proximity to the school itself reinforces the view that treating this event as wholly or largely unrelated to school activities, as Frederick claimed, was at best tenuous.

[21] 127 S Ct at 2622. Chief Justice Roberts noted, in what was likely an amusing understatement, that "[n]ot all the students waited patiently." Id.

visible from the school itself, bearing the words "BONG HiTS 4 JESUS."

As soon as the banner appeared, Deborah Morse, the school principal, approached the group and demanded that they take the banner down. All except Joseph Frederick complied, at which time Morse confiscated the banner and told Frederick to report to her office. He did so, and Principal Morse proceeded to suspend him from school for ten days, subsequently asserting that she did so because of the way in which the banner encouraged illegal drug use in violation of a preexisting written school policy. Frederick appealed his suspension to the Juneau School District Superintendent, who described the banner's message as "a fairly silly message promoting illegal drug usage in the middle of a school activity," but nevertheless reduced the suspension to the eight days that Frederick had by that time served.[22] Upon further administrative appeal, the Juneau School District Board of Education upheld the suspension, and Frederick then brought suit in the U.S. District Court for the District of Alaska, alleging a denial of his First Amendment rights and seeking injunctive relief against the Board of Education and monetary damages against Morse and various other school officials.

Frederick's suit was dismissed by the District Court, which agreed with the Superintendent and the School District Board of Education that suspending a student for advocating drug use during a school activity was allowable under the First Amendment, especially in light of the Supreme Court's 1986 decision in *Bethel School District No. 403 v Fraser*.[23] The Ninth Circuit reversed, however, relying in significant part on *Tinker*, and concluding that only a "risk of substantial disruption," a risk it found not present here, could justify restricting what would otherwise be Frederick's constitutionally protected speech. Moreover, the Ninth Circuit found that both the law and the violation of it by Morse were sufficiently clear to support the conclusion that Morse was not entitled even to qualified immunity. The Ninth Circuit, consequently, reinstated Frederick's Section 1983 damages action against Morse, and it was in that posture that the case arrived at the Supreme Court.

The Supreme Court reversed the Ninth Circuit, with Chief Justice Roberts writing for a majority comprised of himself and Justices

---

[22] Id at 2623.

[23] 478 US 675 (1986).

Scalia, Kennedy, Thomas, and Alito. The Chief Justice agreed with
the school authorities that Frederick's actions had taken place during a school activity, and agreed as well that the message, although
perhaps "cryptic" to some, was reasonably interpreted as encouraging the use of illegal drugs, in particular, marijuana.[24] And for the
majority this was sufficient. The Court explicitly rejected the applicability in this context of the "substantial disruption" standard
set forth *Tinker*, concluding that the school's legitimate interest in
prohibiting advocacy of the use of illegal drugs allowed it to restrict
that advocacy regardless of whether there had been (or was likely
to be) substantial disruption or not. Moreover, the majority concluded, the nature of the school context and the more or less compelling interest[25] in dealing with the problem of juvenile drug use
warranted relaxation in the school context of what would otherwise
be the extraordinarily high standards for restricting the advocacy
of unlawful conduct.[26] Frederick's statement, for the majority, was
just the kind of statement that school officials had a constitutionally
legitimate interest in controlling without regard to an empirical
assessment of its likely consequences. Needless to say, the Court
included in its opinion what is by now the ritual incantation in every
case involving public schools and the First Amendment: *Tinker*'s
statement that "[i]t can hardly be argued that either students or
teachers shed their constitutional rights to freedom of speech or

---

[24] The Chief Justice, perhaps unwilling to rely on his own interpretation of a message
expressed in language that may have been unfamiliar to him, made reference to *Guiles v
Marineau*, 461 F3d 320, 328 (2d Cir 2006), a case in which the Second Circuit had
commented upon the lower court decision in *Morse v Frederick* itself, agreeing that Frederick's sign was "a clearly pro-drug banner." 127 S Ct at 2625. But the Chief Justice also
rejected the view that the banner conveyed a political or religious message, concluding
that "this is plainly not a case about political debate over the criminalization of drug use
or possession." Id. Yet although "[n]ot even Frederick argue[d] that the banner conveys
any sort of political message," id, it is hard to see why Frederick's juvenile sympathy with
marijuana use is any less political than, for example, Paul Robert Cohen's juvenile criticism
of the Selective Service System in *Cohen v California*, 403 US 15 (1971), *Hustler* magazine's
juvenile criticism of Rev. Jerry Falwell in *Hustler Magazine v Falwell*, 485 US 46 (1988),
or Valarie Goguen's juvenile use of the American flag as a political fashion statement in
Smith v Goguen, 415 US 566 (1974).

[25] The ambiguous language in the text is intentional. Quoting *Veronia School District 477
v Acton*, 515 US 646, 661 (1995), the Court in *Frederick* described the interest in deterring
drug use by schoolchildren as an "'important—indeed, perhaps compelling' interest." 127
S Ct at 2628.

[26] The Chief Justice did not refer to *Brandenburg v Ohio*, 395 US 399 (1969) (per curiam),
or *Hess v Indiana*, 414 US 105 (1973), by name, but he did explicitly accept and quote
the acknowledgment in Justice Stevens's dissent (127 S Ct at 1643, 2645) that "our rigid
imminence requirement ought to be relaxed at schools." 127 S Ct at 2629.

expression at the schoolhouse gate."[27] But having offered the oblig-
atory recognition that students have at least *some* free speech rights
in the public schools, the majority then concluded that Frederick
and other public school students did in fact shed at the schoolhouse
gate what would outside of the school context be their largely uncontroversial right to advocate the use of illegal drugs.

At no point in the Court's opinion did Chief Justice Roberts
suggest that the advocacy of illegal drugs was per se a substantially
disruptive act, or was likely to cause disruption. The advocacy of
illegal drug use in the public schools thus emerges not as an application of *Tinker*'s substantial disruption requirement, but rather
as an exception to it. And for the Chief Justice and the majority,
the exception was based not on any special characteristics of advocating illegal conduct in general in the schools, but only on the
even more special characteristics of the advocacy of illegal drug use.
Here the majority offered an extended empirical policy discussion
of the way in which teenage drug use was a major national problem,
and the emphasis the majority placed on the size and gravity of the
school drug problem strongly suggests that for the majority it was
drug use and perhaps drug use alone whose advocacy may constitutionally be restricted in the public schools without satisfying either
Brandenburg's stringent standard in general for the restriction of
advocacy, or the *Hess* gloss in particular on just how imminent
imminence need be in order to justify restriction. Indeed, this drug-
specific interpretation of *Frederick* becomes even clearer when we
look at Justice Alito's concurring opinion, joined by Justice Kennedy, which emphasized more explicitly than had the majority that
it was the particular dimension of drug use that for Justices Alito
and Kennedy was dispositive.[28] To Justice Alito, the outcome in

---

[27] *Tinker*, 393 US at 506, quoted in abbreviated form in *Frederick*, 127 S Ct at 2627. It
is interesting to speculate as to the extent to which *Tinker*'s lingering importance is a
function of its having included a pithy and eminently quotable phrase. If we engage in
the thought experiment of holding constant all of the features of an array of cases except
the presence of a statement (or slogan) with such quote-worthy characteristics (or its
equivalent, such as the "fire in a crowded theater" phrase from *Schenck v United States*,
249 US 47 (1919), or Justice Powell's observation in *Gertz v Robert Welch*, 418 US 323,
339 (1974), that "[u]nder the First Amendment there is no such thing as a false idea"), it
is plausible to hypothesize that quotability bears a causal relation both to subsequent
citation and to actual influence on subsequent case outcomes. Cf. Richard A. Posner,
Cardozo: A Study in Reputation (Chicago, 1990) (arguing that literary flair bears a relationship to a judge's reputation and subsequent influence).

[28] Justice Alito also limited his support for the outcome to cases, such as this one (to
him), in which the speech could not "plausibly be interpreted as commenting on any

Frederick was justified by the fact that "illegal drug use presents a grave and in many ways *unique* threat to the physical safety of students."[29] Thus, for Justice Alito the majority opinion "does not endorse any further extension"[30] beyond those to be found in the existing cases—*Fraser, Hazelwood School District v Kuhlmeier,*[31] and now *Frederick*—from the basic principle set forth in *Tinker*.

Justice Thomas, writing only for himself, also concurred, arguing that the First Amendment was simply inapplicable to student speech in the public schools.[32] Lamenting that *Tinker* had gotten the entire enterprise of judicial scrutiny of school discipline decisions started in the first place, Justice Thomas would simply have allowed school discipline based on the content of a student's speech to be free of First Amendment constraint so long as the speech took place at the school or at school-sponsored events. In reaching this conclusion, Justice Thomas relied heavily on the history of public schooling in the United States, a history that included the principle of *in loco parentis*, and a history that Justice Thomas interpreted as traditionally, and prior to *Tinker*, allowing to teachers and school administrators the unrestricted ability to enforce discipline, obedience, and etiquette in the schools. "In short, in the earliest public schools, teachers taught, and students listened. Teachers commanded, and students obeyed. Teachers did not rely solely on the power of ideas to persuade; they relied on discipline to maintain order."[33] For Justice Thomas, the lesson of "the history of American public education" was that "it cannot seriously be suggested that the First Amendment 'freedom of speech' encompasses a student's right to speak in public schools."[34]

The dissents were of two strikingly different varieties. Justice

---

political or social issue, including speech on issues such as 'the wisdom of the war on drugs or of legalizing marijuana for medical use.'" 127 S Ct at 2636 (Alito, concurring, and quoting from Justice Stevens's dissent). But it remains to be seen whether Justice Alito will apply this rarified (and rare) standard of political commentary to the full range of free speech issues. See note 24.

[29] 127 S Ct at 2638 (Alito, J, concurring) (emphasis added).

[30] Id.

[31] 484 US 260 (1988).

[32] 127 S Ct at 2629 (Thomas, J, concurring).

[33] Id at 2631 (Thomas, J, concurring). Obviously schools vary, but I suspect I am not the only pre-*Tinker* public school student for whom Justice Thomas's description appears to paint a picture of student discipline that is, shall we say, not entirely recognizable.

[34] Id at 2635 (Thomas, J, concurring).

Breyer would not have reached the First Amendment issue at all.[35] Deeming the case capable of decision solely on the basis of the potential Section 1983 damages claim against Morse that the Ninth Circuit had explicitly reinstated, Justice Breyer would have found her clothed in qualified immunity, and on these facts not liable for damages at all. "This Court need not and should not decide this difficult First Amendment issue on the merits. Rather, I believe that it should simply hold that qualified immunity bars the student's claim for monetary damages and say no more."[36] Justice Stevens, however, joined by Justices Souter and Ginsburg, dissented on the merits. The dissenters were "willing to assume" that advocacy of illegal drug use might be restricted in the public schools without having to satisfy the *Tinker* "substantial disruption" standard, but they disagreed with the majority's conclusion that Frederick's actions amounted to the advocacy of illegal drug use. For the dissenters, Frederick's propositionally "ambiguous" stunt could not reasonably be interpreted as advocating anything.[37] And even if

[35] 127 S Ct at 2638 (Breyer, J, concurring in the judgment in part and dissenting in part).

[36] Id. All of the Justices agreed with Justice Breyer's conclusion that damages were an inappropriate remedy in this case. See 127 S Ct at 2643 (Stevens, J, dissenting). Consistent with my theme in this article, the unanimity on this point is likely a consequence of the fact that not even the Justices who dissented on the merits were comfortable with the conclusion that there was clear law on the issue which Principal Morse could be deemed to have violated.

[37] Justice Stevens's interpretation of Frederick's banner seems implausible except under an especially narrow and plainly First Amendment-soaked definition of the word "advocacy," a conclusion reinforced by Justice Stevens's view that restriction is permissible only if the speech "expressly advocates conduct that is illegal and harmful to students." 127 S Ct at 2644 (Stevens, J, dissenting). Frederick may not have expressly advocated or incited drug use, but it seems plain that he endorsed it, celebrated it, sympathized with it, and trivialized the seriousness of it. None of these is advocacy as such, but all seem just the kind of behavior that troubled the school, and that troubled the majority. Moreover, the existence of a culture of celebration, sympathy, and endorsement, coupled with a culture that minimized the seriousness or harm of the act, is likely at least as causal of increased drug use as explicit advocacy. Putting aside the question whether marijuana use among high school students is or should be treated as a problem, it seems likely that the widespread existence of messages like Frederick's would be as causal of increased marijuana use as widespread movie images of cigarette smoking by dashing actors and alluring actresses would be of increased cigarette smoking and as widespread television portrayals of African-Americans as lazy and shiftless would be of racial discrimination against them. Thus, there are two disagreements between the majority and the dissenters on the merits. One is the disagreement about whether Frederick's banner advocated anything, or instead was just attention-grabbing nonsense. And on this the dissent's view that it was *only* the latter seems implausible. The other disagreement, however, is not about the facts but about the law, and this is a disagreement about how much of *Brandenburg* enters through the schoolhouse gates. In saying something pretty close to "none," the majority is plainly in disagreement with the dissent in this legal point, because the dissent appears to be saying "some."

Frederick's behavior could be understood as advocacy, the dissent argued, the advocacy was the kind of nondisruptive political statement that to them fell well within the scope of the original *Tinker* principles.[38]

II. THE STATE OF THE LAW

Although some critics assailed the Court for ignoring precedent in rejecting Frederick's First Amendment claim,[39] it is difficult to resist the conclusion that the majority largely built on and extended a moderately long-standing trend. The Court in *Tinker* did uphold the First Amendment rights to students who wore black armbands to school to protest the Vietnam War, but the Court has never in the ensuing thirty-nine years held that students retain very many free speech rights once they pass through the schoolhouse gates.[40] In *Bethel School District No. 403 v Fraser*,[41] the Court permitted disciplining a high school student who had made a sexually suggestive speech as part of a student government campaign, relying not on the *Tinker* standard that allowed such discipline when there is an actual risk of substantial disruption, but on its belief that a school could permissibly restrict sexually offensive or indecent speech[42] without regard to the presence of actual or likely disrup-

---

[38] Justice Stevens wheels out the hoary claim, common in vast numbers of free speech controversies in court and in public discourse, that officials often restrict messages simply because they "disagree" with them. 127 S Ct at 2644, 2645 (Stevens, J, dissenting). As here, however, officials rarely if ever restrict messages because they disagree with them independent of consequences. Rather, officials object to messages because they fear the consequences of those messages, whether those consequences be causing psychic pain, or increasing the likelihood of illegal acts, or fomenting overthrow of the government, or, as in the case of nineteenth-century obscenity regulation, of leading teenage boys to masturbate. Officials often exaggerate the harm or the likelihood of those consequences, and that is one of the underlying justifications for the First Amendment itself, but the claim that officials often restrict messages because of some kind of mysterious consequence-independent disagreement seems far more of a slogan than reality.

[39] See Hans Bader, *Campaign Finance and Free Speech: Bong HiTs 4 Jesus: The First Amendment Takes a Hit*, 2006–07 Cato Sup Ct Rev 133, 141–50; Erwin Chemerinsky, *Turning Sharply to the Right*, 10 Green Bag 2d 423, 430 (2007); Ronald Dworkin, *The Supreme Court Phalanx*, New York Review of Books 92 (Sept 27, 2007).

[40] A possible exception is *Board of Education v Pico*, 477 US 853 (1982), arguably recognizing a sliver of free speech protection in the context of public school libraries, but at best only with respect to politically inspired removal of books already selected on nonpolitical grounds by library professionals.

[41] 478 US 675 (1986).

[42] And thus speech understood by the existing doctrine to have less than full First Amendment protection, and accordingly permitting a range of otherwise impermissible content-based noncriminal sanctions. See *FCC v Pacifica Foundation*, 438 US 726 (1978); *Young v American Mini Theatres, Inc.*, 427 US 50 (1976).

tion, whether substantial or not. And in *Hazelwood School District v Kuhlmeier*,[43] the Court upheld school administration control over the content of a student newspaper, relying in part on the Court's belief that the school ought to be able to retain control of the content of an official school publication that would be understood to "bear the imprimatur of the school,"[44] and in part on the way in which managing the content of a newspaper that was a central component of a for-credit journalism course seemed little different to the Court from managing the content of any other classroom exercise.

This is not to say that the *Frederick* court might not have convincingly distinguished *Fraser* and *Kuhlmeier*, had it been so inclined. The former, although couched in terms of indecency and sexual offensiveness, nevertheless fits well within *Tinker*'s substantial disruption rationale in ways that Frederick's antic did not. And *Kuhlmeier*'s focus on the student newspaper as a component of a course and as an official school publication seems quite different from the unsupervised and unofficial context in which Frederick and his friends unfurled their banner. But although a plausible argument could thus be made that *Frederick* resembled *Tinker* more than it did *Fraser* and *Kuhlmeier*, the opposing argument is also plausible. And according to this argument, *Tinker* is somewhat of an orphan case substantially abandoned by its successors. It did uphold the in-school free speech rights of students, and some of *Tinker* undoubtedly remains, but the tone of the subsequent cases, so the argument goes, is decidedly in the other direction. In other words, the argument that *Fraser* and *Kuhlmeier* are exceptions to *Tinker* in a way that *Frederick* is not (or should not be) is at best no stronger than the argument that it is *Tinker* that is the exception and *Fraser* and *Kuhlmeier* the rule. So while arguments of constitutional substance can be made against (and for) the *Frederick* holding, the argument that in some way the Court was especially disrespectful to the demands of stare decisis[45] seems implausible in light of the post-*Tinker*

---

[43] 484 US 260 (1988).

[44] Id at 271.

[45] Which is not to imply that the Court has *ever* been very respectful of the alleged demands of stare decisis, contemporary rhetoric notwithstanding. See Frederick Schauer, *Has Precedent Ever Really Mattered in the Supreme Court?* 25 Ga St L Rev (forthcoming 2008).

cases,[46] and implausible in light of the conclusion that the pre-*Frederick* cases are best understood as being roughly as supportive of the *Frederick* holding as they are of the *Frederick* dissent.

Indeed, the precedential plausibility (which is decidedly *not* the same as substantive correctness) of the *Frederick* outcome is reinforced by the Court's small likelihood of being very much more receptive to the in-school rights of teachers than it is of students. Although the Court in 1979 did uphold the First Amendment rights of a teacher who had been disciplined for the manner of her complaints to a school administrator,[47] and although the Court's even earlier and more important holding in *Pickering v Board of Education*[48] recognized the First Amendment rights of a teacher to speak in a public forum on a matter of public concern, the Court's recent history of resisting the on-the-job free speech claims of public employees generally[49] would make it highly unlikely that teachers will fare any better, at least at the primary and secondary level, than did the students in *Frederick*, *Fraser*, and *Kuhlmeier*.

In addition, the result in *Frederick* is consistent with a long line of cases emphasizing that students do indeed shed quite a few of their Fourth Amendment rights at the schoolhouse gate. Starting with *New Jersey v T.L.O.*[50] in 1985, and continuing since then,[51] the Court has consistently upheld the substantial relaxation in the school context of what would otherwise be the rights of citizens to object to searches without warrants or without sufficient probable cause. Thus, when these search and seizure cases are combined with the earlier student speech cases, what emerges from *Frederick* is best understood as the hardly unexpected outcome of a long-standing

---

[46] It should be acknowledged, however, that the college and university cases exhibit a different pattern. See, e.g., *Papish v Board of Curators of University of Missouri*, 410 US 667 (1973); *Healy v James*, 408 US 169 (1972). It would be a mistake, therefore, to take the college and university cases as indicating very much, if at all, about the student speech cases at the primary and secondary school level.

[47] *Givhan v Western Line Consolidated School District*, 439 US 410 (1979).

[48] 391 US 563 (1968).

[49] See especially *Garcetti v Ceballos*, 126 S Ct 1951 (2006). See also *City of San Diego v Roe*, 543 US 77 (2004); *Waters v Churchill*, 511 US 661 (1994). Thus, the tenor of the more recent public employee speech cases is significantly less speech-protective than that of somewhat earlier cases such as *Rankin v McPherson*, 483 US 378 (1987), and the ambiguous *Connick v Myers*, 461 US 138 (1983). See generally Note, *Public Employee Speech*, 120 Harv L Rev 273 (2006).

[50] 469 US 325 (1985).

[51] See *Board of Education v Earls*, 536 US 822 (2002); *Vernonia School District 47J v Acton*, 515 US 646 (1995). See also *Ingraham v Wright*, 430 US 651 (1977) (corporal punishment).

trend toward treating the schools as a domain in which the individual constitutional rights of students as citizens function as only a minimal constraint on the educational and disciplinary decisions of school teachers and administrators.

III. LOOKING DOWN

My goal here is not to assess whether the Court in *Frederick* reached a correct or an incorrect constitutional decision.[52] Rather, I want to scrutinize *Frederick* not in terms of what it decided, but from the perspective of what it did *not* decide. And what *Frederick* did not decide, tellingly, is what standard school administrators should employ in deciding when to discipline students for verbal acts of in-school misbehavior, or what standard lower courts should use when such discipline is challenged on First Amendment grounds. In short, those who seek guidance from the Supreme Court—whether they be judges, lawyers, teachers, or school administrators—about what the law is are certainly no better off after *Frederick* than before, and indeed they are arguably worse off.

The uncertainty and confusion sown by *Frederick* are especially apparent with respect to *Tinker*'s substantial disruption standard. The *Tinker* structure itself was moderately plain. Students were free under the First Amendment to protest in school and during school hours, but could be restricted if their protest activities were reasonably likely to cause "substantial disruption" to school activities. *Fraser* muddied the waters considerably in concluding that the grounds for restricting a sexually suggestive speech by a student could be the sexual inappropriateness of the speech itself rather than the disruption that was or might be caused by it,[53] and *Kuhl-*

---

[52] It is worth suggesting, however, that the most plausible resolution of the question of student speech may resemble the resolution hinted at in Justice Brennan's opinion in *Board of Education v Pico*, 477 US 853 (1982). There Justice Brennan, in the context of a school library book removal controversy, appeared to conclude that routine book selection and removal choices, even when viewpoint based, are inevitable and thus constitutionally permissible, save for judicial oversight when the motivations for removal are more partisan, more political, and more external to the decisions of primary professionals such as librarians and teachers. Much the same may apply to school disciplinary decisions, which are again commonly and almost inevitably viewpoint based, and which may as a practical matter be beyond realistic judicial scrutiny except in the extreme cases in which the viewpoint-based discipline is overly partisan or is substantially influenced by political forces outside the school. See Frederick Schauer, *Principles, Institutions, and the First Amendment*, 112 Harv L Rev 84 (1998).

[53] Because the Court in *Fraser* talked of "indecency," and made oblique reference to the lesser constitutional protection in general for indecent but not legally obscene speech (cf.

meier added to the uncertainty in holding that the grounds for restricting the content of a student newspaper could again be other than the likelihood of substantial disruption when the content restriction was based on the instructional dimensions of a school activity and on the way in which a newspaper could be taken as a statement of the school itself, or at least as bearing the imprimatur or endorsement of the school. After *Frederick*, the status of the *Tinker* standard is even less certain, for now the advocacy of illegal drug use also need not be likely to produce substantial disruption in order to be subject to restriction. The current state of the law, as best it can currently be divined, is consequently that students retain free speech rights in the public schools unless their speech is of an offensively sexually suggestive nature, or unless their speech is part of a school curricular activity where the content of the speech is part of the activity itself, or unless the speech might reasonably be understood as bearing the imprimatur of the school itself, or unless the speech advocates illegal drug use, or unless the speech is reasonably likely in the reviewable opinion of school administrators to cause substantial disruption in the school. Even though *Tinker*'s "substantial disruption" standard is itself less than precise, and even though there remains uncertainty about the extent to which the likelihood of substantial disruption is a determination for school officials to make or whether instead it is a more or less independently judicially assessable question of constitutional fact,[54] it is now even less clear just when the substantial disruption standard even applies, and to which forms of restriction it is applicable.

That the law is this uncertain is problem enough, but the uncertainty does not end there. Although the Court's opinion hinges on the advocacy of illegal drugs, the implications for other cases are at best murky. The Court in *Frederick* emphasizes the special problem of drug use in the schools and among teenagers, but is the advocacy of illegal acts that are not a special problem for high school

---

FCC v Pacifica Foundation, 438 US 726 (1978); *Young v American Mini Theatres, Inc.*, 427 US 50 (1976)), *Fraser* does not itself support the proposition that schools are allowed to restrict nonsexual forms of offensive speech. But nor does it reject it.

[54] See *Hurley v Irish-American Gay, Lesbian, and Bisexual Group of Boston*, 515 US 557, 567 (1995); *Bose Corp. v Consumers Union of United States, Inc.*, 466 US 485, 499 (1984); *Jacobellis v Ohio*, 378 US 184, 189 (1964). In saying that discipline can be justified if it "can reasonably be understood" to advocate illegal drug use, 127 S Ct at 2624, the Court, again more obliquely than directly, seems to be suggesting that determining the meaning of the student speech is initially and primarily for school officials, but the extent to which that determination remains reviewable by a trial court or on appeal remains frustratingly uncertain.

students—terrorism, for example, or even murder or bank rob-
bery—included within the *Frederick* exception? If a student in school
and during school hours expresses public sympathy with the September 11 bombers, for example, and suggests that it might be a
good idea if American students engaged in similar acts, must discipline for that speech meet the *Brandenburg/Hess* incitement standard, or is a lower standard (of imminence? of explicitness? of likely
consequent actions?) applicable, and, if so, what is it? The *Frederick*
majority, and even Justice Stevens in dissent, suggested, perhaps
uncontroversially, that *Brandenburg* might be inapplicable in the
school setting, but we are not told what that standard for incitement
or advocacy in the schools might be, and to which forms of advocacy
it would be applicable.

It is a plausible reading of the majority opinion in *Frederick* that
advocacy of illegal drug use is sui generis, and that *Frederick* is not
to be understood as dealing with any other form of advocacy of
illegal conduct. And this reading becomes even more plausible in
light of Justice Alito's concurring opinion.[55] But if this is the most
accurate reading of *Frederick*, then advocacy of illegal or disruptive
conduct other than illegal drug use would still have to be shown
to be substantially disruptive or shown to meet the undefined lower-
than-*Brandenburg/Hess* standard in order to be subject to constitutionally permissible disciplinary action. But I suspect that this is
not what Chief Justice Roberts had in mind. Yet even indulging in
the possibly doubtful assumption that the *Frederick* majority would
be unwilling to extend the *Frederick* holding to all advocacy of illegal
conduct, or even to all advocacy of serious or especially dangerous

---

[55] It is conceivable that Justice Alito's opinion, especially because it was joined by Justice
Kennedy, will come to have a status somewhat akin to that of Justice Powell's concurrence
in *Branzburg v Hayes*, 408 US 665 (1972). Although Justice Powell did join the majority
opinion in the 5–4 decision in *Branzburg*, his separate concurrence suggested a degree of
First Amendment–motivated scrutiny for journalists' claims of privilege that cannot be
found in the outright rejection of such privileges in the majority opinion. Because Justice
Powell's vote was necessary to make up a majority, it came to be accepted that his concurring opinion was part of the law, see, e.g., *Shoen v Shoen*, 5 F3d 1289, 1292–93 (9th
Cir 1993); *von Bulow v von Bulow*, 811 F2d 136, 142 (2d Cir 1987), even though there is
no basis for granting such status to the concurring opinion of a Justice who had actually
joined the majority opinion. See *In re Grand Jury Subpoena (Miller)*, 397 F3d 964, 968–72
(DC Cir 2005); *McKevitt v Pallasch*, 339 F3d 530, 531–32 (7th Cir 2003). When there is
no majority opinion, the law is determined by the narrowest rationale justifying the outcome, *Marks v United States*, 430 US 188, 193–94 (1976), but the *Marks* principle is
inapplicable when there is in fact an opinion of the Court joined by a majority of sitting
Justices. But although the holding in *Frederick* is what is actually contained in the majority
opinion, it would come as little surprise if lawyers for students attempted to "*Branzburg*"
the majority opinion by limiting it to what can be found in Justice Alito's concurrence.

illegal conduct, important open questions remain. Given the majority's justification for creating the "advocacy of illegal drug use"
exception to *Tinker*, a narrower reading than one encompassing all
advocacy of illegal conduct would still allow restrictions on the
advocacy of those species of illegal conduct that represent a special
problem in the schools or for those of school age. We might ask,
for example, whether *Frederick* encompasses the advocacy of Col-
umbine-style killings (even with the same cryptic form of advocacy
that was present in *Frederick*), or the advocacy of alcohol use (especially while driving), or the advocacy of bullying. All of these
targets of advocacy are illegal, and all are special problems in the
schools, but the Court in *Frederick* tells us nothing about how it
might answer these questions, apart from either suggesting, oddly,
that it is advocacy of illegal drug use alone that justifies separate
treatment, or suggesting, less oddly but less helpfully, that there
might be other types of advocacy that fit the *Frederick* mold, but
which the court will deal with only if and when such cases come
before it.

Criticizing the Court for leaving questions unanswered or for
not resolving future uncertainties and ambiguities is banal. Indeed,
it is perhaps the easiest form of criticism of any judicial decision.
In the normal course of things, complaining that a Supreme Court
opinion leaves the law unclear is the cheapest form of cheap shot.
And were the stock of actual school speech cases ones in which
students were disciplined for advocating on school premises the
commission of crimes of illegal drug use, the Court's approach, for
all of its uncertainties and ambiguities, and for all the questions left
unanswered, would be less open to criticism, at least on guidance
grounds. Under such circumstances, *Frederick* would at least have
given a concrete answer to a question frequently arising in actual
litigation. But in reality the question the Court answered was one
virtually unique to the case before it. And by answering that unique
question, and studiously answering no other, the Court said virtually
nothing relevant to the large number of school speech cases that
actually occupy the lower courts, and have done so regularly since
Tinker.

Many of these actual student speech cases, it turns out, do not
resemble *Frederick* at all. An examination of *all* of the reported
primary and secondary school student speech cases since January
1, 2000, in both the state and the federal courts, reveals, perhaps

not surprisingly in a post-Columbine world, that the largest number of cases in some way or another involve apprehension of or threats of student violence.[56] Some of these cases arise in the context of restrictions on T-shirts or jackets, and others are about public speeches, but most are about student writing, including classroom assignments, that suggest to teachers and administrators that the writer has violent tendencies, or is contemplating violent acts. And although the administrators' disciplinary actions have been upheld by the courts in most of these cases, it is telling that virtually none of these cases involve protests, as in *Tinker*, or substantial disruption, as *Tinker* discusses, or sexual offensiveness, as in *Fraser*, or student publications, as in *Kuhlmeier*, or advocacy of drugs, as in *Frederick*, or indeed advocacy or endorsement of any kind. Rather, the cases involving violence represent a large body of decisions in which the lower courts are left to draw attenuated inferences from the Supreme Court cases, but in which those cases turn out to give remarkably little direct guidance.

Much the same can be said about most of the other student speech cases of the past seven years. Quite a few of those cases deal with questions of student criticism of administrators, principals, athletic coaches, and school policies,[57] a category as to which Supreme Court guidance is even more elusive. Is it substantially disruptive when students in a school newspaper or orally or on T-shirts criticize teachers and administrators, as many teachers and administrators, not surprisingly, appear to believe? Does the First Amendment allow restrictions based on the need for discipline, order, and obedience,

---

[56] *Boim v Fulton County School District*, 494 F3d 978 (11th Cir 2007); *Porter v Ascension Parish School District*, 393 F3d 608 (5th Cir 2004); *Newsom v Albemarle County School District*, 354 F3d 249 (4th Cir 2003); *S.G. v Sayreville Board of Education*, 333 F3d 417 (3rd Cir 2003); *Lavine v Blaine School District*, 279 F3d 719 (9th Cir 2002); *D.F. v Board of Education of Syosset Central School District*, 386 F Supp 2d 119 (EDNY 2005); *Griggs v Fort Wayne School Board*, 359 F Supp 2d 731 (ND Ind 2005); *Porter v Ascension Parish School Board*, 2004 US Dist LEXIS 1175 (MD La 2004); *Demers v Leominster School Department*, 263 F Supp 2d 195 (D Mass 2003); *D.G. v Independent School District No. 11*, 2000 US Dist LEXIS 12197 (ND Okla 2000); *Emmett v Kent School District No. 415*, 92 F Supp 2d 1088 (WD Wash 2000); *Pangle v Bend-Lapine School District*, 10 P3d 275 (Ore Ct of App 2000); *State v Douglas D*, 626 NW2d 725 (Wis 2001).

[57] *Lowery v Euverard*, 497 F3d 584 (6th Cir 2007); *Pinard v Clatskaniie School District*, 467 F3d 755 (9th Cir 2006); *Walker-Serrano v Leonard*, 325 F3d 412 (3rd Cir 2003); *Doninger v Niehoff*, 514 F Supp 2d 199 (D Conn 2007); *Layshock v Hermitage School District*, 496 F Supp 2d 587 (WD Pa 2007); *Lueneburg v Everett School District No. 2*, 2007 US Dist LEXIS 51189 (WD Wash 2007); *Lowry v Watson Chapel School District*, 206 US Dist LEXIS 76854 (ED Ark 2006); *Posthumus v Board of Education*, 380 F Supp 2d 891 (WD Mich 2005); *Killion v Franklin Regional School District*, 136 F Supp 2d 446 (WD Pa 2001); *J.S. v Bethlehem Area School District*, 807 A2d 847 (Pa 2002).

or is a student as free, at the school, to criticize a teacher, publicly and in harsh and offensive terms, as a citizen in a public forum is to criticize the President? Again, this is a category of cases for which the existing stock of Supreme Court decisions provides virtually no answer. Nor do those decisions offer much guidance with respect to student speech that may be racially or religiously or otherwise personally offensive, as with the many cases involving Confederate flag apparel,[58] or neo-Nazi symbols,[59] or messages that are or are perceived to be antigay, or anti-Arab, or otherwise potentially offensive to some group.[60] And although antiabortion messages of some sort or another[61] would appear to fit within the *Tinker* principle of political protest, the typical justification for such restrictions on the grounds of offensiveness once again leaves the lower courts in need of more guidance than they have thus far received.[62]

---

[58] *Castorina v Madison County School Board*, 246 F3d 536 (6th Cir 2001); *Denno ex rel Denno v School Board*, 218 F3d 1267 (11th Cir 2000); *West v Derby County Unified School District No. 260*, 206 F3d 1358 (10th Cir 2000); *B.W.A. v Farmington R-7 School District*, 508 F Supp 2d 740 (ED Mo 2007); *Bragg v Swanson*, 371 F Supp 2d 814 (SD W Va 2005).

[59] *Depinto v Bayonne Board of Education*, 514 F Supp 2d 633 (DNJ 2007); *Governor Wentworth Regional School District v Hendrickson*, 421 F Supp 2d 410 (DNH 2006); *Ponce v Cocorro Independent School District*, 432 F Supp 2d 969 (W D Tex 2006).

[60] *Harper v Poway Unified School District*, 445 F3d 1166 (9th Cir 2006); *Zamecnik v Indian Prairie School District #204 Board of Education*, 2007 US Dist LEXIS 94411 (ND Ill 2007); *Nixon v Northern Local School District Board of Education*, 383 F Supp 2d 965 (SD Ohio 2005); *Barber v Dearborn Public Schools*, 286 F Supp 2d 847 (ED Mich 2003); *Sypniewski v Warren Hills Regional Board of Education*, 2001 US Dist LEXIS 25388 (DNJ 2001); *Smith v Novato Unified School District*, 150 Cal App 4th 1489 (Ct of App, 1st Dist, 2007). Cf. *Bowler v Town of Hudson*, 514 F Supp 2d 168 (D Mass 2007) (student display of video depicting hostage beheading by Al Qaeda terrorists). Perhaps the most bizarre case is *Sonkowsky v Board of Education*, 2002 US Dist LEXIS 6197 (D Minn 2002), in which a student was disciplined for sending a message that was hostile to the Minnesota Vikings professional football team.

[61] *M.A.L. v Kinsland*, 2007 US Dist LEXIS 6365 (ED Mich 2007); *Raker v Frederick County Public Schools*, 470 F Supp 2d 634 (WD Va 2007); *K.D. v Filmore Central School District*, 2005 US Dist LEXIS 33871 (WD NY 2005).

[62] An interesting feature of virtually all the cases I examined is their political distance from *Tinker*. Whereas *Tinker*, to oversimplify, involved conservative school administrators restricting liberal or left-wing political protest, such cases are entirely absent from the array of the past seven years. Some of the recent cases in fact have no political valence at all, such as those involving dress codes with no obvious political dimension. See *Canady v Bossier Parish School Board*, 240 F3d 437 (5th Cir 2001); *Bar-Navon v School Board of Brevard County*, 2007 US Dist LEXIS 2044 (MD Fla 2007); *Brandt v Board of Education*, 420 F Supp 2d 921 (ND Ill 2006); *Alwood v Clark*, 205 US Dist LEXIS 17733 (SD Ill 2005); *Littlefield v Forney Independent School District*, 108 F Supp 2d 681 (ND Texas 2000). With respect to the remainder, however, the overwhelming political configuration is that of conservative students being restricted by (presumably) somewhat more liberal teachers and administrators. And although I have skipped over the cases involving student religious speech (e.g., *Peck v Baldwinsville Central School District*, 426 F3d 617 (2d Cir 2005); *Bannon v School District*, 387 F3d 1208 (11th Cir 2004)), because of the obvious Establishment

Not surprisingly, testosterone being what it is and teenagers being what they are, there are, to be sure, quite a few cases involving sexual speech, and these are cases that involve only questions of application of the lessons of *Fraser*.[63] And two cases in the last seven years do involve speech that advocates, endorses, or celebrates the illegal use of drugs and alcohol.[64] Apart from these cases, however, the gap between the issue that the Supreme Court took on in *Frederick* and the issues that have dominated the lower court litigation about student speech is vast. As the cases below the Supreme Court show, therefore, there are multiple recurring issues in the domain of student speech, but these issues are not the ones that the Court decided, either directly or indirectly, to address.[65] Instead, the Court elected to hear a highly unrepresentative case, and having done so then proceeded to issue a series of opinions, including the opinion of the Court, that gave virtually no additional guidance to lower state and federal courts on how the cases that actually do arise with some frequency in the lower courts ought to be decided.

The *Frederick* Court's nonguidance on issues of student speech and its nonanswer to any of the important questions about student speech are troubling for multiple reasons. In the first place, the topic as a whole is anything but rare, and there is in fact a quite considerable quantity of school speech cases in the lower courts, approximately 600 since *Tinker*.[66] Moreover, given the likely reluc-

---

Clause complications, their inclusion would likely make the contrast with *Tinker* even more dramatic. It is impossible to determine whether this political shift from *Tinker* is a function of the kinds of cases that are brought or a change in the nature of the school environment itself, but it is certainly true that the *Tinker*-paradigm case has essentially vanished.

[63] *Caudillo v Lubbock Independent School District*, 311 F Supp 2d 550 (ND Tex 2004); *Smith v Mount Pleasant Public Schools*, 285 F Supp 2d 987 (ED Mich 2003); *Coy v Board of Education of North Canton City Schools*, 205 F Supp 2d 791 (ND Ohio 2002); *Anderson v Milbank School District*, 2000 US Dist LEXIS 19418 (DSD 2000).

[64] *Guiles v Marineau*, 461 F3d 320 (2d Cir 2006); *Boroff v Van Wert City Board of Education*, 220 F3d 465 (6th Cir 2000).

[65] None of the amicus briefs in *Frederick*, nor any of the briefs of the parties, nor the petition for certiorari, nor the brief in opposition to the grant of certiorari, troubled to tell the Supreme Court just what the terrain of lower court cases looked like. Not surprisingly, all of these filings cited only the occasional lower court case in support of the argued position, leaving the Court to do its own homework if it wanted, preferably before granting certiorari but certainly before deciding how broad or narrow an opinion to issue, to survey the field. There is no evidence, however, that the Court routinely undertakes such a task, seemingly preferring simply to guess about the types of cases that its ruling will affect.

[66] In the thirty-eight years since *Tinker*, that case has been cited (based on a LEXIS search of both state and federal courts conducted on December 14, 2007) 1,767 times. Subtracting the eighty-one citations in the Supreme Court leaves 1,686 citations of the

tance of students and their parents to litigate to trial cases involving typically short periods of suspension rather than, say, expulsion, it may be reasonable to infer that the reported school speech cases represent a smaller percentage of school speech controversies than the reported libel cases against the media, say, represent of defamation controversies.

The upshot of this is that there are a substantial number of litigated controversies, and certainly a much larger number of never-litigated concrete disputes, whose outcome is arguably affected by the Supreme Court's nonguidance. That *Frederick* is the first school speech case the Court has taken and decided since *Kuhlmeier* in 1989 thus carries special significance because of the very fact that the Court takes such cases so rarely. And given the Court's decreasing output of opinions in general, there is little reason to suspect that much less than another eighteen years will pass before the Court takes and decides another such case.

Thus, on a topic on which there is a considerable amount of disputation and litigation, it appears that the Court took the wrong case, or at least a highly unrepresentative one, and, having done so, proceeded to decide that case as narrowly as possible. It decided a case in which the official justification for restricting student speech—advocacy of illegal drugs—is almost never one offered in cases of student speech; and it decided a case in which the speech itself—Frederick's somewhat bizarre banner—is vastly different from those forms of discipline-attracting student speech—Confed-

---

case in the state courts and in the lower federal courts. I then, using a random number generator, sampled a random one hundred of these 1,686 cases, and it turned out that thirty-six of the one hundred were student speech cases. Applying this 36 percent to the 1,686 total citations produced an estimate of approximately 600 reported school speech cases in total since *Tinker*, a sum premised on the safe assumption that it is inconceivable that a student speech case would not cite *Tinker*. A stratified (by five-year segments) random sample indicated a slight but steady decline since *Tinker* in the rate at which such cases arise, but the sixty-one since January 1, 2000, show that student speech remains a frequently litigated topic. Moreover, a similar analysis reveals that there are in the lower courts more school speech cases than obscenity cases (especially in the past ten years, when prosecutions for adult obscenity have declined precipitously), than defamation cases (as to which the Media Law Resource Center reports fewer than twenty trials per year in recent years), or than incitement (or advocacy) cases. This is not to say that school speech is in some larger way more important than these other topics. Obscenity law casts its shadow over broadcast indecency, zoning of adult establishments, and child pornography, for example, just as *Brandenburg* and *Sullivan* have shaped much of the modern First Amendment. Nevertheless, the large quantity of school speech cases, a quantity that would be even larger were we to include teachers as well as students and larger yet if we add colleges and universities, shows that it is a mistake, possibly a mistake the Court itself makes at times, to draw conclusions about the frequency with which an issue arises from the number of Supreme Court cases that deal with it.

erate flags, Nazi images, fantasies of violence, and criticism of school officials, most frequently—that characterize most of the actual disputes and actual litigation in the lower courts.

It is true that an unrepresentative case can still be the occasion for valuable guidance for other cases, even though such guidance may be risky insofar as a court mistakenly assumes representativeness.[67] But assuming sufficient efforts by the Supreme Court to compensate for this bias, the Court could still use an unrepresentative case that happens to come before it as the occasion to provide needed guidance for other and different cases. *Frederick*, however, is an example of just the opposite sort of judicial behavior. Having taken an unrepresentative case, the Court proceeded to decide it as narrowly as possible, on the basis of facts highly unlikely to be repeated, under circumstances in which a concurring opinion— Justice Alito's—will inevitably cast doubt on whether the majority opinion even means as much as its says it means.[68] At the very least, this state of affairs will leave lower courts with less guidance on how to decide such cases than they might desire. Even more importantly, however, it is virtually inconceivable that the teachers, administrators, school lawyers, and student speech advocates who deal with these issues regularly will feel more knowledgeable or confident after *Frederick* about what the law is. That they and the lower court judges who must deal with their actions will feel even more uncertain about what to do is by far the most likely consequence.

IV. A Larger Trend

Frederick may be unrepresentative of school speech cases, but it is hardly unrepresentative of the larger problem of guidance avoidance. In recent years the Court has appeared especially unconcerned with the guidance aspect of its work, and has perhaps taken to heart a bit too much the importunings of those who would have it act minimally and decide merely "one case at a time."[69]

---

[67] See Frederick Schauer, *Do Cases Make Bad Law?* 73 U Chi L Rev 883 (2006). See also Neal Devins and Alan Meese, *Judicial Review and Nongeneralizable Cases*, 32 Fla St U L Rev 323 (2005); Jeffrey J. Rachlinski, *Bottom-Up versus Top-Down Lawmaking*, 73 U Chi L Rev 933 (2006).

[68] See note 55.

[69] See note 11. See also Cass R. Sunstein, *Radicals in Robes: Why Extreme Right-Wing Courts Are Wrong for America* (Basic Books, 2005).

Judicial minimalism may have some virtues, including avoiding the dangers of prematurely deciding an issue as to which there is rapid technological change,[70] securing agreement among Justices with co-incident views about the right outcome but divergent views about the rationale,[71] leaving broad and important questions to be decided by the political branches of government,[72] and not deciding controversies about which the Court has no concrete information.[73] But these virtues, if indeed they are virtues, come at a price.[74] A minimal decision of necessity provides less information about the Court's preferred resolution of cases similar but not (virtually) identical to the one actually decided, just as a maximal decision lays down broad rules encompassing many cases other than ones just like the one decided. To adopt the course of minimalism, therefore, is to adopt the course of nonguidance. And for the Supreme Court to adopt the course of nonguidance, and thus to decide only seventy controversies a year while leaving countless others undecided and unguided, seems at the very least to be an inefficient use of judicial resources.[75] More importantly, adopting the path of nonguidance

---

[70] This consideration has at times explicitly surfaced in the cases dealing with electronic communications technology. See, e.g., *Denver Area Educational Telecommunications Consortium v FCC*, 518 US 727 (1996).

[71] See Sunstein, *Leaving Things Undecided* (cited in note 11).

[72] See Young, *Judicial Activism and Conservative Politics* (cited in note 11).

[73] See *Valley Forge Christian College v Americans United for Separation of Church and State, Inc.*, 454 US 464, 472 (1982); William A. Fletcher, *The Structure of Standing*, 98 Yale L J 221, 222 (1988); Steven Shavell, *The Appeal Process as a Means of Error Correction*, 24 J Legal Stud 379, 417 (1995).

[74] And this assumes that judicial minimalism in fact brings the touted virtues, which on the record thus far seems rather doubtful. It is not as if, for example, the Court's minimalist exercises have produced more agreement, greater decisional accuracy, or better decisions by the political branches. What some of the Court's minimalism *has* produced, however, is a smaller effect for some of its erroneous decisions, but this is a virtue that proponents of minimalism are loathe to acknowledge, in part because it makes the calls for minimalism look like outcome-dependent preferences rather than politically neutral calls for universally desirable judicial behavior. Were we to acknowledge, however, that there is nothing unseemly about designing the judicial environment to maximize substantively desirable outcomes or consequences, see Frederick Schauer, *Neutrality and Judicial Review*, 23 L & Phil 217 (2003), we might be more willing to have a debate about minimalism that directly confronted the question whether minimalism might be a desirable approach for some courts and not for others, and at some times but not at others.

[75] Which is not to say that conceiving of the Court solely in decision-making and not in rule-making (or guiding) terms does not have its supporters. See, e.g., Edward A. Hartnett, *A Matter of Judgment, Not a Matter of Opinion*, 74 NYU L Rev 123 (1999). But it is difficult to understand why a court whose role is so defined decided only seventy cases a year, and with very extensive opinions, rather than, say, hundreds, with commensurately briefer explanations for its judgments.

relinquishes the coordinating and certainty-providing benefits that justify the law itself,[76] and in addition gives up almost all of the advantages of having certain types of issues decided by the non-majoritarian and law-guided institutions that we call courts.[77] If it is wise, for example, that courts determine the scope and strength of the free speech rights of students and teachers, then it would seem wise as well for the courts to make such determinations more often than once every eighteen years. The Supreme Court can do this best not by deciding more school speech cases. There are, after all, numerous other calls on the Court's scarce decisional resources. But the Court can still achieve much the same effect by guiding, influencing, or even dictating outcomes for cases other than the one it actually hears. If instead it decides an unrepresentative case and then says nothing of value about other cases and other controversies, it relinquishes the guidance function that provides much of the justification for why such an important institution makes so few decisions.

This is not to suggest that the Court ought to be concerned *only* about its guidance function. Even those of us who see some virtue in advisory opinions and some vices in the "case or controversy" requirement[78] would not go that far. But it is to suggest that the guidance function has an important place in our thinking about the role of the Supreme Court. Treating minimalism as a preeminent or even just highly important judicial value comes at a high price, therefore, and it is a price that the current Court seems all too willing to pay. To put it that way, however, is to oversimplify. In fact, the Court's seeming unconcern for the guidance function has a number of relatively distinct aspects, and it is worth exploring them separately.

Perhaps most important is the Court's increasing unwillingness to recognize the benefits as well as the costs of relatively rigid substantive rules. In the same Term that the Court decided *Frederick*, for example, it eliminated, in *Leegin Creative Leather Products, Inc.*

---

[76] For an extensive development of this argument, see Larry Alexander and Frederick Schauer, *Law's Limited Domain Confronts Morality's Universal Empire*, 48 Wm & Mary L Rev 1579 (2007).

[77] See Frederick Schauer, *Judicial Supremacy and the Modest Constitution*, 92 Cal L Rev 1045 (2004).

[78] See Frederick Schauer, *Giving Reasons*, 47 Stan L Rev 633 (1995). See also Michael C. Dorf, *Dicta and Article III*, 142 U Pa L Rev 1997 (1994); Evan Tsen Lee, *Deconstitutionalizing Justiciability: The Example of Mootness*, 105 Harv L Rev 605 (1992).

v PSKS, Inc.,[79] the long-standing rule[80] under which resale price maintenance agreements were considered per se violations of the Sherman Act, without regard to whether a particular agreement did or did not have anticompetitive effects. As with any rule,[81] of course, a per se antitrust rule will produce an erroneous outcome in some cases, but at times the advantages of fostering reliance and certainty—the advantages of reliable guidance—will justify the occasional suboptimal result. But the Court in *Leegin* thought otherwise. Over the vigorous dissent of Justice Breyer, joined by Justices Stevens, Souter, and Ginsburg, Justice Kennedy for the majority opened the door to evidence in individual cases, including this one on remand, that the particular resale price maintenance agreement would in fact be pro-competitive. This outcome will be good news for the Leegin Creative Leather Products Company, for some economists, and for some lawyers, but it may be bad news for those who may desire from the Supreme Court or from antitrust doctrine a clear statement as to just which practices are permitted and which are not.

In rejecting a per se (or "bright-line") rule, *Leegin* is of a piece with other recent cases. In *United States v Booker*,[82] for example, the Court substantially softened the mandatory aspect of the Federal Sentencing Guidelines, a course continued even more recently in cases such as *Kimbrough v United States*[83] and *Gall v United States*.[84] In *Gonzalez v Carhart*,[85] the Court, in upholding the federal Partial Birth Abortion Ban Act of 2003,[86] articulated a preference, and arguably not just in the abortion context of *Carhart*, for as-applied rather than facial challenges, in effect leaving the determination of the constitutionality of a statute to be made on a case-by-case basis

---

[79] 127 S Ct 2705 (2007).

[80] *Dr. Miles Medical Co. v John D. Park & Sons Co.*, 220 US 373 (1911).

[81] See Frederick Schauer, *Playing by the Rules: A Philosophical Examination of Rule-Based Decision-Making in Law and in Life* (Clarendon/Oxford, 1991).

[82] 543 US 220 (2005).

[83] 128 S Ct 558 (2007).

[84] Id at 586 (2007). Further post-*Booker* fine-tuning of the now-advisory nature of the Federal Sentencing Guidelines and their state counterparts can also be seen in cases such as *Rita v United States*, 127 S Ct 2456 (2007), and *Cunningham v California*, 127 S Ct 856 (2007).

[85] 127 S Ct 1610 (2007).

[86] Pub L No 108-105, 117 Stat 1201 (codified at 18 USC § 1531 (Supp IV 2004)).

rather than in a more generalized or "wholesale" manner.[87] And although the Supreme Court announced in *Crawford v Washington*[88] that any use of "testimonial" evidence against a criminal defendant triggered the protections of the Confrontation Clause of the Sixth Amendment, regardless of the existence of a hearsay exception, subsequent elaborations of *Crawford*[89] have shown a Court satisfied with a case-by-case development of the "testimonial" standard rather than the articulation of a clear rule or test or definition even on a topic that arises more than daily in everyday criminal trials.

These and other recent cases exemplify two related but distinct themes of nonguidance. First, they express some hostility for rigid rules coming from elsewhere, whether that "elsewhere" be the Federal Sentencing Guidelines as in *Booker* or the Court's own long-standing doctrines, such as the per se antitrust rule rejected in *Leegin*. And, second, they embody a related reluctance on the part of the Court itself to issue rulings in rulelike fashion, preferring instead narrow decisions over broad ones, incremental steps rather than general pronouncements, case-by-case development of the law rather than rules of general application, and vague standards rather than precise rules. In all of these dimensions, *Frederick* is exemplary, but it hardly stands alone.

These two forms of guidance skepticism—skepticism about the value of guiding rules set by others, and skepticism about the wisdom of the Court itself accompanying its rulings with its own guiding rules—are increasingly combined with another impediment to telling lower courts and frontline actors just what the law is in an effective manner. And that impediment is the proliferation of multiple opinions and the consequent increase in the number of cases in which there is no majority opinion at all. Given the large numbers of school districts in which racial assignment is an issue, for example, the absence of a majority opinion in *Parents Involved in Community Schools v Seattle School District No. 1*[90] cannot but contribute to uncertainty on the part of those school districts about which uses of

---

[87] *Carhart* is also consistent in this regard with *Planned Parenthood of Southeastern Pennsylvania v Casey*, 505 US 833 (1992), which replaced the considerably clearer trimester approach of *Roe v Wade*, 410 US 113 (1973), with the rather less crisp, and thus less predictable, focus on whether a state law placed an undue burden on the right to an abortion.

[88] 541 US 36 (2004).

[89] *Davis v Washington*, 547 US 813 (2006); *Hammon v Indiana*, 547 US 813 (2006).

[90] 127 S Ct 2738 (2007).

race, if any, are permissible, and which are not.[91] As with Justice Powell's decisive solo opinion in *Regents of the University of California v Bakke*,[92] a nonmajority opinion can at times provide some degree of short- or intermediate-term clarity, but that requires a degree of rulelike directness in the dispositive opinion itself, something rarely seen these days.[93] And even when the opinion is as clear as Justice Powell's in *Bakke*, it can hardly inspire confidence in those who must plan their actions in light of the prevailing law when the guidance of the Court rests so heavily on the opinion of a single Justice and also on the length of that Justice's likely tenure on the Court.

It has not always been so. *Miranda*'s instructions to the police may stand out as among the Court's strongest guidance performances, but *Miranda* does not stand alone. The original Fourth and Fifth Amendment exclusionary rules,[94] for example, did not have a "good faith" exception,[95] and in the past there have been more per se antitrust rules than now. The Court rejected Justice Marshall's proposed "sliding scale" for equal protection analysis[96] in favor of the more rigid but also more predictable focus on levels of scrutiny. And turning to the First Amendment itself, the background against which *Frederick* was decided, we not only see relatively clear rulelike statements such as the actual malice rule coming out of *New York Times Co. v Sullivan*,[97] but the ubiquity of three- and four-part tests for obscenity,[98] for nonverbal political com-

---

[91] It is not without interest that it is Justice Kennedy whose opinion concurring (largely) only in the judgment contributes to the lack of a majority opinion, that it is Justice Kennedy who writes for the majority in *Leegin*, and that Justice Kennedy both wrote for the majority in *Carhart* and joined the important plurality in *Casey*. The causation is tricky here, because it is not apparent whether an allergy to crisp rules drives Justice Kennedy's position, or whether instead it is a function of being the so-called swing vote on a sharply divided Court. But regardless of the causation, it seems clear that Justice Kennedy's votes and opinions are at the center of the Court's increasing reluctance to provide clear guidance to lawyers, judges, and litigants alike.

[92] 438 US 265 (1978).

[93] Thus, we see the (favorable) comment that Justice Kennedy's view "may also be more tied to context and less generalizable across cases." Heather K. Gerken, *Justice Kennedy and the Domains of Equal Protection*, 121 Harv L Rev 104 (2007).

[94] *Miranda*, 384 US at 444, 478–79; *Mapp v Ohio*, 367 US 643 (1961).

[95] As is now the case after *United States v Leon*, 468 US 897 (1984).

[96] See *Massachusetts Board of Retirement v Murgia*, 427 US 307, 317 (1976) (Marshall, J, dissenting); *Marshall v United States*, 414 US 417, 432–33 (1974) (Marshall, J, dissenting); *San Antonio School District v Rodriguez*, 411 US 1, 98–110 (1973) (Marshall, J, dissenting).

[97] 376 US 254 (1964).

[98] *Miller v California*, 413 US 15 (1973).

munication,[99] and for commercial speech,[100] among others. Such tests are frequently mocked,[101] of course, and I make no claim that they provide the clarity and guidance we typically associate with, say, *Miranda*, Section 16(b) of the Securities Exchange Act of 1934,[102] or the Internal Revenue Code. But such tests perform a valuable function in structuring the analysis, and a lower court (or advocate before a lower court) required to go through prescribed steps in a prescribed order is likely to feel more guided by the Supreme Court than is the case with student speech cases after *Frederick*, cases in which even a conscientious judge is uncertain about whether and when to look for evidence of a likelihood of substantial disruption, and equally uncertain about whether something like student expressions of the desirability of violence are to be governed by *Frederick*, by *Tinker*, by *Brandenburg*, or by some yet-to-be-articulated mélange of all of these considerations.

IV. CONCLUSION: IN SEARCH OF EXPLANATION

The Court's increasing abandonment of its guidance function is in a way puzzling. If, as the political scientists tell us, Supreme Court Justices seek to maximize the effect of their own policy preferences,[103] then we might expect to see a Court composed of Justices with such preferences striving to ensure that their policy preferences will have the greatest impact. And then we might expect to see more guidance and more rules, for surely a Supreme Court that lays down rules to be followed will see more of the policy behind those rules

---

[99] *Texas v Johnson*, 491 US 397 (1989); *United States v O'Brien*, 391 US 367 (1968).

[100] *Central Hudson Gas & Elec. Co. v Public Service Commission of New York*, 447 US 557 (1980).

[101] See, e.g., Daniel A. Farber, *Missing the "Play of Intelligence,"* 36 Wm & Mary L Rev 147 (1994); Morton J. Horwitz, *The Supreme Court, 1992 Term—Foreword: The Constitution of Change: Legal Fundamentality Without Fundamentalism*, 107 Harv L Rev 30, 98 (1993); Robert F. Nagel, *The Formulaic Constitution*, 84 Mich L Rev 165 (1985).

[102] 15 USC § 78p (2004). I use this example because Section 16(b)'s attempt to deal with the problem of insider trading by imposing restrictions on precisely designated classes of insiders trading within precise time periods is in marked contrast with the substantially looser and more standard-like approach of SEC Rule 10b-5, 17 CFR 240.10b-5 (2006), a rule whose target is similar to that of Section 16(b).

[103] See, e.g., Saul Brenner and Harold J. Spaeth, *Stare Indecisis: The Alteration of Precedent on the U.S. Supreme Court, 1946–1992* (Cambridge, 1995); Jeffrey A. Segal and Harold J. Spaeth, *The Supreme Court and the Attitudinal Model Revisited* (Cambridge, 2002); Harold J. Spaeth and Jeffrey A. Segal, *Majority Rule or Minority Will* (Cambridge, 1999); Thomas G. Hansford and James F. Spriggs II, *The Politics of Precedent on the U.S. Supreme Court* Princeton, 2006).

put into practice than a Court that simply makes a context-specific ruling about the particular case before it.

Yet although shying away from the guidance function may diminish the impact of a majority's policy preferences, there are possibly other factors at work. And one of them is likely to be the incentives that, at least in part, guide the behavior of individual Justices.[104] More particularly, the incentive of reputation may have an explanatory role to play here. Those who have the ability to make or break judicial reputations—lawyers, other judges, law professors, historians, and journalists, most prominently—rarely focus on the Court as an institution. Yes, there is talk of the Warren Court, the Burger Court, the Rehnquist Court, and now the Roberts Court, but such talk pales in comparison to the evaluation of individual Justices and their performance, and at that point it is the individual performance that matters. Rare is the praise for the Justice who subjugated her or his own point of view in order to help make a clear majority (or unanimity), and even rarer is the praise for the Justice whose opinion is nonliterary, crystal clear, and oversimplified, even though these are among the most important hallmarks of an opinion likely to guide successfully. Instead, those who influentially evaluate the performance of Supreme Court Justices celebrate subtlety, nuance, context, and complexity, or increasingly they celebrate simply reaching the right result. And sometimes they celebrate reaching the right result with eloquent phrasing: Justice Brennan in *New York Times Co. v Sullivan*.[105] Chief Justice Warren in *Brown v Board of Education*.[106] Justice Harlan in *Cohen v California*.[107] Justice O'Connor in *Planned Parenthood v Casey*.[108] And, more recently, and for those who agree with the outcome, very possibly Justice Thomas in *Parents Involved in Community Schools*. But almost never do the reputation-makers celebrate the kind of straightforward rule-making language for which we would praise a drafter of a statute or a regulation, and almost never do they celebrate the Justice who simplifies, even perhaps at the expense of

---

[104] See Richard A. Posner, *How Judges Think* (Harvard, 2008); Frederick Schauer, *Incentives, Reputation, and the Inglorious Determinants of Judicial Behavior*, 68 U Cin L Rev 616 (2000).

[105] 376 US 254 (1964).

[106] 347 US 483 (1971).

[107] 403 US 15 (1971).

[108] 505 US 833 (1992).

reaching a more criticizable result in the particular case. And as long as this is so, we should not be surprised that Supreme Court Justices—who are, after all, human beings with human motivations and goals—would have little reason to take the guidance function more seriously.

Moreover, the guidance function may be among the earliest goals to be jettisoned by a deeply divided Court, especially one in which there are one or more genuine swing votes. Under circumstances of deep division, individual Justices may well have reason to want to keep things unclear for the time being, hoping that changes in the Court's personnel may produce outcomes more to their liking.[109] Guidance may be important, but most Justices will probably believe that clear guidance (and therefore more outcomes) to what they believe is the wrong result is inferior to simply less guidance. Uncertainty, after all, is for most of us preferable to certain or widespread error.

If some of these speculations about the causes of decline in attention paid to the guidance function turn out to be sound, then there may be little that can be done. But much the same can be said about the arguable futility of most forms of criticism of the Court. So if we put aside such a pessimistic view about the possibility that criticism may ever make a difference, the question is whether a particular form of criticism might make a difference. In earlier times, it was considered appropriate for commentators to criticize the craft of even those Supreme Court decisions with which they agreed. That tradition seems to have waned in recent decades, but dealing with that issue is for another occasion. On this occasion, however, and in the particular context of *Morse v Frederick*, it may be worthwhile noting that if there is a place left for criticism of the craft of the Supreme Court, then perhaps criticism of the craft (or lack thereof) of the Supreme Court in giving guidance to the lower courts, guidance to legislators, guidance to executive and administrative officials, and guidance to the teacher in the classroom and the cop on the beat still has its place. And if such criticism for poor guidance is appropriate, or might become appropriate, there seems no better place to start than with the Court's decidedly nonguiding opinion in *Morse v Frederick*.

---

[109] Cf. Mark Ramseyer, *The Puzzling (In)Dependence of the Courts: A Comparative Approach*, 23 J Legal Stud 721 (1994) (explaining how permitting or restricting judicial independence may be a function of assessments of future political alignments).

KENNETH L. KARST

FROM CARBONE TO UNITED HAULERS: THE ADVOCATES' TALES

The first full Term of the full Roberts Court[1] produced news headlines with its decisions on abortion rights, campaign financing, and
affirmative action in public schools. Two months before the end of
the Term, however, the Court issued a decision that was important
even though it attracted little public attention. In the *United Haulers*
case,[2] a 6–3 Court upheld the constitutional power of two New
York counties, taking part in a comprehensive system of waste management, to require haulers to deliver locally created waste to a
publicly owned facility that would process the waste, sort it, and
distribute it for disposal.[3] The subject of "flow control," as this sort
of ordinance is described, may not interest many reporters,[4] but in

---

Kenneth L. Karst is David G. Price and Dallas P. Price Professor of Law Emeritus, UCLA
School of Law.

Author's note: My thanks to Stephen Yeazell and Eugene Volokh for their comments
on a draft of this article. I am also indebted—again—for the assistance of Jennifer Lentz,
a research librarian par excellence.

[1] The first full Term, that is, of a Court including both Chief Justice Roberts and Justice
Alito.

[2] *United Haulers Ass'n, Inc. v Oneida-Herkimer Solid Waste Management Authority*, 127 S
Ct 1786 (2007).

[3] The plant was owned and operated by the defendant Authority, which was formed
under state law to manage waste in Oneida and Herkimer Counties. It serves 78 municipalities in the Mohawk Valley, including Utica. Elizabeth McGowan Washington, *The
Ebb and Flow: Results of Supreme Court's United Haulers Ruling Begin to Sink In*, 13 Waste
News, no 1, at 1 (May 14, 2007).

[4] Here I imitate the practice of Chief Justice Rehnquist: "[H]e would regularly discuss
at judicial conferences the less celebrated cases of a Court Term, pointing out the inter-

the law's academy some will see *United Haulers* not as just another incident along the Court's tour through the Dormant Commerce Clause, but as a Noteworthy Decision. By the time these words are in print, editors of constitutional law casebooks will have added the case to their new editions or supplements,[5] and teachers of the subject will have had fun with it in the classroom. In this article, however, the case's doctrinal contribution to the Dormant Commerce Clause will play what another academy[6] would call a supporting role.

The main characters in this story are the advocates who litigated the case in the Supreme Court, and especially the advocates on the counties' side. Those lawyers had an obstacle to overcome. As recently as 1994 the Supreme Court had decided a case that looked very much like the one before the Court in *United Haulers*. In *C & A Carbone, Inc. v Clarkstown*[7] the Court, by a 6–3 vote, had struck down a flow control ordinance requiring all solid waste found in the town to be delivered for processing in a new and privately owned processing station. In the Court's view, Clarkstown had discriminated against interstate commerce, in presumptive violation of the Dormant Commerce Clause. Because the ordinance forbade haulers to take waste out of the state for processing, it was, said Justice Kennedy for the Court, "just one more instance of local processing requirements that we have long held invalid."[8] The *Carbone* dissenters, in an opinion by Justice Souter joined by Chief Justice Rehnquist and Justice Blackmun, emphasized that the transfer station serving Clarkstown was "essentially a municipal facility,"[9] part of a public health and safety operation in its infancy. The private builder-operator was allowed to run the new plant for five years, charging a high processing price that would recover its construction costs. After those five years, it

---

esting aspects of legal craft implicated in those cases that might be overlooked." John G. Roberts, Jr., *In Memoriam: William H. Rehnquist*, 119 Harv L Rev 1, 2 (2005). The *Harvard Law Review* did not include this decision in its November 2007 treatment of the Court's 2006 Term.

[5] The first to come my way are Kathleen M. Sullivan and Gerald Gunther, *Constitutional Law* (16th ed 2007), using *United Haulers* (p 199) as a principal case, and William Cohen, Jonathan D. Varat, and Vikram Amar, *Constitutional Law, Cases and Materials* (2007 Supp to 12th ed), using *United Haulers* (p 22) as a note case.

[6] Yes, I do mean the Academy of Motion Picture Arts and Sciences.

[7] 511 US 383 (1994).

[8] Id at 391. Here Justice Kennedy rounded up the usual precedents, including *Minnesota v Barber*, 136 US 313 (1890), *Foster-Fountain Packing Co. v Haydel*, 278 US 1 (1928), *Toomer v Witsell*, 334 US 385 (1948), and *Pike v Bruce Church, Inc.*, 397 US 137 (1970).

[9] 511 US at 419.

was bound by contract to turn over the plant to the town for a nominal ($1.00) price. The *Carbone* majority saw this arrangement as no more than "a financing measure"[10] and was unmoved by Justice Souter's argument that the purpose of the flow control ordinance was not economic protectionism, but fulfillment of the town's public responsibility to promote health and safety.

Because flow control had been so prominent a feature of modern efforts at comprehensive waste management, *Carbone* set a cat among the pigeons in that field.[11] Law journals all over the country picked up the issue with commentary expressing dismay—or, alternatively, suggesting ways for local communities to get around the decision's stringent limit.[12] Yet the ordinances challenged in the

---

[10] Id at 393.

[11] The main theme, among waste management specialists, was uncertainty. "Welcome to the wild post-*Carbone* world, where gyrating prices and legal battles have stalled projects, brought bond ratings down and have wreaked general havoc." Bob Sanders, *Supreme Court Decision Has Changed Trash-Disposal Landscape*, 18 New Hampshire Bus Rev 29 (1996). "The realities of *Carbone* are very clear: the future of solid waste management will be nothing like its past." H. Lanier Hickman, *Life After Carbone*, 38 World Wastes 16 (May 1995).

In New York alone, 38 municipalities and solid waste authorities had flow control plans authorized by the legislature since 1975. The *Carbone* decision "suddenly imperiled New York State's long-term solid waste strategy, the viability of many new municipal waste treatment facilities around the state, and the bond ratings of these same municipalities." Jim Gertner, *Waste Overhaul*, Empire State Report (Aug 1994), p 21. Gertner quoted the director of the state's main legislative committee on the subject: "Basically, it has turned the issue of municipal waste upside down." Id. The legislative counsel for the Solid Waste Association of North America said that *Carbone* had undermined the basis for an integrated waste management system, including waste reduction, recycling, waste-to-energy, and landfills. *Supreme Court Rulings Affect Waste Industry*, American City & County (July 1994), p 14. "Flow control is essential if there is to be a reduction in solid waste and greater reliance on recycling, composting and hazardous waste collection." Jeffrey L. Esser, *The Flow Control Debate: A Time to Act*, 11 Gov't Finance Rev no 2, p 3 (April 1995). *Carbone* "jeopardizes at least 6 billion dollars of debt secured by municipal revenue bonds that rely on flow control ordinances to direct garbage to government-financed facilities . . . . The ruling discourages cities from implementing waste reduction and recycling programs, which seldom pay for themselves, in favor of landfilling waste." Barrie Tabin and Carol Kocheisen, *Cities Take Hit on Flow Control*, 17 Natl Cities Weekly 11 (Natl League of Cities, May 23, 1994).

[12] Among many examples, see Eric S. Peterson and David N. Abramovitz, *Municipal Solid Waste Flow Control in the Post-Carbone World*, 22 Fordham Urban L J 361 (1995); Maryellen Surhoff, *Solid Waste Flow Control and the Commerce Clause: Circumventing Carbone*, 7 Albany L J Sci & Tech 185 (1996); Benjamin D. Allen, *Trash in the Courtroom: The Problem of Solid Waste Control Ordinances After Huish Detergents, Inc. v. Warren County*, 16 J Natural Resources & Envtl L 307 (2001–02); Natasha Ernst, *Flow Control Ordinances in a Post-Carbone World*, 13 Penn St Envtl L Rev 53 (2004). For a thoughtful critique of the Supreme Court's waste management jurisprudence in decisions leading to *Carbone*, see Robert R. M. Verchick, *The Commerce Clause, Environmental Justice, and the Interstate Garbage Wars*, 70 S Cal L Rev 1239 (1997). On the expansion of the "discrimination" element of the Dormant Commerce Clause in these cases, see David S. Day, *The "Mature" Rehnquist Court and the Dormant Commerce Clause Doctrine: The Expanded Discrimination*

United Haulers case were not the product of any such strategy of evasion; they had been adopted five years before *Carbone* was decided. The federal district court, taking *Carbone* at face value, initially granted summary judgment to the United Haulers and their co-plaintiffs who challenged the two counties' flow control ordinances. The Second Circuit, however, distinguished between forcing haulers to use a privately owned processing plant (as in *Carbone*) and forcing haulers to use the Authority's publicly owned plant.[13] In the Second Circuit's view, *Carbone* did not stand for "a *per se* prohibition against flow control laws."[14] Here the counties were not protecting a local private business against interstate competition, but favoring their own governments in the course of protecting their residents' health and safety. Thus, the counties' flow control ordinances were "not discriminatory under the Dormant Commerce Clause."[15] Eventually,[16] the Supreme Court affirmed the Second Circuit. Chief Justice Roberts wrote for the Court, embracing the public-private distinction.[17] Justice Alito, dissenting, found this

---

Tier, 52 SD L Rev 1, 8–21 (2007). Catherine Gage O'Grady powerfully criticized the Court's decision in *Carbone* for its failure to distinguish between protectionism—the real villain in such cases—and "discrimination" against interstate commerce. Catherine Gage O'Grady, *Targeting State Protectionism Instead of Interstate Discrimination Under the Dormant Commerce Clause*, 34 San Diego L Rev 571, 603–08 (1997).

In an excellent treatment of the *United Haulers* case while it was under consideration by the Supreme Court, Bradford Mank called upon the Court to "abandon the rigid per se approach of Carbone" and to adopt Catherine Gage O'Grady's "protectionism" approach. Bradford C. Mank, *Are Public Facilities Different from Private Ones? Adopting a New Standard of Review for the Dormant Commerce Clause*, 60 SMU L Rev 157, 196–98 (2007). Mank was severely critical of *Carbone*, but not optimistic about its possible overruling.

[13] *United Haulers Ass'n, Inc. v Oneida-Herkimer Solid Waste Management Authority*, 261 F3d 245 (2d Cir 2001).

[14] Id at 256.

[15] Id at 263.

[16] The Second Circuit had remanded the case to the district court for determination whether—assuming the ordinances did not discriminate against interstate commerce—they passed the "balancing" test of *Pike v Bruce Church, Inc.*, 397 US 137, 142 (1970): whether the incidental burdens of the law on interstate commerce are "clearly excessive in relation to the putative local benefits" of the law. The district court, finding a complete lack of evidence that the counties' ordinances imposed any cognizable burden on interstate commerce, granted summary judgment to the counties. The Second Circuit, reviewing de novo, affirmed; assuming for argument that the flow control ordinances did burden commerce in some way, the court held that any such burden was "modest" in comparison with the ordinances' "clear and substantial" local benefits. 438 F3d 150, 160 (2d Cir 2006). Because this decision was in conflict with the Sixth Circuit's decision in *National Solid Wastes Management Ass'n v Daviess County*, 434 F3d 898 (2006), the Supreme Court granted certiorari in *United Haulers*, 127 US 35 (2006). The next spring, the Court affirmed both of the Second Circuit's judgments.

[17] Chief Justice Roberts, having rejected the claim of discrimination against interstate commerce, proceeded (joined only by Justices Souter, Ginsburg, and Breyer) to "*Pike*

distinction unacceptable and argued that the case should be governed by *Carbone*; he was joined by Justices Stevens and Kennedy.

I. United Haulers in the Shadow of Carbone

The most useful starting point for examining the work of the advocates in 2007 is recognition that the case bore an extremely close resemblance to *Carbone*. The one difference in *United Haulers*—and, for the Court, the crucial distinction—was that the flow control facility was owned by a government agency. But even this turns out to be a matter of characterization; Justice Souter's dissent in *Carbone* argued persuasively that the facility should be seen as the city's, operated by a private company just long enough to pay off the costs of its construction. Consider these statements in the opinions that the two cases produced.

Justice Kennedy, for the Court, in *Carbone*; partially quoted by Justice Alito, dissenting, in *United Haulers*:

> The essential vice in [local processing laws] is that they bar the import of the processing service. . . . The flow control ordinance has the same design and effect. It hoards solid waste, and the demand to get rid of it, for the benefit of the local processing facility.[18]

Justice Souter, dissenting, in *Carbone*:

> The outstanding feature of the [laws] reviewed in the local processing cases is their distinction between two classes of private economic actors according to location, favoring [local busi-

---

balancing," see note 16 supra, and agreed with the Second Circuit's conclusions.

Justice Scalia, concurring, repeated his intention to vote to strike down laws that facially discriminate against interstate commerce. With the rest of the majority, he agreed that the flow control ordinance before the Court did not so discriminate: "None of this Court's cases concludes that public entities and private entities are similarly situated for Commerce Clause purposes." 127 S Ct at 1799. He did not join the Court in upholding the ordinances against the *Pike* balancing test; absent discrimination against interstate commerce, he will vote to strike down only those laws that closely match laws previously held invalid.

Justice Thomas had joined Justice Kennedy's majority opinion in *Carbone*, but in *United Haulers* he concurred in the result, saying he now believed *Carbone* was wrongly decided. He reaffirmed his intention to proceed in all cases on the basis that the Constitution provides for no such thing as a Dormant Commerce Clause. Assuming that a state or local law burdens interstate commerce, or even discriminates against it, Justice Thomas will not vote to strike down the law, but will leave any remedy to Congress. He added, "as the debate between the Court's opinion and the dissenting opinion reveals, no case law applies to the facts of this case." 127 S Ct at 1801. After *United Haulers*, of course, some case law does apply.

[18] 511 US at 392; 127 S Ct at 1803.

nesses]. . . . [T]he Court struck down these local processing laws
as classic examples of the economic protectionism the dormant
Commerce Clause jurisprudence aims to prevent.[19]

Chief Justice Roberts, for the Court, in *United Haulers*:

As our local processing cases demonstrate, when a law favors in-
state business over out-of-state competition, rigorous scrutiny is
appropriate because the law is often the product of "simple economic protectionism." . . . Laws favoring local government, by
contrast, may be directed toward any number of legitimate goals
unrelated to protectionism.[20]

Justice Souter, dissenting, in *Carbone*:

The local government . . . enters the market to serve the public
interest of local citizens quite apart from private interest in private gain. Reasons other than economic protectionism are accordingly more likely to explain the design and effect of an ordinance that favors a public facility.[21]

Justice Souter, dissenting, in *Carbone*:

[The flow control ordinance] finances whatever benefits it confers
on the town from the pockets of the very citizens who passed it
into law.[22]

Chief Justice Roberts, for the Court, in *United Haulers*:

Here, the citizens and businesses of the Counties bear the costs
of the ordinances.[23]

Justice Alito, dissenting, in *United Haulers*:

[T]his Court has long recognized that "a burden imposed by a
state upon interstate commerce is not to be sustained simply
because the statute imposing it applies alike to the people of all
the States . . . ." . . . It therefore makes no difference that the

---

[19] 511 US at 416.

[20] 127 S Ct at 1795–96.

[21] 511 US at 421.

[22] Id at 425.

[23] 127 S Ct at 1797.

flow-control laws at issue here apply to in-state and out-of-state businesses alike.[24]

Justice Thomas, concurring, in *United Haulers*:

> This distinction [between regulations favoring local private business and regulations favoring local government] is razor thin.[25]

Justice Alito, dissenting, in *United Haulers*:

> The public-private distinction . . . is both illusory and without precedent. . . . The Court exalts form over substance in adopting a test that turns on this technical distinction . . . .[26]

Justice Souter, dissenting, in *Carbone*:

> Clarkstown's transfer station is essentially a municipal facility, built and operated under a contract with the municipality and soon to revert entirely to municipal ownership.[27]

Justice Alito, dissenting, in *United Haulers*:

> The preferred facility in *Carbone* was, to be sure, nominally owned by a private contractor who had built the facility on the town's behalf, but it would be misleading to describe the facility as private.[28]

Often, in the quoted statements, one Justice's thrust is another's parry. That alone might suggest a strong similarity between the two cases. But we need not rest such a conclusion on inference. In *United Haulers*, four Justices (the three dissenters and Justice Thomas[29]) explicitly said the two cases were indistinguishable. If we add Justice Souter to the group sharing this opinion, then we have a majority for that view. And we should, indeed, add Justice Souter; the point of departure for his *Carbone* dissent was that the mandated processing was done in what should be seen as a *public*

---

[24] Id at 1811.

[25] Id at 1802.

[26] Id at 1814.

[27] 511 US at 419.

[28] 127 S Ct at 1804.

[29] Id at 1802 (Thomas, J, concurring) (seeing "no basis" for the majority's distinction of *Carbone*).

facility. In the Conference, when *United Haulers* was discussed and decided, and later when the opinions were being circulated, no doubt Justice Souter had the good grace to suppress any temptation to say "I told you so."

A personal note: When *Carbone* was decided, I didn't bat an eyelash. In classroom teaching, I treated it as the majority had described it: another in the long series of cases in which the Court had invalidated laws requiring local processing of milk, shrimp, cantaloupes, what have you. Studying the materials of the *United Haulers* case, I came to regret that I had not given Justice Souter's *Carbone* dissent the attention it deserved. My interest in the advocates' role increased as I worked my way through many of the briefs and the oral argument. The perspective emphasized here is that of the advocates, looking at *United Haulers* as they constructed their briefs and planned the oral arguments they would offer to the Court. In drafting this article I have not consulted these lawyers. In offering their tales, I have imagined their possible thought processes. As even Justice Scalia might agree, my imagining follows venerable precedent. The Pardoner's Tale and the Wife of Bath's Tale were imaginary.

II. The Initial Head Count: Estimating Justices' Likely Leanings

Of the nine Justices who had participated in *Carbone*, six remained on the Court that would decide *United Haulers*: Justice Souter (author of the *Carbone* dissent) and all five Justices who had joined in Justice Kennedy's opinion for the Court holding the ordinance to be a discrimination against interstate commerce. Missing were the two other *Carbone* dissenters, Chief Justice Rehnquist and Justice Blackmun, along with Justice O'Connor, who had said the *Carbone* ordinance was not discriminatory, but joined in the result because the law imposed an undue burden on interstate commerce. These three had been replaced, respectively, by Chief Justice Roberts, Justice Breyer, and Justice Alito. The leading lawyers for the *United Haulers* plaintiffs were understandably optimistic. Evan Tager, who would sign the plaintiffs' briefs and present their oral argument, was quoted in a widely read blog as saying he was "confident" of the Court's decision.[30] Any such estimate implies a pre-

---

[30] The blogger was Roger Kamholz. See http://docket.medill.northwestern.edu/ar-

diction, or at least a guess, about the likely votes of individual Justices—and, given the extent that *United Haulers* resembled *Carbone*, Tager's statement did not seem like overconfidence.

Let us consider the Justices one by one, as they might be considered by the *United Haulers* advocates in briefing and arguing the case. Whether or not a Justice's vote might be readily predictable, some of the factors mentioned here might suggest lines of emphasis in briefing and arguing the case.

Chief Justice Roberts had not participated in a case involving flow control, either as a judge or during his service as Principal Deputy Solicitor General. In addition to representing the United States, he had considerable experience as a lawyer for business clients, at least some of whom surely were not enthusiasts for government regulation. At his confirmation hearing he had said he was a devotee of judicial modesty,[31] but, as we shall see, in this case an appeal to that generality was available to both sides. One datum of interest is that Chief Justice Roberts had been a clerk for Chief Justice Rehnquist during the era when Rehnquist was a regular dissenter from the Court's numerous decisions holding waste management laws invalid as discriminations against interstate commerce.[32] In one such dissent, Chief Justice Rehnquist had lamented that, in this whole series of cases, the Court "refuses to acknowledge that a safe and attractive environment is the commodity really at issue."[33] In another dissent he had remarked that, in the law before

---

chives/003884.php. Tager, a well-known Supreme Court advocate, is co-chair of appellate and Supreme Court practice for Mayer Brown, LLP.

[31] Early in his appearance before the Senate Judiciary Committee, he referred to

> my view that a certain humility should characterize the judicial role. Judges and justices are servants of the law, not the other way around. Judges are the umpires. Umpires don't make the rules; they apply them. . . . And I will remember that it's my job to call balls and strikes and not to pitch or bat.

"*I Come Before the Committee with No Agenda. I Have No Platform*," NY Times (Sept 13, 2005), A1, at 28. Of course, any ballplayer will confirm that different umpires have different strike zones.

[32] This dissenting pattern began in the leading case on the subject, *Philadelphia v New Jersey*, 437 US 617, at 629 (1978) (Justice Rehnquist, joined by Chief Justice Burger). It continued unabated through *Chemical Waste Management, Inc. v Hunt*, 504 US 334, 349 (1992); *Fort Gratiot Sanitary Landfill, Inc. v Michigan Dep't of Natural Resources*, 504 US 353, 368 (1992) (joined by Justice Blackmun); *Oregon Waste Systems, Inc. v Dep't of Environmental Quality*, 511 US 93 (1994) (joined by Justice Blackmun); and *Carbone*, 511 US at 410 (joining, along with Justice Blackmun, in Justice Souter's dissent).

[33] *Chemical Waste Management* (cited in note 32) at 350. In this dissent Chief Justice Rehnquist had commented that the state could have avoided any problem with the Dormant Commerce Clause by taking over the waste management facility, and relying on the

the Court, the state was "exercising its legitimate police powers in regulating solid waste disposal."[34] In still another dissent, he had expressed admiration for a state's "comprehensive approach" to waste disposal.[35] Would these Rehnquist dissents be persuasive to the new Chief Justice? How should the counties' lawyers seek to appeal to him?

Justice Stevens had been one of the Court's leaders in its campaign to rid the land of state-enforced discriminations against interstate commerce. He had written for the Court in several of these Dormant Commerce Clause cases, including one that invalidated a Michigan restriction on the import of waste.[36] In the waste disposal cases in which Chief Justice Rehnquist dissented, Justice Stevens had been in the majority—prominently including *Carbone* itself. In *Carbone*, as the senior Justice in the majority, presumably he had selected Justice Kennedy to write the opinion of the Court—a tactic often used in the hope of cementing the views of the Justice who is thus tapped. Finally, Justice Stevens can claim to stand among the Court's strongest devotees of adherence to precedent. Somehow, the counties' lawyers would have to convince him that *United Haulers* was different. The public/private distinction seemed their only hope—and a faint hope, at that.

Justice Scalia was no friend of the Dormant Commerce Clause, but he had joined with Justice Stevens in all of the previous waste disposal cases; they all fell within the area he defined as facial discrimination against interstate commerce. Yet, in a post-*Carbone* Dormant Commerce Clause case involving a claim of discrimination—not in the field of waste disposal[37]—he had embraced a public/private distinction along lines that might be seen to resonate with the Second Circuit's holding in *United Haulers*. Would this notion be transferable here, despite the case's resemblance to *Carbone*?

Justice Kennedy had joined in the Court's expansion of the "discrimination" element of the Dormant Commerce Clause from the

---

"market participant" doctrine to allow it to govern later disposal of the waste. 504 US at 351.

[34] *Oregon Waste Systems* (cited in note 32) at 112.

[35] *Fort Gratiot Sanitary Landfill* (cited in note 32) at 369.

[36] Id. The petitioners had focused on the *Carbone* precedent. In starting with the waste "crisis," the respondent counties wisely agreed with the advice of an old hand: "Accentuate the affirmative features of *your* case, don't let the other side write your brief or even shape it." Frederick Bernays Wiener, *Effective Appellate Advocacy* 107 (1950).

[37] *General Motors Corp. v Tracy*, 519 US 278, 312 at 313 (1997) (Scalia, J, concurring).

time he was appointed—an experience that culminated in his assignment to write for the Court in *Carbone*. Although his opinion did not explicitly engage Justice Souter's dissent, Justice Kennedy referred to the privately owned disposal plant as the town's facility—and, of course, he found no reason to uphold the flow control ordinance. The public/private distinction seemed likely to have hard going with Justice Kennedy.

Justice Souter surely seemed a good bet for a vote supporting the validity of the counties' flow control ordinances. He had argued that the facility in *Carbone* should be seen as public, and that flow control was a valid means of fulfilling local government's responsibilities for promoting health and safety. Much of his *Carbone* dissent would be adaptable for use in an opinion upholding the counties' flow control ordinances.

Justice Thomas had joined the Court in *Carbone*. Because of this vote, he might have been seen as another Justice who would vote against the counties. Furthermore, he seemed generally skeptical of the utility of government regulation. But in a 2005 concurring opinion he had declared the Dormant Commerce Clause to be an improper basis for holding a state law invalid—in every case.[38] Put him down as a vote to uphold the ordinances.

Justice Ginsburg, too, had joined the Court in *Carbone*. She might be more receptive to the view Justice Souter had expressed in his dissent in that case, now that the flow control facility before the Court was indisputably public. She would also be seen as having a generalized sympathy with government regulation in the realms of health and safety.

Justice Breyer had replaced Justice Blackmun, who had joined with Rehnquist in a number of the dissents noted above, notably including *Carbone*. Even so, there was no reason to assume that Justice Blackmun's view would carry much weight with his successor. Justice Breyer had joined the Court shortly after *Carbone* was decided. In his academic career before he became a judge, he had specialized in administrative law and government regulation of business. Like Justice Ginsburg, he had no general antipathy toward government regulations aimed at serving important public interests. He might even see this flow control law as an institutional relative of a public utility's monopoly. To the extent that Justice Breyer

---

[38] *American Trucking Ass'n v Michigan Pub. Serv. Comm'n*, 45 US 429, 439 (2005).

resembled the caricature of a "justice Justice" (as opposed to a "law Justice"[39]), he might respond favorably to a demonstration of the value of flow control in modern waste management.

Justice Alito had replaced Justice O'Connor. During his service as a judge of the Third Circuit, he had participated in the invalidation of New Jersey flow control regulations that required the deposit of waste with each district's designated local facility, which might be either private or public.[40] The regulations thus differed only slightly from the ordinance in *Carbone*.[41] Judge Stapleton, writing for the unanimous circuit panel, parsed the *Carbone* opinion and held that the New Jersey regulations discriminated against interstate commerce, "accomplish[ing] on a district level substantially what Clarkstown's flow control ordinance accomplished on a local level. They favor the district's designated facilities at the expense of out-of-state providers of processing and disposal services that would otherwise compete for the opportunity to service solid waste generated within the district."[42] Perhaps this experience had prepared Justice Alito to be skeptical of "public good" claims in justification of flow control ordinances that prevented the processing of waste outside the regulating counties.[43]

My tally at this point, which I take with a grain of salt—well, more than a grain—suggests this possible estimate of the lineup, before the *United Haulers* briefs were written:

Most likely to uphold: Justices Souter and Thomas

---

[39] I have heard that one commentator attached the "justice Justice" label to Justice Breyer at an academic gathering. Surely, all this is a matter of degree. Every judge, at the very least, claims to be a "law judge," and it is rare to find a judge who is impervious to a strong showing that some law makes good sense, or is useless.

[40] The waste might be deposited elsewhere, but only if the depositor compensated the local favored district for the revenue thus lost.

[41] *Atlantic Coast Demolition & Recycling, Inc. v Board of Chosen Freeholders of Atlantic County*, 48 F3d 701 (3d Cir 1995).

[42] Id at 712.

[43] Later in the same year as *Atlantic Coast*, then-judge Alito concurred when another Third Circuit panel, over one member's dissent, remanded a flow control case to the district court for further findings concerning possible discrimination against interstate commerce. *Harvey & Harvey, Inc. v County of Chester*, 68 F3d 788 (3d Cir 1995). The panel majority (Judge Becker, joined by Judge Alito) suggested that a flow control could be upheld if the designated facility had been selected in a system of competitive bidding open to out-of-state businesses. Contrary to the dissenter's suggestion, the majority said, *Carbone* "did not establish a *per se* rule subjecting all flow control ordinances to strict scrutiny." Id at 801. The Supreme Court denied certiorari, 516 US 1173 (1996), but the case was settled, and never reached final disposition on the merits.

Most likely to invalidate: Justices Stevens and Kennedy
Leaning to uphold: Justices Ginsburg and Breyer
Leaning to invalidate: Justice Alito
Too close to predict: Chief Justice Roberts and Justice Scalia

III. The Briefs

In a recent forum, Justice Alito remarked that an effective brief was one that provided a "road map" for decision[44]—by which he surely meant a line of argument that would help the Justices to understand the important issues in a case, to reach a decision, and to produce an opinion that was coherent and persuasive. The plaintiff haulers had been arguing from the earliest days in the trial court that this case was *Carbone* all over again. In paraphrase of the common real estate slogan, their opening brief argued: precedent, precedent, precedent.[45] They said that adoption of the Second Circuit's public/private distinction "would effectively overrule *Carbone*."[46] The effects of the counties' export ban on interstate commerce would be the same as the effect of the *Carbone* ordinance, preventing the export of waste for disposal. The haulers also said that a decision for the counties would equally support monopolies for publicly owned shrimp processing plants, slaughterhouses, milk pasteurizing plants, etc., covering the whole range of local processing cases invoked in the *Carbone* opinion.[47] After the counties had their say, the haulers did offer slightly different phrasing, but it all came back to the argument that the "formalistic" public/private distinction was irreconcilable with the Court's decisions, and that this case was, for all important purposes, a rerun of *Carbone*.[48]

The haulers' amici offered other arguments as well, appealing to concerns about efficient markets and fairness. They suggested that

---

[44] Justice Alito spoke on August 7, 2000, to a large group of faculty and students at Pepperdine University's law school, where he had taught a summer course in advanced constitutional law. His fellow panelists were Carter Phillips, a prominent Washington lawyer who has argued many cases in the Supreme Court, and Kenneth Starr, the school's dean; the interlocutor was Professor Douglas Kmiec. For C-Span's version, see http://www.c-span.org/videoarchives.asp?CatCodePairs=.&ArchiveDays=100; also available at http://law.pepperdine.edu/news/082007_WFSLecture.jsp.

[45] Brief for Petitioners, *United Haulers Ass'n v Oneida-Herkimer Solid Waste Management Authority* 13–41 (public/private distinction is "formalistic" at 25).

[46] Id at 37.

[47] Id at 27–36.

[48] Reply Brief for Petitioners, *United Haulers*, 2–18 ("formalistic" at 9).

the "theoretical" and "myopic" public/private distinction made by the Second Circuit would distort "the current efficient and environmentally protective interstate waste disposal system."[49] The main distortion anticipated in this brief was that if *United Haulers* were decided for the counties, "[n]ew facilities will undoubtedly be structured so as to incorporate public ownership," to hoard disposal facilities that would gather "monopoly profits" for local communities,[50] thus jeopardizing the financial well-being of "host communities" that have been disposing of waste from other localities, including such exporters as New York City.[51] In their view, the principal response to health and safety concerns about waste disposal should be a nationwide free market—the "efficient and environmentally protective" system described by the amici.

Let us imagine the thought processes of the counties' lawyers as they designed the presentation of their case. Two lines of argument surely were dismissed out of hand. First, although at least some of them must have thought *Carbone* had been wrongly decided, it would be silly to put that suggestion in a brief. Justice Souter might nod in assent, but they had to consider the effect of an anti-*Carbone* screed, not just on Justice Kennedy, *Carbone*'s author, but also on Justices Stevens, Scalia, and Ginsburg, who had joined in the Kennedy opinion.[52] Far better to persuade them that differences between the two cases justified a different result here. The second argument that would have been left on the shelf was that the counties, as participants in the market for waste processing, were entitled to rely on the "market participant exception" from the Dormant Commerce Clause.[53] Some commentators, and even some judges,[54] had found room for such an argument as one way around *Carbone*'s demands—but the argument plainly was not appropriate in *United Haulers*. The ordinances before

---

[49] Brief of Amici Curiae National Solid Wastes Management Ass'n, American Trucking Ass'ns, Inc., and National Ass'n of Manufacturers, *United Haulers*, 12–17.

[50] Id at 16 (new facilities' structuring), 17 (monopoly profits).

[51] Id at 14. To avoid blushing, they did not suggest that New York City itself would seek to hoard the business of waste disposal.

[52] Presumably Justice Thomas would vote to uphold the ordinances even if the counties failed to make their case on "discrimination." See text at note 38.

[53] On this exception, see Donald H. Regan, *The Supreme Court and State Protectionism: Making Sense of the Dormant Commerce Clause*, 84 Mich L Rev 1091, 1193–1202 (1986); Dan T. Coenen, *Untangling the Market-Participant Exemption to the Dormant Commerce Clause*, 88 Mich L Rev 395 (1989).

[54] See the decisions criticized in Stanley E. Cox, *Garbage In, Garbage Out: Court Confusion about the Dormant Commerce Clause*, 50 Okla L Rev 155, 189–207 (1997).

the Court were not offers to buy or sell anything; rather, they *commanded* the deposit of locally created waste in the public processing facility, and they imposed criminal responsibility on those who did not comply. This was a plain case of market regulation.

At the outset, the counties sought to create a mood that would infuse their main arguments. They related in some detail the health and safety disasters produced by minimally regulated dumping of waste.[55] Those events had led to enormous cleanup costs and litigation under federal law to pass the costs on to the generators of waste—both private businesses and local governments. They rightly called the situation a "crisis" in waste management.[56] The creation of the bi-county Authority, and the two counties' flow control ordinances, were reactions to the crisis. Three interrelated themes characterize the counties' arguments: First, the public/private distinction is valid; the counties were not discriminating against interstate commerce, but serving public interests in health and safety. Second, the federal courts should avoid meddling in areas where they do not belong. Third, flow control is vital to any comprehensive effort to manage waste disposal. As they made all these arguments, the counties and their amici would relate them to the crisis they had faced.

Flow control requiring waste processing in a publicly owned facility does not discriminate against interstate commerce. Counsel for the counties did not need the haulers' brief to remind them of their need to distinguish *Carbone*. Justice Souter's *Carbone* dissent had argued that the town's ordinance was not "protectionist," and so there was no discrimination against interstate commerce. Clarkstown's purpose in flow control, he argued, was public: the promotion of health and safety. The Second Circuit's public/private distinction resonated with Justice Souter's point—but which way did that cut? The counties would need to argue that, although Justice Souter had made his point explicitly, the *Carbone* majority had not rejected his argument but ignored it. Justice Kennedy's opinion for the Court

---

[55] Examples were: identification of 44 dump sites with "varying degrees of threat to public health and environment"; "closure of drinking water wells near several of these facilities"; identification by federal and state authorities of 12 of the sites as "inactive hazardous waste disposal sites." Brief for Respondents, *United Haulers*, 3–4.

[56] Id at 4. See also Brief for the states of New York, Arkansas, California, Connecticut, Delaware, Hawaii, Illinois, Iowa, Kentucky, Maine, Maryland, Michigan, Minnesota, Mississippi, Missouri, Montana, Nevada, New Hampshire, New Jersey, North Dakota, Oregon, Rhode Island, Tennessee, Vermont, Virginia, and West Virginia as Amici Curiae in Support of Respondents, *United Haulers*, 1.

had not even mentioned the Souter dissent—arguably a breach of etiquette, but one that opened the door for the counties in *United Haulers*. They might—and did—argue that the *Carbone* majority had left undecided the question now before the Court: whether a flow control system requiring waste processing at a publicly owned and operated facility discriminated against interstate commerce. Their answer to that question was, of course, no. The public authority had taken over the responsibility for processing waste, not to provide advantages to local private interests, but to protect the public's health and safety, and also to reduce their residents' and businesses' risks of liability.[57] This line of argument—first, denying that *Carbone* had decided the present issue, and, second, asserting that the ordinances in *United Haulers* were not "protectionist" but public-spirited—was central to the counties' doctrinal claim. Surely, however, their lawyers understood that, to escape the charge that the public/private distinction was formalistic, they needed to offer support from other arguments, some institutional and others more clearly substantive.

Judicial modesty suggests affirmance of the Second Circuit's decision. The supporting institutional argument would center on the role of the federal courts. A number of writers had portrayed the recent expansion of the Dormant Commerce Clause as a rebirth of the spirit of the *Lochner* era, when the federal judiciary closely scrutinized economic regulations that would interfere with the operation of a free market.[58] The charge deserved to be taken seriously. Enlarging the definition of "discrimination against interstate commerce," with its strong presumption of invalidity, federal courts had been striking down state and local economic regulations unless those

---

[57] Federal law imposes liability on the generators of waste for harms cased by improper disposal. Resource Conservation and Recovery Act of 1976, 42 USC § 6901 et seq; Comprehensive Environmental Response Compensation and Liability Act of 1980, 42 USC § 9601 et seq. The counties' ordinances had taken possession of local waste to reduce this potential liability. Brief for Respondents, *United Haulers*, 18–23.

[58] E.g., Lisa Heinzerling, *The Commercial Constitution*, 1995 Supreme Court Review 217, 268–75 (citing *Carbone* as an example at 269); Cox, 50 Okla L Rev at 214–20 (cited in note 54); C. M. A. McCauliff, *The Environment Held in Trust for Future Generations or the Dormant Commerce Clause Held Hostage to the Invisible Hand of the Market?* 40 Vill L Rev 645 (1995); *The Supreme Court, 1993 Term*, 108 Harv L Rev 23, 153 (1994) (discussing *Carbone*). For an analysis of Dormant Commerce Clause decisions as a revival of the spirit of *Lochner* (but not discussing waste management decisions), see Richard H. Fallon, Jr., *The "Conservative" Path of the Rehnquist Court's Federalism Decisions*, 69 U Chi L Rev 429, 470–71 (2002). One irony is that Chief Justice Rehnquist himself was a consistent dissenter from opinions in the waste management field that indulged the *Lochner* spirit. See notes 32–34, and accompanying text.

governments could demonstrate that their laws were clearly necessary to achieve local interests of major importance.[59] A separate
criticism of this development was founded on federalism: the national government (i.e., the federal judiciary) increasingly had been
overriding state sovereignty in an area where states traditionally had
been accorded deference. Chief Justice Rehnquist's reference to
waste disposal regulation as a "police power" issue[60] was a pointed
complaint against the heavy burden of persuasion imposed on local
governments in those cases.

In *United Haulers*, the counties and their amici sought to convince
the Justices that the flow control ordinances before them lay at the
center of any sensible definition of state police power, and that a
decision invalidating these ordinances would exemplify the worst
sort of federal judicial meddling. The counties' amici states put it
clearly: the hauler's argument "intrudes unnecessarily on the States'
sovereignty and threatens to federalize basic decisions about how
the States exercise their police powers."[61] Yet, if the counties could
say that a Justice avoids "activism"[62] by deferring to legislative judgment—that is, voting to uphold the law before the Court—the
haulers could reply that the way to avoid "activism" is to refrain
from changing legal doctrine—that is, voting to follow the *Carbone*
precedent. So, the counties' institutional argument about judicial
modesty—which had been made only summarily by Clarkstown in
Carbone itself[63]—would need reinforcement by an appeal to considerations of a purely substantive nature.

Flow control is essential to comprehensive waste management. Among
waste management professionals, even after *Carbone*, flow control
continued to be regarded as an indispensable ingredient in the com-

---

[59] "Especially in the arena of waste and trash disposal, the dormant commerce clause
has become a major instrument of judicial activism . . . ." Jenna Bednar and William N.
Eskridge, Jr., *Steadying the Court's Unsteady Path: A Theory of Judicial Enforcement of Federalism*, 68 So Cal L Rev 1447, 1462 (1995) (discussing *Carbone*).

[60] In his 1994 dissent in *Oregon Waste Systems* (cited in note 32), decided along with
Carbone.

[61] Brief for the States of New York, et al, *United Haulers* (cited in note 56), at 3.

[62] I do recognize the subjectivity in uses of this word. For the well-supported view that
a majority of the Court largely abandoned judicial modesty in the full Roberts Court's
first Term, see Adam Cohen, *Last Term's Winner at the Supreme Court: Judicial Activism*,
NY Times (July 9, 2007) (on line). Cohen did not discuss *United Haulers*—perhaps because
he was aware of the large reservoir of readers' indifference to the subject of trash.

[63] Brief for Respondent, *C & A Carbone, Inc. v Town of Clarkstown*, 1993 WL 433043,
30.

prehensive waste disposal systems that local governments needed—
all local governments, all over the country.[64] This substantive claim
about the value of the regulation was crucial to the counties' case,
and, in my opinion, was the most important message for the counties
to convey to the Court.[65] In doctrinal terms, the Justices' understandings of the purposes and effects of flow control would strongly
influence their treatment of the issue of "discrimination" and also
the "*Pike* balancing" inquiry. And judicial deference to local legislative power would be easier to sell if the counties could persuade
the Justices of the value of their publicly managed flow control.
That argument required them to explain the relation of flow control
to an integrated system of waste management designed to increase
recycling, reduce the volume of nonrecyclable waste, turn green
waste into compost, and facilitate the disposition of hazardous waste.
In short, the counties needed to bring to the Justices an appreciation
of flow control from the regulators' point of view—as Clarkstown
had not been able to do in *Carbone*.

An ideal set of arguments for the respondents in *United Haulers*
would weave all three of these themes together. In their briefs,
counsel for the counties and their principal amici curiae did remarkably well in achieving this ideal. Their doctrinal arguments
about the Dormant Commerce Clause were consistently supported
by references to the virtues of federal judicial modesty and the
tradition of upholding local regulations to promote health and
safety. All these positions, in turn, were supported by explanations
of the public interest in flow control.

As Justice O'Connor suggested in her *Carbone* concurrence, the
"discrimination" and "*Pike* balancing" strands of modern Dormant
Commerce Clause analysis typically overlap.[66] A good example, well
outside the field of waste management, is *Kassel v Consolidated
Freightways Corp.*,[67] where a divided majority struck down a state
law limiting the length of trucks. The law provided for minor exceptions, largely favoring local interests. Justice Powell's plurality

---

[64] See the literature cited in notes 11 and 12.

[65] The suggestion here and in the succeeding paragraphs of the text illustrates what
Justice Thomas said should lie outside the courts' ken. He lamented that "application of
the negative Commerce Clause turns solely on policy considerations, not on the Constitution." 127 S Ct at 1799.

[66] "[T]here is no bright line separating the two categories of analysis." 511 US at 404–05.

[67] 450 US 662 (1981).

opinion concluded that the law failed the test of *Pike* balancing—
to use today's language.[68] Justice Brennan's concurrence said that
sort of judicial interest balancing was inappropriate, but he found
the law to be "protectionist" and thus invalid. The case is well
adapted to classroom teaching about the Dormant Commerce
Clause, because Justice Powell supported his balancing argument
by showing that the state's safety claims were undermined by evidence of local favoritism,[69] and Justice Brennan supported his protectionism argument with a showing that the state's claims about
safety were not weighty.[70] In *United Haulers*, the counties' demonstration of the public's interests in health and safety would help
them to avoid a conclusion that discrimination ("economic protectionism") was their ordinances' purpose or effect—and so to distinguish *Carbone*. The same public purposes (now labeled "interests") could be weighed on the counties' side of the *Pike* balance.
In pursuing both of these doctrinal goals, the counties would find
support in a persuasive argument about the need for flow control
in a comprehensive system of waste management. If the weakness
of a legitimate reason for regulation suggests that the lawmakers
had a "bad" purpose, the opposite is also true.[71]

The counties' brief reviewed the Court's waste management decisions, and along the way articulated the public/private distinction.
The brief also set forth several public (i.e., not "protectionist")
purposes for the counties' decision to take responsibility for the
sorting function, crucial to the system of waste management. Those
purposes included (i) assuring processing that would protect health
and safety, (ii) protecting their residents and businesses from liability
under federal law for improper disposal of waste,[72] and (iii) through
an integrated waste management system, pursuing the goals of waste

---

[68] Justice Powell would not admit to "balancing"—no doubt because that locution might
cause him to lose Justice Blackmun's vote—but balancing is what he did.

[69] 450 US at 676–77.

[70] Id at 681–82.

[71] Even *Philadelphia v New Jersey* (cited in note 32), the fountainhead for the Court's
series of waste management decisions, was followed by an "exception" in *Maine v Taylor*,
377 US 131 (1986). A restatement of the principle of *Taylor* might be this: A really
important reason for discriminating against interstate commerce is a good enough reason
to do just that.

[72] The counties pointed out that a system in which private haulers were allowed to haul
waste to low-cost processors would expose the counties' residents and businesses—as "generators" of waste—to liabilities under federal law for harms caused by mismanagement of
waste. Brief for Respondents, *United Haulers*, 38.

reduction and recycling—interests "antithetical to private sector waste interests, and uniquely governmental."[73] These arguments were designed to counter the charge of "discrimination" against interstate commerce, and also to provide a strong weight on the state's-interest side of the *Pike* balancing formula. Here, after noting the dangers of leaving waste control decisions in private hands,[74] the counties devoted three pages to the importance of flow control in an integrated system of waste management. The Authority serving the two counties operates not only the processing plant at issue here, but seven other facilities, each aimed at providing various parts of the "waste stream" with appropriate forms of treatment, aimed at reducing the total volume of waste, maximizing recycling, composting of green waste, and specialized treatment of hazardous waste.[75] All these facilities are financed by the processing plant's high fees for accepting nonrecyclable waste—the same fees that encourage the generators of waste to practice recycling. The private sector would not, and could not, achieve this sort of integrated treatment of waste; the system was "possible only through a system of regulation."[76]

Two briefs amici curiae in support of the counties were especially effective in relating doctrinal arguments to the realities of waste disposition. First, consider the brief for two New York counties' waste management agencies that were using flow control,[77] along with the association that represents hundreds of the state's public waste management officials. This brief was, in form, heavily doctrinal, but at every turn it drew in arguments addressed to the role of the federal judiciary and arguments demonstrating the utility of flow control. The opening paragraph of the brief is a carefully constructed plea for judicial modesty on the part of federal courts:

> This case presents an attempt by the petitioners to expand the sweep of the dormant Commerce Clause far beyond the bound-

---

[73] Id at 17.

[74] The concerns are several. Profit-driven private activity will not allow local governments to protect their residents against liability for mismanaged waste. Nor will a privately managed system serve the interests of waste reduction and recycling; rather it will "shore up the old structure of the waste markets, in order to protect the position of low-cost landfills in those markets." Id at 33.

[75] Id at 36. The counties' lawyers had made sure that all these functions were put into evidence at the trial. The two-county Authority's eight facilities also include some landfills.

[76] Id at 37.

[77] The brief was joined by one of those counties.

aries recognized in this Court's precedents and at the expense
of traditional police powers. The waste-management ordinances
challenged here are community regulations, enacted pursuant to
the police power, that benefit only a public entity that is itself
acting pursuant to that police power. To condemn such a law as
"discriminatory" under the dormant Commerce Clause would
enlarge that doctrine in ways that defy this Court's established
police power jurisprudence and impair the constitutional balance
between national and local authority.[78]

The introduction to the brief goes on to make the substantive point
that flow control is needed to subsidize vital public programs (recycling, waste reduction, waste-to-energy conversion, or disposal of
hazardous waste) "that would not otherwise be economically sus-
tainable."[79] In short, said these amici, "The basic purpose of flow
control is *the cleansing of the waste stream*. . . . The waste that
emerges from the flow-control process is cleaner, safer, and less
voluminous than the waste that enters it."[80] The present action, said
the amici, is brought by haulers who want to dump at lower-priced
landfills that offer no such services. Their appeal to the Dormant
Commerce Clause "elevates the parochial self-interest of a few private trash haulers over local communities' authority, within their
police powers, to manage their own waste for the public good."[81]

After these introductory remarks, the brief responds to the appeal
of the haulers' amici to the virtues of a free market. The amici
counties note that, without flow control, the communities would
face a serious "free rider" problem. Putting this economic argument
into common language, these amici say the haulers are claiming
"that the Commerce Clause grants them and their customers a

---

[78] Brief for the Onondaga County Resource Recovery Agency, the Dutchess County Resource Recovery Agency, the County of Dutchess, and the New York State Association for Solid Waste Management as Amici Curiae in Support of Respondents, *United Haulers*, 1.

[79] Id at 2. The brief notes that not all local waste management programs offer all of these services. Id at 11 n 4.

[80] Id at 3 (italics in original).

[81] Id at 4. A parallel "free rider" issue was presented in an antitrust case considered by the Court during the same period as *United Haulers, Leegin Creative Leather Products, Inc. v PSKS, Inc.*, 127 S Ct 2705 (2007). In *Leegin*, a 5–4 Court overruled a long-standing rule of per se prohibition of resale price maintenance, replacing it with the "rule of reason" applied in other antitrust cases. Leegin, the producer, had argued that a minimum-price contract was needed to protect specialty stores offering high customer services (such as attractive display) against "free rider" discount houses that let customers pick out the goods at the high-end shops, but buy from them at cut prices. The *Leegin* majority opinion, accepting this free rider argument, was written by Justice Kennedy and joined by Justice Alito—both dissenters in *United Haulers*. Justice Stevens joined the dissent in *Leegin*.

constitutional license to avoid paying their fair share of the cost of a basic public service—a claim that, if extended to other public services, would eviscerate local government."[82] Only then do the amici reach the doctrinal questions of "discrimination" and "*Pike* balancing." Reinforcing the Second Circuit's public/private distinction, they emphasize that in this context local governments' purposes and operations diverge from those of private businesses, and—referring back to their own economic arguments—that "governmental entities, unlike private ones, have a legitimate role in mitigating 'public good' and 'free-rider' problems."[83] They go on to invoke the language of federalism: For the Court to treat local waste management authorities as "no different from commercial businesses would be to ignore the constitutional commitment to local sovereignty and reserved powers."[84]

In the other amici brief most worthy of note, the State of New York, represented by Solicitor General Caitlin J. Halligan,[85] was joined by twenty-five other states, all of whose attorneys general signed the brief.[86] The fact that twenty-six states were asking the Court to affirm the Second Circuit surely carried its own weight as an appeal to the values of federalism. But the principal authors of this brief made sure to emphasize the advantages of local government's comprehensive regulation of waste management and the vital contributions of flow control to such an integrated system. Of course the brief makes these points in arguing their doctrinal case, but a careful reading demonstrates that the authors know that their main job is to convince the Justices that flow control is not a grab for local economic advantage, but the necessary instrument of an important public purpose.

The amici states note that at least half of the states had authorized local governments to enact flow control ordinances—including eight states that had not joined in this brief.[87] Then the amici im-

---

[82] Id at 11.

[83] Brief for Amici Counties, *United Haulers* (note 78 supra), at 18.

[84] Id.

[85] Solicitor General Halligan also participated in the oral argument.

[86] Brief for the States of New York, et al, note 56 supra, *United Haulers*.

[87] Id at 2. The haulers themselves told the Court that 39 states and the District of Columbia had authorized flow control laws, by way of emphasizing the laws' potential nationwide effects as impediments to interstate commerce. Brief for Petitioners, *United Haulers*, 39 and n 12

mediately appeal to the principles of federalism and judicial modesty:

> [A]mici states—whether or not they use flow control—are united in believing that this choice should be left to each State's legislature, which should be free to experiment with different approaches to solid waste management. . . .
>
> [I]n this case, by seeking to extinguish a State's right to supplant the private sector—which includes both local and out-of-state firms—in an area of legitimate public concern, petitioners would stretch the dormant Commerce Clause far beyond its anti-protectionist purpose. Because petitioners' approach intrudes unnecessarily on the States' sovereignty and threatens to federalize basic decisions about how the States exercise their police power, it should be rejected and the decision below affirmed.[88]

After making these general points, the amici turn to their doctrinal arguments rejecting the charge of "discrimination" and supporting the ordinances in relation to *"Pike* balancing."

The central feature of the amici states' argument that the counties' ordinances did not discriminate against interstate commerce is a demonstration that flow control is designed, not for local economic profit, but as the keystone for a number of public purposes. They begin with their version of the public/private distinction. True, the counties had deliberately displaced the private sector in waste processing. But:

> Sometimes, the general welfare will be inconsistent with private, profit-driven activity. The private sector might offer an alternative that in the short term is cheaper but in the long run inflicts significant costs on the public at large, rather than a product that is pricier in the short term but mitigates the harmful and expensive long-term consequences. Allowing the private sector to operate in this situation would trigger a race to the bottom in which only the cheap, but more harmful, alternative would survive.[89]

This is a consideration of major importance, reinforced later in the

---

[88] Brief for States of New York, et al (note 56), 2–3. The brief noted that Congress had approved local regulation of waste management, and said that this law "confirms that in the area of local waste management, the dormant Commerce Clause should not be extended beyond its core function of preventing protectionism." Id at 8–9 (quote at 9).

[89] Id at 11.

brief.[90] General Halligan returned to it during the oral argument.[91]

The amici states distinguish *Carbone* as an example of the generality that laws favoring local private firms do cause concerns about protectionism. In *Carbone*, they say,

> Flow control was not part of an integrated waste-management scheme; it was merely a way to pay off the private firm that had built the station. Because that purpose was protectionist, and because flow control advanced no legitimate governmental interests, the ordinance was invalid.[92]

One can imagine Justice Souter reading these words. Part of him might want to say "Don't blame me," but any such inclination would have to be squelched during the discussions of *United Haulers* that lay ahead in the Conference.

After this tour through the public/private distinction, the amici states turn to what I have called the main business at hand: providing the Justices with a particularized demonstration of the public benefits of flow control as "part of an integrated solid waste management plan."[93] The counties gave their Authority full control of the initial processing (sorting) of waste in order to "match the best management method to each component of solid waste," and to give local residents and businesses an economic incentive to recycle and to shift to use of recyclable materials. (Recycled waste was accepted either free or at below-market cost.) As a result,

> The Authority accepts and recycles dozens of types of waste products, many of which are not commonly recycled by other public or private waste-management programs because of their unprofitability. Flow control plays a vital role in providing these benefits.[94]

---

[90] See text following note 94.

[91] See text following note 110.

[92] Brief for States of New York, et al, *United Haulers* (note 56), 13. Amici also distinguished *Carbone* by pointing out the extreme unlikelihood that the counties' publicly owned flow control plant would inspire "retaliation" by other states—one of the usual concerns about discrimination against interstate commerce. A law requiring flow control in a public facility risks huge liabilities under federal law for improper waste handling. Thus a local community is likely to insist on flow control only as part of a comprehensive waste management plan that requires a large commitment of public resources. Id at 14.

[93] Id.

[94] Id at 13–14 (indented quote at 14).

Thus, the amici argue, flow control, far from being economically inefficient as the haulers argued, makes excellent economic sense for the counties and their residents:

> Their goal is not simply to offer the cheapest disposal service, but to offer one with the most value. The Authority charges a higher price for processing some kinds of solid waste—and none for other services such as recycling even though they cost more to provide—in part to encourage the counties' citizens to reduce or recycle their waste. Overall, the better services are worth the higher price. [Here the amici quote a report by the federal Environmental Protection Agency calling integrated waste management "cost-effective."[95]] . . . And without flow control, all of the profitable waste-management business would go to private firms and the Authority would be burdened with only the high-cost, low-revenue services like recycling.[96]

These arguments are what was once called "result-oriented." Good for them.[97]

When the amici states turn to interest balancing, they strike a note that echoes Justice O'Connor's remark in *Carbone* about the overlap between applications of the "*Pike* balancing" and "discrimination" doctrines of the Dormant Commerce Clause.[98] Invalidation of a law on the basis of *Pike* balancing largely has been limited to the case in which a state or local law has a disparately severe impact on interstate commerce in relation to its impact on local commerce—as exemplified by the *Pike* case itself. It is this disparate impact that suggests a serious inquiry into the legitimate interests that are said to justify the law; absent such a justification, a court would properly suspect a protectionist motive for the law. If there

---

[95] EPA Office of Solid Waste III-78 (1995). Of course, in 1995 the E in EPA was widely understood to stand for "Environmental," not "Entrepreneurial."

[96] Brief of the States of New York, et al, *United Haulers* (note 56), 15. Here the amici states were responding to the haulers' argument featuring state-owned shrimp processing plants, slaughterhouses, etc. See text at note 47. The amici states said that, given those hypothetical services, there would be

> no apparent reason to ban the private sector from profiting. . . . Private waste processing is different because it may fail to provide services such as recycling that—while unprofitable—benefit the public. That is why waste processing is traditionally a governmental function.

Id at 15–16.

[97] When I was in law school, and Felix Frankfurter's academic disciples were in full flower, this term was always uttered with a sneer. Times have changed.

[98] See note 66 and accompanying text.

were no such disparity of impact, the amici states say, the law should be upheld, for there would be "no cognizable burden" worth balancing against the legitimate interests. They continue:

> To hold otherwise would be to turn the dormant Commerce Clause into a free-ranging license to second-guess virtually any state law on the ground that it is not economically efficient— that is, that its burdens on commerce generally (not interstate commerce in particular) outweigh its benefits.
> . . . For example, here petitioners ask this Court to invalidate the local laws because, in their view, it is more effective to process the counties' solid waste elsewhere. Thus, in their view, a court must decide whether, as a policy matter, the benefits of the local laws for public health and the environment outweigh the economic drawbacks they postulate. The courts are ill-equipped to handle this sort of inquiry.[99]

The amici states thus come full circle to the subjects with which they opened: the demands of federalism and the demands of judicial modesty.

IV. The Oral Argument

For the right kind of reader, the transcript of the *United Haulers* oral argument[100] is entertaining—but perhaps this category of readers does not have many members.[101] The Justices were well primed, as Justices these days usually are. Some of them framed their questions in ways suggesting a purpose to convince each other, thus reinforcing the cliché that the oral argument is the first meeting of the Conference. All three of the oral advocates—Evan Tager for the haulers, Michael Cahill for the counties, and Caitlin Halligan for the amici states—did the profession proud. They were thoroughly prepared, articulate, able to stay on message, and cool in circumstances of considerable challenge. Some of the challenges would be called rudeness if we were talking about anyone but a Justice. In my annotated copy of the transcript, I find such com-

---

[99] Brief of States of New York, et al, *United Haulers* (note 56), 177–19.

[100] References to the *United Haulers* oral argument on January 8, 2007, are taken from the transcript available at http://www.supremecourtus.gov/oral_argument_transcripts .html. It is labeled "Official—Subject to Final Review." I have made minor changes of punctuation and spelling: for example, "petitioners' argument" in place of "petitioner's argument."

[101] During the writing of this article, when I have told a few friends about my own entertainment, I have encountered more bemused looks than indications of shared interest.

ments as "Good response" noted in the margins next to the words of all three of these advocates—usually for their answers to particularly probing questions. In *United Haulers*, the oral advocates satisfied the highest standards of craft.[102]

In examining the oral argument, we shall follow the same three-part division of subjects used above in discussing the briefs for the counties and their amici: the doctrinal questions raised by "discrimination" and "*Pike* balancing" in the context of public ownership of the flow control facility; concerns about the demands of judicial modesty; and the utility of comprehensive waste management (and of flow control in particular).

Discrimination, burdens on commerce, and the public/private distinction. Evan Tager, for the haulers, led with the argument from precedent: the "outright embargo" in this case was at least as severe an impediment to interstate commerce as was the ordinance in *Carbone*.[103] Indeed, he said, "this case is almost on all fours with *Carbone*."[104] Michael Cahill, for the counties, did not dispute the ordinances' effect on interstate commerce, but argued that the Court had never held, in this context, that public service is comparable to private enterprise.[105] After Cahill had spoken the first two sentences of his oral argument, Justice Alito asked whether the Court's local processing decisions would come out differently if the facilities for pasteurization of milk, or processing of shrimp, etc. had been publicly owned.[106] Cahill answered in the affirmative. This variety of

---

[102] For an accomplished advocate's suggestion to "ignore all guidance in the abstract and focus instead on the particulars of the case at hand," see John G. Roberts, Jr., *Thoughts on Presenting an Effective Oral Argument*, School Law Rev 7-1 (Natl School Boards Ass'n 1997).

[103] Transcript of oral argument, *United Haulers*, 2–3.

[104] Id at 9. Perhaps Tager had read the words of the younger John Roberts:

> If you believe the result you seek is compelled by a recent Supreme Court decision, ignore all advice about how to structure the perfect argument; begin and end with that controlling decision.

Roberts at 7-1 (cited in note 102).

In a colloquy of some length, Justice Ginsburg made clear that she did not think the Court in *Carbone* had considered the validity of a publicly owned waste transfer facility. Id at 9-11. Tager agreed that the *Carbone* majority had not explicitly decided that issue, for it was "focusing on the consequences of putting up barriers to interstate commerce, of putting up embargos and local processing requirements." Id at 10-11.

[105] Transcript of oral argument, *United Haulers*, 26.

[106] In the Pepperdine forum (note 44), he had remarked that "It is extremely difficult to get a question in," once the Justices get going, and that a Justice who has a question must look for an "opportunity" to ask it. The *United Haulers* transcript amply supports

hypothetical was to make repeated appearances in the argument. Pressed by Justice Scalia to say whether a compulsion to buy from a publicly owned hamburger stand would be different, Cahill said the state would have to have a very good reason. However, under further questioning by Justice Souter, he said he meant only that there would be an in-state political check on such a law's adoption; he agreed that such a scheme would not constitute discrimination under the Commerce Clause.[107] Caitlin Halligan, arguing for the amici states in support of the counties, said that a law establishing a publicly owned hamburger monopoly might, indeed, give an advantage to some local private interest—and if it did so, then strict scrutiny, *Carbone*-style, would be appropriate. But, she argued, nothing like that was present in *United Haulers*, where the lower courts had found that the primary burden of the flow control ordinances was on local interests.[108] When Justice Kennedy asked her how a publicly owned milk processing plant should be treated, she attempted to answer, but was interrupted twice by Justice Kennedy and once by Justice Stevens before she could respond.[109] When she did start to distinguish the export bans previously held invalid, Justice Stevens stopped her again, saying, "This is an export ban." Then she got the first part of a sentence out, and he interrupted to say, "Your case involves an export ban. All the trash has to be processed in your tipping facility." At last she was allowed to answer:

> It does, . . . and to the extent that's what you are characterizing as an export ban, that's certainly correct. What the Court has found problematic about export bans [is] either that they are put in place to create local [jobs or local] economic opportunities, for example, the timber cases or the shrimp cases.
>
> That's not what you have here. There's no allegation that the purpose of these [ordinances] is to foster or promote local industry. In fact, the only plaintiffs in this case are local haulers themselves.[110]

---

both of these conclusions. My guess is that Justice Alito thought he had better ask this question right away, for he might have no other opportunity.

[107] Transcript of oral argument, *United Haulers*, 33–35. Cahill repeated this conclusion in response to Justice Scalia's later hypothetical about a state-owned pasteurization plant. He agreed that the Commerce Clause might limit the application of such a law, but only as a matter of *Pike* balancing; this was not the sort of discrimination that faced virtually certain invalidation. Id at 39–40.

[108] Id at 45–46.

[109] Id at 46–47.

[110] Id at 47–48.

When Chief Justice Roberts replied, "Well, there is an allegation that you charge above market rates to pursue particular economic goals that the municipality has," Halligan responded:

> For a different basket of services, Your Honor. A basket of services that includes a wider range of goals that the private sector has no interest in providing.
> To return to the question of whether or not this is an inappropriate benefit for the citizens, I would argue that there is a meaningful distinction between government taking an action which benefits the citizens as a whole . . . [and] a law that benefits a local private economic interest and is intended to do so.[111]

For the counties and their amici, the question of "discrimination" was inextricably bound to the Second Circuit's public/private distinction. They were arguing that the purpose and effect of their flow control ordinances were not to confer special advantages on local private interests, but to produce the public benefits of a comprehensive waste management system. In the oral argument, they made this point repeatedly. The counties and their amici had argued in their briefs that the main concern of the Dormant Commerce Clause was the sort of protectionism that advantaged local private interests, and during Tager's argument for the haulers, Justice Breyer supported that position, saying, "Protectionism is when a state favors its own producers."[112] Justice Souter, speaking of *Carbone*—now describing the position of the majority opinion from which he had dissented—added that the private operator of the flow control plant in Clarkstown "was being protected so it could make money, . . . [and] being protected handsomely."[113] Tager responded by suggesting a hypothetical case that showed the similarity between *Carbone* and the case at hand:

> But it would be equally protected, Your Honor, if the government owned the facility but said, "you keep all the tipping fees until it's paid off, and take a nice profit on top, too."[114]

A purely doctrinal analysis of the oral argument brings two points into bold relief. First, any Justices who concentrated on the effects

---

[111] Id at 48–49.

[112] Id at 12.

[113] Id at 13.

[114] Id.

of flow control on out-of-state disposal facilities—the "export ban"—would be inclined to conclude that *United Haulers* was, as the haulers argued, a rerun of *Carbone*. Second, unless the Justices could be persuaded to overrule *Carbone*—an outcome that no one expected—they would decide for the counties only if they were persuaded by the public/private distinction made by the court of appeals. What the counties needed to demonstrate was that this distinction was not "formalistic,"[115] but necessary to preserve the ability of local governments to fulfill their responsibility to safeguard health and safety. Ultimately, this argument would require the counties to show that flow control was needed in a comprehensive plan for waste management. But a logically prior step would be to convince the Court that the regulation of waste management lies within what Chief Justice Rehnquist, in 1994, had called the state's "police powers."[116]

Federalism and judicial modesty. Chief Justice Rehnquist's choice of words was a shorthand way of making two points. First, with a view toward federalism, the reference emphasized the primacy of state and local regulation in the field of waste management. Second, the "police powers" language suggested judicial modesty: in this field of regulation, courts should pay considerable deference to the judgment of legislative bodies. In the Rehnquist view, the two points converged: federal courts should defer to the judgment of state and local policymakers about waste management. During the *United Haulers* oral argument, Michael Cahill for the counties and Caitlin Halligan for the amici states found several opportunities to argue along these lines, regularly relating their points about federalism and judicial modesty to the public/private distinction, which had become the case's doctrinal center. As to federal-state relations, Cahill reminded the Justices that Congress had called on states and local governments to take responsibility for the safe management

---

[115] Some of the haulers' arguments attracted similar charges of "formalism." Justice Ginsburg remarked on the haulers' agreement that "if the county took over all of the garbage disposal business [including hauling], there wouldn't be any commerce problem, right? But if it does something less, there is?" Id at 11. Tager started to answer, but was interrupted by questions from other Justices, and never got back to Justice Ginsburg's point. Later, Chief Justice Roberts suggested that Tager's argument could be called "formalistic," because he had agreed that if the municipality arranged for a voluntary sort of flow control, providing free dumping at its waste processing plant and financing the facility through tax revenues, "that would be okay." Tager answered: "There are certain ways you do things and certain ways you can't do things." Id at 15.

[116] See text at note 60.

of solid waste, and had reinforced this admonition by imposing liability on those who handled waste in an unsafe manner.[117] This rather general point about federal-state relations produced no objection, for Cahill made clear that the counties were not arguing that Congress had authorized discrimination against interstate commerce. Rather, Congress did "recognize that the states do have the sovereign power to act, and they expected the states to act in this way."[118] So, the counties' flow control ordinances were "fulfilling national objectives" of recycling and waste reduction.[119]

The demands of judicial modesty, which had been contested in the briefs, were further contested in the oral argument. Before Evan Tager could get past his introductory statement, Justice Breyer asked him whether application of the *Carbone* precedent to this case would imply the invalidity of publicly owned electricity or gas monopolies all over the country. Eventually, Tager said he thought those cases would call for "the same principle . . . ." He might have had *Carbone* in mind, but we shall never know; before he could finish the sentence, Justice Breyer said, "Yeah, I think it would. The same principle would apply."[120] Justice Souter later joined in, suggesting that a win for the haulers would put a great many public utility monopolies at risk.[121] Later, Justice Stevens said to Tager, "What I guess we really don't know is whether Justice Breyer's parade of horribles are cases in which the municipality was able to provide the service more cheaply, if it subsidized it, in which case there's no burden on commerce, or were they prohibitions against competition . . . ."[122] After a brief byplay, Tager went back to Justice Stevens's point and described the Court's earlier local processing

---

[117] Transcript of oral argument, *United Haulers*, 38–39. In defending the public/private distinction, Cahill had previously argued that the counties, through their publicly owned flow control facility, were protecting their residents and businesses against potential liability under federal law. See text at note 57.

[118] Id at 39.

[119] Id at 35.

[120] Id at 4–6 (quoted language at 6). In the *Atlantic Coast* case (cited in note 41), with Justice Alito on the panel, the Third Circuit had previously considered an argument of this sort. The panel did suggest that a public utility monopoly would not be a discrimination against interstate commerce if the monopoly had been granted in competitive bidding that was open to out-of-state applicants. 48 F3d at 715.

[121] Transcript of oral argument, *United Haulers*, 19–21. Tager suggested that, although strict scrutiny would be required for such monopolies, perhaps in the public utility arena the courts might conclude that the utilities passed that difficult test. Id at 23.

[122] Id at 24.

cases as involving laws that "basically so obstruct interstate commerce as to require the virtual per se rule."[123]

The haulers' persistent reliance on the *Carbone* precedent was more than a suggestion that the Court avoid doctrinal novelty. Tager was also arguing that the public/private distinction would set the Court on an "unworkable" effort "to determine what is a traditional governmental function" entitled to deference as an exercise of the police power.[124] The haulers' argument that the Second Circuit's public/private distinction was "formalistic" sounded the same warning. When Chief Justice Roberts commented that a distinction between public and private actors might "make all the difference" in determining whether some action would implicate, for example, the First Amendment,[125] Tager responded,

> Well, I just think you are going to be walking into so many line-drawing problems . . . [such as,] are you going to require 100 percent public ownership, or a majority interest? 50–50? Once you go down this road, I think it is just opening a huge can of worms[126] when the focus ought to be, What is the impact on interstate commerce? What we have here . . . is an absolute embargo."[127]

But Justice Souter soon repeated his counteralarm about expanding the courts' role: "If we accept your argument [rejecting the public/private distinction] . . . every municipal utility in the United States is going to fall."[128]

During Michael Cahill's argument for the counties, Chief Justice Roberts raised two other cautions about overextending the federal judiciary's capacity. First, he put to Cahill the case of 50–50 public/private ownership: "Is that covered by the Commerce Clause cases or not?" Cahill said that such a scheme would "not be unconstitutional . . . . [W]hen government is actually in the transaction, when it's providing a service directly to the people, . . . it's a public

---

[123] Id at 13.

[124] Id at 11–12.

[125] Id at 14. The Chief Justice was referring by inference to the "state action" limitation under the Fourteenth Amendment.

[126] Id at 14. Any reader who smiles at this composite metaphor should engage in some self-examination. In similar circumstances, would we attain greater purity? Other parts of this colloquy between the Chief Justice and Evan Tager appear in note 115.

[127] Id at 14–15.

[128] Id at 17–18.

service." Justice Souter, perhaps thinking this response would not satisfy a doubting listener, said, "Why isn't the better answer that it *would* be subject to Commerce Clause analysis and that would fall," and that to survive, the ownership of a disposal monopoly would have to be "100 percent government." Cahill readily took the hint: "We don't have 50 percent ownership. We don't have any private ownership anywhere. . . . That's a case that isn't here today. But the question was, What if there was, and I don't think the answer is automatic one way or the other."[129] Justice Scalia then suggested a possible analogy: government usually has no sovereign immunity "when the government is engaging in a commercial activity." Cahill replied, "I think it is a reasonable rule. But I don't think that we're engaging in commercial activity in this particular case."[130]

The Chief Justice's second caution came in reply to Cahill's argument that the counties' publicly owned flow control facility should not be subjected to the tough scrutiny demanded for cases of "discrimination" against interstate commerce, but rather to the *Pike* formula, which would balance the adverse impacts on interstate commerce against the benefits of the ordinance. The Chief Justice said,

> So then, the Commerce Clause would become the vehicle by which we would develop federal law about what's appropriate for municipal governments to do and what's not appropriate? We could decide it may be appropriate to run waste facilities but not to run milk pasteurization? I don't know how we would do that.[131]

Cahill responded with a different version of the demands of judicial self-control:

> I don't know how you would do that either, Your Honor, but you would be led into that by accepting the petitioners' argument that public services and private sector services are comparable under the Commerce Clause.[132]

Still agreeing that it was not advisable to extend judicial power, Cahill said:

---

[129] Id at 28–29.

[130] Id at 29–30.

[131] Id at 40.

[132] Id.

> [I]f the petitioners' idea—that any government service could be
> challenged under the dormant Commerce Clause simply because
> there's a private entity out there that says they could do the same
> thing—were accepted, the definition of discrimination would be
> changed from differential treatment of economic interests to differential treatment of government *or* economic interests.[133]

When Caitlin Halligan stood up to speak for the twenty-six states
as amici curiae, she immediately presented the same argument.
Treating the public/private distinction as established law, she said
the petitioners' "novel" theory would "trigger near fatal scrutiny
every time the government takes over, to the exclusion of all private
actors . . . ."[134] Later she returned to this position. The petitioners,
she said, were proposing to apply the "discrimination" label to a
government's action to benefit all its citizens.

> For the dormant Commerce Clause to reach that far would be
> unprecedented. It would implicate not only electricity but . . .
> for example, government decisions to provide prisons and correctional services through a public system as opposed to a private
> one. What about school bus services? Car insurance?[135]

At this point, Chief Justice Roberts had heard enough about those
slippery slopes, and interjected one of his own:

> [O]n the other side, they have the hamburger case or the milk
> processing cases. How do we decide whether this is one of the
> traditional governmental services, the police, the prisons, whatever, or is it one of these [i.e., hamburgers, or milk processing],
> that looks more like regular market participation?

Halligan began her answer by referring to a 1905 opinion stating
that the regulation of waste management was an essential function
of local government, within the police power.[136] As to the mythical
state hamburger monopoly that had been haunting the oral argument, she said the proposal of such an ordinance would be opposed
by local interests that would be disadvantaged, and "there would

---

[133] Id at 41–42. I have added the emphasis to "or."

[134] Id at 43.

[135] Id at 49.

[136] *California Reduction Co. v Sanitary Reduction Works*, 199 US 306 (1905). In that case
the Court had no occasion to explore any potential relevance of the Dormant Commerce
Clause.

be a political process check." The Court should, indeed, "look for discrimination that is protectionist in nature, whether it is, as the Court has said, forthright or ingenious."[137] The respondents and their amici had already argued that "protectionism" in this sense referred to the protection of local private interests, not the protection of public health or safety.

Most of these questions about the judicial function are variations on a perennial theme in constitutional argumentation: the stopping-place problem. In oral arguments, a common question from the bench takes this form: If we decide this case for you, where will it all lead? The oral argument in *United Haulers* exemplified this pattern. Would a decision for the haulers mean the end of public utility monopolies, or even public prisons or school buses? Would a decision for the counties mean endless litigation to define which functions are "traditionally public," or "public" at all—for example, the 50–50 ownership of a waste facility? All the Justices *say* they believe in judicial modesty, and all advocates must talk the talk. In this respect, the subject of discrimination against interstate commerce resembles the subject of racial discrimination. In *Washington v Davis*,[138] the Court famously held that a law's racially disparate effect did not amount to the sort of racial discrimination that required strict judicial scrutiny. That sort of scrutiny was required only for deliberate racial discrimination. Justice White, writing for the Court, concluded his discussion of the issue in an oft-quoted passage. A principle requiring strict scrutiny of a law that has racially disparate effects

> would be far reaching and would raise serious questions about, and perhaps invalidate, a whole range of tax, welfare, public service, regulatory, and licensing statutes that may be more burdensome to the poor and to the average black than to the more affluent white.[139]

In other words, where would it all end? Students of constitutional law are taught that if they want to persuade the Supreme Court to buy an equality argument (or, for that matter, a liberty argument),

---

[137] Transcript of oral argument, *United Haulers*, 50.

[138] 426 US 229 (1976).

[139] Id at 248.

they have to be ready to identify a stopping place for the principle they propose.

The importance of flow control in a comprehensive plan for waste management. The counties' doctrinal argument for the public/private distinction and their efforts to encourage "police-powers" reasoning about municipal waste management were both supported by substantive claims about the need for flow control legislation. A casual reading of the oral argument might suggest that the eleven participants in the conversation—the three counsel, and all the Justices except Justice Thomas—were narrowly focused on Commerce Clause doctrine. Certainly, the public/private distinction was always nearby. But most of the participants were concerned, along the way, with the question whether the flow control legislation made good sense as a matter of waste management policy. Justice Breyer, who had intervened early to ask Evan Tager about the implications of the haulers' argument for public utility monopolies,[140] later posed a "question" that must have sounded to Tager rather like an argument:

> Here, I take it, the reason [for these flow control ordinances is that the counties] wanted their municipal facility to charge a higher price for the non-recyclable rubbish, and that will encourage people to segregate the rubbish and thereby have more . . . recyclable rubbish, and therefore overall pay less.
>
> And that's why they want to do it, and of course that's not going to work [without flow control]. If somebody comes in from out of state and charges a lower price for all of the non-recyclable rubbish—or, you know, all rubbish—it just won't work.[141]

Tager started his reply by saying that the same argument had been made in *Carbone*, and that "it doesn't matter who owns the facility." Second, and still closely focused on doctrine, he said that the argument made by Justice Breyer ultimately might be used to suggest that the ordinances could survive strict scrutiny, "but the question here is, Do we apply strict scrutiny or not?" Up to this point in his response, my guess is that Tager had made no converts. But he went on in a vein that was more substantive—and, I suggest, more persuasive:

---

[140] See text following note 119.

[141] Transcript of oral argument, *United Haulers*, 16.

And then, of course, the question turns on, Can it be met in nondiscriminatory ways? The answer is, Very well. Since *Carbone* was decided, the municipalities have been living with no flow control—virtually every one in the country—yet recycling has gone up in . . . that intervening period.

Indeed, the best way to accomplish recycling is to charge volume-based fees . . . between the haulers and . . . the generators. . . . There are plenty of communities all over the country that are charging what is known as a batch fee . . . . [N]one of these communities have flow control . . . .

They can also impose regulations directly on the generators and directly on the haulers to make sure they're doing these things.[142]

Michael Cahill, from the moment he started his argument for the counties, was caught up by questions focused on the public/private distinction. But eventually he touched on the substantive values in flow control: "We've asked our public to separate their wastes, and we've asked our haulers to collect it in a way that's consistent with the programs that we've established."[143] Justice Scalia answered:

You could do that by requiring all trash pickup to segregate recyclable and non-recyclable, and if it's going to cost each householder just as much trouble, then there could be competition and you would have achieved you goal. No?

Cahill replied:

No, Your Honor. There is no competition between our program and [what is] offered by the private sector. What we do is different [from] what the private sector offers, ...[144]

Later, in making the point that the counties were "fulfilling national objectives," he identified them as

reduc[ing] the amount of waste we generate, and recycl[ing] as much as possible. That is not necessarily something the private sector would do. A landfill is not built to discourage the amount of waste that comes through it. Our system is designed to try to

---

[142] Id at 17. Here Justice Souter led the discussion back to Justice Breyer's initial point about pubic utilities. See text following note 119.

[143] Transcript of oral argument, *United Haulers*, 31.

[144] Id at 31.

change the habits of our citizens—[Justice Kennedy broke in, saying that Commerce Clause doctrine makes clear that "a State has no interest in what happens out of state." Cahill continued:] We are not attempting to regulate what goes on in other states. . . . We are attempting to protect our own citizens by reducing the liabilities that they may incur if that waste is shipped anywhere outside the counties. We hope to give them a better solution for disposal than they would get from the marketplace.[145]

At this point Justice Souter more or less took over the discussion, saying, "I will assume that the government does have some basic health and safety objectives and the objective to protect its citizens here." Cahill said "Yes." (Wouldn't you?) Justice Souter then set out the point more fully:

If the government tries to pursue these policies solely by private inducement, trash haulers may say, We don't want to deal on those terms; we can haul somewhere else, in another county, another State, what-not.

By taking on the job itself, the government in effect is guaranteeing that to the extent it can protect its citizens, induce respect for environmental policy, and so on, it will do so without any cessation of service? There's a kind of assurance of service plus the objectives that the government gets by running the plant itself. And isn't that sort of the nub of all of your points?

Cahill agreed, and went on to emphasize the role of flow control in effective waste management:

[W]e're attempting to implement a comprehensive solid waste plan. With the passage of Federal legislation on these environmental matters touching on waste in the 1970s, . . . there was a new message . . . which to [waste] generators meant, . . . you better watch where this [waste] goes and you better be careful because liability could attach to you. . . . And that's what we've done. Any time a government . . . [puts] a plan together to dispose of solid wastes, whether like ours it uses several different technologies to try to address different parts of the waste stream, you have to have the cooperation of the people who collect the waste. If [they] could drive it away to anywhere they please, the plan is no plan; the plan is just a suggestion.[146]

---

[145] Transcript of oral argument, *United Haulers*, 35–36.

[146] Id at 37–38.

A few minutes later, he added,

> [T]he approach that Oneida-Herkimer has taken . . . is tailored
> to our local situation. It's not something that the marketplace
> would provide if the government were not there.[147]

As I mentioned, the brief of the amici states was especially strong
in demonstrating the importance of flow control in a comprehensive
waste management plan such as the one before the Court. But when
it was the turn of Caitlin Halligan to speak for those amici, she
appeared to recognize that the preceding discussions had centered
on the appropriateness of the public/private distinction, and the
parties' competing versions of the demands of judicial self-restraint.
Appropriately, she devoted most of her time to these two subjects.
Near the end of her argument, however, she saw an opportunity to
reinforce the counties' claim about the need for their flow control
ordinances. She was speaking to the question whether the ordinances' objectives—encouraged by federal and state laws—could be
served by other means. (As she noted, this question would be relevant either to the question of discrimination or to the outcome of
Pike balancing.) Halligan found an answer in the Second Circuit's
conclusion, following the district court's finding that "there was no
other option that presented itself in the record that the counties
. . . could use to address their liability concerns and to encourage
recycling across a very wide range of products."[148] It would be hard
to find a source more persuasive than a finding of the district court.

For those who might think they can tell how a case will be decided
by listening to (or reading) its oral argument, *United Haulers* presented a puzzle. The preliminary tally I suggested earlier[149] (trying
to avoid reliance on hindsight) does seem bolstered as to the Justices
estimated to be likely to join one side or the other or to be "leaning"
one way or the other. As for the votes of Chief Justice Roberts or
Justice Scalia, I doubt that the oral argument would have permitted
anyone outside the Court to make even a tentative prediction. The
Chief Justice had posed challenging questions to both sides, and
Justice Scalia, who enjoys give-and-take exchanges for their own
sake, had engaged in them with all the advocates.

---

[147] Id at 41.

[148] Id at 50–51.

[149] In the text following note 30.

V. Advocacy and the Opinions

In his opinion for the Court, Chief Justice Roberts began by taking note of the "solid waste 'crisis'" that had engendered the bi-county Authority and the counties' legislation. After setting out the majority's view that *Carbone* had not extended to a publicly owned facility, in six crisp, clear-cut paragraphs he rejected the haulers' central claim that the flow control ordinances constituted discrimination against interstate commerce.[150] Then, writing for a plurality of four Justices, the Chief Justice concluded that the ordinances passed the *Pike* balancing test: their environmental benefits to the counties' citizens outweighed "any arguable burden" on interstate commerce—a phrasing that suggests skepticism that there were any such burdens.[151] A majority of six Justices thus affirmed the lower courts' decisions, and five of them fully embraced the Second Circuit's public/private distinction. In *United Haulers*, the Supreme Court has turned a corner on the subject of flow control.[152]

After some months of immersion in materials of the *United Haulers* case, I remain impressed by the effectiveness of the advocates in conveying their messages to at least seven—maybe eight—of the Justices.[153] The main points in the Chief Justice's opinion had been highlighted in the briefs of the counties and their amici, and stoutly maintained in the oral argument. The majority's adoption of the public/private distinction follows the counties' arguments about the scope of *Carbone* and about the meanings of "discrimination" in the Court's precedent decisions under the Dormant Commerce Clause. This is an opinion that is largely doctrinal, and thus—if one thinks only of existing doctrine—fair game for the dissent's complaints. But, at the very outset of the Chief Justice's majority opinion, he presents the theme that (I have argued) was the most important

---

[150] This opinion is written fluently and sparingly; it bears the stamp of an experienced advocate.

[151] There was no opinion of the Court on the issue of *Pike* balancing. See note 17.

[152] If *United Haulers* portends a new chapter in the story of the law of waste management, perhaps it also portends a new, anti-*Lochner* chapter in the story of the Dormant Commerce Clause. In another perspective, the decision is a modest contribution to the story of the Roberts Court. When the October 2006 Term began, how many Court watchers would have expected a case producing this particular division of the Justices?

[153] Justice Thomas had foreclosed any attempt to persuade him, and perhaps Justice Scalia was similarly impervious. If the counties had utterly failed to show that flow control helped to protect public health and safety, would Justice Scalia still have concluded that the ordinances did not discriminate against interstate commerce? Surely he would say yes—and that ends speculation. Yet . . . .

contribution of the briefs for the counties and their amici, and served as a subtext for much of the oral argument. He recounts some aspects of the waste "crisis" faced by local governments, and moves on to a capsule explanation of the reasons why the counties formed their waste management Authority and adopted their ordinances. Along the way, the Chief Justice briefly states the workings of the system of flow control, including its purposes and its effects within a system of comprehensive waste management.[154] Any reader sympathetic to the briefs for the counties and their amici is likely to nod repeatedly, as the opinion takes account of the main points of those briefs. Yet, the Chief Justice never goes into detail about the need for flow control—perhaps because such an exposition would threaten to lead the argument into a morass of explanation, thus diluting the doctrinal value of a public/private distinction. Furthermore, he surely thought it important to avoid the impression that the majority had departed from *Carbone* in the face of strong criticism.

The Chief Justice concludes with a nod to the point made in Chief Justice Rehnquist's earlier dissents, and a strong endorsement of the counties' version of the demands of judicial modesty:

> The Counties' ordinances are exercises of the police power in an effort to address waste disposal, a typical and traditional concern of local government. . . . There is a common thread in [the haulers' arguments as to "discrimination" and "*Pike* balancing"]: They are invitations to rigorously scrutinize economic legislation passed under the auspices of the police power. There was a time when this Court presumed to make such binding judgments for society, under the guise of interpreting the Due Process Clause. See *Lochner v. New York*, . . . We should not seek to reclaim that ground for judicial supremacy under the banner of the dormant Commerce Clause.[155]

Similarly, all the essentials of Justice Alito's dissent had been highlighted in the haulers' brief and oral argument. First, he argued that the case before the Court was no different from *Carbone*. The *Carbone* Court had referred to the privately owned transfer station as the town's facility.[156] In any case, the effects of the counties'

---

[154] 127 S Ct at 1790–92.

[155] Id at 1798.

[156] Id at 1803–05.

ordinances on interstate commerce were identical to the effects of Clarkstown's ordinance, and the ordinances' discriminatory means could not be trumped by the bare existence of a legitimate legislative goal.[157] The majority's public/private distinction was an innovation—hardly a sign of judicial modesty.[158] Having established strict scrutiny as the appropriate standard of review, Justice Alito asserts that the counties' legitimate goals could be achieved by nondiscriminatory regulation. At this point he cites *Carbone*'s recommendation of uniform safety regulations, general taxes, or municipal bonds.[159] But, like the Chief Justice, he does not seriously engage the argument that flow control plays a central role in comprehensive waste management—perhaps because such an analysis would invite detailed refutation and would concede implicitly that a good enough justification would serve to excuse discrimination against interstate commerce.[160]

As Justice Alito's dissent makes clear, in no sense was the majority's result foreordained. A contrary decision was not merely imaginable; after all, five Justices came to believe that *United Haulers* did not differ significantly from *Carbone*.[161] The haulers' amici had predicted that a departure from *Carbone* would produce a rash of flow control legislation featuring publicly owned transfer facilities.[162] That result is not yet certain, but seems likely to come true.[163]

---

[157] Id at 1806–07.

[158] Id at 1810–11.

[159] Id at 1810.

[160] One analogy here is the saying of trial lawyers that, in many a case, there is a witness whose testimony would be highly relevant, but who is never called. One side, of course, fears that the witness's testimony will favor their opponents. But the other side also refrains from calling the witness, for fear that disclosure of the witness's personal qualities, or something else the witness might blurt out, will be adverse. My thanks to Stephen Yeazell for suggesting this analogy.

[161] See the text at note 29. Justice Souter joined the opinion of the Court, but if you think he saw *United Haulers* as different from *Carbone*, I offer to sell you my interest in the Brooklyn Bridge.

[162] They argued that if the counties should prevail in *United Haulers*, "there can be little doubt that counties and municipalities will quickly move to take advantage of the conversion option [to public-owned flow control facilities] wherever possible." Brief of Amici Curiae National Solid Wastes Management Ass'n, American Trucking Ass'ns, Inc., and National Ass'n of Manufacturers, *United Haulers*, 17.

[163] Some local governments are already moving toward publicly owned flow control facilities. See, e.g., Laura Incalcaterra, *Rockland May Take Advantage of Court Ruling, Challenge Garbage Rules*, Journal News (Westchester County, NY) (May 4, 2007), 1B (on line). Just fewer than 20% of U.S. disposal facilities are publicly owned, and it will take several years before conversions to public ownership take hold. See Stephen Ursery, *A New Era*, 38 Waste Age 24 (June 1, 2007). Yet, waste management specialists are speculating that

The *Carbone* precedent, although not overruled, has been locked in a doctrinal corner, not to die at once but to wither away.

The question then arises: If the Court has preserved *Carbone*'s form while depriving it of substantive importance, would it have been simpler to say that Justice Souter was right in 1994, and that *Carbone* should be overruled? No. An opinion along those lines would provide no "stopping place" to guide the lower courts. It would leave open, for determination case by case, the question whether the particular measure before the court provides enough public management, or public involvement, for the flow control regulation to escape the "per se rule" for discrimination. For one example—one among many possibilities for joint public and private action—consider the hypothetical "50–50" division of public and private ownership that was suggested in the oral argument. Would that be enough government participation to avoid application of *Carbone*'s strict rule to a flow control ordinance? Considering the public/private distinction in relation to what I have called judicial modesty—that is, the aim of reducing the role of the federal courts—the sharp line drawn in the *United Haulers* opinion makes good sense. As the Chief Justice remarked, interstate commerce, "whether engaged in by private or public entities," is subject to congressional regulation, including protection that might "limit state use of exclusive franchises."[164] Recognizing the difficulty of persuading Congress to act, we might put the question before the Court in these terms: Which way should the inertia of the national legislative process lean? In *United Haulers*, the Court puts the burden on those who would seek relief from municipal regulation that deploys publicly owned flow control facilities.

Justice Alito's dissent, quoted earlier, commented that the Court's "technical distinction" of *Carbone* "exalts form over substance."[165] A technical distinction is not unusual when the Court is adopting a new substantive position, but for some reason does not want to

---

more communities will, indeed, turn to the kind of flow control the Supreme Court upheld. Id. See also Washington, 13 Waste News (cited in note 3).

Presumably, a privately owned facility will also pass muster under the Dormant Commerce Clause's "discrimination" test if the facility's selection is made in a process of competitive bidding open to out-of-state bidders.

[164] 127 S Ct at 1797 n 7. Today no Justice disagrees with this remark. For an academic view to the contrary, specifically discussing waste management issues, see Norman R. Williams, *Why Congress May Not "Overrule" the Dormant Commerce Clause*, 53 UCLA L Rev 153 (2005).

[165] 127 S Ct at 1804.

overrule a prior decision.[166] Reliance on a "razor thin" distinction, then, is nothing new. Justice Kennedy, who (on April 30) joined the *United Haulers* dissent that condemned this practice, had used it with aplomb (on April 18) in his own opinion for the Court in *Gonzales v Carhart*.[167] Anyone who heard an echo at that time might have been recalling Justice Kennedy's use of the same technique six years earlier in *Nguyen v INS*.[168] Most readers of this *Review* will be able to identify similar examples in the work product of many another Justice, from John Marshall[169] to Louis Brandeis[170] and beyond. For at least a century, the ability to craft distinctions has been nourished in American law schools—and a good thing, too. Some consistencies *are* foolish; imagine a social world in which Emerson's hobgoblin scared all of us out of our good sense.

Another way to put this point is to confess, explicitly, my own view that *Carbone* was a (forgivable) mistake; I further confess that this view is formed thirteen years late, after studying the briefs and argument in *United Haulers*. Surely, the path to *Carbone* was paved with good intentions. The decision was a plausible extension of a series of waste management cases[171] in which local greed seemed a likely explanation of local processing requirements.[172] In *United Haulers*, the counties and their amici confronted the Justices with vivid descriptions of the real world of waste management. Apparently, some Justices heard a wake-up call. Yet, even if you were a Justice now persuaded that the federal judiciary should stop contributing to the waste management crisis, you would still face a

---

[166] One such reason might be the wish to avoid losing one or more votes in the majority. A famous example is Justice Scalia's opinion for a closely divided Court in *Employment Division v Smith*, 494 US 872 (1990), announcing a radically restricted view of the Free Exercise Clause of the First Amendment, but setting out particularized exceptions that undoubtedly were designed to avoid overruling some well-known precedents.

[167] 127 S Ct 1610 (2007). In this opinion Justice Kennedy was joined by Chief Justice Roberts and Justice Alito.

[168] 533 US 53 (2001).

[169] Compare *Gibbons v Ogden*, 9 Wheat (22 US) 1 (1824), with *Willson v Black-Bird Creek Marsh Co.*, 2 Pet (27 US) 245 (1829).

[170] Compare *Buck v Kuykendall*, 267 US 307 (1925), with *Bradley v Public Utilities Comm'n*, 289 US 92 (1933).

[171] See note 32 and accompanying text.

[172] *Philadelphia v New Jersey* (cited in note 32) only barely deserves placement in this category. For a thoughtful analysis of interests that were burdened and benefited by the New Jersey law in that case, and similar analyses of *Carbone* and other related cases, see Geoffrey R. Stone, Louis M. Seidman, Cass R. Sunstein, and Mark V. Tushnet, *Constitutional Law* 314–19 (3d ed 1996).

serious problem. How could the Court depart from the rigidity of *Carbone* without upsetting the venerable structure of doctrine built on the idea of discrimination against interstate commerce? That idea, after all, had become a central pillar of the Dormant Commerce Clause. In 2001, in *United Haulers* itself, the Second Circuit had suggested an answer that provided a clear stopping place: the distinction between public and private ownership. As a result, some waste management officials had already begun to breathe a little more easily.[173]

Until the day when insiders' memoirs come to be published, we shall not know just how the *United Haulers* result and the Justices' opinions came to be. One factor, hard to evaluate, is the possibility that perceptions—among waste management specialists, or more generally among informed citizens—about the waste crisis had changed significantly in the years since *Carbone*. But my sense of the case is that the advocates deserve a lot of credit for defining issues of consequence and for sharpening the debate on those issues. If all cases before the Supreme Court were presented at a comparable level of performance, the nation would be well served.

---

[173] Speaking of the Second Circuit's 2001 decision, an official of Ulster County, New York, said it was already "changing the way we look at the law, changing the way everybody is looking at flow control laws. . . . I think it's a moral obligation and a contractual obligation that we have with the county and our bondholders [to explore the flow control option]." Jim Johnson, *Going Against the Flow*, 8 Waste News, no 11, at 3 (Sept 30, 2002).

M. TODD HENDERSON

FROM SERIATIM TO CONSENSUS AND BACK AGAIN: A THEORY OF DISSENT

When John Roberts acceded to the position of Chief Justice of the United States, he stated that one of his top priorities was to reduce the number of dissenting opinions issued by members of the Court.[1] Roberts believes dissent is a symptom of dysfunction.[2] This belief is shared with many Justices past and present, the most famous of whom is his predecessor John Marshall, who squelched virtually all dissent during his thirty-five years as Chief Justice.[3] One of their arguments is that dissent weakens the Court by exposing internal divisions.[4] The Court would be better, perhaps more efficient at deciding cases and making law, if it spoke with one voice. This is

M. Todd Henderson is Assistant Professor, The University of Chicago Law School.

AUTHOR'S NOTE: Thank you to the Sarah Scaife Foundation, the Microsoft Corporation, the George J. Phocas Fund, and the John M. Olin Foundation for research support. Daniel Klerman, Alison LaCroix, Martha Nussbaum, James Oldham, Judge Richard Posner, and Geoffrey Stone gave many helpful comments. Ali Beyer and Jason Lawrence provided research support.

[1] See Hope Yen, *Roberts Seeks Greater Consensus on Court*, Wash Post (May 21, 2006), available at http://www.washingtonpost.com/wp-dyn/content/article/2006/05/21/AR2006 052100678.html; see also, Chief Justice John Roberts, Address to Georgetown University Class of 2006 (May 21, 2006), available at http://www.law.georgetown.edu/webcast/ eventDetail.cfm?eventID=144.

[2] See Address to Georgetown University, Class of 2006 (cited in note 1).

[3] See Part II.C. As discussed below, Marshall used leadership, example, and other techniques to discourage dissent and build a collegial and consensus Court. There was some dissent, but as shown herein, it was trivial.

[4] Learned Hand believed that dissent "cancels the impact of monolithic solidarity on which the authority of a bench of judges so largely depends." Learned Hand, *The Bill of Rights* 72 (1958).

a common refrain in American constitutional history. Justice Louis Brandeis famously wrote that "[i]t is more important that the applicable rule of law be settled than that it be settled right," stating that he would join opinions he disagreed with just for the sake of settling the law.[5] Other Justices have called dissents "subversive literature"[6] and "useless,"[7] and, we presume, acted just like Brandeis.

Another reason for the hostility to dissent is that dissent enables the majority to be bolder in its decision, because it is not forced to compromise. In a speech at Georgetown Law School, Chief Justice Roberts explained that "[t]he broader the agreement among the justices, the more likely it is a decision on the narrowest possible grounds."[8] Of course, this does not tell us the why this is good. We can guess it has something to do with Bickel's "passive virtues" and Sunstein's one-case-at-a-time minimalism. But whatever the reason, Roberts, like Marshall before him, believes that limiting dissent will help him achieve his unstated goals.

To other past and present Justices, most famously Chief Justice Harlan Stone and Justice William Brennan, dissent is a healthy, and even necessary, practice that improves the way in which law is made.[9] We get better law, ceteris paribus, with dissent than without.[10] Their counter position rests in part on two ideas: first, dissents communicate legal theories to other Justices, lawyers, political actors, state courts, and future Justices, and have sometimes later won the day

---

[5] *Burnet v Coronado Oil & Gas Co.*, 285 US 393, 406 (1932) (Brandeis, J, dissenting).

[6] In an interview, Stewart characterized dissents in this way, quoting an unnamed law professor of his. See Robert Bendiner, *The Law and Potter Stewart: An Interview with Justice Potter Stewart* (American Heritage), available at http://www.americanheritage.com/articles/magazine/ah/1983/1/1983_1_98.shtml ("Q: Isn't it a matter of concern, then, that the government should tempt people into committing an offense? A: It's a matter of great concern to me. I wrote a dissenting opinion in a similar case, but it was a dissenting opinion, and when I went to law school we had a professor who said dissenting opinions are nothing but subversive literature.").

[7] See *Northern Sec. Co.·v United States*, 193 US 197, 400 (1904) (opinion of Justice Oliver Wendell Holmes, the "Great Dissenter").

[8] See Yen, *Roberts Seeks Greater Consensus on Court* (cited in note 1).

[9] See William J. Brennan Jr., *In Defense of Dissents*, 37 Hastings L J 427, 438 (1986) (defending dissents on multiple grounds and calling dissent a "duty"); see also Ruth Bader Ginsburg, *Speaking in a Judicial Voice*, 67 NYU L Rev 1185 (1992) (presenting several arguments justifying the current practice of frequent dissenting opinions); Ruth Bader Ginsburg, *Remarks on Writing Separately*, 65 Wash L Rev 133 (1990) (same).

[10] Cass Sunstein makes a more general case for the value of dissent in all aspects of decision making in a recent book. See Cass R. Sunstein, *Why Societies Need Dissent* 210–11 (2006) ("Organizations and nations are far more likely to prosper if they welcome dissent and promote openness.").

as a result of this; and, second, dissents are essential to reveal the deliberative nature of the Court, which in turn enhances its institutional authority and legitimacy within American governance. Justice Brennan describes the first idea as Justices "contributing to the marketplace of competing ideas" in an attempt to get at the truth or best answer.[11] Chief Justice Charles Evans Hughes captured this latter point when he observed that dissent, when a matter of conviction, is needed "because what must ultimately sustain the court in public confidence is the character and independence of the judges."[12]

So who is right? Is dissent a symptom of a dysfunctional Court or of a healthy one? Is dissent essential to getting the best possible legal rule or does it lead to murky or bad legal rules? Throughout its history, the Supreme Court has sometimes issued predominantly unanimous opinions, while at other times it has often issued separate opinions. Since the trend is toward the latter, one might conclude that there has been learning and evolution—that the practice today is better than the practice in the past. But the almost thousand-year history of separate opinions by English courts gives us reason to doubt this. Another possibility is that judicial practices are tailored to the times. If we believe this, then we must ask what it is about the times that leads to any particular practice.

I conclude that there is no simple answer to the question of how courts should decide cases or deliver opinions. Issuing dissenting opinions is not a natural condition or even the most effective, efficient, or rational system for making law. But the elimination of dissents would not move the Court in the direction of a better state of discourse. Instead, the style of appellate decision making reflects the power-accumulating tendencies of courts and the law generally. There is no neutral answer to the question of how courts should communicate their decisions. Style reflects power, and the Court's choice of style is about the Court's power.

This is not a new idea in philosophy: Michel Foucault and others tell us that truth is not determined in a vacuum, but rather is re-

---

[11] Brennan, 37 Hastings L J at 438 (cited in note 9) ("Through dynamic interaction among members of the present Court and through dialogue across time with the future Court, we ensure the continuing contemporary relevance and hence vitality of the principles of our fundamental charter.").

[12] Charles Evans Hughes, *The Supreme Court of the United States* 67–68 (1928).

vealed only through an exercise of power.[13] So too here. The Court has no army, no guns, and no bureaucrats to enforce its will, so its power must come from somewhere else.[14] Its power resides in the only place where the Court communicates with those on the outside—its opinions.[15] The content of opinions is an essential element of this power, but so is the style or manner in which they are issued. And because decisions are an exercise of power, we should expect the manner in which the Court communicates its decisions to reflect the Court's power.[16] In other words, the presence or absence of separate opinions depends on the goals of the Court.[17]

To test this hypothesis, I briefly examine the history of dissent.[18] I show that the manner in which appellate law is made has changed several times throughout Anglo-American legal history in an attempt to increase the power of courts over other forms of dispute resolution. The Supreme Court, and its predecessors in England, sometimes issued dissents and sometimes spoke largely with one voice. In each case, the choice about which style to use was made with an eye toward bringing more business or more interesting business or more influential business to the court.

A change in the delivery of opinions designed to increase the power of "Law" has happened at least three times on a grand scale: (1) the change from seriatim opinions to an "opinion of the court" in England circa 1760; (2) a similar change in the U.S. Supreme

---

[13] Here I draw on Foucault's "power/knowledge" dynamic. See Michel Foucault, *Power/Knowledge: Selected Interviews and Other Writings, 1972–1977* (1980).

[14] Hand, *The Bill of Rights* (cited in note 4).

[15] The power of the Supreme Court manifests itself in many forms, including in structural prestige and the reputation of individual Justices, but is expressed through only one form: the written legal opinion.

[16] As is the case for automobiles, architecture, toothbrushes, and most other things in life, for legal opinions, form follows function. Architect Louis Sullivan of the Chicago School made the phrase "form follows function" famous by christening a new style of architecture for skyscrapers that emphasized exposing the structural realities of buildings instead of hiding them behind adornments. See Louis Sullivan, *The Tall Office Building Artistically Considered*, Lippincott's Magazine (Mar 1896).

[17] This raises the obvious question of how we can speak of the goals and objectives of "the Court" when it is composed of individuals and when we normally don't think of multimember bodies in this way. The idea here is that the Court is just a proxy for the overall sociological and subconscious forces at work.

[18] Foucault would call this a "genealogical" study of dissent. Genealogy is the process of looking to the past for an explanation or greater understanding or appreciation of the present. By looking at the reasons (underlying or overt) dissent is encouraged, tolerated, or squashed at a given time by courts, genealogy may provide us with the perspective to call the conventional wisdom about dissent into question.

Court upon the ascendancy of John Marshall to Chief Justice in 1801; and (3) the development of a tradition of writing separately during the New Deal era, which has persisted to the present.[19] In each of these examples, the change of discourse was a power play designed to increase the role of law in shaping the norms of society. England's abandonment of seriatim opinions was designed to increase the reach of law into the regulation of commercial activity; the Supreme Court's similar change in the era of Marshall was intended to increase the role of the Court generally and to assert the authority of the judiciary in the fledgling days of American democracy; and the rise of dissent in the New Deal era was necessary to expand the influence of the Court and law in deciding disputes previously addressed by other, extrajudicial means.

Those seeking to control "truth" in each instance used a change in discourse to achieve power within their society for themselves, their class, or their group.[20] This does not necessarily mean that there were explicit or even conscious plans by those making the change. The Court and the individual Justices did not necessarily intend the consequence, but they were affected by sociological forces beyond their ken.

This article is organized as follows. Part I explores the relation between discourse and power, and how this impacts our conceptions of truth. The goal is to put the opinion-delivery practices of the Supreme Court in the context of their larger role in formulating the legal framework through which truth in our society is determined. Part II examines the Anglo-American history of dissenting opinions. The takeaway is that dissent and unanimity norms are merely tools used to increase the power of the Court and law. Part III describes current practices, focusing on the change from the Rehnquist to the Roberts Court.

---

[19] The evolution of appellate discourse may be roughly analogous to the theory of "punctuated equilibrium" in evolutionary biology. See Niles Eldredge and Stephen Jay Gould, *Punctuated Equilibria: An Alternative to Phyletic Gradualism*, in T. J. M. Schopf, ed, *Models in Paleobiology*, 82–115 (1985). Changes in style, tone, approach, length, etc. occur gradually over the years, and then there is a sudden change that precipitates a dramatic reordering of the predominate discourse. In this view, the changes of Mansfield and Marshall were the legal equivalents of the asteroids that destroyed the dinosaurs and the trilobites. The theory has been applied in the public policy context. See Frank Baumgartner, et al, *The Destruction of Issue Monopolies in Congress*, 87 Am Pol Sci Rev 673 (1993) (showing that government policies in some areas are characterized by long periods of stability, which are disrupted by rare but significant shocks).

[20] Lawrence M. Friedman, *A History of American Law* 29 (1985) ("In modern times, law is an instrument; the people in power use it to push or pull toward some definite goal.").

Roberts's desire to move the Court toward unanimity might be seen as a countermove in this historical vector of more power for courts and law. His discursive move, which doesn't appear to be working, is also about the Court's power, but it may be about *decreasing* the Court's power. Although somewhat unique in the history of the Court, his attempt to deemphasize the Court's role in social disputes appears to be consistent with his jurisprudential philosophy. Here again, we see that discourse is power, whether for greater or lesser.

I. Discourse, Power, and Truth

Law is to a great extent what judges say it is,[21] and how they say it is one of the primary sources of legal authority. In our society law is often synonymous with power, and it greatly influences the pursuit of "truth."[22] Not only do laws define the locus of acceptable conduct, but they also set the framework in which truth is determined. Whether the issue is the veracity of a litigant's claim or the impact of a business merger on consumer well-being, law establishes the rules whereby competing claims of truth are weighed. This was not always the case. In other societies, at other times, various forms of truth existed outside or above the law. Religion or magic often was the source.[23] Law has displaced these forces so that "the characteristic of our Western societies [is] that the language of power is law."[24]

But the law does much more than this. Law constructs much of modern discourse. It authorizes some to speak and some views to be taken seriously, while marginalizing or excluding others. The

---

[21] H. L. A. Hart, *The Concept of Law* 138 (1961) ("A supreme tribunal has the last word in Saying what the law is and, when it has said it, the statement that the court was 'wrong' has no Consequences within the system: no one's rights or duties are thereby altered.").

[22] Here we see the intuition of Max Weber, whose famous speech to Munich University students, *Politics as a Vocation*, introduced the concept that the state has a monopoly on the legitimate use of physical violence. See Daniel Warner, *An Ethic of Responsibility in International Relations* 9–10 (1991).

[23] It is well known that religious or pseudo-religious entities have historically been rivals of law. See, for example, Friedman, *History of American Law* at 52, 65 (cited in note 20) ("[C]hurches . . . worked . . . as rivals of courts."). In England, this tradition survived well into the nineteenth century, and it is arguably still true in some advanced nations, and definitely true in other societies. See id at 202 ("In England [in the 1800s], ecclesiastical courts had jurisdiction over marriage and divorce, and the church had an important role in family law.").

[24] Foucault, *Power/Knowledge* at 201 (cited in note 13).

law frames discourse that affects all citizens through the creation of "episteme"—historically enduring discursive regularities that act as perception grids within which thought, communication, and action can occur. Court rules, the Federal Rules of Civil Procedure, the Federal Rules of Evidence, and the delivery of opinions are all legal "grids" within which truth is produced. In other words, discourses generate truth. As Foucault writes:

> Each society has its regime of truth, its "general politics" of truth: that is, the type of discourse which it accepts and makes function as true; the mechanisms and instances which enable one to distinguish true and false statements, the means by which each is sanctioned; the techniques and procedures accorded value in the acquisition of truth; the status of those who are charged with saying what counts as true.[25]

Law is the "general politics" of the modern era, and legal opinions are the fundamental discourse of this politics. Initially lower courts establish the rules for how the truth will be determined in a particular case. Then appellate courts act as an additional guardian of a particular form of truth by acting as a normalizing influence over the lower courts. The Supreme Court fills this same normalization role vis-à-vis the appellate courts. The result is the creation of a regularized and legalized form of truth.[26]

Appellate judges determine the boundaries of what is proper and improper for individuals in particular cases, for lower courts, and for the practice of law in general.[27] This legal grid is not usually

---

[25] Id at 131.

[26] This concept of "truth" is divergent from any conventional definition. Historically the word "truth" was synonymous with "fact" or "actuality." In this traditional world, truth is neutral and reveals itself only when the corrupting forces of power are absent. Perhaps this understanding of truth explains why for most of Anglo-American history legal judgments were made in public, openly and extemporaneously by each judge, where there was no possibility of "backroom dealing." This type of discourse was used under the guise of trying to avoid (or show) the influence or coercion of power. But truth cannot exist independently of power. In the police station, the courtroom, the statehouse, the workplace, and throughout modern society, law is the power that enables the production of knowledge and the determination of truth.

[27] The law does more than allow truth to be revealed in a certain way. Law is one of the most powerful discourses in that it claims not only to reveal the truth, like science, but also to consecrate it as the Law, the sole source of legitimate physical power. In this context, an appellate opinion is a source of truth and a representation of power, not so much as an evaluation of the "facts" of a particular case, but rather what "facts" are acceptable within the legal grid that the court creates. It is up to the lower courts to determine the truth, but the appellate court enables the truth to be discovered in a particular way.

transparent or obvious to the lay public, but it is the locus of acceptable legal behavior within which society is required to function. Things or actions inside this set of behaviors are accepted as true and proper; those outside are punished. This is true not only for specific legal rules (e.g., briefs submitted within a set period of days are accepted, those outside are not), but also for society more broadly (e.g., burning a flag is protected "speech," while burning a cross is generally not).[28] In other words, judges—and especially appellate judges—determine what is "normal" and what is "abnormal" in our society in subjects ranging far beyond the narrow world of the courtroom. In this way, law is a normalizing force and a judicial opinion is a normalizing act.[29]

Appellate opinions achieve this role of normalization in several ways. First and foremost, the opinion seals the fate of the parties before the court and establishes a precedent for actors in future cases. In addition, the opinion delineates the bounds of acceptable reasoning for lower courts. This control is exercised not only over the substantive decision, but also over details of procedure, including what witnesses may testify and what evidence judges and juries may consider. Finally, the opinion will set the broad boundaries of acceptable legal conduct and argument: law students learn by reading appellate opinions, lawyers plan cases and strategies by studying appellate opinions, and judges decide cases by following previous appellate opinions. The content, the structure, and tone of judicial opinions influence all these players in the practice of law. Courts therefore determine the scope of their own authority through their discourse.

This discourse among litigants, judges, lawyers, academics, students, and the public is greatly influenced by the manner in which appellate opinions are issued. The most important influence on this discourse is the presence or absence of separate opinions. There are many ways of deciding and announcing the result of a legal dispute: there could be a collection of opinions from each judge

---

[28] This is not exactly correct. Burning a cross and burning a flag are both protected to some extent; what differentiates the treatment of these two acts of speech is the existence of threat in the former case. Cross burning can be prohibited *only* when it is a threat. In theory, the state could prohibit flag burning if it was viewed as a threat, but this is much more difficult to imagine. The end result in most cases will be that burning a flag is OK, while burning a cross is not.

[29] See Michel Foucault, *Discipline and Punish* 187–92 (1975) (using hospitals as a prototypical example of the growth of normalization through record keeping and other forms of documentary power).

without an opinion of the court as a whole (seriatim opinions, as was the tradition in England for hundreds of years); there could be a single unsigned opinion with no permitted dissent (unanimous, per curiam opinions issued without a public vote, as is the current practice in civil law countries such as Germany and France);[30] or there could be an opinion of a majority of the judges (either signed or unsigned) along with any concurring or dissenting opinions (as is primarily the practice in American federal and state courts).[31]

The structure of appellate opinions is an integral part of the creation of legal truth grids. A unanimous opinion (9–0) by the Supreme Court will foster a much different reaction than a 5–4 decision with several scathing dissents. Unanimous opinions settle the law. Lower courts may try to carve out small areas of disagreement within the legal grid, but the message of the Court is that this issue is decided and will not be reconsidered any time soon. No foreseeable changes in Court personnel or attitude are likely to change the votes of five Justices. By contrast a 5–4 decision will send quite a different message to lower courts and to lawyers who want to challenge the precedent. Challenges may be fruitful when a change in the Court's membership makes the vote uncertain or when a compelling case forces one or two Justices to reconsider their vote. Therefore, dissenting opinions are more likely to create uncertainty. This uncertainty will produce a much different process for determining "truth."[32]

The resulting discourse—be it ambiguous, disputed, apparently unassailable, or obscure—determines, or at least greatly influences, our conception of legal "knowledge" and the determination of legal "truth." Throughout history the process of deciding cases, of establishing how the "truth" will be determined, has changed, and with it the legal discourse has changed. Seriatim opinions were common at certain times and in certain nations, while unanimous opinions dominated at other times and in certain countries or legal

---

[30] Continental law (and the law in Japan, China, and other non-Anglo-American countries) is not made by judges but is contained mostly in written statutory codes. In the common law system, in contrast, a great deal of law is made by the opinions of judges. Friedman, *History of American Law* at 22 (cited in note 20).

[31] For an analysis of the difference between these styles, see Ginsburg, *Speaking in a Judicial Voice* at 67 (cited in note 9); Ginsburg, *Remarks on Writing Separately* at 133 (cited in note 9).

[32] This analysis is true, of course, only in a legal system in which judges express their differences in public through concurring and dissenting opinions. In France and Germany, all opinions carry the same discursive impact because disagreement is not published.

systems. But what determines the shape of appellate discourse, and why do we see different types of discourse at different times and across different societies?

II. A Brief History of Dissent

There are only three widely used ways in which multijudge courts have delivered judicial decisions over nearly a thousand years of Anglo-American jurisprudence. The first is the seriatim delivery of the judgment of each judge individually. This practice prevailed in Great Britain for nearly all of its history, from the time of William the Conqueror to the present day. It also was common in U.S. courts (both state and federal) at the Founding. The second is delivering an "opinion of the court," with no publicly revealed vote or separate opinions. This practice has been used twice: by Lord Mansfield of the King's Bench in England and (more or less) by John Marshall of the U.S. Supreme Court. Finally, the modern practice in the United States is a hybrid, in which an opinion of a majority of the court is issued, but judges decide individually whether to "write separately."

A. THE ENGLISH EXPERIENCE

For almost a thousand years, decisions of multimember courts in England were delivered orally by each judge seriatim and without any prior intracourt consultation.[33] The opinions, the sum of which would amount to the legal rule in the case, were not even published until the early seventeenth century. Prior to that time, case reports were the written compilation of the notes of prominent lawyers at the trial, who recorded, to the best of their ability, the proceedings of the court and the orally delivered opinions of the judges. Because more than one lawyer might take notes on a particular case, there were often multiple, and perhaps conflicting, reports. These reports, covering a huge swath of English legal history dating back to at least the reign of King Edward I and going forward to at least the reign of Henry VIII, were originally published in raw form, and were used by lawyers as source material and precedent. The unedited and unabridged compilations were massive and did not present a coherent picture of the law. Lawyers

---

[33] See, for example, William H. Rehnquist, *The Supreme Court* 40 (2001).

and judges had a difficult time even knowing the legal rule from a case.[34] "Precedent" was virtually unknown because it implies the existence of a set of judgments available to parties and judges. Abridgments of leading cases appeared by the late fifteenth century,[35] but the quality varied tremendously, and no systematic court "reports" were issued until Edward Coke published his case notes in 1609.[36] (There were no "official" case reports until the late eighteenth century, and the regular practice of issuing official court reports of cases did not become regular until the mid-nineteenth century.) The "poverty of the law reports," as C. H. S. Fifoot writes, contributed to the lack of clarity of the law.[37] This had many bad effects, but, as shown below, the lack of clarity did not become a crisis until the rise of commerce in the mid-seventeenth century.

Even after Coke and his contemporaries formulated the issuance of reports of judicial decisions, the practice of each judge delivering his opinion seriatim continued. Although tradition and a sense of efficiency sustained this practice, we can only speculate as to its origins. One possibility is concern about concealed power. Oral delivery by each individual judge may be a more accountable method of deciding cases than decisions made in seclusion, because judgments made in the open and without explicit caucus among the judges may be less likely to be (or appear to be) infected by corruption or collusion or the influence of the monarch. As critics

---

[34] William Murray, who practiced before the Court of Chancery in the mid-eighteenth century (when reporting was still poor in equity courts), wrote: "It is a misfortune attending a court of equity, that the cases are generally taken in loose notes, and sometimes by persons who do not understand business, and very often draw general principles from a case, without attending to particular circumstances, which weighed with the court in the determination of these cases." James Oldham, *English Common Law in the Age of Mansfield* 366 (2004).

[35] The first abridgment was made by Nicholas Statham, Baron of the Exchequer under Edward IV, in around 1470. 8 *The Cambridge History of English and American Literature*, chap XIII sec 9 (1907) ("As the number of the Year Books increased, it became convenient to make classified abridgments of their leading cases. The first of these was made, about 1470, by Nicholas Statham, baron of the exchequer under Edward IV").

[36] Edward Coke, who served as Chief Justice of the Court of Common Pleas and then the King's Bench, became the first English jurist to publish his opinions, in 1609. His cases became Volume I of the English Reports. These were his personal account of the cases, and they are generally considered to be misleading, often reporting what he wanted the result or reasoning to be instead of what it actually was. See, for example, J. H. Baker, *New Light on Slade's Case*, 29 Cambridge Law J 213 (1971) (showing how Coke's reporting introduced inaccurate distortions into the law).

[37] See Cecil H. S. Fifoot, *Lord Mansfield* 89 (1936).

complained after certain American courts departed from the seriatim tradition, forcing individual judges to give their account
provided a basis to hold judges accountable, which in turn gave
them an incentive to work hard and do well.[38]

The long and unbroken tradition of delivering opinions seriatim
was changed unilaterally with the ascendancy of William Murray,
known as "Lord Mansfield," to the position of Lord Chief Justice
of the King's Bench in 1756.[39] Mansfield introduced a procedure
for generating agreement and consensus among judges and then
issuing caucused opinions. The judges met collectively in the secrecy of their chambers, worked out their differences into a compromise decision, and then wrote what was to be delivered as an
anonymous and unanimous "opinion of the court." Mansfield
made this dramatic change in an attempt to bring clarity to the
law in order to bring English commercial law in line with prevailing practices in trades and in other countries.[40] He succeeded.
Jim Oldham, the world's leading Mansfield scholar, summarizes
his accomplishment: "[Mansfield] established the basic principles
that continue to govern the mercantile energies of England and
America down to the present day."[41]

During the Middle Ages and until Mansfield, the law governing
business affairs—known as "the law merchant"—was administered
by special lay courts at "fairs" set up on trade routes, in trade
centers, or that traveled across Europe.[42] The law merchant was

---

[38] Thomas Jefferson, a strong critic of the "opinion of the court," wrote: "An opinion
is huddled up in conclave, perhaps by a majority of one, delivered as if unanimous, and
with the silent acquiescence of lazy or timid associates, by a crafty chief judge, who
sophisticates the law to his own mind, by the turn of his own reasoning." *Letter from
Thomas Jefferson to Thomas Ritchie* (Dec 25, 1820), in Paul L. Ford, ed, 10 *The Writings
of Thomas Jefferson* 169, 171 (1899).

[39] Murray served as Lord Chief Justice from 1756 to 1788. The King's Bench was one
of three common law courts in England at the time. Although there were rival courts of
various royal and nonroyal statures, the King's Bench was the most important common
law court in the land. Appeals were possible but largely unknown, and therefore the King's
Bench had the ultimate say in most matters, especially those of a commercial nature.

[40] Friedman, *History of American Law* at 133 (cited in note 20). Mansfield recognized
the importance of the law merchant, which was based largely on commercial customs in
practice in some areas since the Middle Ages, and incorporated it into general rules of
application within the larger common law.

[41] Oldham, *Law in the Age of Mansfield* at 10 (cited in note 34).

[42] Edmund Heward, *Lord Mansfield: A Biography of William Murray, 1st Earl of Mansfield
(1705–1793) Lord Chief Justice for 32 Years* 99 (1979); Friedman, *History of American Law*
at 28 (note 20) ("There were many types of merchant courts, including the colorful courts
of piepowder, a court of the fairs where merchants gathered."). Recent scholarship casts
doubt on the view that the law merchant was a system of private ordering among merchants

distinct from the common law because it was international in scope and based largely on trade-specific customs that were unique to the commercial setting. The law merchant consisted primarily of semicodified customs that developed over the course of many years and many thousands of transactions.[43] It also existed in various treaties and legal codes set out by scholars and merchants in trade centers, like Rhodes, Barcelona, and Visby.[44]

In many cases, this customary law differed from the more structured formalities of English common law.[45] For example, the common law gave tremendous advantages to parties enforcing a written contract "sealed by the party against whom the claim was made," but in fair courts this rule was generally waived.[46] In general, the customs and practices of trades were the law of commerce on the Continent, which was foreign to judges, juries, and judgments in English courts. Lord Holt, who preceded Mansfield as Chief Justice, noted when describing why the "law" should be insulated from the influence of merchants: "no protagonist, however influential, [should] be permitted to dictate the terms upon which his dispute should be resolved."[47] In this respect, England differed substantially from the rest of Europe, where trade guild law was well incorporated into the body of general law.[48] As could be ex-

---

that was somehow superior to modern commercial law. See, for example, Emily Kadens, *Order Within Law, Variety Within Custom: The Character of the Medieval Merchant Law*, 5 Chi J Intl L 38, 63 (2004) (describing the law merchant as a "layer of laws and practices that included legislative mandates, broad-reaching customs, and narrow trade usages").

[43] For a modern example, see Lisa Bernstein, *Private Commercial Law in the Cotton Industry: Creating Cooperation Through Rules, Norms, and Institutions*, 99 Mich L Rev 1724 (2001) (describing the private commercial law used by merchants in the cotton industry).

[44] In the famous case *Luke v Lyde*, Lord Mansfield cited to various laws of the sea, including Rhodian Laws, the Consolato del Mare (Barcelona), and the laws of Visby. See Bridget Murphy, *Luke v Lyde*, 2003 Auckland U L Rev 2 (2003).

[45] Edward Coke, who preceded Lord Mansfield on the King's Bench by 150 years, declared in 1608 that "the Law Merchant is part of this realm," see 1 Edward Coke, *Institutes of the Laws of England* 182a (1648), but this did not mean that customary commercial law was fully incorporated into the common law or that common law courts stepped aside and let merchant courts settle disputes. A century and a half after Coke made this statement the common law was largely ignorant and disrespectful of the law merchant. See W. S. Holdsworth, *The Rules of Venue, and the Beginnings of the Commercial Jurisdiction of the Common Law Courts*, 7 Colum L Rev 551, 561–62 (1914) ("It was not till the common law obtained in Lord Mansfield a judge who was a master of [foreign writings on commercial customs] that the rules deducible from the many various commercial customs which had come before the courts were formed into a coherent system, and completely incorporated with the common law.").

[46] See Heward, *Lord Mansfield* at 100–101 (cited in note 42).

[47] Fifoot, *Lord Mansfield* at 9 (cited in note 37).

[48] See Heward, *Lord Mansfield* at 99–101 (cited in note 42).

pected, this procedural difference made law courts less valuable for resolving commercial disputes.

The unprecedented growth in trade and commerce during the eighteenth century made the usefulness of courts in settling commercial law disputes an especially acute problem. In the fifty years before Mansfield became Chief Justice and for the fifty years after, international commerce became essential to the success of England's expanding empire.[49] As Dr. Samuel Johnson noted in 1756, the same year Mansfield was called to the bench, "there was never from the earliest ages a time in which trade so much engaged the attention of mankind, or commercial gain was sought with such general emulation."[50] At this time "the place of the Law Merchant in English law was considerably unsettled . . . [because] very few general rules and principles had been established to which isolated decisions could be adjusted."[51] English courts were not viewed as being equipped to offer a valuable service to commercial parties. The inadequacy of common law courts is apparent from commentary by merchants at the time. One influential guide for merchants noted that "[t]he right dealing merchant doth not care how little he hath to do in the Common Law."[52] Others advocated the establishment of specialty courts, impugning the law courts for not understanding commercial issues and creating confusion with their opinions.[53]

The divergence between formal and informal law, between common and commercial law, was a problem *for law courts* since their inadequacy simply pushed commercial disputes to other forums of dispute resolution. Courts were, from the perspective of busi-

---

[49] See P. Marshall, *The Eighteenth Century* (1988) 53 (noting that during the period 1697 to 1815 exports increased much faster than population growth or economic growth as a whole).

[50] See Fifoot, *Lord Mansfield* at 4 (cited in note 37).

[51] Murphy, *Luke v Lyde* at 4 (cited in note 44).

[52] John Marius, *Advice Concerning Bills of Exchange* (Early English Books Online, Electronic Reproduction, Ann Arbor, MI, 1999).

[53] John D. Cary, *An Essay on the State of England in Relation to Its Trade* (printed by W. Bonny, 1695, Early English Books Online, Electronic Reproduction, Ann Arbor, MI, 1999) (advocating "Courts of Merchants . . . for the speedy deciding all differences relating to Sea Affairs, which are better ended by those who understand them, than they are in Westminster-Hall."); see also Josiah Child, *A Discourse About Trade* (printed by A. Sowle, 1689, Early English Books Online, Electronic Reproduction, Ann Arbor, MI, 1999) ("it is well if, after great expenses of time and money, we can make our own Counsel (being Common Lawyers) understand one half of our Case, we being amongst them as in a Foreign Country.").

ness interests, overly formal and out of touch with the reality of commerce. The growth of commercial transactions in number, size, and complexity only exacerbated the problem.[54] As commerce became more demanding of law, the hodgepodge of courts (e.g., courts of law, courts of equity, law merchant courts, ecclesiastical courts, etc.) regulating commerce added to the misfit between common law adjudication and the needs of business. This manifested itself in two ways.

First, different courts made different rules, creating uncertainty for businesses. There were over seventy law "courts" operating in London in the late eighteenth century, and these were administered by almost 800 judges.[55] Although this plethora of courts gave plaintiffs a wide range of options to find the best venue for their claim, the lack of a centralized or systematic reporting system made the mishmash of courts a nightmare for anyone looking for clear legal rules. Even with a modern database like Westlaw, English judges and litigants at the time would have had difficulty determining the rule for any particular case. The plight of businessmen planning their affairs without legal counsel would have been nearly hopeless.

Even when we narrow the number of courts to the most important ones,[56] this still leaves three—Common Pleas, Exchequer, and King's Bench—all of which had overlapping jurisdiction.[57] Decisions from these courts were not binding on other courts,[58]

---

[54] For example, during the time when Lord Mansfield was Chief Justice the number of cases involving promissory notes or bills of exchange increased about 100 percent per year, over three times the increase in cases overall. Heward, *Lord Mansfield* at 53 (cited in note 42).

[55] See Patrick Colquhoun, *A Treatise on the Police of the Metropolis* 383–88 (5th ed) (describing 9 supreme courts, 4 ecclesiastical courts, 17 courts for the City of London, 8 courts for the City of Westminster, 14 courts for the part of the city lying in the County of Middlesex, 8 courts in the Borough of Southwark, 18 courts for small debts, 1 court of oyer and terminer, 4 courts of general and quarter sessions of the peace, 10 courts for the police petty matters, and 5 corners' courts. These were overseen by 753 judges. Id at 389. This does not include the innumerable merchants' courts, private arbitration proceedings, and other methods for resolving disputes.

[56] These three courts were the primary source of the common law during this period, despite being responsible for only a small percentage of cases. See Oldham, *Law in the Age of Mansfield* at 12 (cited in note 34).

[57] These courts, comprised of four judges each, had overlapping jurisdiction, and therefore competed for cases. As Daniel Klerman argues in a recent paper, competition was fierce, since judges were paid by the case. See Daniel M. Klerman, *Jurisdictional Competition and the Evolution of the Common Law*, 74 U Chi L Rev 1179, 1189–90 (2007).

[58] Oldham, *Law in the Age of Mansfield* at 366 (cited in note 34) ("Decisions from another court would be looked to only as advisory or as a means of persuasion.").

meaning there were (at least) three relevant sources of legal precedents for any particular dispute. According to Oldham, "[t]he horizontal structure of the English general courts, with three common law courts, each court operating largely independently of the others, inhibited growth of the notion of binding precedent."[59] In addition, separate equity courts, specifically the Court of Chancery, existed as an alternative to law courts. Although the equity courts had limited jurisdiction, they were available for many commercial law disputes. To complicate matters, equity courts typically had even worse reporting than the law courts.[60]

It is not surprising that these many courts competed with each other for business. They did so not only for the reputational benefits, but for cash, since judges were paid by the case.[61] According to a recent study, judges therefore had an incentive to rule in favor of plaintiffs because they were the party that chose the venue in most common law cases.[62] Plaintiffs also had an incentive to choose a venue that increased their prospects, regardless of the impact on future cases, which could be brought in other courts. If a business wanted to enforce a contract without a sealed, written document, it could bring an action at a merchant fair instead filing a formal pleading with a law court. And if a business had an equitable action to bring—for example, that a contract should be enforced despite technical defects—it would have to do so in Chancery, where this argument was allowed, as opposed to the law courts. In this way, the various courts competed for the business of commercial dispute resolution. By making favorable rules or procedures, courts could attract more disputes (taking market share from competing courts) and perhaps encourage more suits due to reduced transaction costs (growing the pie).

Second, even within a specific court jurisdiction, the use of seriatim opinions added a layer of confusion. Instead of mani-

---

[59] Id at 365.

[60] William Murray, who practiced before the Court of Chancery in the mid-eighteenth century (when reporting was still poor in equity courts), wrote: "It is a misfortune attending a court of equity, that the cases are generally taken in loose notes, and sometimes by persons who do not understand business, and very often draw general principles from a case, without attending to particular circumstances, which weighed with the court in the determination of these cases." Id at 366.

[61] See Klerman, *Jurisdictional Competition* at 9–11 (cited in note 57) (showing that fees paid to judges per case were substantial and sufficient to bias their decisions in favor of plaintiffs, who chose the venue).

[62] Id.

festing a binary win-loss character, opinions were a collection of "for" and "against" arguments. To determine whether one had won or lost a case, and, more importantly, what the rule of the case was and how strong the precedent was, it was necessary to count heads. In complex commercial disputes, this was not an easy matter. Moreover, interpreting past cases to plan future arguments was also exceedingly complex given the plethora of opinions on every subject and the often highly nuanced differences among them. Accordingly, during this period the law became much more "confusing and remote to merchants and businessmen."[63] Thus the nascent commercial law of England was uncertain, exactly the opposite of what businesses needed to thrive.

From the perspective of eighteenth-century merchants what was needed was someone or something to bring more certainty to commercial dealings, simplify legal proceedings, and create a simple set of rules that could be applied to all transactions.[64] According to Mansfield, the law of business "ought not to depend on subtleties and niceties, but upon rules easily learned and easily retained because they are dictates of common sense. . . ."[65]

From the perspective of courts what was needed was a way to bring the business of commercial regulation to law courts—to increase the market share of law courts.[66] Mansfield's strategy was to make the decisions of his court (that is, his product) more attractive to potential litigants (that is, potential customers). To do this, Mansfield adopted the best practices of competitors. He created a set of general principles based on the valuable services that rival courts offered business litigants. These general principles included the requirement of good faith (from equitable courts) and the use of trade custom (from the law merchant or fair courts). Mansfield believed that the international nature of commerce meant that commercial law must be the "same all over the world"[67]

---

[63] Friedman, *History of American Law* at 95 (cited in note 20).

[64] Id at 58 ("The merchant's idea of a good legal system was one that was rational and efficient, conforming to his values and expectations—traits that neither lay justice neither the baroque extravagances of English procedure [at law courts] supplied.").

[65] *Hamilton v Mendes*, 2 Burr 1214 (1761).

[66] Friedman, *History of American Law* at 18 (cited in note 20). Mansfield wanted not only to take cases from other courts, but also from the legislature. See Jack N. Rakove, *Original Meanings: Politics and Ideas in the Making of the Constitution* 211 (1997) (describing Mansfield as engaged in a "project of defending . . . traditional modes of adjudication against the perceived vices of legislation.").

[67] *Pelly v Royal Exchange Assurance Co.*, 1 Burr 341, 347 (1757).

and that England therefore had to move its formal law in the direction of traditional practices in other countries. "He . . . encouraged the development of legal rules that would support a commercial economy that was increasingly dependent on paper credit and that was vigorously involved in international trade."[68] Related to this was his view that legal rules should be understood by those "who must obey [them]."[69] The normative underpinning of Mansfield's revolution was certainty: "the great object in every branch of law, but especially in mercantile law, is certainty."[70]

But Mansfield needed a mechanism to deliver certainty. He found it in the "opinion of the court." The reform of the common law of commerce was possible only with an assertion of judicial power through a united court speaking in a single voice. Mansfield's expertise and clarity provided a certain statement of the law that drew cases to his court—no longer would multiple courts and numerous judges produce different opinions subject to nuance and ambiguity. A single court would hear and decide the fundamental issues of commercial law, decide them once and for all without dispute or ambiguity, and provide the certainty and stability needed for commercial transactions.[71]

The arc of the famous case *Luke v Lyde* is instructive. After a merchant ship was captured at sea and then recaptured, the privateer, ship owner, and captain litigated, in the absence of a formal contract, what was owed to whom. Mansfield originally heard the case alone in the assizes of Devonshire, but he removed it to London for a hearing before the whole court of the King's Bench so that he could make it "a Case" or a more useful precedent for other merchants.[72] According to Burrow's account:

> [Mansfield] said he always leaned (even where he had himself no doubt) to make cases for the opinion of the Court; not only for the greater satisfaction of the parties in the particular case

---

[68] Oldham, *Law in the Age of Mansfield* at 365 (cited in note 34).

[69] Id at 124.

[70] *Milles v Fletcher*, 1 Doug 231, 232 (1779).

[71] Mansfield's application of equitable principles to commercial disputes was extremely controversial. In fact, Mansfield's successors—such as Kenyon, Thurlow, and Eldon—all opposed this reform, and it was not until 1873 that the Supreme Court of Judicature was established and endowed with both equitable and legal powers. See Judicature Act of 1873, § 24.

[72] See James Oldham, *Review: From Blackstone to Bentham: Common Law versus Legislation in Eighteenth-Century Britain*, 89 Mich L Rev 1637, 1645 n 32 (1991).

> but to prevent other disputes, by making the rules of law and
> the ground upon which they are established certain and no-
> torious.[73]

The new "truth" about commercial law could be discovered only
by an exercise of power—the power to change the discourse of
the law, to change the form to adapt to the new function.

Mansfield's success can be measured in several ways. For one,
as a result of his legal innovations, Mansfield's court flourished.
Prior to Mansfield's discursive change, very few commercial cases
came before law courts such as the King's Bench.[74] As a result of
the consolidation of power through the focusing of legal discourse,
Mansfield created a forum that was conducive to handling commercial cases, and "business flowed into his court."[75] The number
of "commercial cases" handled by the King's Bench increased more
rapidly than the overall growth rate of the docket as a whole. For
example, the number of commercial cases handled by the King's
Bench grew by 30 percentage points more than all other cases
during Mansfield's time on the bench.[76] More specifically, the
number of cases involving promissory notes, which are essential
elements for international trade, rose fivefold, from about three
per year during the beginning of Mansfield's tenure to about fifteen per year at the end. Cases involving "bills of exchange" and
various monetary disputes saw similar increases, while common
law standards, like trover and trespass, increased at much lower
rates.[77]

Another measure of Mansfield's success is his impact on legal

---

[73] *Luke v Lyde*, 2 Burr 882, 887, 97 Eng Rep 614, 617–18 (KB 1759).

[74] Fifoot, *Lord Mansfield* at 13 n 1 (cited in note 37).

[75] Heward, *Lord Mansfield* at 173 (cited in note 42). Other factors contributed to the
success of the King's Bench at attracting cases to the court. Mansfield was a very hard
worker and, by all accounts, operated his court with a ruthless efficiency. See Oldham,
Law in the Age of Mansfield at 5 (cited in note 34) ("[H]e took particular care that this
should not create delay or expense to the parties; and therefore he always dictated the
case to the Court, and saw it signed by counsel, before another case was called; and always
made it a condition in the rule, that it should be set down to be argued within the first
four days of the term.").

[76] According to Heward, the number of commercial cases (e.g., "goods sold and delivered," "money," "promissory notes," "policy of assurance," and "bills of exchange") grew
105 percent, from 217 during the period 1761–65 to 444 during the period 1776–80,
whereas the total number of other cases grew 75 percent (134 to 235) over the same
periods. See Heward, *Lord Mansfield* at 105–06 (cited in note 42).

[77] Trover, or an action for the taking of property, went from 32 to 44, trespass from 7
to 16. See id.

thinkers and legal aggregators of the day. Blackstone, the greatest of these, wrote, just nine years after Mansfield became Chief Justice, that "the learning relating to . . . insurance hath of late years been greatly improved by a series of judicial decisions, which have now established the law."[78] Judge Buller, writing seven years after Mansfield stepped down, described the impact:

> Before [Mansfield] we find that in Courts of law all the evidence in mercantile cases was thrown together . . . and they produced no established principle. From that time we all know the great study has been to find some certain general principles . . . not only to rule the particular case then under consideration, but to serve as a guide for the future.[79]

Writing with more historical perspective, Oldham writes that Mansfield was one of the two "most important judicial figures in the law of bankruptcy,"[80] and the elucidator of the fundamental legal principles of insurance and negotiable instruments, where his chief contribution was "cogency."[81] Mansfield brought, "with considerable success," merchant customs "harmoniously" into the common law.[82] Mansfield accomplished the reform of commercial law—in fact, the capture of commercial regulation by law—in part through an alteration of legal discourse.[83] Clarity, which commerce demanded as a precondition for using law courts, was achieved by changing opinion-delivery practices in a way designed to unify the judicial voice.

The change from seriatim opinions to opinions of the court was short-lived. On the retirement of Mansfield, Lord Kenyon put an end to the practice, and the judges returned to the practice of seriatim opinions.[84] The reason for Kenyon's decision can be found in his theory of judging. Kenyon believed in a traditional

---

[78] See William Blackstone, 2 *Commentaries on the Laws of England* *461.

[79] *Lickbarrow v Mason*, 2 TR 63, 74; 100 ER 35 (1787).

[80] Oldham, *Law in the Age of Mansfield* at 107 (cited in note 34).

[81] Id at 124, 163.

[82] Id at 365, 368.

[83] Id at 365 ("[Mansfield] strove with considerable success to absorb the customs of merchants into the common law.").

[84] Until recently they delivered their opinions seriatim, each Lord reading aloud his judgment and the reasons for it. The Lords no longer routinely deliver five separate opinions, although they do more frequently announce separate opinions than does our Supreme Court. J. H. Baker, *Introduction to English Legal History* 204–11 (1990).

common law approach to deciding cases; he viewed law and equity as separate and considered an incremental approach, rather than a broad, theoretical one, as the way to reach the best results.[85] Kenyon seldom wrote opinions and rarely gave reasons for his judgments, preferring to decide cases one at a time on the narrow facts before him, rather than announce broad legal rules.[86] This stands in stark contrast with Mansfield's attempt to fuse common law and equity and to announce principles of law from cases in an attempt to increase court power.[87] As one account describes Kenyon's legacy, he is most remembered for "restor[ing] the simplicity and rigour of the common law."[88] These views about judicial minimalism were known to Mansfield, who worried so much about Kenyon's views and the impact they would have that he lingered on the King's Bench long after he planned retirement in the hopes that someone other than Kenyon would be appointed to succeed him.[89] Kenyon's restoration of seriatim persevered until very recently in all multimember English courts.[90]

B. EARLY AMERICAN PRACTICES

England's long tradition of seriatim opinions crossed the Atlantic along with much of the common law during the formative

---

[85] See George T. Kenyon, *The Life of Lloyd, First Lord Kenyon, Lord Chief Justice of England* 391 (1873) (noting that Kenyon favored the traditional common law approach over Mansfield's attempt to fuse law and equity and discern abstract theories from cases); see also John Lord Campbell, *The Lives of the Chief Justices of England: From the Norman Conquest Till the Death of Lord Tenterden* 96 (1874) (noting Kenyon's preference for a traditional common law, case-by-case approach).

[86] See Kenyon, *The Life of Lloyd* at 390–91 (cite in note 85). Here we see a similarity with the views of Chief Justice Roberts and his views about the role of the Supreme Court. Roberts also appears to be trying to innovate in opinion-delivery practices to achieve his goals, just as Kenyon did. See Part III.B.

[87] See id at 391 (noting that Kenyon favored the traditional common law approach over Mansfield's); see also Campbell, *Lives of the Chief Justices of England* at 96 (cited in note 85).

[88] See Campbell, *Lives of the Chief Justices of England* at 96 (cited in note 85).

[89] See Kenyon, *The Life of Lloyd* at 166 (cited in note 85).

[90] The Law Lords, who serve as the Supreme Court of Great Britain in some cases, routinely delivered opinions seriatim, with each of the five judges announcing an individual judgment with reasons. See Louis Blom-Cooper and Gavin Drewry, *Final Appeal: A Study of the House of Lords in Its Judicial Capacity* 81–82, 523 (1972). This practice recently waned. See also Paterson, *The Law Lords* 109–10 (1982) (noting that the Lords no longer routinely deliver five separate opinions).

stages of American judicial development.[91] Early American jurists learned the law by studying the English common law, and therefore adopted many of its practices and institutions. In addition, many of the state courts were established before Mansfield's discursive innovation, so in every state court and in the early years of the Supreme Court, American judges continued the practice of seriatim opinions.[92]

But Mansfield's change was evident to American courts and judges, so in some cases it was emulated. In several states, Mansfield's practice was adopted as a way to increase the power of the courts vis-à-vis the other branches of government. Jurists in these states saw how Mansfield had increased the power of the King's Bench at the expense of other forms of power, and were eager to emulate this power grab. For example, in Virginia soon after the Revolution, Judge Edmund Pendleton became the chief judge of the court of appeals.[93] Pendleton admired Mansfield and "considered him as the greatest luminary of law that any age had ever produced."[94] Pendleton introduced Mansfield's practice of "making up opinions in secret & delivering them as the Oracles of the court."[95]

This practice was widely criticized by Thomas Jefferson and other Republicans. Due to this political pressure, upon the ascension of Judge Spencer Roane to Judge Pendleton's seat on the bench some years later, the practice ceased and the tradition of seriatim opinions was quickly reinstated.[96] Roane shared Jeffer-

---

[91] Friedman, *History of American Law* at 112 (cited in note 20) ("To fill the gap [in American law at the beginning], English materials were used, English reports cited, English judges quoted as authority.").

[92] See Scott D. Gerber, ed, *Seriatim: The Supreme Court Before John Marshall* (1998); see also David P. Currie, *Review of Seriatim: The Supreme Court Before John Marshall*, 105 Am Hist Rev 1301, 1301 (2000) (noting that "the justices of the time deliver[ed] their opinions seriatim.").

[93] *Letter from Thomas Jefferson to Justice William Johnson* (Oct 27, 1822), in Merrill D. Peterson, ed, *Thomas Jefferson: Writings* 1460–63 (1984).

[94] Id. Mansfield was a hero to many early colonial lawyers, so it is not surprising that his experiment with unanimous, anonymous opinions would be something they were willing to try. See Friedman, *History of American Law* at 109 (cited in note 20) ("One of the cultural heroes of the American legal elite was England's Lord Mansfield.").

[95] Id.

[96] See Donald G. Morgan, *The Origin of Supreme Court Dissent*, 3 Wm & Mary Q 353, 354 (1953) ("In Virginia . . . Judge Pendleton, taking Mansfield as his model, had instituted the secret, unanimous opinion in the state bench; his successor, Judge Roane, had abolished the practice.").

son's view about the role of the judiciary, which is best expressed in a letter he sent to Roane after the decision in *Marbury v Madison*: "The constitution, on this hypothesis, is a mere thing of wax in the hands of the judiciary, which they may twist, and shape into any form they please."[97]

Thomas Jefferson's role in returning to seriatim opinions in Virginia courts is not surprising, because he was a vocal critic of courts and the threat to democracy an aggrandizement of judicial power posed.[98] This battle against Judge Pendleton in Virginia foreshadowed a battle with John Marshall over the same issue regarding the way the Supreme Court delivered opinions. In fact, this single issue would become one of the predominant political issues of the age, embroiling the nation's legal system for a decade and threatening the political stability of the young nation.[99] The winners of the battle—Marshall and the Federalists—would use their victory over the form of legal discourse to build much of what we recognize as the American legal system. The Supreme Court and its relation with the other branches of government looks the way it does today because of Marshall's ability to carry the day with respect to how legal opinions should be issued from the bench.

Jefferson praised the seriatim system of announcing the law for four reasons: (1) it increased transparency and led to more accountability, (2) it showed that each judge had considered and understood the case, (3) it gave more or less weight to a precedent based on the vote of the judges, (4) and it allowed judges in the future to overrule bad law based on the reasoning of their predecessors.[100] The overarching rationale for Jefferson's preference was to limit what he viewed as the undemocratic power of courts.

---

[97] *Letter from Thomas Jefferson to Spencer Roane* (Sept 6, 1819), in Paul Leicester Ford, ed, *The Works of Thomas Jefferson* (1904–5).

[98] See generally Richard E. Ellis, *The Jeffersonian Crisis: Courts and Politics in the Young Republic* (1971).

[99] See generally James F. Simon, *What Kind of Nation: Thomas Jefferson, John Marshall, and the Epic Struggle to Create a United States* (2003). Jefferson and Marshall battled repeatedly over the extent of judicial power in the early Republic. See, for example, id at 285 (noting that Jefferson criticized Marshall's opinion in *Cohens v Virginia*, writing to Judge Spencer Roane: "The great object of my fear is the federal judiciary. . . . Let the eye of vigilance never be closed.").

[100] In this final capacity, dissenting opinions act as an "antiprecedent" that allows future judges to base their decision to overrule the previous opinion based on established legal reasoning.

First, Jefferson argued for a return to seriatim opinions to increase the transparency of the decision-making process in order to reign in the power of the judiciary. In Jefferson's view, the practice of issuing an "opinion of the court" insulated any single Justice from criticism. In this way, "judicia[l] perversions of the Constitution will forever be protected."[101] Opinions of the Court were the shield that insulated the Justices from obloquy and perhaps even impeachment. Jefferson described the practice of issuing opinions as an entire Court without a public vote as a "most condemnable" practice in which the Justices "cook[ed] up a decision in caucus and deliver[ed] it by one of their members as the opinion of the court, without the possibility of our knowing how many, who, and for what reasons each member concurred."[102] In Jefferson's view it was not only the particular decisions that were to be condemned but also the process, which "smother[ed] evidence" and allowed the Justices to decide important questions without "justify[ing] the reasons which led to their opinion."[103]

Second, Jefferson worried that judges were lazy, aloof, or otherwise absent from decision making on important legal questions. Jefferson reasoned that requiring a judge to write out his argument for each case would provide sufficient incentive for each judge adequately to consider the legal merits of the case. Jefferson wrote:

> Let [each judge] prove by his reasoning that he has read the papers, that he has considered the case, that in the application of the law to it, he uses his own judgment independently and unbiased by party views and personal favor or disfavor.[104]

Third, Jefferson wrote that multiple opinions not only "communicated [the law] by [the judges] several modes of reasoning, it showed whether the judges were unanimous or divided, and gave accordingly more or less weight to the judgment as a precedent."[105] Jefferson wanted a vote. "Why should not every judge be asked his

---

[101] *Letter from Thomas Jefferson to James Pleasants* (Dec 1821), in Paul Leicester Ford, ed, 10 *The Writings of Thomas Jefferson* 198–99 (1892–99).

[102] Id.

[103] Id.

[104] *Letter from Thomas Jefferson to Justice William Johnson* (March 4, 1823), in Henry A. Washington, ed, 7 *The Writings of Thomas Jefferson* 278–79 (1853–54).

[105] *Letter from Thomas Jefferson to Justice William Johnson* (Oct 27, 1822), in Merrill D. Peterson, ed, *Thomas Jefferson: Writings* 1460–63 (1990).

opinion, and give it from the bench, if only by yea or nay? . . . it would show whether the opinions were unanimous or not and thus settle more exactly the weight of their authority."[106] This practice of dissent by vote only was occasionally practiced in the early years of the Court[107] and has been advocated by some modern commentators.[108] To Jefferson, who was fearful of the aggrandizement of power in the judiciary,[109] this would allow the legislature or other courts to respond appropriately to the decision—follow it, evade it, or bypass it with legislation or constitutional amendment—based on the "strength" of the opinion. Dissent, with or without opinion, would serve this function.

Finally, Jefferson acknowledged that temporal communication between current and future judges allowed for bad law to be overturned more easily.[110] Jefferson knew of English cases in which decisions had occasionally been overruled based on "dissents" in previous seriatim opinions. Jefferson acknowledged this when he wrote that "[i]t sometimes happened too that when there were three opinions against one, the reasoning of the one was so much the most cogent as to become afterwards the law of the land."[111] This is the most powerful justification for dissent. In fact, Jefferson was foreshadowing to an extent the future of the Supreme Court and the power of dissenting opinions when he called for this sort of deliberation from judge to judge across time. To take just two of the many examples from Supreme Court history, dissents in cases such as *Lochner v New York*[112] and *Plessy v Ferguson*[113] were instrumental in changing the law many years in the future.[114]

---

[106] *Letter from Thomas Jefferson to Justice William Johnson* (June 6, 1823), in Henry A. Washington, ed, 7 *Writings of Thomas Jefferson* at 293–98 (cited in note 104).

[107] For example, in *Herbert v Wren*, 11 US 370 (1813), Justice Johnson dissented from the opinion of the Court, but did not state his reasons.

[108] Richard A. Posner, *The Federal Courts: Challenge and Reform* 174 (1996).

[109] Thomas Jefferson strongly disagreed with Alexander Hamilton's characterization of the judiciary as the "least dangerous branch." See Clinton Rossiter, ed, *The Federalist Papers* (No 78), 392–99 (Alexander Hamilton) (1999).

[110] Of course, dissenting opinions can be used to overturn "good" law too.

[111] *Letter from Thomas Jefferson to Justice William Johnson* (Oct 27, 1822), in Merrill D. Peterson, ed, *Thomas Jefferson: Writings* 1460–63 (cited in note 105).

[112] *Lochner v New York*, 198 US 45 (1905).

[113] *Plessy v Ferguson*, 163 US 537 (1896).

[114] The overruling of laissez-faire constitutionalism based on Justice Holmes's dissent in *Lochner* was the first time in Supreme Court history that a fundamental jurisprudential doctrine was overruled on the basis of a prior dissenting opinion. Similarly, it was Justice

For these reasons perhaps, but more likely out of tradition, the Supreme Court, like most of the state courts, initially emulated the seriatim practice of their brethren on England's courts. The fact that decisions of the Supreme Court were issued as a collection of separate opinions, with each Justice issuing an opinion with reasons for the decision, also limited the Court's power. Just as in the King's Bench before and after Mansfield, this style of opinion delivery created substantial uncertainty and instability in the law.[115]

Calder v Bull, a classic case from the pre-Marshall Supreme Court, demonstrates this perfectly.[116] Decided in 1798, the Court considered whether a statute passed by the Connecticut legislature overturning a state court probate decision violated the Ex Post Facto Clause of the federal Constitution.[117] Four Justices wrote opinions on the ex post facto issue, and the holding was therefore highly confused. The modern interpretation of the collection of seriatim opinions is that the constitutional clause applies only to retroactive punishment, but, according to David Currie, "the practice of seriatim opinions . . . make[s] it difficult to say that this was the holding of the Court . . . ."[118] Currie goes on to conclude that "*Calder* illustrates the uncertainty that can arise when each Justice writes separately . . . ,"[119] and that "[t]he practice of seriatim opinions . . . weakened the force of the [Court's] decisions."[120]

The result of this practice was a weak and divided Court unable to assert any real authority.[121] Although the Federalists, including

Harlan's lone dissent in *Plessy* that would later provide much of the eloquent ammunition against "separate but equal" laws. With the words "the Constitution is color blind, and neither knows nor tolerates classes among citizens," Harlan set the stage for *Brown v Board of Education*, 347 US 483 (1954), and much of the civil rights movement. This is the power of dissent, for good or bad.

[115] As noted by Professor David Currie, seriatim opinions may be beneficial in that they may provide more information germane to predicting future outcomes. See David P. Currie, *The Constitution in the Supreme Court: The First Hundred Years, 1789–1888* 14, n 61 (1985) ("Yet seriatim opinions actually may give us a better basis for predicting later decisions.").

[116] 3 US 386 (1798).

[117] Id at 387 (interpreting Art I, § 10).

[118] Currie, *Constitution in the Supreme Court* at 44 (cited in note 115).

[119] Id at 45.

[120] Id at 55.

[121] Furthermore, the circuit-riding duties of the Justices eroded the spirit and morale of the Court, contributing to its ineffectiveness. These duties were especially draining of the Justices' energy because of the difficulty of traveling during this era. When John Jay referred to a lack of "energy" on the Court, it was riding circuit that was the likely culprit. Thus Congress, state legislatures, and state courts were the dominant policy makers during this period.

the first Chief Justice, John Jay, wanted to assert the Court's power to ensure the supremacy of federal law, Anti-Federalist antipathy toward the federal judiciary continued to dominate the political scene.[122]

The weakness of the Court was demonstrated by the negative reception of many of its early opinions. Characteristic of the hostility to the Court during this period was the reaction of the Anti-Federalists to the Court's opinion in *Chisholm v Georgia*.[123] *Chisholm* held that a state was not immune to suit by a private citizen in federal court.[124] Legislators in Georgia responded to this decision by introducing a constitutional amendment to restrict the power of federal courts to hear suits against states brought by citizens of other states. This amendment quickly became the Eleventh Amendment to the Constitution.[125] With this severe blow to the institutional power of the Court, Chief Justice Jay abandoned his leadership of the Court in order to become governor of New York.[126] When asked by President John Adams to resume his duties in 1800, Jay refused on the grounds that the Court lacked any prestige or authority and would be unable to earn the "public confidence and respect."[127]

Following Jay's departure and the brief leadership of John Rutledge,[128] Oliver Ellsworth was appointed as Chief Justice. Ellsworth

---

[122] See, for example, Ellis, *Jeffersonian Crisis* at 12 (cited in note 98) ("Throughout George Washington's first administration the federal judiciary tried to avoid becoming engaged in political controversies or becoming entangled in questions outside its immediate jurisdiction.").

[123] *Chisholm v Georgia*, 2 US 419 (1793).

[124] Id.

[125] US Const, Amend XI ("The judicial power of the United States shall not be construed to extend to any suit in law or equity, commenced or prosecuted against one of the United States by citizens of another state, or by citizens or subjects of any foreign state."). This was one of only two constitutional amendments that was adopted explicitly to repudiate a Supreme Court decision—the other being the Sixteenth Amendment (federal income tax), which was in response to the Supreme Court's decision in *Pollock v Farmers' Loan*, 158 US 601 (1895), which declared the federal income tax of 1894 unconstitutional.

[126] Similarly, Robert H. Harrison refused an appointment to the Court in 1789 to become chancellor of Maryland. See Friedman, *History of American Law* at 133 (cited in note 20).

[127] Richard Morris, *John Jay, the Nation, and the Court* (1967). Jay "left the bench perfectly convinced that under a system so defective it would not obtain the energy, weight, and dignity which are essential to its affording due support to the national government, nor acquire the public confidence and respect which, as a court of laws resort of the justice of the nation, it should possess." 4 *The Correspondence and Public Papers of John Jay* 285 (1893).

[128] John Rutledge was appointed by President Washington in 1795. Rutledge participated

was an advocate of a stronger central government. In order to increase federal power, Chief Justice Ellsworth attempted to initiate a policy of handing down opinions per curiam—anonymous and unanimous opinions that would emulate Mansfield's opinion of the court. Ellsworth believed that by issuing decisions that would speak for the Court as a whole without dissent, the power of the Court, and thereby the power of the national government, would be increased. This reform was unsuccessful in part because of the lack of political will on the part of those opposed to seriatim opinions, in part because Ellsworth's tenure as Chief Justice was brief due to illness, and undoubtedly for other reasons as well.[129] The seed, however, that would allow the growth of national power had been sowed.

When Ellsworth left office, the future of the Court was not clear. This was in part because the Supreme Court's very existence was questioned at the Founding. Although eventually established as a tri-equal branch of government, the creation of a national court was contested at the Constitutional Convention of 1787. The delegates realized the need for a stronger national government than existed under the Articles of Confederation, but many representatives considered the existing state courts as sufficient for interpreting national laws and thought the federal judiciary to be a potential "source of tyranny."[130]

In the end, Federalists, who envisioned a national judiciary to settle interstate disputes, were victorious.[131] The Supreme Court was their reward. By modern standards this was a substantial expression of national power, but for the first decade of its existence it remained untapped as the Supreme Court was largely ignored by lawyers, politicians, and the public. The Court was not provided with a chambers and the job of Chief Justice was refused by several prominent statesmen. According to the first Chief Justice, John Jay, in its first ten years the Court "lacked energy, weight, and dignity."[132]

in two cases as Chief Justice before his nomination was defeated in the Senate in December of 1795.

[129] See William G. Brown, *The Life of Oliver Ellsworth* (1905).

[130] See Rakove, *Original Meanings* at 186 (cited in note 66) (describing the position of the Anti-Federalists as articulated by "Brutus," a New York writer responding to the Federalist Papers).

[131] See id.

[132] Morris, *John Jay* at 81 (cited in note 127). See also Robert P. Frankel, Jr., *Judicial Beginnings: The Supreme Court in the 1790s*, 4 History Compass 1102, 1104 (2006).

Everything changed with the appointment of John Marshall as Chief Justice in 1801.

C. THE ERA OF UNANIMITY

In 1800, the year of Ellsworth's retirement from the Court, the Federalists, who had dominated politics since 1789, were on the way out. The Federalists were advocates of a strong central government, were skeptical of state powers, and distrusted direct democracy. By contrast, Jefferson's Republicans emphasized the decentralized authority of the states and the people. With the defeat of Federalist John Adams by Jefferson in the election of 1800, the power of the central government seemed to be on the wane. The outgoing Federalists, however, were not content to entrust the Constitution to Jefferson's Republicans.

Realizing that they were about to lose control of the only two branches of government with any power, the Federalists looked to secure control of the third branch as a possible bulwark of national power. The branch that they seized, however, needed serious reform in order to be strong enough to counteract, or at least curtail, the power of the new president and the Republican-controlled Congress. During its first sixteen terms, the Court heard only about sixty cases, only about ten were of any significance, and when the government moved to Washington in 1800, the Court had "no library, no office space, no clerks or secretaries," and heard cases on the first floor of the Capitol, "adjacent to the main staircase."[133] For these reasons, and because the power of the Court to interpret the Constitution was not clear at this time, Alexander Hamilton described the judiciary as "beyond comparison the weakest of the three branches."[134]

1. *The Marshall Court.* The Federalist reform came in two forms: the outgoing Federalist Congress passed the Judiciary Act of 1801, and lame duck President Adams appointed John Marshall as Chief Justice. Each of these acts was intended not merely to secure Federalist control of the Court, but to increase the power of the Court at the expense of the legislative and executive branches.

The Judiciary Act doubled the number of circuit courts (from

---

[133] Jean Edward Smith, *John Marshall: Definer of a Nation* (1996).

[134] Clinton Rossiter, ed, *The Federalist Papers* (No 78), at 464–65 (Alexander Hamilton) (1999).

three to six) and created sixteen new judgeships.[135] This was intended to do two things to increase Federalist control over the judiciary. First, it gave outgoing President Adams a chance to populate the federal courts with Federalists. Second, it eliminated the circuit-riding duties of Supreme Court Justices, who previously had sat on both the Supreme Court and on the three circuit courts. This was designed to increase the Court's prestige and to increase the desirability of being a Supreme Court Justice.

Riding circuit was a major impediment to an energetic and collegial Court. Relieved of their duties to travel and sit on other courts, the Justices could live together in Washington, develop strong relationships, and work in a more united way on important issues, giving the Court the "energy" that Jay claimed it lacked. This reform was not effective, however, because the Republican-controlled Congress repealed the Act in 1802, and Supreme Court Justices continued to ride circuit until 1869.

The Federalist plan to control the judiciary therefore rested principally on the appointment of John Marshall as Chief Justice of the United States. This was not lost on Marshall. The day Jefferson was inaugurated, Marshall wrote to Charles Cotesworth Pinckney: "Of the importance of the judiciary at all times, but more especially the present I am fully impressed. I shall endeavor in the new office to which I am called not to disappoint my friends."[136]

Marshall was an "ardent nationalist." He wrote that "I was confirmed in the habit of considering America as my country and Congress as my government. . . . I had imbibed these sentiments so thoroughly that they constituted a part of my being."[137] Despite his firm belief in the national government, Marshall was a reluctant political actor. Marshall entered politics following Shays' Rebellion of 1786 only because he felt that the nation was in danger of collapse.[138] Marshall viewed Republican control of the government

---

[135] The Sixth Circuit only got one additional judge. The Act also created ten new district courts, overseen by existing district court judges, who were federalists. These were the famous "midnight judges." See David R. Stras, *Why Supreme Court Justices Should Ride Circuit Again*, 91 Minn L Rev 1710, 1719–21 (2007) (describing the Judiciary Act of 1801 as the "Midnight Judges Act").

[136] *Letter from John Marshall to Charles Cotesworth Pinckney* (Mar 4, 1801), in 6 *The Papers of John Marshall* 89 (1990).

[137] John Stokes Adams, ed, *John Marshall: An Autobiographical Sketch* 9–10 (1937).

[138] Smith, *John Marshall* at 5 (cited in note 133).

as dangerous to his conception of the nation. The "gloomy views"[139] of Federalists upon Jefferson's ascendancy were captured in a letter Marshall wrote to a Congressman from Massachusetts at the time: "I feel that real Americanism is on the ebb."[140] Marshall carried his national spirit to the Court.

Unlike the failed attempt with the Judiciary Act, this tactic of the Federalists proved to be a tremendous success. Marshall found a ready historical example of how courts could increase their power in the experience of Lord Mansfield, who was a "cultural hero of the American legal elite" at that time, and whose reform in the early 1760s was recent history for the Founders.[141] Marshall increased the power of the Court vis-à-vis the other branches of government by dramatically altering the way the Court decided and announced its opinions, just as Mansfield had done, and for the same reasons.

In an expression of raw political power, Marshall abandoned the tradition of seriatim opinions and established an "Opinion of the Court" that would speak for all Justices through a single voice.[142] This change was viewed as an "act [] of audacity" and "assumption [] of power."[143] Marshall used his leadership skills and the power of persuasion to convince the other five members of the Court that they should abandon the practice of issuing seriatim opinions. Cases were now decided by private conference in which the Justices reached a compromise position. An opinion, commanding an unknown vote, was drafted by an anonymous Justice and then issued under the name of "John Marshall" who signed for the Court: "For the first time the Chief Justice disregarded the custom of delivery of opinions by the Justices *seriatim*, and, instead, calmly assumed the function of announcing, himself, the views of that

---

[139] J. Beveridge Jr., *The Life of John Marshall* 15 (1919) ("Of all the leading Federalists, John Marshall was the only one who refused to 'bawl,' at least in the public ear; and yet, as we have seen and shall again find, he entertained the gloomy views of his political associates.").

[140] *Letter from John Marshall to Harrison Gray Otis* (Aug 5, 1800), in 4 *The Papers of John Marshall* at 204–05.

[141] Friedman, *History of American Law* at 109 (cited in note 20).

[142] See, for example, Rehnquist, *The Supreme Court* at 40 (cited in note 33) ("Marshall, in what one of his biographers calls 'an act of audacity,' changed this tradition in the Supreme Court of the United States so that an opinion for the Court was delivered by only one of the justices.").

[143] Beveridge, *Life of John Marshall* at 16 (cited in note 139).

tribunal."[144] Marshall's great discursive revolution, which would cause fundamental shifts in the power of American government, began boldly with the Court's decision in *Talbot v Seeman*.[145]

Although the question presented in *Talbot* was on its face a simple admiralty issue regarding payments owed in cases of salvage, the context of the case required the Court to take sides in a political debate about a raging "quasi-war" with France. The ship involved in the case was the *Amelia*, which was owned by Seeman, a resident of a neutral city-state in the war between England and France. The ship, an armed merchant ship carrying some English goods, had been captured by the French and then recaptured by Talbot, the captain of the American frigate *Constitution*.[146] Talbot sued seeking salvage rights—half the value of the cargo. Seeman argued that the ship was neutral and in no danger of being condemned by the French, and that there was no service rendered and therefore no salvage rights owed.

The controversy required the Court not only to decide the narrow question about whether the risk of condemnation was sufficient to justify payment to Talbot, but also to interpret conflicting congressional and presidential actions regarding America's role in the quasi-war with France. In short, the Court was being asked to make a highly political statement in the guise of a salvage case.

The case required the Court to decide two questions: (1) was the seizure by Talbot legal? and (2) did Talbot provide a valuable service to Seeman? Federalists, who were proponents of the war with France, argued strongly for Talbot; Republicans, who wanted to avoid foreign entanglements and defended neutral shipping, supported Seeman.[147] The Court answered both questions in the affirmative, but did so in a manner designed to placate everyone, thereby allowing the Court to increase its power. Marshall convinced the other Justices that:

> [i]f a complex, politically charged case like *Talbot* could be resolved with a single opinion, not only would the holding enjoy greater legitimacy, but the identity of the Supreme Court as

---

[144] Id.

[145] 5 US 1 (1801).

[146] This is the famous "Old Ironsides." See http://www.ussconstitution.navy.mil.

[147] To add to the mystique of the case, on appeal from a district court ruling for Talbot, Federalist Alexander Hamilton represented Talbot, while Republican, and Hamilton's archenemy and eventual murderer, Aaron Burr, represented Seeman.

[the] nation's highest tribunal would become manifest and its prestige would be enhanced enormously.[148]

The Court's decision reveals not only the compromise the Court needed to reach to speak with one voice but also the need to prevent a political backlash against the Court's new power play. The Court held for Talbot (a victory for the Federalists), but it reduced Talbot's salvage claim to one-sixth of the ship's value (down from the traditional half) and then allowed Seeman to deduct his costs from this amount (a rarity), making the damages nominal (a victory for the Republicans). Marshall established the power of the Court to decide whether congressional statutes authorized seizure of vessels of foreign powers and what role the executive had in foreign policy,[149] while insulating the decision (and thus his assertion of power) from critics. Acceptance of the decision, which Jefferson and the Republicans did reluctantly, opened the door for the Court to assert, just two years later, the power of judicial review in *Marbury v Madison*.

Thus was born the "Opinion of the Court," which, in a revised form, survives to this day. The Court now had weight and dignity as well as energy, and it was not subject to political sniping. John Jay's challenge was met, and the Court was able to assert itself as a tri-equal branch of government.[150] This innovation—a paradigmatic shift in legal discourse—initiated a new era of Supreme Court power. The result was a focusing of the power of the national judiciary, and consequently, a shift in the locus of power from the nonlegal to the legal, and from the states to the federal government. This evolution in the *function* of law was enabled through a change in the *form* in which law is established and delivered. In 1801, the form of legal discourse transmogrified to adapt to law's new role in the emerging modern world.

During his first ten years as Chief Justice, Marshall "wrote" 90

---

[148] Smith, *John Marshall* at 293 (cited in note 133).

[149] In an oft-quoted passage, the Court wrote: "The whole powers of war being, by the Constitution of the United States, vested in Congress, the Acts of that body can alone be resorted to as our guides in this enquiry." See *Talbot v Seeman*, 5 US at 28.

[150] See William J. Brennan, Jr., *In Defense of Dissents*, 37 Hastings L J at 427 (cited in note 9) ("This change in custom at the time consolidated the authority of the Court and aided in the general recognition of the Third Branch as co-equal partner with the other branches. Not surprisingly, not everyone was pleased with the new practice.").

TABLE 1
DISSENTING BEHAVIOR OF CHIEF JUSTICES

Chief Justice	Dates of Service	No. of Cases	No. of Chief Justice Dissenting Opinions	Dissent Proportion (%)
Marshall	1801–35	1,187	3	0
Taney	1836–63	1,708	38	2
Chase	1864–73	1,109	33	3
Waite	1874–87	2,642	45	2
Fuller	1888–1909	4,866	113	2
White	1910–20	2,541	39	2
Taft	1921–29	1,708	16	1
Hughes	1930–40	2,050	46	2
Stone	1941–45	704	95	13
Vinson	1946–52	723	90	12
Warren	1953–68	1,772	215	12
Burger	1969–85	2,755	184	7
Rehnquist	1986–2005	2,131	182	9
Roberts	2005–present	104	3	3

SOURCE.—Westlaw SCT database.

percent of the opinions for the Court.[151] The only opinions that were not issued under his name during this period were in cases in which Marshall tried the case below while riding circuit,[152] had a personal interest in the case,[153] or dissented from his fellow Justices.[154] Although Marshall dissented occasionally, he generally led by example and acquiesced to the compromise position. This is demonstrated by comparing Marshall with his successors. As shown in Table 1, in the history of the Court, Marshall is the Chief Justice least likely to dissent.

Marshall's plan was a dramatic success. From 1801 to 1835, Justices filed very few dissenting opinions from the hundreds of opinions of the Court (Fig. 1), and the Court decided such fundamental legal issues as the supremacy of federal law, judicial re-

---

[151] Opinions were issued under Marshall's name in all cases in 1801, 1805, and 1806; in 91 percent of cases in 1803; 89 percent in 1804; 90 percent in 1807; 83 percent in 1808; 88 percent in 1809; 73 percent in 1810; and 58 percent in 1812. Over the next 23 years, Marshall accounted for only about 40 percent of opinions. This remains about four times as many opinions as are written by Chief Justice Rehnquist.

[152] See, for example, *Stuart v Laird*, 5 US 299 (1803).

[153] See, for example, *Martin v Hunter's Lessee*, 14 US 304 (1816).

[154] See, for example, *Bank of the U.S. v Dandridge*, 25 US 64 (1827).

FIG. 1.—Dissenting opinions in the Supreme Court during the Marshall Court (1801–35).
Source: Westlaw Supreme Court database (SCT-OLD).

view,[155] the implied powers of the national government,[156] the
Court's power over state court decisions implicating federal questions,[157] and federal power over interstate commerce[158] without
much dispute, open challenge, or reversal by the political branches.

In fact, it was not until 1804, when President Jefferson appointed Justice William Johnson, who would be known as the
"First Dissenter," that the first dissenting opinion was recorded.[159]
Jefferson recognized this change in discourse as a blatant attempt
to counteract the results of the congressional and presidential elec-
tions, and to increase the power of the judiciary. "The Federalists,"
he wrote "retreated into the Judiciary as a stronghold, the tenure
of which renders it difficult to dislodge them."[160] In order to
counter the lack of political accountability in the Court, Jefferson
urged Republican appointed judges to revert to the practice of
seriatim opinions.[161] Most famously, in a series of letters between
Jefferson and Johnson in 1822, the former urged the latter to

---

[155] *Marbury v Madison*, 5 US 137 (1803).

[156] *McCulloch v Maryland*, 17 US 316 (1819).

[157] *Martin v Hunter's Lessee*, 14 US 304 (1816) (Marshall recused himself because he was
personally involved in this case; Joseph Story wrote the opinion); *Cohens v Virginia*, 6
Wheaton 264 (1821).

[158] *Gibbons v Ogden*, 22 US 1 (1824).

[159] See *Herbert v Wren*, 11 US 370 (1813). Johnson's first dissent was tentative: the report
states that he dissented but "did not state his reasons." Id at 382.

[160] Charles Warren, 1 *The Supreme Court in United States History* 193 (1926).

[161] For example, many of Jefferson's letters cited above were correspondence between
Jefferson and Justice Johnson in which Jefferson extolled the virtues of traditional seriatim
opinions.

dissent in nearly every case. This was somewhat successful at breaking Marshall's grip on the Court. As shown in Figure 1, the number of dissenting opinions increased in the later years of the Marshall Court as Jefferson appointees began to disrupt the practice of unanimity. After ten years of near unanimity, the next twenty-five years saw an increased number of dissenting opinions.

Notwithstanding the increase in the number of dissents, there was still only one dissent in about every twenty-five cases decided during the Marshall Court, the lowest percentage in the history of the Court. Notably, of the fifty-two dissenting opinions issued during the Marshall Court, Jefferson appointees William Johnson and Brockholst Livingston authored almost 60 percent.[162] Although law at the time of the Marshall Court was considered less political than it is today, even at this early time dissent was seen as a political act. Still, Johnson sided with Marshall far more often than not, joining the opinion of the Court 96 percent of the time.[163] According to legal historian Lawrence Friedman, even Johnson was under Marshall's "spell."[164]

Although Marshall effectively controlled the discourse of the Court, he did not dominate its "thinking."[165] Instead, Marshall effectively led the Court. Marshall established and maintained an atmosphere during conferences that was conducive to compromise. After a decision was reached, Marshall managed the public and political perception through the issuance of unanimous and anonymous opinions. The opinions carried greater authority, and individual Justices were shielded from outrage or impeachment charges.[166]

---

[162] Johnson and Livingston (Jefferson appointees) authored 20 and 9, respectively; Thompson (Monroe appointee) authored 6; Baldwin and McLean (Jackson appointees) authored 6 and 2, respectively; Story and Duvall (Madison appointees) authored 4 and 1; Chase (Washington appointee) authored 3; Marshall and Washington (Adams appointees) authored 3 and 1.

[163] Johnson heard approximately 977 cases during his time on the Court (1805–33); he dissented or wrote seriatim 39 times (or in 4 percent of cases). See David G. Morgan, *The Origin of Supreme Court Dissent*, 10 Wm & Mary Q 353, 377 (1953).

[164] Friedman, *History of American Law* at 128 (cited in note 20).

[165] Herbert A. Johnson, *The Chief Justiceship of John Marshall, 1801–1835* 51 (1997) (noting that there is "undeniable evidence that Chief Justice Marshall did not dominate his colleagues; the domination theory has been so thoroughly refuted that Professor David Currie referred to it as the story of 'John Marshall and the six dwarfs.'").

[166] Although the call to impeach a Supreme Court Justice for a particular decision seems outrageous today, during this era such charges were frequently threatened and occasionally levied against judges. For example, in 1805 Associate Justice Samuel Chase was impeached

This "authority" was simply assumed by Marshall, and it has remained virtually unquestioned for over 200 years. Many powerful individuals have tried to usurp it—President Jefferson tried to impeach Justice Chase; President Jackson refused to enforce decisions with which he disagreed; President Lincoln refused to enforce a writ of habeas corpus issued by Chief Justice Taney; several presidents either increased or proposed enlarging the Court to alter its power;[167] and numerous representatives and senators have proposed curtailing Supreme Court power through legislation[168]—but none has succeeded in undoing the institutional

---

by the House and tried in the Senate. The ground for the impeachment was Chase's handling of several criminal trials in which he tried to implement the Adams administration's attempts to silence political foes. However, the charges against Chase were shown to be politically motivated and he was acquitted in the Senate. Judge Charles Pickering was not so lucky. A Federalist judge who "had committed no 'high crimes and misdemeanors'" but was "a drunk, seriously deranged," and overtly political in his handling of cases, was impeached and convicted in 1804. See Friedman, *History of American Law* at 129–30 (cited in note 20). This impeachment, like that of Alexander Addison, a Federalist judge from Pennsylvania who "harangued grand juries on political subjects" and was impeached and removed from office in 1803, was Jefferson's attempt to create a "bogeyman" to threaten judges into good behavior. Id at 129. Historians believe that it was largely effective, much like Roosevelt's "Court-packing plan" 150 years later. Id at 129, 132 ("The failure of [the Chase] impeachment was not a clear-cut victory for either side. . . . The judges won independence, but at a price. Their openly political role was reduced.").

[167] The number of Supreme Court Justices was originally set at six. See Judiciary Act of 1789, 1 Stat 73 (1789). Changes in the number of Justices have been made or proposed many times for political reasons. For example, when Jefferson was elected in 1800, the outgoing Federalist Congress reduced the number of Justices to five, but this was increased to six and then seven by Republicans in Congress to give Jefferson two appointments. Andrew Jackson got two appointments when the Court grew to nine in 1837. Antislavery forces increased the Court to ten, but then after the Civil War, the Republicans reduced the number to seven to ensure Democrat Andrew Johnson would not get any appointments. When a Republican, U.S. Grant, was elected in 1868, the Republicans gave him two new Justices to appoint, expanding the Court back to nine. His nominees quickly made an impact, voting to reverse the Court's recently created precedent in the *Legal Tender* cases. More recently, Franklin Delano Roosevelt's Court-packing plan did not succeed in increasing the number of Justices, but it did cause enough Justices to reverse opposition to the New Deal to achieve the results intended.

[168] For example, Senator Charles Sumner of Massachusetts was concerned that the Supreme Court would hold Congress's reconstruction laws unconstitutional, so he introduced a bill in 1869 that would dramatically curtail the Supreme Court's jurisdiction: "The judicial power extends only to cases between party and party . . . and does not include the President or Congress, or any of their acts . . . and all such acts are valid and conclusive on the matters to which they apply; . . . and no allegation or pretence of the invalidity thereof shall be excuse or defense for any neglect, refusal, or failure to perform any duty in regard to them." See *Congressional Globe*, 41st Cong, 2d Sess, at 2895 (1869). Senator Lyman Trumbell of Illinois proposed a similar, albeit more narrow, limitation on the Court in 1868 and 1869, arguing that the reconstruction acts were "political in character" and the Court had no jurisdiction to pass upon them. See 40th Cong, 2d Sess, at 1204, 1428, 1621 (1868); see also 41st Cong, 2d Sess, at 3, 27, 45, 96, 152, 167 (1869). Senator Richard M. Johnson of Kentucky proposed giving the Senate appellate jurisdiction in cases in which the government was a party, allowing the Senate to effectively overrule Supreme

authority created in large part by Marshall's discursive change.

Marshall was able to achieve the power of unanimity and effectuate a fundamental change in legal discourse based, at least in part, on his personal leadership skills. Marshall was revered for his ability to lead and to relate to others. Biographers describe him as able to "inspire confidence and trust" and "able to elicit a warm and supportive response from others."[169] In a famous quote, fellow Justice Joseph Story responded to questions about Marshall's motives on the Court: "I love his laugh—it is too hearty for an intriguer."[170] Whether Marshall had a strategy or whether he was an "intriguer" is a question without an easy answer. Jefferson famously accused Marshall of deliberately manipulating the Constitution to achieve his own ends,[171] and some modern observes agree, viewing his early opinions as highly political.[172]

Marshall had nationalist tendencies, but so did his predecessor Chief Justice Ellsworth and many of his successors. But only Marshall was able to implement these tendencies so effectively in practice. What made Marshall different was his ability to assert the type of personal leadership necessary to achieve the goal of strong national power. But there were many "conditions of possibility" that enabled this change. Marshall and his fellow Justices were able to achieve considerable unanimity because of their similar socioeconomic backgrounds. Justices were drawn entirely from the cadre of practicing lawyers or the government elite. All of the Justices were propertied gentlemen and each had a strong sense of nationalism, a concern for private property rights, and accepted traditional principles of the legal profession of the era.[173] In ad-

---

Court opinions. See Annals of Congress, 17th Cong, 1st Sess, Dec 12, 1821, Jan 14 and 15, 1822. In response to the Supreme Court's rejection of much progressive legislation in the pre-New Deal period, Senator Robert M. LaFollette, Sr. of Wisconsin proposed a constitutional amendment that would allow two-thirds of the Senate to overrule any decision of the Court. See Cong Rec, 67th Cong, 2d Sess, at 9073 (1922), reprint of LaFollette's speech before the American Federation of Labor.

[169] Johnson, *Chief Justiceship* at 121 (cited in note 165).

[170] Smith, *John Marshall* at 291 (cited in note 133).

[171] "In Marshall's hands the law is nothing more than an ambiguous text to be explained by his sophistry into any meaning which may subserve his personal malice." *Letter from Jefferson to Madison* (May 25, 1810), in M. Smith, ed, *The Republic of Letters: The Correspondence Between Thomas Jefferson and James Madison* 64 (1995).

[172] See, for example, Akhil Reed Amar, *Marbury, Section 13, and the Original Jurisdiction of the Supreme Court*, 56 U Chi L Rev 443 (1989); John V. Orth, Book Review: *John Marshall and the Rule of Law*, 49 SC L Rev 633, 636 (1998) ("Marshall did seem to have a strategic vision of forcing . . . the national government to govern the nation.").

[173] Johnson, *Chief Justiceship* at 96–97 (cited in note 165).

dition, for the first several decades of Court history, the Justices all lived in the same boardinghouse in Washington. This living arrangement added to the collegial nature of the Court and helped foster similar views among the Justices. Whatever the exact mix of reasons, Marshall was able to increase the power of the Court in no small part through a change in the discourse of the Court.

2. *The continuing tradition.* Unlike the experience with the "opinion of the court" in England, the unanimity consensus continued to a great extent even after Marshall left the Court in 1835. Although the number of separate opinions increased slightly after Marshall resigned, the practice of unanimity dominated the Supreme Court for over 100 years (Fig. 2).

The unanimity discourse of Marshall changed over time. By 1814, Marshall did not sign the vast majority of opinions, but instead authored only about 50 percent. This was still significant (compared to the approximately 15 percent of opinions authored by Chief Justice Rehnquist during his tenure), but it represented a changing of the guard. Furthermore, Jefferson appointees, who were hostile to Marshall, were beginning to assert their power, and other factors led to a decline in the collegiality of the Court. For example, by 1827, under pressure from Republicans and because newly appointed Justices established their own residences in Washington, the "boardinghouse Court" was abolished. This undermined attempts to maintain unanimity.[174] As factions developed within the Court, the percent of cases with a dissenting opinion increased from 4 percent under Marshall to nearly 10 percent under his immediate successors.

Despite these changes, the period from the end of Marshall's tenure in 1835 to the beginning of Harlan Fiske Stone's appointment in 1941 saw little change in the discourse of Supreme Court opinions.[175] Table 2 shows the frequency of dissenting opinions during each Chief Justiceship.

Until 1941, the rate of dissent remained relatively constant at less than 10 percent. Two primary factors seem to explain this result. First, the traits and leadership of the Chief Justices who

---

[174] Id at 110–11.

[175] "Yet, neither [Justice] Johnson nor any later justices could or would undo Marshall's work. Doctrine changed; personalities and blocs clashed on the Supreme Court; power contended with power; but these struggles all took place within the fortress that Marshall had built." Friedman, *History of American Law* at 134 (cited in note 20).

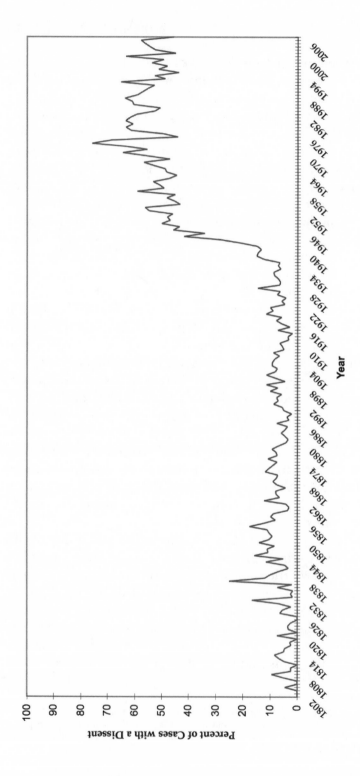

Fig. 2.—Supreme Court cases with a dissenting opinion: 1802–2006

TABLE 2
DISSENTING PROCLIVITY

Chief Justice	Dates of Service	Percent of Opinions with a Dissent
Marshall	1801–35	4
Taney	1836–63	9
Chase	1864–73	9
Waite	1874–87	6
Fuller	1888–1909	7
White	1910–20	5
Taft	1921–29	7
Hughes	1930–40	9
Stone	1941–45	27
Vinson	1946–52	48
Warren	1953–68	50
Burger	1969–85	59
Rehnquist	1986–2005	56
Roberts	2005–present	47

succeeded Marshall; and, second, the legal atmosphere of the period and the type of cases heard by the Court.

As for leadership, each Chief Justice from Marshall to Stone came from similar backgrounds,[176] had remarkable leadership skills, and was committed to unanimity. Melville Fuller (1888–1910) was an "excellent social leader . . . blessed with conciliatory and diplomatic traits."[177] Justice Oliver Wendell Holmes characterized Fuller as a great Chief Justice because of his ability to conduct the business of the Court without much dissent.[178] Likewise, Chief Justice Edward White (1910–20) was a former Senate majority leader blessed with a "genial temperament and adroit logrolling skills that permitted him to mend fences and reinforce consensus norms in Court."[179] Following White was the legendary consensus builder, William Howard Taft (1921–29). Taft "hated dissenting opinions, wrote very few himself, and made every effort to dissuade others from writing them."[180]

---

[176] Marshall, like his successors, was first and foremost a lawyer. He spent a career representing business interests in Virginia, and, like most contemporaries of the bench and bar, was a significant property owner. See Charles F. Hobson, *The Great Chief Justice: John Marshall and the Rule of Law* 74 (1996).

[177] Sheldon Goldman, *Constitutional Law and Supreme Court Decision-Making* 178 (1982).

[178] Id at 178–79.

[179] James Watts, *Edward Douglas White*, in Leon Friedman and Fred Israel, eds, 3 *The Justices of the United States Supreme Court 1789–1969* (1969).

[180] Edward White, *The American Judicial Tradition* 180 (1976).

Taft explained, "I don't approve of dissents generally, for I think in many cases where I differ from the majority, it is more important to stand by the Court and give its judgment weight than merely to record my individual dissent where it is better to have the law certain than to have it settled either way."[181] Taft imparted this tendency to his successor Charles Evans Hughes (1930–40). Hughes discouraged dissent in order to shield internal divisions from public view.[182] In a personal letter to another Justice, Hughes explained why he would join the majority opinion despite his strong reservations about the outcome: "I choke a little at swallowing your analysis; still I do not think it would serve any useful purpose to expose my views."[183]

In terms of case characteristics, most of the cases heard by the Court during this period were straightforward common law or admiralty cases that were less contentious than most modern cases.[184] *Talbot* was the rare admiralty case that posed contentious political questions. Most Supreme Court cases were not like *Talbot*. Most of the Court's decisions were able to garner consensus in part because the common law provided numerous precedents. Federal courts did not have general federal question jurisdiction to hear matters arising under the Constitution and laws of the United States until 1875. It was not until after *Erie* in 1938, when federal common law was abandoned, that the Court would routinely handle difficult, and politically sensitive, constitutional issues.[185] This change from a common law court of last resort to a constitutional court caused a dramatic increase in the percentage of cases with a dissenting opin-

---

[181] Walter Murphy, *Elements of Judicial Strategy* 61 (1964).

[182] Henry Abraham, *The Judicial Process* 230 (1986).

[183] Id at 224.

[184] Of the nearly 400 cases decided by the Supreme Court between 1801 and 1833, less than 50 (or about 12 percent) were "constitutional" cases, according to Professor David Currie. See Currie, *Constitution in the Supreme Court* at 65–193 (cited in note 115) (collecting and treating these cases; number counted by author). The most common cases during this time were traditional common law cases: property (17 percent), admiralty/prize cases in which the Court was an instance court (15 percent), procedure (15 percent), family law (10 percent), and contracts (9 percent). Chief Justice Rehnquist also describes nineteenth-century Supreme Court jurisprudence as largely run of the mill by today's standards, noting that the Court spent considerable time during the 1860s and 1870s on railroad bond cases. See Rehnquist, *The Supreme Court* at 90–91 (cited in note 33).

[185] *Erie Railroad Co. v Tompkins*, 304 US 64 (1938). Prior to 1938, many constitutional questions of great import were decided, but the Supreme Court docket consisted mainly of routine common law and admiralty cases. Some of the more famous dissents of the early period arose in the tough constitutional questions. See, for example, *Lochner v New York*, 198 US 45 (1905); *Scott v Sanford*, 60 US 393 (1857); and *Plessy v Ferguson*, 163 US 537 (1896).

ion. In its first 150 years, the Court rarely dealt with disputes involving civil liberties, as we understand them today. The first cases to uphold civil liberties were *Ex parte Milligan*[186] and *Ex parte Garland*,[187] which were not decided until 1866. There would be more contentious cases during the next few decades, including the upholding of "separate but equal laws" in *Plessy v Ferguson*[188] in 1896 and the free speech cases during World War I,[189] but the Court's cases were generally not politically contentious in the modern sense until the New Deal.

D.   THE RISE OF DISSENT

The long-standing practice of virtual unanimity was abandoned as abruptly as it was begun. With the ascendancy of Harlan Fiske Stone to Chief Justice in 1941, the Court began a trend of writing separate opinions in most cases (Fig. 2). Several possibilities may explain this change, but one stands out. Stone tolerated and even encouraged dissent out of personal preference and practice. Stone was the first academic appointed to hold the position of Chief Justice, and this background made him more likely to encourage open debate. This academic pedigree combined with his personality, which favored debate and confrontation, were evident in his frequent dissents as an associate Justice. This proclivity to dissent continued when Stone was appointed Chief Justice—Stone was much more likely to dissent himself compared to his predecessors and remains the Chief Justice most likely to dissent (Table 1). Just as Chief Justices from Marshall to Taft encouraged unanimity by their own practice of acquiescing in opinions with which they did not fully agree, so did Chief Justice Stone and his successors lead by example by issuing a substantial number of dissenting opinions themselves.

It is Stone's leadership that scholars argue caused the end of

---

[186] 71 US 2 (1866).

[187] 71 US 333 (1866).

[188] 163 US 537 (1896).

[189] See, for example, *Abrams v United States*, 250 US 616 (1919) (holding that an amendment to the Espionage Act of 1917 that made it a crime to criticize the government did not violate the First Amendment). *Abrams* is no longer good law. See *Brandenburg v Ohio*, 395 US 444 (1969) (holding that the government cannot punish potentially inflammatory speech unless it threatens "imminent lawless action").

the consensus norm.[190] For example, the most prominent study of dissent in the political science literature concludes that, as in the case of John Marshall and the rise of the unanimity norm, it was the leadership of Chief Justice Stone that was most responsible for the change.[191] Other possible explanations examined by the authors were the change in docket from mandatory to discretionary review, the shift in the type of cases argued before the Court, the internal politics of the Court, and large-scale changes in the Court's personnel at the time. Let us look at some of the theories considered and rejected.

First, the authors examined the role of the Judiciary Act of 1925 and the move to a discretionary docket. Although it is possible that this would create more dissent because only difficult cases would be granted certiorari, the authors conclude that this change was not responsible for the increase in dissents. They base this on the fact that the rise in dissents did not occur until 1942, many years after passage of the Act.[192] The time gap may be sufficient evidence that the direct or only cause of the change was not the Judiciary Act. It does not, however, eliminate the change in jurisdiction as a "condition of possibility" that contributed to the change in discourse.

Another explanation considered and rejected by the authors was the increase in the Supreme Court caseload. The authors reject this explanation because of timing. Although they observe a dramatic increase in caseload results in less time to build consensus and construct compromises, they conclude that the growth in the caseload was not dramatic until the 1960s, twenty years after the rise of dissent. But the authors' data confuse the rise in *federal cases*, which started in the 1960s, and the rise in the number of Supreme Court cases, which occurred much earlier and then subsequently decreased. The data presented in Figure 3 show a growth in Supreme Court cases following the Civil War and then a decrease by the time of the Stone Court (1941–45).

The data suggest that the change in the number of cases is inversely related to the number of dissenting opinions. The five-fold increase in Supreme Court decisions in the 1860s was not

---

[190] Thomas Walker, et al, *On the Mysterious Demise of Consensual Norms in the United States Supreme Court*, 50 J Pol 361, 362 (1988).

[191] Id.

[192] Id at 364–65.

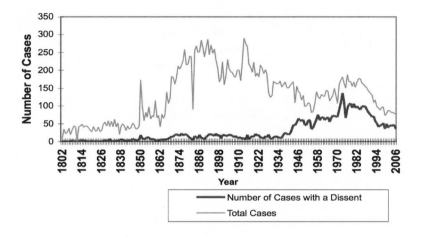

FIG. 3.—Total number of cases and cases with a dissenting opinion in the Supreme Court: 1802–2006.

accompanied by an increase in dissenting opinions. By contrast, the drop in the number of Supreme Court cases following the Judiciary Act of 1925 corresponds well with the increase in dissenting opinions. In addition, the Rehnquist Court heard fewer cases per year than any Court of the last 100 years, but nearly 50 percent of all opinions had a dissent; the Roberts Court appears to be following a similar pattern. This inverse relation suggests that it was more likely the change in the type of cases that resulted in more dissenting opinions rather than the change in the number of cases.

The authors also briefly considered this possible explanation when they compared the type of cases heard by the Stone Court and its predecessor, the Hughes Court. The authors concluded that there was not a significant increase in the type of cases they describe as "dissent prone." But their analysis ignored the fundamental change in the role of the Court post-*Erie*. By the time of Stone's appointment as Chief Justice, the Court was becoming a constitutional rather than a common law court. Certainly, the increase in contentious cases in the 1940s made for a more fertile ground for dissent. It was at this time that "the cutting edge debate [of] constitutional law shifted from . . . economic regulation . . . to claims of civil liberties violations on behalf of various kinds of dissidents."[193] The growth in dissent-prone cases was caused in part by the fact that during this time the Court issued a series of decisions that extended the protections of the Bill of Rights to the states through the Fourteenth Amendment.[194] But like the possible causes noted above, this explanation cannot be viewed in a vacuum. Both the law and society were in great flux at this time. The rise of New Deal constitutionalism replaced the long history of *Lochner* constitutionalism, and Holmes's dissent in *Lochner* came to be revered after it became the law of the land in 1937. Dissent had proved to be a powerful weapon for change. Furthermore, this era saw the rise of legal realism. During the majority of Supreme Court history, the Court had acted as a sort of an Oracle of the Law. In the grand formal style, the Justices would, through their internal debate, derive the correct answer or the "truth" of the law.

This idea that there was a discoverable and objective truth behind the law began to evaporate in legal academic circles by the 1920s. Although Holmes had argued in his Lowell Lectures on the common law in 1881 that many extralegal matters affect the

---

[193] Rehnquist, *The Supreme Court* at 174–75 (cited in note 33).

[194] The "incorporation" of the Bill of Rights via the Fourteenth Amendment is a controversial constitutional question. In a recent essay, David Strauss notes that the issue "went from being a subject of intense controversy—probably the most controversial issue in constitutional law between the mid-1940s and mid-1950s, and one of the most controversial for a decade or more thereafter—to being a completely settled issue." See David A. Strauss, *Common Law, Common Ground, and Jefferson's Principle*, 112 Yale L J 1717, 1746 (2003). Although the first right to be incorporated, the Takings Clause, occurred in the late nineteenth century, see *Chicago, Burlington & Quincy Railway Co. v Chicago*, 166 US 226 (1897), the period around Stone's tenure saw the greatest activity of incorporation by the Court. See *Gitlow v New York*, 268 US 652 (1925) (incorporating freedom of speech clause); *Near v Minnesota*, 283 US 697 (1931) (incorporating freedom of the press clause); *Powell v Alabama*, 287 US 45 (1932) (incorporating right to assistance of counsel in capital criminal cases); *DeJonge v Oregon*, 299 US 353 (1937) (incorporating freedom of assembly clause); *Cantwell v Connecticut*, 310 US 296 (1940) (incorporating free exercise of religion clause); *Everson v Board of Education*, 330 US 1 (1947) (incorporating establishment of religion clause); *In re Oliver*, 333 US 257 (1948) (incorporating public trial right); *Wolf v Colorado*, 338 US 25 (1949) (incorporating unreasonable search and seizure clause). The incorporation parade paused for a decade or so before resuming in the civil rights era of the sixties and seventies. See *Gideon v Wainwright*, 372 US 335 (1963) (incorporating right to assistance of counsel in all felony cases); *Pointer v Texas*, 380 US 400 (1965) (incorporating right to confrontation of adverse witnesses); *Klopfer v North Carolina*, 386 US 213 (1967) (incorporating right to speedy trial); *Washington v Texas*, 388 US 14 (1967) (incorporating right to compulsory process to obtain witness testimony); *Duncan v Louisiana*, 391 US 145 (1968) (incorporating trial by impartial jury); *Rabe v Washington*, 405 US 313 (1972) (incorporating notice of accusation). Some rights have not been incorporated (yet). See *Curtis v Loether*, 415 US 189 (1974) (addressing right to jury trial in civil cases); *Presser v Illinois*, 116 US 252 (1886) (rejecting incorporation of Second Amendment).

law more than abstract logic or natural law, it was not until forty years later that this would become a mainstream idea in the legal academy. Coincidentally, the rise of legal realism was centered at Yale and Columbia during the late teens and early 1920s when future Chief Justice Stone was dean of the Columbia Law School (1910–23). Stone was educated in, and as dean participated in the creation of, a vastly different legal world than that known by his predecessors. The broad social forces that led to the New Deal, the rise of legal realism, and the change in the cases heard by the Court greatly contributed to Stone's attitudes about law and about how "truth" should be determined.

By 1941, the Court was also populated with a more diverse (at least intellectually diverse) group of Justices than at any earlier time. During the 1920s when Stone ascended to the Court, the legal realists and the new process for deciding the law were well represented on the Court by Justice Brandeis. Brandeis, like Holmes, was revered for his powerful dissents and his passion for change in the law. Dissenting in *Gilbert v Minnesota*, Brandeis first suggested that the liberties protected by the Fourteenth Amendment should include civil liberties as well as property rights.[195] This period of history was a wellspring for change in the law and it was at the Supreme Court that the reformers were able, by building upon the reasoning of past dissenting opinions, to effect their revolution.

Chief Justice Stone admired the practice of dissent and its recent history in the Court. He knew the power of Holmes and Brandeis to shape the law through dissent, and he encouraged the practice.[196] Therefore, compared to earlier Chief Justices who sought compromise and unanimity, Stone could be seen as an ineffective "leader." Under his leadership, conference debates among the Justices were often heated and filled with controversy.[197] Stone

---

[195] See *Gilbert v Minnesota*, 254 US 325 (1920).

[196] The most startling example of this power comes from the cases *Minersville School District v Gobitis*, 310 US 586 (1940), and *West Virginia Board of Education v Barnette*, 319 US 624 (1943). In *Gobitis*, Chief Justice Stone dissented from an eight-member majority holding that Jehovah's Witnesses could be expelled from public school for failing to salute the flag during the Pledge of Allegiance. *Gobitis*, 310 US at 601–02. In the very next term, five Justices were persuaded by Stone's dissent, and voted to overrule *Gobitis* in a case again involving Jehovah's Witnesses and the Pledge. *Barnette*, 319 US at 642.

[197] David Danelski, *The Influence of the Chief Justice in the Decisional Process of the Supreme Court*, in Joel Grossman and Richard Wells, eds, *Constitutional Law and Judicial Policy Making* (1980).

argued that "[t]he right of dissent is an important one and has proved to be such in the history of the Supreme Court . . . I do not think it is the appropriate function of a Chief Justice to attempt to dissuade members of the Court from dissenting in individual cases."[198] The "history" that Stone was referring to was the recent vindication of Holmes's dissent in *Lochner*. Stone was a new breed of lawyer at the helm of the law's most powerful entity during a fundamental change in our understanding of legal reasoning. Law was now more like politics, and Stone was willing to assert the Supreme Court as a political branch. Stone achieved this revolution in part by encouraging the use of dissenting opinions, just as Marshall implemented his revolution by introducing consensus. The means were different, but the ends were the same.

Stone increased the power of the Court, and thus achieved the same results as Marshall, but for different reasons and in different circumstances. Both Marshall and Stone sought a more active role for the Court. To increase the power of the Court specifically and the law generally, Stone encouraged debate and controversy, rather than suppressing it as Marshall was required to do, to accomplish the same end. Only by empowering the Court to act even *without unanimity* could Stone extend the reach of the Court from primarily economic matters into the realm of civil liberties.

It is not necessary to say that Stone *knew* that increasing tolerance for dissent would have the impact it did on the Court's role. The practice no doubt seemed natural and reflected the mood of the times and of the Justices then on the Court. But when viewed in light of the other discursive changes, it seems clear that these explanations are just "conditions of possibility" that undergird the true explanation for the practice.

After Stone's brief tenure as Chief Justice, the unanimity rule was dead for good—in spite of immediate steps to reverse the trend. To replace Stone as Chief Justice, President Truman chose Fred Vinson, who was known for his sociable and likable personality.

> Although Truman admired Vinson's record . . . his personality was the most important factor influencing the decision to appoint him. . . . His sociability and friendliness, his calm, patient, and relaxed manner, his sense of humor, his respect for

---

[198] Alpheus Mason, *Harlan Fiske Stone: Pillar of the Law* 608 (1956).

the views of others, his popularity with the representatives of many factions, and his ability to conciliate conflicting views and clashing personalities and to work out compromises were qualities that Truman admired. Even more important, those personal qualities seemed to the President to fit the needs of the situation inside the Supreme Court. Dissension and dissent were on the rise . . . Vinson seemed capable of unifying the Court and thereby improving its public image.[199]

But the other eight Justices had all been influenced by Stone and were proponents of legal realism. They were aware too that dissent had enabled them to expand their role and power over policy issues. Once the genie was out of the bottle, it was impossible to put it back in.[200] Instead of working toward compromise and consensus, the Vinson court became known as "nine scorpions in a bottle."[201]

The "failure" of Vinson need not be viewed as a personal failure of leadership. The context in which each of these Chief Justices tried to lead was different for a variety of reasons. Even Marshall would not have achieved unanimity in the Supreme Court of Vinson's day. The Vinson Court and the Marshall Court both existed during a period of legal revolution. At the time of Marshall, however, the Court and the Justices were certain about the role of law. Marshall redirected the Court toward a more active political role. Had Marshall been Chief Justice in Stone's time, he likely would have led the change from unanimity to the dissent norm. In both cases, it was the end result—increased authority for the law and the Court—that was important, not the means.

In contrast to the end of the Marshall Court, during the Stone and later Courts, the dispute was not only about the political nature of the Court, but about the broader role of law in society. Achieving unanimity in this context is much more difficult and might have had the opposite effect. The Justices, despite somewhat similar backgrounds, had very different perspectives on such social issues as the rights of women, segregation, and abortion. In addition, the Court does not act in a political vacuum. The issuance

---

[199] Richard Kirkendall, *Fred M. Vinson*, in Leon Friedman and Fred Israel, eds, 4 *The Justices of the United States Supreme Court 1789–1969* 2641 (1969).

[200] See, for example, Rehnquist, *The Supreme Court* at 148 (cited in note 33) ("Brought in as a mediator, Vinson largely failed in this task.").

[201] Robert Steamer, *Chief Justice: Leadership and the Supreme Court* 19 (1986).

of unanimous, per curiam opinions "deciding" particularly thorny issues might provoke extrajudicial or even extralegal responses. Justice Frankfurter portended the surge in dissents in one of his first opinions, written in 1939. Frankfurter praised the seriatim tradition in England, calling it a "healthy practice," but noting that the Court's workload prohibited the Justices from doing it in every case.[202] He suggested that the Court use the seriatim approach "when an important shift in constitutional doctrine is announced after a reconstruction in the membership of the Court."[203] This idea—that all Justices should be heard from on big questions—originated with Madison, who wrote in an 1819 letter:

> I could have wished also that the Judges had delivered their opinions seriatim. The case was of such magnitude, in the scope given to it, as to call, if any case could do so, for the views of the subject separately taken by them. This might either by the harmony of their reasoning have produced a greater conviction in the Public mind; or by its discordance have impaired the force of the precedent now ostensibly supported by a unanimous & perfect concurrence in every argument & dictum in the judgment pronounced.[204]

Frankfurter's suggestion is notable because it previews both the constitutional showdowns to come and the role of dissent (if not seriatim) in giving the Court legitimacy to decide these disputes. As Jefferson noted when advocating the writing of separate opinions, dissent allows judges in the future to overrule bad law based on the reasoning of their predecessors, in essence allowing the Court, and thus the law and lawyers, to play a more political role by essentially mollifying the losing parties and encouraging a continuing legal discourse. Of course, achieving unanimity on contentious political issues might have been preferred by the winners ex post, but if the issues were too contentious and the opposition too strong to achieve, ex ante both sides of the debate would prefer the option value imbedded in a world with dissent. Dissent allows the Court to continue in its active role post-legal realism.

---

[202] *Graves v New York ex rel O'Keefe*, 306 US 466, 487 (1939) (Frankfurter, J, concurring).

[203] Id.

[204] See Letter from James Madison to Spencer Roane (Sept 2, 1819), reprinted in Philip B. Kurland and Ralph Lerner, eds, *The Founders' Constitution, Article 1, Section 8, Clause 18, Document 15* (1987).

III. Recent History: To Seriatim and Back Again?

The last fifty years of Supreme Court history since the time of Chief Justice Stone have been characterized by a proliferation of dissents.[205] During the first 140 years of Court history there were dissents in less than 7 percent of cases; since then, there have been dissenting opinions in more than half of all cases.[206] Chief

---

[205] Not only has the number of dissents increased, but so has the vitriol. When Justices did dissent during the Marshall Court, they did so reluctantly and apologetically. This was in part due to the collegial atmosphere that existed in the "boardinghouse Court." Compare several opening sentences from dissenting opinions during this period. Those Federalist Justices that supported Marshall's change in discourse wrote cautiously when dissenting. See *Bank of the United States v Dandridge*, 25 US 64, 90 (1827) (Marshall, J, dissenting) ("I should now, as is my custom, when I have the misfortune to differ from this Court, acquiesce silently in its opinion . . . ."); *Mason v Haile*, 25 US 370, 379 (1827) (Washington, J, dissenting) ("It has never been my habit to deliver dissenting opinions in cases where it has been my misfortune to differ from those which have been pronounced by a majority of this Court."); *Drown v United States*, 12 US 110, 129 (1814) (Story, J, dissenting) ("In this case, I have the misfortune to differ in opinion from my brethren."). By contrast, the two most frequent dissenters during Marshall's reign, Justice Johnson and Justice Livingston, both Jefferson appointees and strongly opposed to Marshall's change to unanimous opinions, did not hesitate to criticize the majority when dissenting. See *Kirk v Smith*, 22 US 241, 294 (1824) (Johnson, J, dissenting) ("The reasoning upon this cause, must be utterly unintelligible to those who hear it. . . ."); *United States v Smith*, 18 US 153, 163 (1820) (Livingston, J, dissenting) ("In a case affecting life, no apology can be necessary for expressing my dissent from the opinion which has just been delivered."). Even these attacks on the majority pale by comparison to the lack of respect shown fellow Justices by modern dissenters. See *Lee v Weisman*, 505 US 577 (1992) (Scalia, J, dissenting) (writing that the majority opinion was "oblivious to our history," "incoherent," a "jurisprudential disaster," and "nothing short of ludicrous."). This type of name calling and hyperbolic rhetoric is a far cry from the day when Justices rarely had the courage to dissent, and when they did, the guilty feelings compelled them to apologize publicly. As Roscoe Pound noted long ago, such vitriolic denunciation of other Justices is "not good for public respect for courts and law and the administration of justice." Roscoe Pound, *Cacoethes Dissentiendi: The Heated Judicial Dissent* 39 ABA J 794, 795 (1953). Although Judge Posner has argued that Justices should dissent because dissents play (have played) an integral part in the development of law, Posner agrees with Pound that the acerbic dissent is both unnecessary and destructive. See Richard A. Posner, *The Federal Courts: Challenge and Reform* 356–57 (1996). Posner criticizes Justices as being more concerned about their individual role and less concerned with the institutional role of the Court. In cases that are relatively straightforward, Posner agrees with Justice Taft that a definitive rule that may not be perfect or even "correct" is often better than an uncertain rule. "In such a case a dissent will communicate a sense of the law's instability that is misleading." Id. Accusing judges of worrying about their own legacy and ego, Posner writes that "[f]rom an institutional perspective it is better for the disagreeing judge not to dissent publicly [in a case which he knows will not be reconsidered soon], even though such forbearance will make it more difficult for someone to write the judge's intellectual biography." Id at 357.

[206] From 1801 to 1940 (Marshall to Hughes) there were approximately 1,231 cases with dissents out of a total of approximately 17,811 (~7 percent); from 1941 to 1997 (Stone to Rehnquist) there were about 3,877 cases with dissents out of a total of approximately 7,434 (~52 percent). From 1801 to 1940 (Marshall to Hughes) there were approximately 1,231 cases with dissents out of a total of approximately 17,811 (~7 percent); from 1941 to 1997 (Stone to Rehnquist) there were about 3,877 cases with dissents out of a total of approximately 7,434 (~52 percent).

Justices from Stone to Rehnquist made no attempt to return to a Court of consensus. Chief Justice Rehnquist spoke of dissent in matter-of-fact terms[207] and Justice William Brennan wrote of dissent as a "duty."[208] The dissent norm continues to this day.[209]

A. THE MODERN HYBRID APPROACH

Although opinions are still issued as "opinions of the court" and separate opinions are designated as concurrences or dissents, the practical effect has been a change back to writing separately—back nearly to the tradition of seriatim. For example, in *Turner Broadcasting System v FCC*, the decision was announced as follows:

> Kennedy, J., announced the judgment of the Court and delivered the opinion of the Court, except as to a portion of Part II-A-1. Rehnquist, C.J., and Stevens and Souter, JJ., joined the opinion in full, and Breyer, J., joined except insofar as Part II-A-1 relied on an anticompetitive rationale. Stevens, J., filed a concurring opinion. Breyer, J., filed an opinion concurring in part. O'Connor, J., filed a dissenting opinion in which Scalia, Thomas, and Ginsburg, JJ., joined.[210]

Dissents, once reserved for only the most profound differences of opinion, are now commonplace.

There are several reasons why dissenting opinions might be so common today. Most simply, there is inertia and custom. Perhaps once the practice develops it is hard to stop; dissent becomes the discourse of law and will continue to be so until another fundamental shift in power. This tendency to follow the norm was one of the reasons the age of consensus lasted for almost 100 years after the death of Marshall. In a classic defense of dissents, Justice Brennan argued that while a Justice's "general duty is to acquiesce in the rulings of th[e] court," it was a "duty" (and not "an egoistic act") for Justices to dissent.[211]

---

[207] William H. Rehnquist, *The Supreme Court: How It Was, How It Is* 302–03 (1987).

[208] Brennan, *In Defense of Dissents*, 37 Hastings L J at 437–38 (cited in note 9).

[209] In 1995 majority opinions represented 43 percent of all opinions. See Posner, *Federal Courts* at 358 (cited in note 108). See also Figure 3.

[210] *Turner Broadcasting System v FCC*, 520 US 180 (1997).

[211] Brennan, *In Defense of Dissents*, 37 Hastings L J at 437–38 (cited in note 9). Justice Brennan and Justice Marshall were two of the Court's most frequent and famous dissenters. Not only did these two Justices significantly add to the number of dissenting opinions, but they also introduced a new practice in the Supreme Court—the publishing of dissents

There are also potential political reasons. Vehement dissents may signal a political drift within the Court that threatens the stability of the law. The audience for these dissents would be other Justices, the public, the press, advocacy groups, and the Congress. Dissents signal that the Court is headed down a dangerous path. In this way, dissents can be viewed as a way of marshalling groups to influence the appointment/confirmation process.

Dissent is a tool to seize power within the Court. The minority Justices can silently acquiesce (as was the tradition for the first century and a half of Court history) or they can alert Court stake-holders about the "errors" of a decision. To do the former creates a perception that the ruling is settled law and that no changes in Court personnel will alter the result. To do the latter can weaken the precedent and thus encourage judicial or political responses. Like-minded lower court judges may feel emboldened by the dis-sents, and attempt to narrow the rulings. Dissents also commu-nicate to Justices in the future (either current or new members of the Court), providing them with logic and support for voting to reverse or narrow the holding.

Another reason for the continuing use of dissents is the com-monly held belief that dissents make the law better or make better law. This is based on the power of famous and not-so-famous dissents throughout history to shape the Court's future holdings. Think of the success of Holmes's dissent in *Lochner* and Harlan's dissent in *Plessy*.[212] As Justice Brennan argued, dissents are offered

---

from petitions filed with the Court. During the past 30 years there were hundreds of dissents from petitions published by Justice Brennan and Justice Marshall. These dissents were occasionally in protest of a denial of certiorari, but the vast majority was dissents from denials to review sentences of capital punishment. In each case for death penalty review received by the Court, Justice Brennan and Justice Marshall published a dissent that simply stated that in their view capital punishment violated the cruel and unusual provision of the Eighth Amendment. This practice was in plain violation of well-established Court precedent. The Justices were making an overtly political statement—a statement to the public and to the future.

[212] Although the law would be less great without the dissents of Brandeis and Holmes, these influential and often graceful expositions of the law as how it should be are by far the exception from the mass of pointless dissents. An example of the inefficient use of separate opinions is the opinions of Justice Frankfurter. John P. Frank studied the separate opinions of Justice Frankfurter, the most frequent concurring Justice in the history of the Court. Frank found that Frankfurter's opinions were almost never cited by anyone. See John P. Frank, *Marble Palace: The Supreme Court in American Life* 126 (1958). Frank con-cluded that this was a waste of energy and talent and led to unnecessary ambiguity and uncertainty in the law. Even Justice Holmes, who was known as the "Great Dissenter," remarked that dissents are in most cases "useless and undesirable." *Northern Securities Co. v United States*, 193 US 197, 400 (1904). Therefore, Holmes was reluctant to dissent and discouraged the practice in all but the most necessary circumstances. Like the boy who

as a corrective in "the hope that the Court will mend the error of its ways in a later case."[213] In addition, dissents may enable lower courts or future coalitions of Justices to narrow a majority opinion that sweeps too broadly. Brennan views these as essential components of judicial determination of the "truth." Therefore, Brennan criticized Chief Justice Marshall as "shut[ting] down the marketplace of ideas" when he instituted the consensus norm. This marketplace of legal ideas, Brennan argued, is necessary for the creation of quality legal decisions. In this way, Brennan sees the publication of multiple opinions as analogous to legal argument within the courtroom.[214]

But this isn't the whole story. The criticism of Marshall and the distinction that Brennan draws between the current and past practice of dissent is flawed. The Supreme Court is a normalizing entity within the larger perspective of modernity: like all other forms of modern power, the Court is about the power of domination, the power of lawyers and judges and citizens over others—the "governmentalization" of society. The current practice of dissent can be seen as achieving exactly the same results as Marshall's consensus norm—an increase in Court power. To achieve these ends, the Court has adopted various discursive practices through-

---

cried wolf, the more one dissents, the less likely dissents are to be seriously considered. Familiarity of dissent breeds contempt.

[213] Brennan, *In Defense of Dissents*, 37 Hastings L J at 430 (cited in note 9). A classic example of this in our era is the dissenting opinion of then–Associate Justice Rehnquist in *Garcia v San Antonio Metropolitan Transit Authority*, in which he wrote that the states' rights principles he and the other dissenters were advocating were "a principle that will, I am confident, in time again command the support of a majority of this court." 469 US 528, 580 (1985). After the Court's stunning series of 5–4 decisions over the past decade upholding the rights of states against federal interests, Rehnquist has proved to be quite a prognosticator.

[214] Another possible explanation for continued dissents is the rise of the law clerk and the expansion of opinions to resemble law review articles. As the length and legal extent of an opinion increases with more and more arguments and footnotes, so does the grounds for possible disagreement among the Justices. Finally there is the possibility that modern Justices are generally more apt to desire individual recognition. Supreme Court Justices now have their own jurisprudence that is studied in law schools and debated in the legal literature. Furthermore, legal biographies, monographs, and speeches are increasingly popular so as to tempt individual Justices to create their own legacy of judicial opinions. Justice Scalia and Judge Posner both agree that personal recognition is often the motivating force behind the trend of frequent dissenting opinions. See Antonin Scalia, *The Dissenting Opinion*, J S Ct Hist 33–44 (1994); Posner, *Federal Courts* at 356–57 (cited in note 205). The power of ego should not be underestimated. See, for example, Rehnquist, *The Supreme Court* at 141 (cited in note 33) (commenting on Justice Frankfurter's proclivity to write separately, and noting the rise in the judicial ego), especially when Justices are so underpaid relative to what they could earn in the private legal world. Without riches, it is understandable that Justices seek individual power and fame.

out its history depending on the circumstances of society at the time. When Marshall took control of the Court, there existed a power vacuum at the national level. The consensus norm was a way for the Court to achieve not only power vis-à-vis the other branches of government, but also power in the form of "governmentalization." By increasing the authority of the Court, law as an institution was able to intrude into previously uncharted territory. Lawyers and judges became more important. The discourse of law was forever altered in favor of greater judicial authority over other forms of government and the lives of individual citizens.

At first blush, the rise of the dissenting opinion seems to offer a counterexample to this theory of Supreme Court normalization. Published separate opinions allow the eleven circuit courts and hundreds of lower federal and state courts to offer their own narrower (or broader) interpretation of an opinion. In addition, dissents enable future Justices to overrule an opinion and reverse the trend of the law. By limiting the authority that comes with a 9–0 opinion, dissents undermine the normalizing power of the Court. Even Supreme Court Justices recognize this impact. In controversial cases, the Court will go out of its way to try to achieve a unanimous result. For example, in *Clinton v Jones*, a highly politicized case involving a conflict between the power of the executive and the judiciary, the Court achieved a 9–0 majority in order to strengthen the Court's decision.[215] A 5–4 opinion with only "conservative" Justices in the majority would have been highly criticized as a political attempt to undermine the power of the president.[216] The result instead has been an acceptance that only can come when the Court seems united and apolitical.

Justice Scalia recently wrote about the role of dissenting opinions in these cases. Scalia argued that dissenting opinions augment the prestige of individual Justices while allowing "genuine" una-

---

[215] *Clinton v Jones*, 520 US 681 (1997). In fact this was an 8–0–1 majority in which Justice Breyer concurred with the majority. However, Justice Breyer's opinion reads more like a dissent. Breyer probably joined the majority primarily to achieve unanimity, while writing separately in order to undercut the majority opinion or to offer future Supreme Court Justices an antiprecedent, or to offer lower court judges an escape hatch around the decision. Other examples of this need abound. See, for example, *United States v Nixon*, 418 US 683 (1974) (requiring President Nixon to turn over the Watergate tapes); *Cooper v Aaron*, 358 US 1 (1958) (requiring states to abide by federal desegregation law).

[216] See, for example, *Bush v Gore*, 531 US 98 (2000) (reserving, 5–4, the recount of the ballots in the 2000 presidential election by the Florida Supreme Court).

nimity to have great force when most needed.[217] As an example of when unanimity was "most needed," Scalia cites to *Brown v Board of Education.*[218] Although in *Brown* and *Clinton* unanimity was necessary to achieve political acceptance, in the majority of cases decided today, dissent provides the same result. Ironically, the practice of dissent provides the Court as an institution with a public and political acceptance it would be unable to achieve with per curiam opinions.

This goes back to the point Chief Justice Charles Evans Hughes made about what is needed to "sustain the court in public confidence."[219] The credibility of the Court in general is enhanced when it reveals, at least to a degree, the integrity of its deliberative decision-making process. Kevin Stack argues that the "Supreme Court's legitimacy depends in part upon the Court reaching its judgments through a deliberative process."[220] Decision making at the Court is secret. Only the nine Justices attend the conference of Justices, and the circulation of draft opinions is kept hidden from public view. Given the secrecy of the Supreme Court process for deciding cases, "dissent is necessary to expose the deliberative character of the Court's decision-making."[221]

In Stack's view, majorities, concurrences, and dissents offer a published version of the behind-the-scenes debate in the Supreme Court conference room. This public airing of the deliberative process lends legitimacy to the institution. This cuts to the heart of Jefferson's criticism of opinions of the court. Jefferson encouraged the use of seriatim opinions in order to expose each Justice to public view, so they would have to consider and reason through each case. With individual opinions, Justices expose their competence and legal analysis to the world for criticism. In this way, dissenting opinions arguably create better Justices. With their reputation or career on the line, Justices have the incentive to consider each case carefully.

But this account is not complete. Dissent is not just about modernity's quest for deliberative democracy or necessary for the

---

[217] See Scalia, *Dissenting Opinion*, J S Ct Hist at 33–44 (cited in note 214).

[218] 347 US 483 (1954).

[219] Hughes, *Supreme Court* at 67–68 (cited in note 12).

[220] Kevin M. Stack, *The Practice of Dissent in the Supreme Court*, 105 Yale L J 2235, 2236 (1996).

[221] Id at 2246.

proper functioning of a Supreme Court. It is also about the type of law being practiced before the Court. Dissent is not only necessary to ensure the legitimacy of the Court, but also gives law the *authority* to resolve controversial social issues—it ensures a particular type of Court legitimacy. Just as the opinion of the court was necessary to increase the power of the Court during the Marshall era, dissent is the strategy that enables the Court and the law in general to maintain its institutional power given the highly political nature of the cases the Court decides today. Dissent ensures legal control over society just as the unanimity norm was necessary to achieve the same result in the early nineteenth century. In this light, unanimity and dissent are means to achieve the same ends—increased power and a greater role of normalization for courts and lawyers.

In order to test this hypothesis, let us compare the origin of unanimity and the origin of modern dissent. Despite the long history of openness in the judicial process, Lord Mansfield instituted a change to unanimity in order to achieve greater legal control over the commercial law. Chief Justice Marshall seized upon this same power to increase the reach of the judiciary into new realms. This extension was not simply a greater centralization of power, but also an increase in establishment of broad norms and the enabling force behind modernity's juridical monarchy. For one hundred years, the unanimity consensus existed in part because of this purpose, but the inertia of institutional processes and the culture of the legal profession also perpetuated the norm. During this time, the Supreme Court was deciding similar types of cases. On common law and primarily economic matters, the Court was generally accepted as legitimate despite the secrecy of its process.

But then, in the early 1940s, the conditions of possibility were such that a departure from the consensus norm was necessary. The origin of law evolved from natural law to legal realism—politics entered the law *explicitly* for the first time. But legal realism was a symptom of a broader change in society. Issues never before considered as properly before the Court were thrust into the discourse of the law. This change precipitated a crisis for both the law and the Court.

How is it possible to address these often highly political subjects without sacrificing judicial integrity? The partial answer was dissent. Separate opinions not only show society that the process of decision making is legitimate, but also allow those who oppose a particular result to take comfort that the result may someday be reversed. This is Brennan's idea of dissent as a corrective force. The corrective force of dissents is a two-way street. Both good and bad law is subject to the force of criticism, depending on the prevailing political attitude of the Court. Dissents therefore preserve the ability of the Court to maintain its normalizing power. The vulnerability of precedents based on less than a unanimous judgment makes the Court and the law invulnerable.

Imagine a per curiam opinion that overruled all affirmative action programs or established a constitutional right to an abortion, where the absence of dissent reflected mere conformity rather than actual agreement. Such an opinion would be criticized in part because of Stack's notion of legitimacy, but also because opponents of the opinion would have no legal grounds to continue the fight. A unanimous opinion is so strong as to be susceptible only to constitutional amendment or impeachment of individual Justices, both of which are unlikely.[222] By contrast, dissent allows lower courts, lawyers, and politicians to measure the weight of the opinion and to plan a political or legal counterattack. Dissents lead to ambiguity and hope of change, both of which are fertile ground for legal fights and more lawyers. Litigation strategy often depends on the strength of precedents or the voting records of the current Justices. Without such possibilities for counterattack, the opinion would carry more weight, but the integrity of law and the Court might well come under siege from more dangerous political forces.[223] Possible political reactions are impeachment, change in

---

[222] Jefferson wrote about how difficult impeachment would be, and how this interplays with judicial discourse. See *Letter of Thomas Jefferson to Edward Livingston*, in Lipscomb and Bergh, eds, 16 *The Writings of Thomas Jefferson: Memorial Edition* 114 (1903–04) ("I . . . [am] against caucusing judicial decisions, and for requiring judges to give their opinions *seriatim*, every man for himself, with his reasons and authorities at large, to be entered of record in his own words. A regard for reputation, and the judgment of the world, may sometimes be felt where conscience is dormant, or indolence inexcitable. Experience has proved that impeachment in our forms is completely inefficient."); see also *Letter from Thomas Jefferson to Spencer Roane*, in Paul Leicester Ford, ed, *The Works of Thomas Jefferson* (1904–05) ("For experience has already shown that the impeachment it has provided is not even a scarecrow. . . .").

[223] For example, Bork proposed congressional review of Supreme Court decisions or curtailing the scope of judicial review. See Robert H. Bork, *Our Judicial Oligarchy*, 67 First Things 21, 21 (1996). Bork argued that "[t]he most important moral, political and cultural decisions affecting our lives are steadily being removed from democratic control," and that a "change in our institutional arrangements" is the only thing that "can halt the transformation of our society and culture by judges." Id. His solution: "Decisions of courts

Court composition or jurisdiction,[224] or a constitutional amendment.[225] Congress's power is robust here, as the Constitution grants it the "power to decide how much appellate jurisdiction, and of what sort, the Supreme Court would enjoy."[226]

Dissent undermines the force of an opinion, and allows opponents to hope for the day when they will control the Court. Paradoxically by undermining the authority of the Court, dissent increases the power of the Court and the law by insulating it from potential political attacks. Dissent keeps potentially extrajudicial subjects such as abortion and affirmative action within the purview of the law courts, in just the same way that Mansfield brought commercial disputes into the ambit of the King's Bench.

B. THE ROBERTS GAMBIT?

At his confirmation hearings, Chief Justice Roberts expressed a narrow conception of the role of the Court in public policy matters. Using a baseball analogy, Roberts defined the Supreme Court's role as simply "calling balls and strikes," rather than deciding the fundamental rules of the game. He distinguished himself from Justices Antonin Scalia and Clarence Thomas, by proffering himself as, to use Cass Sunstein's terms, a "minimalist" rather than a Scalia or Thomas-like "visionary." Some doubt the seriousness of this claim, but Roberts has stated publicly that he wants the Court to return to a Marshall-like consensus norm. Critics object to his proposed reform of discourse. Geoffrey Stone recently opined that Supreme Court opinions are not about deciding outcomes but announcing legal principles that will give guidance to lower courts, police, citizens, and so on—they are the creators of

---

might be made subject to modification or reversal by majority vote of the Senate and the House of Representatives. Alternatively, courts might be deprived of the power of constitutional review." Id. This point of view is a departure for Bork, who argued previously that a veto over the Supreme Court was dangerous because it could be used destructively to overturn the "Court's essential work." See Robert H. Bork, *The Tempting of America: The Political Seduction of the Law* 55 (1997) ("If two-thirds of the Senate might have overruled Dred Scott, then perhaps it is imaginable that two-thirds might have overruled a case like *Brown v Board of Education.* That depends on the passions of the moment, but is obvious that unpopular rulings may be easily overturned as improper ones. There is, after all, no reason to think that over time the Senate will be a more responsible interpreter of the Constitution than the Court.").

[224] See note 168.

[225] See note 125.

[226] See Friedman, *History of American Law* at 142 (cited in note 20).

legal truth grids, and small or narrow grids are unhelpful. Stone writes:

> Whenever the Supreme Court decides a case "narrowly," resolving only the particular dispute before it, it leaves the rest of the society and rest of the legal system in the dark. When the Supreme Court leaves important issues unresolved, everyone else must guess about what they can and cannot do under the law. Lower courts are free to disagree with one other, with the result that the scope of constitutional rights will vary randomly from state to state and district to district throughout the nation. Unnecessary uncertainty is not a healthy state of affairs when it comes to the freedom of speech, the freedom of religion, or the right of the people to be secure against unreasonable searches and seizures. It may be easier for the Court to decide cases "narrowly," but it creates chaos for everyone else in the system.[227]

Stone also echoes Jefferson. He writes that opinions without dissent are an "abdication" of judicial responsibility to expose judicial decision making to public critique: "The legitimacy of the judicial branch rests largely on the responsibility of judges to explain and justify their decisions in opinions that can be publicly read, analyzed, and criticized." Consensus decisions that paper over differences do not do this. Here we see Jefferson's arguments about transparency and accountability. Stone also believes dissent is essential to overruling bad law, and he, like Jefferson, cites examples of cases in which results we think are right were first suggested in earlier dissents.[228] Squelching dissent would "degrade the quality of the Court's work and undermine the public's and the legal profession's ability to evaluate the seriousness and persuasiveness of the Court's reasoning. In the long run, it would undermine the Court itself."[229]

---

[227] Geoffrey Stone, *Chief Justice Roberts and the Role of the Supreme Court*, University of Chicago Faculty Blog (Feb 2, 2007), available at: http://uchicagolaw.typepad.com/faculty/2007/02/chief_justice_r.html.

[228] Id. ("It is also important to note that some of the most influential opinions in the history of the Supreme Court were concurring and dissenting opinions. Although they did not command the support of a majority of the Justices at the time, they eventually won the day because of the force of their reasoning. Familiar examples, to name just a few, include Justice Harlan's famous dissenting opinion in *Plessy v Ferguson*, the pivotal dissenting and concurring opinions of Justices Holmes and Brandeis in a series of free speech decisions following World War I, and Justice Robert Jackson's landmark concurring opinion in the *Steel Seizure* case.").

[229] Id.

Although Jefferson and Stone make the same arguments about the value of dissent, remember that Jefferson wanted to *decrease* the power of the Court, while Stone presumably wants to *increase* it or, at least, keep it the same. This exposes these arguments, as well as the arguments of their opponents—Marshall and Roberts, respectively—for what they are: justifications for a particular political role for the Court. The critiques are instrumental only. Neither Jefferson nor Stone believes that dissent makes better law in the abstract, but rather that separate opinions from that of the Court were necessary for an expression of their particular preference for the locus of legal power. Jefferson wanted a weak Court so power could be located in the legislature, presidency, and the states, and dissent was the means to weaken the Court given its institutional position at the time. Stone wants a strong Court and dissent appears to be the means to strengthen the Court at this time.

To put it another way, taking Chief Justice Roberts at his word, the preference for unanimity does not obviously sit well with the current stable of cases—it seems implausible to suggest that Roberts can achieve unanimity on questions of race, gender, school choice, homosexual rights, the War on Terror, and other politically contentious issues. So what is his rhetoric about? One possibility is that Roberts wants to decrease the power of the Court in American society, and his mechanism for that is same as that urged by Mansfield, Marshall, and Stone, just in the opposite direction.[230]

IV. Conclusion

It is not surprising that we observe opinion-delivery practices of Anglo-American courts suited to the particular times. This fact seems almost self-evident, but it does rebut claims that the current practice of writing separately is theoretically and ceteris paribus superior to other methods. The lesson from history is that allowing or forbidding dissent is not about getting better law per se, but about achieving some defined role for courts. This role is typically, but not always, more power over disputes.

We have seen that the history of debates about the opinion-delivery practices of Anglo-American courts has been about court power. Those arguing for the right to dissent have sometimes been

---

[230] Roberts's move is perhaps analogous to that of Lord Kenyon.

about limiting court power (e.g., Jefferson) and sometimes about increasing it (e.g., Brennan). We should view the proposal from Chief Justice Roberts in this light. Roberts's nostalgia for the Marshall era of unanimity is about reducing the power of the Court, both by narrowing individual holdings to open up decision space for other actors, and also to limit the kinds of cases the Court hears. A consensus norm is incompatible with deciding the Court's recent docket of cases, at least in the broad manner in which they have historically been decided. In this day and age, narrowness and minimalism go hand in hand with consensus, while breadth and judicial power go hand in hand with dissent. Of course, it was not always this way, and it may not be again. This pattern of punctuated equilibrium is bound to repeat itself again and again. Dissent is a powerful tool of the law. And because it is a tool, dissent is used to achieve the ends of the law, whatever they may be.

ALISON L. LaCROIX

THE NEW WHEEL IN THE FEDERAL MACHINE: FROM SOVEREIGNTY TO JURISDICTION IN THE EARLY REPUBLIC

Legal historians and constitutional scholars have tended to approach the judiciary acts of 1789 and 1801 as though the two statutes were separated not only by a dozen years but also by a fundamental, unbridgeable conceptual gulf. While the Judiciary Act of 1789[1] is celebrated as "probably the most important and the most satisfactory Act ever passed by Congress," as Justice Henry B. Brown hailed it in 1911, the Judiciary Act of 1801[2] is frequently regarded as a forgettable relic of early national political squabbling.[3] The storied heritage of the 1789 act began with its passage into law more than four months before the Supreme Court convened for its first session,

Alison L. LaCroix is Assistant Professor of Law, University of Chicago Law School.

AUTHOR'S NOTE: I am grateful to William A. Birdthistle and Adam B. Cox for their helpful comments and suggestions. I also thank the Elsie O. and Philip D. Sang Law Faculty Endowment and the Russell Baker Scholars Fund for research support.

[1] An Act to Establish the Judicial Courts of the United States, Ch 20, 1 Stat 73 (1789) (Judiciary Act of 1789).

[2] An Act to Provide for the More Convenient Organization of the Courts of the United States, 2 Stat 89 (1801) (Judiciary Act of 1801) (repealed by Judiciary Act of 1802, 2 Stat 132 (1802)).

[3] Henry B. Brown, *The New Federal Judicial Code*, 36 ABA Rep 339, 345 (1911), quoted in Charles Warren, *New Light on the History of the Federal Judiciary Act of 1789*, 37 Harv L Rev 49, 52 (1923).

and therefore well in advance of the date when the entire federal government can truly be said to have begun functioning;[4] the 1801 act, in contrast, is remembered principally for a pair of controversial distinctions: first, creating the circuit courts to which President John Adams appointed the so-called "midnight judges" on the eve of his departure from office; and second, suffering repeal at the hands of the newly Republican Congress one year later, in the aftermath of the acrimonious election of 1800. As Kathryn Turner Preyer observed, "[A]wareness of the Act seems to have been kept alive chiefly because it must be summoned to serve as the cause of its own repeal in March 1802."[5] If the 1789 act stands for the fulfillment of the "Madisonian compromise" reached at Philadelphia, in which the delegates agreed to postpone the divisive issue of inferior federal courts to the First Congress, the 1801 act represents the failure of compromise, when the first party system collided with unsettled questions regarding the structure of the federal judiciary.[6]

Clearly, the two acts have received quite disparate treatment over the course of the past two centuries. But this difference fails to take into account their meaning and context in light of their shared historical moment. Too often, each judiciary act has been treated as an isolated piece of legislation complete in itself rather than as an intellectual vestige of a particular moment in American legal and political discourse. But the acts have more to tell us than this. Considering the two acts as disjunctive and dichotomous overlooks the vital role that both statutes played in the development of American federalism. Instead of lionizing the 1789 act and attempting to excuse or dismiss the 1801 act, reading the two together offers new insights into the crucial decades between 1787 and 1802, when theorists and politicians struggled to give meaning to the Constitution's phrase, "the judicial power of the United States."

If one regards the years from 1787 to 1802 as a single period

---

[4] The first session of the Supreme Court—attended by only four of the six original Justices—took place in New York on February 2, 1790. See Robert G. McCloskey, *The American Supreme Court* 1–2 (Chicago, 4th ed 2004).

[5] Kathryn Turner [Preyer], *Federalist Policy and the Judiciary Act of 1801*, 22 Wm & Mary Q 3, 3 (3d ser, 1965). See also William E. Nelson, *The Province of the Judiciary*, 37 John Marshall L Rev 325, 336 (stating that "[t]he 1801 Act, as we know, was a failure").

[6] On the Madisonian compromise, see Martin H. Redish and Curtis E. Woods, *Congressional Power to Control the Jurisdiction of Lower Federal Courts: A Critical Review and a New Synthesis*, 124 U Pa L Rev 45, 52–56 (1975); Robert N. Clinton, *A Mandatory View of Federal Court Jurisdiction: A Guided Quest for the Original Understanding of Article III*, 132 U Pa L Rev 741, 763–64 (1984).

and then situates that period at the end of a larger sweep of Anglo-American constitutional ferment, the two judiciary acts take on new significance beyond simply completing the founding settlement. On this view, the importance of the acts lies beyond their immediate consequences for the balance between state and federal judicial power, or even for the broader question of the meaning of union at the dawn of the nineteenth century. Rather, the debate surrounding the judiciary acts implicates federal ideas in the broadest sense— that is, the specifically late eighteenth-century/early nineteenth-century effort to bring together multiple levels of authority within a single government while maintaining lines of demarcation between the levels. In other words, the judiciary acts must be understood as important sites for the development of federal *theory*, not simply as component parts in the heroic story of the construction of the modern American republic.

The passage of the judiciary acts, then, should be examined in the context of the continuing development of American federal ideas *as ideas* in the early republican period. The acts of 1789 and 1801 are vital to the story of federalism because their passage signaled a shift from legislative-focused theorizing, which had characterized the years roughly between 1765 and 1787, to a new emphasis on the role of judicial power in establishing and delineating boundaries between the levels of authority within a multilayered polity.[7]

Some scholars have pointed out the significance of the acts, especially the 1789 act, for establishing the federal judiciary in the separation-of-powers framework.[8] Other commentators have explored the institutional role of the courts, vis-à-vis other actors such as Congress or the states, in maintaining (or, in some cases, confounding) the federal structure.[9] Rather than focusing on judicial

---

[7] On the general shift in focus from legislatures to courts—especially by the Federalists— in the ratification period, see, for example, Nelson, 37 John Marshall L Rev at 340–49 (cited in note 5); Gordon S. Wood, *The Creation of the American Republic, 1776–1787* at 537–38 (W.W. Norton, 1969).

[8] See, for example, Akhil Reed Amar, *America's Constitution: A Biography* 227–32 (Random House, 2005); Wythe Holt, *"To Establish Justice": Politics, the Judiciary Act of 1789, and the Invention of the Federal Courts*, 1989 Duke L J 1421.

[9] See, for example, Larry D. Kramer, *The People Themselves: Popular Constitutionalism and Judicial Review* (Oxford, 2004); Jesse H. Choper, *Judicial Review and the National Political Process: A Functional Reconsideration of the Role of the Supreme Court* 171–259 (Chicago, 1980); Alexander M. Bickel, *The Least Dangerous Branch: The Supreme Court at the Bar of Politics* (Bobbs-Merrill, 1962); Herbert Wechsler, *The Political Safeguards of Federalism: The Role of the States in the Composition and Selection of the National Government*, 54 Colum L Rev 543 (1954).

supremacy at either the horizontal level of separation-of-powers analysis or the vertical level of state-federal relations, however, my analysis seeks to situate the judiciary acts in the context of the Revolutionary and early republican struggles to construct a federal union that was more centralized than the old Confederation but less unitary in its distribution of sovereignty than the British Empire.[10] On this view, the judiciary acts should be understood not only as markers in the retrospective, modern narrative of how the United States came to have the courts that it now has, but as experiments in fleshing out the sometimes ill-defined scheme of federal government that had slowly been emerging in America since the 1760s.

The two acts must be seen on their own terms, as attempts by particular individuals to confront functional questions of governmental authority that more than two decades' worth of thought and debate had left unaddressed. The turn to the judiciary in 1789 represented a subtle but important departure from the prominent role that the legislature had played in the past several decades' theories of divided authority. Anglo-American theorists of the pre- and post-Revolutionary eras had for the most part shared their metropolitan cousins' emphasis on the legislative power as the most significant player in the contemporary constitutional arrangement. Many Americans, however, declined to follow this theory to the conclusion that was increasingly gaining adherents in Britain, among them Sir William Blackstone: namely, that the legislature—specifically, Parliament—possessed complete and indivisible sovereign authority.[11] Consequently, in the transatlantic debates of the 1760s and 1770s, Anglo-Americans began to articulate a vision of political authority that explored new methods of segmenting power among many levels of legislatures, rather than vesting power entirely

---

[10] On the role that theories of empire played in the early Republic, see Daniel J. Hulsebosch, *Constituting Empire: New York and the Transformation of Constitutionalism in the Atlantic World, 1664–1830* at 203–58 (North Carolina, 2005); Peter S. Onuf, *Jefferson's Empire: The Language of American Nationhood* 53–79 (Virginia, 2000).

[11] In Blackstone's view, set forth in his *Commentaries on the Laws of England* of 1765–69, government required a "supreme, irresistible, absolute, uncontrolled authority . . . in which the rights of sovereignty reside." William Blackstone, 1 *Commentaries* *49. For Blackstone, that authority was Parliament, which he described as possessing "sovereign and uncontrolable authority in making, confirming, enlarging, restraining, abrogating, repealing, reviving, and expounding of laws, concerning matters of all possible denominations, ecclesiastical, or temporal, civil, military, maritime, or criminal." Parliament could thus "do every thing that is not naturally impossible." Id.

in one supreme legislature. In so doing, they rejected the growing orthodoxy of domestic British constitutional theory as well as the broader applications of that theory to the British Empire. Not until 1787, however, did the demands of the constitution-drafting process impel American thinkers to put aside the legislative focus of their political heritage and begin experimenting with the judicial power as a key component of the federal arrangement.[12]

To be sure, by 1789, the notion that the judiciary might potentially play a specific, structural role in the architecture of the federal republic remained a highly contested idea. It would continue to be controversial for many years, as the rancor surrounding the 1801 act and its repeal would demonstrate. But the period beginning around 1789 differed from the colonial, Revolutionary, and ratification periods in at least one crucial respect. The final decade of the eighteenth century and the early decades of the nineteenth century witnessed a transformation from *sovereignty* to *jurisdiction* as the central organizing principle—and battlefield—of American federalism.

As I will demonstrate, pre- and postwar debates regarding the essential nature of sovereignty—an inquiry that had occupied political theorists since the early modern era—slowly gave way in the early republican period to a search for the proper jurisdictional arrangement to mediate between the multiple levels of government contemplated in the Constitution. This quest to find the appropriate structural mechanisms to avoid the "solecism" of an *imperium in imperio*, or a government within a government, continued to haunt early republicans, just as it had plagued their predecessors during the Stamp Act crisis of the 1760s and the confrontations between colonial assemblies and royal governors of the 1770s.[13] Yet although they employed this inherited vocabulary, theorists and politicians

---

[12] For a more extended discussion of the origins of American federalism in this period, see Alison L. LaCroix, *A Well-Constructed Union: An Intellectual History of American Federalism, 1754–1800* (PhD diss, Harvard University, 2007).

[13] The "solecism" of *imperium in imperio* was a powerful rhetorical device invoked repeatedly throughout eighteenth-century Anglo-American debates. See, for example, Federalist 20 (Madison with Hamilton), in Jacob E. Cooke, ed, *The Federalist* 128–29 (Wesleyan, 1961) (describing "a sovereignty over sovereigns, a government over governments, a legislation for communities, as contradistinguished from individuals" as "a solecism in theory" and "in practice"). As Daniel Hulsebosch has demonstrated, the pejorative dated back at least to 1720, when Henry St. John, Viscount Bolingbroke, referred to *imperium in imperio* as a "Solecism in Politicks." Daniel J. Hulsebosch, *Imperia in Imperio: The Multiple Constitutions of Empire in New York, 1750–1777*, 16 Law & Hist Rev 319, 340 n 58 (1998), citing [Bolingbroke], *The Country Journal, or the Craftsman*, no 172 (October 18, 1729).

in the 1790s and 1800s conceived of their problem not in terms of
locating the initial source of governmental authority but instead as
a question of delineating the boundaries among the judicial bodies
that would guide the exercise of that authority. This second-generation process sought to fill in gaps and decipher hints left by the
Constitutional Convention. In so doing, early republican theorists
seized on Article III and the Supremacy Clause to guide their efforts
to establish institutions that would carry out the federal project.
The goal of this project was to build a structure to support the
federal aspirations of the Constitution. The material of this structure was a theory of federal jurisdiction.

My analysis examines the rise of jurisdiction as the defining element of American federalism. Beginning around 1789, the organization of the federal judiciary became the locus of debates concerning both the practical and the ideological meaning of
federalism. Commentators as diverse as Alexander Hamilton,
Thomas Jefferson, John Marshall, Theodore Sedgwick, Joseph
Story, and St. George Tucker focused on jurisdiction as they ham-
mered out their own working understandings of federalism and
confronted those of their contemporaries. This account thus challenges the assumption underlying some modern federalism scholarship that nationalization through the federal judiciary is a relatively new, post-1937 phenomenon. My argument demonstrates the
anachronistic nature of such assumptions by highlighting the centrality of the judiciary to the nation's earliest debates concerning
the scope and extent of national power. To be sure, general federal
question jurisdiction did not become a stable fixture of American
law until 1875. That date does not mean, however, that for the
previous eighty-six years any consensus had held that the scope of
federal courts' jurisdiction was limited, and properly so. On the
contrary: viewing the expansion of federal jurisdiction as purely a
post-Reconstruction or a twentieth-century phenomenon ignores
important early republican antecedents to those later developments.
The period between 1787 and 1802 witnessed a transformation in
American constitutional discourse from the language of legislative
power and sovereignty to that of judicial power and jurisdiction.

I. Defining the Judicial Power, 1787–1789

A. BACKGROUND: CONVENTION AND CONSTITUTION

The period between 1789 and 1802 witnessed the increased salience of the judicial power in the ongoing American dialogue regarding the proper arrangement of the layers of governmental power in a federal republic. In order to see this subtle but fundamental transformation in early national modes of thought, we must in a sense undomesticate the judiciary acts by examining them outside the familiar tropes of, on the one hand, the state-versus-federal binary that often preoccupies American constitutional history, and, on the other hand, twentieth- and twenty-first-century debates concerning the scope of modern federal courts' jurisdiction. Without question, those debates are important, and they occupy a deservedly central place in constitutional law and federal courts scholarship.[14] But in order to comprehend the judiciary acts' significance for the historical narrative of federalism's origins, a wider perspective is necessary. This perspective begins with an inquiry into the particular legal and political context in which the acts were created.

When the First Congress convened in April 1789, fifty-four of the congressmen and senators had recently served as members of the Constitutional Convention or of the state ratification conventions.[15] As part of those earlier deliberations, the members would have been involved in discussions concerning two measures that emerged in the course of the debates at Philadelphia and that shaped the role of the judiciary in the new republic. Although the provisions had different aims, taken together they suggested that judicial institutions would feature prominently in the new government that was being cobbled together.

The first such measure, the so-called "Madisonian compro-

---

[14] The literature concerning Congress's power to regulate the scope of federal jurisdiction is enormous. The classic account is Henry M. Hart, Jr., *The Power of Congress to Limit the Jurisdiction of Federal Courts: An Exercise in Dialectic*, 66 Harv L Rev 1362 (1953). More recent analyses include John Harrison, *The Power of Congress to Limit the Jurisdiction of Federal Courts and the Text of Article III*, 64 U Chi L Rev 203 (1997); Akhil Reed Amar, *The Two-Tiered Structure of the Judiciary Act of 1789*, 138 U Pa L Rev 1499 (1990); Akhil Reed Amar, *A Neo-Federalist View of Article III: Separating the Two Tiers of Federal Jurisdiction*, 65 BU L Rev 205 (1985); Clinton, 132 U Pa L Rev at 741 (cited in note 6); Gerald Gunther, *Congressional Power to Curtail Federal Court Jurisdiction: An Opinionated Guide to the Ongoing Debate*, 36 Stan L Rev 895 (1984).

[15] Richard Morris, ed, *Encyclopedia of American History* 145 (Harper & Row, 6th ed 1982).

mise," consisted of a provision that "the National Legislature be empowered to institute inferior tribunals"; the measure was adopted by the convention on June 5, 1787, after substantial debate.[16] It was in the nature of a compromise in that it staved off a motion by John Rutledge of South Carolina to delete all references to inferior federal courts from the draft constitution, but it did not go as far as mandating the establishment of inferior federal courts, as had been proposed in Edmund Randolph's Virginia Plan or South Carolinian Charles Pinckney's draft constitution.[17] Instead, the compromise was incorporated into Article III, which vested the "judicial Power of the United States" in "one supreme Court, and in such inferior Courts as the Congress may from time to time establish."[18]

In addition to the Madisonian compromise, which established the potential for but not the certainty of inferior federal courts, the delegates at Philadelphia and in the state ratifying conventions engaged in a related debate that concerned not the horizontal relationship between Congress and lower federal courts but instead the vertical interaction between the general government and the states. Madison and other delegates such as Pinckney and James Wilson of Pennsylvania feared that the states might continue the unruly and independent behavior that they had displayed throughout the 1780s. A government capable of accommodating multiple levels of authority had been many colonists' desideratum since the 1760s, but the reality of the 1780s forced observers to reconsider the structure of this multitiered polity. How might the state legislatures be checked in their rush to issue paper currency, pass debtor-relief laws, deny the provisions of the peace treaty with Britain, and otherwise follow state rather than larger, national interests?[19]

As his voluminous notes and correspondence before the convention and his comments on the floor at Philadelphia made clear,

---

[16] 1 *The Records of the Federal Convention of 1787* at 125 (Yale, 1966) (Max Farrand, ed). For classic articulations of the Madisonian compromise, see Redish and Woods, 124 U Pa L Rev at 52–56 (cited in note 6); Clinton, 132 U Pa L Rev at 763–764 (cited in note 6).

[17] See 1 *Records of the Federal Convention* 104–05, 119, 124–25; 2 id at 45–46 (cited in note 16).

[18] US Const, Art III, § 1, cl 1.

[19] On the turmoil of the 1780s and its consequences for the drafting of the Constitution, see Wood, *The Creation of the American Republic* at 393–429 (cited in note 7).

Madison believed that he had the answer: the Constitution should grant Congress the power to negative state laws "in all cases whatsoever"—or at least, as other delegates suggested, in situations where Congress deemed the state law in question "improper."[20] In other words, Madison hoped to use the legislative power of the general government to quell the wayward lawmaking tendencies of the several states. After much discussion—including an impassioned defense by Madison, who regarded the negative as "absolutely necessary to a perfect system"—the proposal suffered a series of defeats, culminating in its rejection on July 17 by a vote of seven states to three.[21] Despite the failure of the negative, however, many of Madison's fellow delegates appear to have agreed with his judgment that checks on the "centrifugal tendency of the States" were necessary to prevent them from "continually fly[ing] out of their proper orbits and destroy the order & harmony of the political system."[22] A mechanism had to be found by which the states might be both restrained from exploiting each other and coaxed into aligning their interests with those of the Union.

The mechanism that the delegates settled on was a bold statement of federal supremacy that emerged more or less simultaneously with the demise of the negative.[23] Adopting the language of William Paterson's New Jersey Plan, the delegates drafted what became the Supremacy Clause of Article VI.[24] In contrast to Mad-

---

[20] Madison had aired his proposal for the federal negative in letters to Thomas Jefferson, Edmund Randolph, and George Washington as early as March 1787. The negative was a central feature of the Virginia Plan, which Randolph proposed at an early meeting of the Philadelphia convention. It attracted little controversy or even notice until June 8, at which point Pinckney's motion to expand the scope of Congress's authority from negativing state laws "contravening in the opinion of the National Legislature the articles of Union" to cover laws that Congress simply deemed "improper" galvanized debate. See 1 *Records of the Federal Convention* 164–73, 2 id 25–36 (cited in note 16). For Madison's letters, see 9 *The Papers of James Madison* 317, 369, 383 (Chicago, 1975) (Robert Rutland et al, eds). On the federal negative, see LaCroix, *A Well-Constructed Union* at 217–83 (cited in note 12).

[21] 1 *Records of the Federal Convention* 164 (cited in note 16).

[22] Id at 165.

[23] The final vote on the negative took place on July 17, 1787; immediately thereafter, the delegates took up the provision that would become the Supremacy Clause. See 2 id 28–29. See also Kramer, *The People Themselves* at 74–75 (cited in note 9); Jack N. Rakove, *The Origins of Judicial Review: A Plea for New Contexts*, 49 Stan L Rev 1031, 1046–47 (1997); Jack N. Rakove, *Original Meanings: Politics and Ideas in the Making of the Constitution* 82–83 (Vintage, 1996); Lawrence Gene Sager, *The Supreme Court, 1980 Term—Foreword: Constitutional Limitations on Congress' Authority to Regulate the Jurisdiction of the Federal Courts*, 95 Harv L Rev 17, 46–47 (1981).

[24] US Const, Art VI, cl 2 ("This Constitution, and the Laws of the United States which

ison's scheme, which had embraced a legislative solution to the problem of mediating between the levels of authority within the federal republic, the Supremacy Clause presented the judiciary as a potential site of intergovernmental ordering. In this way, the clause addressed Madison's twin goals, as he subsequently described them in a letter to Jefferson: "1. to prevent encroachments on the General authority. 2. to prevent instability and injustice in the legislation of the States."[25] By identifying "the Laws of the United States" as the "supreme Law of the Land," which would in turn bind the "Judges in every State," the clause spoke the language of court-made law. One reads the Supremacy Clause and thinks of the interpretation of law through processes of adjudication, not the creation of law through the legislative process.

The evidence suggests that at least some members of the founding generation believed that the shift from the negative to the Supremacy Clause as a key federalism-enforcing mechanism meant that the Supreme Court very likely possessed the power to review actions by both state legislatures and state courts.[26] During the convention, Thomas Jefferson, at that time serving as minister to the Court of Versailles, conveyed to Madison his dislike for the negative and suggested that courts rather than Congress might be charged with policing the states. The negative, Jefferson wrote,

---

shall be made in Pursuance thereof; and all Treaties made, or which shall be made, under the Authority of the United States, shall be the supreme Law of the Land; and the Judges in every State shall be bound thereby, any Thing in the Constitution or Laws of any State to the Contrary notwithstanding.").

[25] 10 *Papers of James Madison* 209–10 (cited in note 20).

[26] By "federalism-enforcing mechanism," I mean federalism in the structural, mechanical sense that most concerned Madison: namely, the need to incorporate the states into the general government, and in so doing to move from a confederation—the early modern political philosophers' "system of states"—to a new species of federal republic in which the central government had some independent powers rather than acting merely as a shell for the states. The construction "system of states" is associated with the early modern theorist Samuel von Pufendorf. See Samuel von Pufendorf, *The Law of Nature and Nations: or, a General System of the most Important Principles of Morality, Jurisprudence, and Politics*, trans Basil Kennet (London, 5th ed 1749) (1672), vol 2, bk 7, ch 5, § 18, 682–83. The phrase "judicially enforced federalism" has been used in modern scholarship to refer to courts' acting on behalf of substantive federal values, including "limits on the power of the national government vis-à-vis the states." Larry D. Kramer, *But When Exactly Was Judicially-Enforced Federalism "Born" in the First Place?* 22 Harv J L & Pub Pol 123, 123 (1998). For the source of the related debate regarding the need for the federal government to protect federalism by acting on behalf of the states, see Wechsler, 54 Colum L Rev at 543 (cited in note 9). See also Gerald Leonard, *Party as a "Political Safeguard of Federalism": Martin Van Buren and the Constitutional Theory of Party Politics*, 54 Rutgers L Rev 221 (2001); Larry D. Kramer, *Putting the Politics Back into the Political Safeguards of Federalism*, 100 Colum L Rev 215 (2000).

"proposes to mend a small hole by covering the whole garment."[27] He disapproved of vesting Congress with such a broad—and potentially open-ended—power. Would it not be preferable, Jefferson asked, to rely on a more elegant solution that required less apparatus? "[A]n appeal from the state judicature to a federal court, in all cases where the act of the Confederation controled the question" would "be as effectual a remedy, & exactly commensurate to the defect."[28] For Jefferson, allowing an injured party to appeal from a state court to a federal court was preferable to building an ex ante system of legislative review into the Constitution.

On the floor of the convention, other delegates similarly assumed that the alternative to the negative was case-by-case review by courts. Arguing that including the negative in the Constitution would "disgust all the States," New Yorker Gouverneur Morris articulated the judicial approach: "A law that ought to be negatived will be set aside in the Judiciary departmt. and if that security should fail; may be repealed by a Nationl. law."[29] In other words, judicial review of state law and state-court decisions was at least a possibility for delegates to the convention and their contemporaries.[30]

But this vision of the judicial power of the United States concerned only the Supreme Court. It said nothing about the lower federal courts that Congress might eventually choose to establish, and therefore it provided few definitive answers to the question what the full judicial power of the United States might look like. Explication of those issues awaited the First Congress, where the

---

[27] 10 *Papers of James Madison* 64 (cited in note 20).

[28] Id.

[29] 2 *Records of the Federal Convention* 28 (cited in note 16).

[30] Morris later commented that portions of Article III had intentionally been drafted (by him) to speak in somewhat oblique terms. "[C]onflicting opinions had been maintained with so much professional astuteness, that it became necessary to select phrases, which expressing my own notions would not alarm others, nor shock their selflove, and to the best of my recollection, this was the only part which passed without cavil." Morris to Timothy Pickering (Dec 22, 1814), 3 id at 420. By the nineteenth century, the notion that judicial review had been adopted in place of the negative was a commonplace, at least for some theorists. See, for example, Joseph Story, *Commentaries on the Constitution of the United States* 607 (Hilliard, Gray, abr ed 1833) (describing the federal government's power to check state legislatures as "either a direct negative on the state laws, or an authority in the national courts to overrule such, as shall be manifestly in contravention to the constitution" and concluding that "[t]he latter course was thought by the convention to be preferable to the former; and it is, without question, by far the most acceptable to the states"). See also William E. Nelson, *Changing Conceptions of Judicial Review: The Evolution of Constitutional Theory in the States, 1790–1860*, 120 U Pa L Rev 1166 (1972).

veterans of the ratification debates and their colleagues together took up the question that, among a host of divisive issues that had vexed the Constitutional Convention, had been postponed to be dealt with by the legislature.

In the nineteen months between the end of the convention and the first meeting of Congress, the subject of inferior federal courts had generated prolonged and intense discussion. During the ratification debates in the states, pamphlets and speeches had focused on the issue as one of the key sites of dispute between supporters and opponents of the new constitution.[31] The fervor with which commentators attacked the question of the federal courts suggests that they regarded jurisdictional decisions as central to defining the new republic.

Indeed, the provisions of the Constitution concerning the judicial power gave rise to some of the most vehement disagreements between Federalists and Antifederalists. The establishment of the Supreme Court proved relatively uncontroversial.[32] The prospect of an entirely new echelon of federal courts in addition to the Supreme Court, however, tested many observers' deepest constitutional commitments. In *Federalist* 81, Alexander Hamilton argued that inferior federal courts ought to be viewed merely as ancillae of the Supreme Court and not as independent forces of consolidation. Calling the establishment of federal district courts "highly expedient and useful," Hamilton concluded that "[t]his plan appears to me at present the most eligible of any that could be adopted."[33] A few weeks later, John Marshall offered Virginia's ratifying convention a practical argument for the new courts. "Does not every Gentleman here know, that the causes in our Courts are more numerous than they can decide, according to their present construction?" he asked. The future Chief Justice then exhorted his colleagues to "[l]ook at the dockets. You will

---

[31] Compare, for example, *George Mason Fears the Power of the Federal Courts: What Will Be Left to the States?* in 2 *The Debate on the Constitution: Federalist and Antifederalist Speeches, Articles, and Letters During the Struggle over Ratification, January to August 1788* at 720–29 (Library of America, 1993) (Bernard Bailyn, ed), with *John Marshall on the Fairness and Jurisdiction of the Federal Courts*, in id at 730–41.

[32] See "Introduction: The Constitutional Origins of the Federal Judiciary," 4 *The Documentary History of the Supreme Court of the United States, 1789–1800* at 10 (Columbia, 1992) (Maeva Marcus, ed) (hereafter "*DHSC*").

[33] Federalist 81 (Hamilton), in *The Federalist* 547–48 (cited in note 13).

find them crouded with suits, which the life of man will not see determined."[34]

Yet strong voices such as that of Maryland's Luther Martin lambasted the plan. Permitting Congress to appoint inferior courts "would eventually absorb and swallow up the state judiciaries," Martin insisted, "by drawing all business from them to the courts of the general government, which the extensive and undefined powers, legislative and judicial, of which it is possessed, would easily enable it to do."[35] George Mason of Virginia, meanwhile, feared potential expansion of federal power under Article III. "The inferior Courts are to be as numerous as Congress may think proper," he warned. "Read the second section, and contemplate attentively the jurisdiction of these Courts; and consider if there be any limits to it."[36]

Controversy regarding the establishment of the inferior federal courts thus smoldered during the ratification period, with each side in the debate invoking the first sentence of Article III ("The judicial Power of the United States, shall be vested in one supreme Court, and in such inferior Courts as the Congress may from time to time ordain and establish.") as evidence of either Philadelphian prudence or consolidationist connivance.[37] Few observers could have been surprised, then, when on April 7, 1789, the First Congress took up the issue as its first item of business. Throughout the spring and summer of 1789, public attention was fixed on Federal Hall in Wall Street. As Virginia congressman Alexander White commented in a letter to Madison: "At the inns on the road, I was surprised to find the knowledge which the landlords, and the country people who were at some of them, had acquired of the debates and proceedings of Congress."[38]

---

[34] 2 *The Debate on the Constitution* at 732 (cited in note 31).

[35] Luther Martin's Letter on the Federal Convention of 1787 (The Genuine Information), 1 *The Debates in the Several State Conventions on the Adoption of the Federal Constitution, as Recommended by the General Convention at Philadelphia, in 1787, Together With the Journal of the Federal Convention, Luther Martin's Letter, Yates's Minutes, Congressional Opinions, Virginia and Kentucky Resolutions of '98–'99, and Other Illustrations of the Constitution* 370 (Washington, 1836) (Jonathan Elliott, ed).

[36] 2 *The Debate on the Constitution* 720 (cited in note 31).

[37] US Const, Art III, § 1, cl 1.

[38] White to Madison (Aug 17, 1789), in Warren, 37 Harv L Rev at 65 (cited in note 3).

B. THE JUDICIARY ACT OF 1789

The history of the 1789 act's drafting and passage is well known.[39] A Senate committee comprising ten members (one from each state that had ratified the Constitution and sent senators by that point) produced a first version of the act, which the committee circulated to select attorneys and officials for comment during the summer of 1789.[40] On July 17, the Senate approved the bill by a vote of fourteen to six. The House of Representatives, which had been occupied drafting the amendments that formed the basis of the Bill of Rights, took up the judiciary act on August 24. After extensive debate—much of it concerning the propriety of establishing inferior federal courts at all—and the addition of fifty-two amendments, the House passed the bill on September 17 by a vote of thirty-seven to sixteen. House and Senate then conducted speedy negotiations regarding some of the amendments before sending the bill on to President Washington, who signed it into law on September 24.

The most important provisions of the act for our purposes centered on two structural aspects: the jurisdiction of the Supreme Court and the organization and powers of the inferior federal courts, which the act broke down into the two categories of district courts and circuit courts.[41] As students of *Marbury v Madison* will

---

[39] For a comprehensive discussion of the background to the act, see Maeva Marcus, ed, *Origins of the Federal Judiciary: Essays on the Judiciary Act of 1789* (Oxford, 1992); Warren, 37 Harv L Rev at 49 (cited in note 3). For the debates, see 1 *The Debates and Proceedings in the Congress of the United States; with an Appendix, Containing Important State Papers and Public Documents, and all the Laws of a Public Nature; With a Copious Index (Annals of the Congress of the United States)* (Gales and Seaton, 1834) (hereafter "*Annals*").

[40] The ten senators were Oliver Ellsworth (Connecticut), William Paterson (New Jersey), Caleb Strong (Massachusetts), Richard Henry Lee (Virginia), Richard Bassett (Delaware), William Maclay (Pennsylvania), William Few (Georgia), Paine Wingate (New Hampshire), Charles Carroll (Maryland), and Ralph Izard (South Carolina). Marcus notes that of the ten, "six had been members of the Continental Congress; and five had been members of their state ratifying conventions" and that "[w]ith the exception of Lee and Maclay, all were Federalists." Moreover, "[a]ll but Izard and Wingate had at least some legal training," although she describes only Ellsworth, Strong, and Paterson as having "extensive legal experience." Ellsworth handled the majority of the drafting. 4 *DHSC* at 22–23 (cited in note 32). William Maclay's journal suggests that tempers among the committee members occasionally flared up amidst the intense efforts to produce a draft bill. On June 29, Maclay noted, "Attended at the Hall early. Sent my letters to the post-office; and now for the judiciary. I made a remark where Elsworth [*sic*] in his diction had varied from the Constitution. This vile bill is a child of his, and he defends it with the care of a parent, even with wrath and anger." William Maclay, *Journal of William Maclay, United States Senator From Pennsylvania, 1789–1791* at 91 (D. A. Appleton, 1890) (Edgar S. Maclay, ed).

[41] At least as important, but beyond the scope of this article, are two related issues on

recall, the act sought to grant certain heads of original jurisdiction to the Court in addition to those contained in Article III.[42] The act also established the Court's appellate jurisdiction, which extended to the lower federal courts as well as the state courts.[43] Despite the later salience of Section 25's grant to the Court of the power to review state-court decisions, as demonstrated in such cases as *Martin v Hunter's Lessee*[44] and *Cohens v Virginia*,[45] in 1789 this provision generated less debate than did the architecture of inferior federal courts that the act set up.[46]

The structure of the lower federal courts consisted of two parts: (1) thirteen district courts (one for each of the eleven then-ratifying states, plus Maine and Kentucky, which at that time were still part of Massachusetts and Virginia, respectively), each with its own district judge; and (2) three circuits, each requiring a quorum of two Justices of the Supreme Court and the district judge of the particular district in which the court was sitting at a given time. The district courts possessed exclusive jurisdiction over admiralty cases and cases involving minor federal crimes, as well as concurrent jurisdiction with the circuit or state courts with respect to certain tort suits by aliens and certain suits by the United States.[47] The circuit courts' original jurisdiction, meanwhile, extended to "all suits of a civil nature at common law or in equity, where the matter in dispute exceeds . . . the sum or value of five hundred dollars, and the United States are plaintiffs, or petitioners; or an alien is a party, or the suit is between a citizen of the State

---

which modern commentators frequently look to the 1789 act: (1) the extent of Congress's power over inferior federal courts vis-à-vis the jurisdictional baseline set forth in Article III; and (2) the question of which law applies in federal diversity cases, and the corollary inquiry into the existence or nonexistence of a federal common law. On the former, see the sources cited in note 14 above. On the latter, see Tony Freyer, *Harmony and Dissonance: The Swift and Erie Cases in American Federalism* (NYU, 1981); Julius Goebel, Jr., *Antecedents and Beginnings to 1801* at 229–30 (Macmillan, 1971); Felix Frankfurter and James M. Landis, *The Business of the Supreme Court: A Study of the Federal Judicial System* (Macmillan, 1927); Warren, 37 Harv L Rev at 49 (cited in note 3).

[42] Judiciary Act of 1789 § 13. The provision regarding original jurisdiction was invalidated in *Marbury v Madison*, 1 Cranch 137, 176–79 (1803).

[43] Judiciary Act of 1789 §§ 22, 25.

[44] 14 Wheat 304 (1816) (civil cases).

[45] 19 Wheat 264 (1821) (criminal cases).

[46] 4 *DHSC* at 30–31 (cited in note 32). The membership of the Senate committee represented this diversity of opinion, for Lee and Wingate had both been instructed by their respective state ratifying conventions to resist granting broad powers to the lower federal courts. See id; Goebel, *Antecedents and Beginnings*, 470–71.

[47] Judiciary Act of 1789 § 9.

where the suit is brought, and a citizen of another State."[48] While this jurisdiction was original, however, it was not exclusive but rather concurrent with the state courts. In addition, the circuit courts were given exclusive jurisdiction over all major federal crimes and appellate jurisdiction with respect to district-court cases.[49] Thus, in the words of Julius Goebel, "[i]f the District Courts were viewed primarily as courts of special jurisdiction, the Circuit Courts were erected as courts of general original jurisdiction."[50]

As many modern commentators have noted, the 1789 act did not grant general federal question jurisdiction to the inferior federal courts.[51] Indeed, Congress did not decisively embrace the modern, broadened version of federal question jurisdiction until 1875.[52] To twentieth- and twenty-first-century eyes, this is a startling fact.[53] Yet this sense of surprise results from the assumption that the Judiciary Act of 1789 belongs only to our own age rather than also to the late eighteenth century. After all, the language seems familiar: the act introduced district courts and circuit courts, diversity jurisdiction, amount-in-controversy requirements, and many other staples of a modern federal courts course. As the foregoing discussion illustrates, however, these were not "our" district

---

[48] Id § 11.

[49] Id.

[50] Goebel, *Antecedents and Beginnings* 475 (cited in note 41).

[51] See, for example, Maeva Marcus and Natalie Wexler, *The Judiciary Act of 1789: Political Compromise or Constitutional Interpretation?* in Marcus, ed, *Origins of the Federal Judiciary* 16 (cited in note 39) (stating that "no provision was made [in the 1789 act] for 'general federal question' jurisdiction in the lower federal courts"); Warren, 37 Harv L Rev at 131 (cited in note 3) (stating that "it was eighty-six years before legislation was enacted, in 1875, vesting the Federal Circuit Courts with jurisdiction in all cases arising under the Federal Constitution and laws"). But see Wilfred J. Ritz, *Rewriting the History of the Judiciary Act of 1789: Exposing Myths, Challenging Premises, and Using New Evidence* 59–60, 222 n 9 (Oklahoma, 1990) (Wythe Holt and L. H. LaRue, eds) (arguing that the act's "silence" does not amount to a denial of federal question jurisdiction, although the editors—who took over the manuscript after the author suffered a disabling stroke—take some exception to this claim).

[52] See Act of March 3, 1875, ch 137, § 1, 18 Stat 470 (providing circuit-court jurisdiction "of all suits of a civil nature at common law or in equity . . . arising under the Constitution or laws of the United States, or treaties made, or which shall be made under their authority"). The modern grant of federal question, or "arising under," jurisdiction is now codified at 28 USC § 1331 (providing that "[t]he district courts shall have original jurisdiction of all civil actions arising under the Constitution").

[53] See, for example, William R. Casto, *The First Congress's Understanding of Its Authority Over the Federal Courts' Jurisdiction*, 26 BC L Rev 1101, 1116 (1985) ("In retrospect, the most remarkable limitation upon the lower courts' jurisdiction was the absence of general federal question jurisdiction over civil cases.").

courts or circuit courts. One need only consider the lack of a circuit-court bench, the relative autonomy of the district courts, and the absence of the type of firm appellate hierarchy that exists today to grasp how different the federal courts of 1789 were from those of today.

This pervasive sense of surprise is useful, however, because it demonstrates the importance of historicizing the judiciary act. To ask, "Why didn't Congress grant general federal question jurisdiction until 1875?" is to get the analysis backward. A better, less teleological approach might be to ask, "Why did Congress grant federal question jurisdiction in 1875?"—or, indeed, "Did Congress attempt to grant federal question jurisdiction before 1875?" Such questions permit a more expansive view of the impetus behind the 1789 act, as well as a richer, more contextualized picture of constitutional thought in the early Republic, because they provide a means to connect the 1789 act with the 1801 act—which did, in fact, establish general federal question jurisdiction, albeit only temporarily. The 1801 act's modern identity as a federal-courts trivium could not seem more remote from the grave attention with which the 1789 act is greeted by scholars, law students, and constitutional commentators generally. But the Judiciary Act of 1801—and, perhaps even more important, the vituperative political debate that preceded it in the 1790s—is important precisely because it reminds us of the essential foreignness of jurisdiction theory in the early Republic. Federal jurisdiction is an idea, and like all ideas it had a before and an after, a time when it did not exist and a later time when it did.

Even before President Washington signed the Judiciary Act of 1789 into law, supporters and critics alike had begun to wonder aloud whether a better system might be possible. Madison termed the act "pregnant with difficulties, not only as relating to a part of the constitution which has been most criticised, but being its own nature peculiarly complicated & embarrassing."[54] (When the bill came before the House a few weeks later, however, Madison spoke in its favor; according to published reports, the delegate from Virginia argued that "[t]he bill may not exactly suit any one member of the House, in all its parts—but it is as good as we can

---

[54] Madison to Samuel Johnston (July 31, 1789), 4 *DHSC* at 491 (cited in note 32).

at present make it."[55]) The Antifederalist Elbridge Gerry, representing Massachusetts in the First Congress, said of the judiciary,
"[T]his department I dread as an awful tribunal," citing the federal
courts' broad jurisdiction over common law, equity, and admiralty
cases as well as the potential for abuse of power by judges who
could not be removed by Congress.[56]

In keeping with the controversy that had surrounded the drafting of the act, within a year of its passage two reform plans were
proposed. In December 1790, in response to a request from the
House, Attorney General Edmund Randolph submitted a report
containing recommendations for restructuring the federal judiciary. Randolph's report was followed just over two months later
by a set of amendments to Article III drawn up by New York
congressman Egbert Benson. Neither reform plan made much
headway; on the contrary, both ended their days languishing in
committee.[57] Yet Randolph's plan attracted substantial press notice, suggesting that at least some portion of the public was interested in judicial reform.[58] Both plans will be discussed at greater
length below.

II. Concurrence: Drawing Lines, Again

The intellectual transition from defining questions of political and legal authority in terms of sovereignty to defining them
in terms of jurisdiction manifested itself most profoundly in the
decade following the passage of the Judiciary Act of 1789. Writing
in early September of that year, a few weeks prior to the passage
of the act, Massachusetts congressman Fisher Ames sent a letter
to his friend John Lowell (soon to become federal judge for the
newly created district of Massachusetts) in which Ames detailed a
speech that he had recently delivered on the House floor. Ames's
remarks included the following passage:

> What is jurisdiction? Authority to judge, derived from a su-
> perior power_ The law of the U.S. is the law of the land, but
> not the law of a state_ . . . Many tell me, the state judges must
> decide according to law, & the offences &c are defined by law.

---

[55] Gazette of the United States (Sept 17, 1789), id at 512.

[56] Gerry to John Wendell (Sept 14, 1789), id at 509.

[57] 4 *DHSC* at 168 (cited in note 32).

[58] Id at 124.

> . . . If we ascend to the first principles of the Judicia[l] power,
> I think we shall find them analogous to my doctrine_ . . . .[59]

Ames clearly regarded jurisdiction as the fundamental currency of the federal republic and an ordered system of jurisdiction as the sine qua non of that republic's success. And what was jurisdiction, in Ames's view? "Authority to *judge*, derived from a superior power"—in other words, court-based authority, the source of which was a still higher level of power.

Ames's comments are, it must be said, somewhat elliptical.[60] But they demonstrate the degree to which the concept of jurisdiction occupied the thoughts of politicians and theorists by 1789. The debates of the 1790s, which led to the passage of the Judiciary Act of 1801, centered on a pair of related themes. Both concerned the vertical distribution of authority between the states and the federal government—or, more broadly, between the component entities and the general government in a federal structure. The two themes were, first, the notion of concurrent jurisdiction, according to which bodies at multiple levels of government had the power to hear cases on a given topic or involving a given type of party; and second, the possibility of vesting the lowest-level authorities with the power and duty to carry out the commands of higher-level authorities. In the 1790s, then, commentators explored the possibilities of embracing concurrent jurisdiction in state and federal courts as well as designating the state courts essentially as inferior federal courts.

In some sense, these were new issues. As subjects of the British Empire, Americans had devoted most of their political attention not to institutional arrangements within a largely agreed-upon system but rather to challenging the fundamental nature of the system itself. Thus, members of the colonial opposition had cobbled together an alternative vision that would come to be called "federalism" in their efforts to rebut the hegemonic system of

---

[59] Ames to Lowell (Sept 3, 1789), id at 506 (cited in note 32). Ames had originally begun the second sentence "A power to judge" but replaced it with "Authority to judge." Id.

[60] Ames seems to have been aware that his remarks might not be understood. Writing to Lowell ten days later, Ames commented, "I endeavoured to explain the leading idea or principle of my Speech in Fenno's paper [the Federalist *Gazette of the United States*] . . . not because I was under concern about it's [*sic*] reception with the people_for on a legal question, I never supposed they would have either curiosity or understanding. But I was afraid that the lawyers w^d either hurry over or misconceive my doctrine, and deny it's [*sic*] orthodoxy." Ames to Lowell (Sept 13, 1789), 4 *DHSC* at 507 (cited in note 32).

empire on which metropolitan authorities insisted.[61] Early republicans, meanwhile, viewed their main task as settling on the mechanisms by which the new federal system would be maintained—a
no less important or potentially acrimonious dispute, for the system was so new that its structure would in important respects
determine its substance.

In another sense, however, the questions presented similar quan-
daries to those that had occupied the colonial opposition since the
imperial struggles of the 1760s and 1770s. The crucial issue no
longer concerned the nature of sovereignty in a compound political entity, but the new variable of jurisdiction—Ames's "authority
to judge"—and its allocation among the United States' hard-won
multiple sovereigns. Perhaps, then, it is not surprising that early
republicans thought about these problems through some of the
same intellectual lenses that had served them during the intra-
imperial conflict. As we will see, when Americans in the 1790s
considered how best to arrange their multilayered authorities, they
often returned to familiar notions of *imperium in imperio* and line
drawing.

A. CONCURRENT JURISDICTION; OR, PARALLEL JUDICIAL TRACKS

The idea of concurrent jurisdiction was absolutely central to
the early national efforts to theorize what federalism meant in
practice. Yet various observers used the term in different senses
that proceeded from distinct understandings of the appropriate
baseline distribution of authority between the federal government
and the states. At times, "concurrence" seems to have referred to
very broad notions of how to manage multiple sovereigns operating within the same space; at other times, the term referred to
a more finely grained vision of the institutional distribution of
authority among various levels of courts and legislatures. Moreover, contemporaries disagreed regarding the direction of the sharing of power. Was concurrence in effect when an all-powerful
general government allowed states to exercise some authority over
federal issues, as Alexander Hamilton argued? Or was it the opposite situation, in which a state granted some of its plenary power
to the general government, as Thomas Jefferson maintained? Although the meaning of concurrence remained contested through-

---

[61] See LaCroix, *A Well-Constructed Union* at 18–89 (cited in note 12).

out the early republican period, the term—and the basic concept of overlapping power—informed theorists on all sides of the debate.

In the broadest sense, the term "concurrence" referred in this context to a structure in which multiple levels of government within a single polity possess overlapping authority to regulate, legislate, or adjudicate. This was the sense in which Hamilton employed the label in *Federalist* 32. Addressing the Constitution's grant to Congress of the power to "lay and collect Taxes, Duties, Imposts and Excises," Hamilton reassured skeptics that the states would nonetheless retain the "independent and uncontrolable [*sic*] authority to raise their own revenues for the supply of their own wants"—a power that had been central to the colonies' claims of independence since the 1760s.[62] Because the Constitution "aims only at a partial Union or consolidation," Hamilton reasoned, the states necessarily retained "all of the rights of sovereignty which they before had" and which were not by the Constitution "*exclusively* delegated to the United States."[63] The consequence of such an arrangement would, Hamilton concluded, mean that in certain areas—such as taxation of "all articles other than exports and imports"—citizens might be subject to "a concurrent and coequal authority in the United States and in the individual States."[64] In other words, not all powers associated with the federal government were vested exclusively in the federal government.

Since the 1760s, the taxation issue had implicated questions about overlapping, or concurrent, *legislative* powers. By 1789, however, the debate had shifted to include concurrent *judicial* power. Here, too, Publius had something to say. In *Federalist* 82, Hamilton took up the question of the relationship between the state courts and the federal courts. (Note that at the time that Hamilton was writing, the federal courts comprised only the Supreme Court; however, Hamilton's references to "the national tribunals" suggests that he, like many of his contemporaries, assumed that the First Congress would indeed establish inferior federal courts.[65]) Here again, Hamilton was sanguine about the prospects for con-

---

[62] US Const, Art I, § 8, cl 1; Federalist 32 (Hamilton), in *The Federalist* 199 (cited in note 13).

[63] Id at 200.

[64] Id at 201.

[65] Federalist 82 (Hamilton), in *The Federalist* 553 (cited in note 13).

current jurisdiction. Reading Article III, Section 1 as a nonexclusive description of the "organs" through which the federal judicial power was to be exercised, Hamilton argued that the states retained jurisdiction "of causes of which the state courts have previous cognizance."[66] This concurrence did not extend, however, to "cases which may grow out of, and be *peculiar* to the constitution to be established."[67] The guiding principle for Hamilton, then, was that the state courts might permissibly hear cases "arising under the laws of the union," as long as the Constitution or an act of Congress did not expressly commit that class of case to the federal courts.[68]

Hamilton's justifications for this concurrent judicial power are interesting because they represent a subtle but important shift from some Americans' pre-Revolutionary vision of the proper allocation of authority in a federal government. Beginning in the 1760s, colonists had objected to increased taxation and regulation by Parliament based on their belief that such measures violated what they regarded as the essential structure of the imperial union. That structure, the colonists argued, did not depend on the territory-based view of authority on which metropolitan officials insisted, and which maintained that the colonies were integrated into the British dominions and therefore subject to the full range of regulation by Parliament. Rather, Anglo-Americans argued for a subject-matter conception of political and legal power that allocated jurisdiction among multiple governmental actors (in their case, between Parliament and the colonies' own assemblies), depending on the particular thing or activity to be regulated.[69]

In the colonists' view, this subject-matter approach to authority meant that certain types of issues were the exclusive province of colonial governments and were therefore beyond the power of Parliament (and, in some cases, the Crown) to regulate. Provincial spokespeople denominated these areas of exclusively local regulation variously as "internal" (as opposed to "external"), "special," or "domestic," or as related to locally raised "revenue" that they believed ought to be reinvested locally rather than disbursed into the general accounts of the realm. During the Stamp Act crisis

---

[66] US Const, Art III, § 1, cl 1; Federalist 82, in *The Federalist* 554 (cited in note 13).

[67] Id.

[68] Id at 555.

[69] See LaCroix, *A Well-Constructed Union* at 79 (cited in note 12).

and the ensuing, decade-long cycle of parliamentary legislation and colonial outrage, commentators such as Richard Bland of Virginia put the matter increasingly bluntly. For purposes of external government, Bland acknowledged, "we are and must be subject to the authority of the British Parliament." With respect to internal government, however, Bland contended that "any tax respecting our INTERNAL polity which may hereafter be imposed on us by act of Parliament is arbitrary, as depriving us of our rights, and may be opposed." On this basis, Bland argued, "[T]he legislature of the colony have a right to enact ANY law they shall think necessary for their INTERNAL government."[70] By 1773, members of the Massachusetts assembly were invoking Continental theorists such as Samuel von Pufendorf to support their demands to be treated as coequal entities in a system of states, with a concomitant degree of legislative autonomy within its defined sphere.[71] On the eve of the Revolution, then, American commentators increasingly advocated a governmental architecture that comprised multiple sources of lawmaking authority operating largely in parallel, with each responsible for a specific category of subjects. As a report of the upper house of the Massachusetts assembly described the relationship between that body and Parliament in 1773, "[T]he two Powers are not incompatible, and do subsist together, each restraining its Acts to their Constitutional Objects."[72]

As these comments demonstrate, much prewar Anglo-American thinking about the nature of authority within a compound government centered on what contemporaries viewed as the absolute necessity of setting boundaries between the respective levels of government. Delineation was the order of the day, and a transatlantic obsession with drawing lines—and, indeed, with the rhetoric of line drawing—took hold. The royal governor of Massachusetts, Thomas Hutchinson, declared in 1773, "I know of no Line that can be drawn between the supreme Authority of Parliament and the total Independence of the Colonies: it is impos-

---

[70] Common Sense [Richard Bland], *The Colonel Dismounted: or the Rector Vindicated. In a Letter addressed to His Reverence: Containing a Dissertation upon the Constitution of the Colony* 22–23 (Williamsburg: Joseph Royle, 1764).

[71] See LaCroix, *A Well-Constructed Union* 119–20 (cited in note 12).

[72] Alden Bradford, ed, *Speeches of the Governors of Massachusetts, From 1765 to 1775* at 86–87 (Boston: Russell and Gardner, 1818). See also LaCroix, *A Well-Constructed Union* 90–165 (cited in note 12).

sible there should be two independent Legislatures in one and the same State . . . ."[73] A pseudonymous writer in the *Boston-Gazette and Country Journal* took a different view, stating, "NO *Line can be drawn between the usurped Power of Parliament, and a State of Slavery in the Colonies.*"[74] Advocates of metropolitan supremacy tended to argue for what might be considered a measure of concurrence, insofar as they were willing to permit colonial assemblies to act as subordinate and dependent municipal bodies. Members of the colonial opposition, by contrast, rejected concurrence because they viewed it as a tool of continued metropolitan dominance. The only workable scenario by which the colonies could remain in the empire, they believed, was for provincial and central legislatures to operate along distinct and nonintersecting lines.

By embracing concurrent powers as a natural consequence of the Constitution's structure, Hamilton implied that this strict demarcation along subject-matter lines might not be relevant to the new republic. Indeed, his formulation of the jurisdiction question referred not at all to the separation of authority that had obtained within the British Empire. Rather, his description of those powers suggested a certain degree of ambiguity, at least with respect to concurrent state- and federal-court jurisdiction. State courts might permissibly take cognizance of cases arising under federal law, Hamilton stated, as long as the state had jurisdiction over the persons of the parties. "The judiciary power of every government looks beyond its own local or municipal laws, and in civil cases lays hold of all subjects of litigation between parties within its jurisdiction though the causes of dispute are relative to the laws of the most distant part of that globe," he wrote in *Federalist* 82. "Those of Japan not less than of New-York may furnish the objects of legal discussion to our courts."[75]

According to this line of analysis, subject matter was irrelevant; the only pertinent consideration for a court was whether the parties were physically within its jurisdiction. Such a regime would necessarily lead to overlaps and would therefore run afoul of the parallelism principle articulated by prewar colonial commenta-

---

[73] Bradford, ed, *Speeches of the Governors* at 109 (cited in note 72).

[74] "An Elector," Boston-Gazette and Country Journal (Jan 11, 1773).

[75] Federalist 82 (Hamilton), in *The Federalist* 555 (cited in note 13).

tors.[76] Yet Hamilton took a slightly different approach when he argued that the Supreme Court would necessarily possess appellate jurisdiction over state-court cases involving federal law. "The objects of appeal, not the tribunals from which it is to be made, are alone contemplated" when determining whether a case was eligible for appeal to the Supreme Court, Hamilton wrote. Here, then, the relevant criterion was that the case arose under the law of the United States, not the largely happenstance fact of the geographic location in which it originated. Subject-matter questions were thus largely irrelevant to Hamilton for purposes of expanding state-court jurisdiction to include federal causes of action, but they were dispositive in determining the scope of the Supreme Court's jurisdiction.

The interest in exploring at least the possibility of concurrence as a basis for the federal republic therefore set the constitutional debates of the ratification and early republican periods apart from those of the 1760s and 1770s. Whereas many colonists had resisted concurrence and pressed for subject-matter-specific boundaries between local and metropolitan authorities, Hamilton and other commentators in 1787 treated overlapping boundaries between states and federal government as a potential means of granting a measure of power to the states. This may seem counterintuitive; after all, the colonists viewed concurrence not as an opportunity to stake their claim to a piece of the larger government but as a transfer of power back to Westminster. How, then, could Hamilton present concurrence as an acknowledgment of the states' "primitive jurisdiction"?[77] Consider again his statement in *Federalist 32*: "the plan of the Convention aims only at a partial Union or consolidation," and therefore "the State Governments would clearly retain all the rights of sovereignty which they before had and which were not by that act *exclusively* delegated to the United States."[78] In a world such as that of the 1760s and 1770s, where the central

---

[76] See, for example, John Dickinson's prewar argument against concurrent authority in Parliament and the colonial assemblies over revenue matters. "The single question is whether the parliament can legally impose duties to be paid *by the people of these colonies only* FOR THE SOLE PURPOSE OF RAISING A REVENUE, *on commodities which she obliges us to take from her alone*; or, in other words, whether the parliament can legally take money out of our pockets without our consent." [John Dickinson], *Letters from a Farmer in Pennsylvania, to the Inhabitants of the British Colonies* 26 (Boston: Mein and Fleeming, 1768).

[77] Federalist 82 (Hamilton), in *The Federalist* 555 (cited in note 13).

[78] Federalist 32 (Hamilton), in id 200.

controversy concerned not membership and control of a central government but independence from that government, concurrence provided a means for the center to overreach itself and exert power over the provinces. But perhaps in a world such as that of 1787, where complete union or consolidation appeared to be a possibility, retaining concurrent jurisdiction might reasonably be construed as a victory for the states.[79]

Still, one important difference between the colonial and early republican discussions of concurrence was the institutional focus of each. Whereas the colonists devoted themselves to analyzing competing legislative claims to power (the provincial assemblies vs. Parliament), commentators in the ratification period and afterward increasingly emphasized the judicial side of concurrence. Hamilton's analysis in *The Federalist* contemplated both species of concurrence. Increasingly after 1789, however, the drive to establish the inferior federal courts shifted the emphasis of structural discussions away from issues of legislative competition, with their colonial resonance, and toward the new problem of organizing multiple judiciaries within a single overarching polity. The advent of the lower federal courts added a new urgency to this inquiry. Thus, by 1803, Virginia jurist St. George Tucker could observe that the "grand boundary" that "mark[ed] the obvious limits between the federal and state jurisdictions" coexisted with "some few cases, where, by a special provision contained in the constitution either concurrent, or exclusive, jurisdiction is granted to the federal government."[80] Notably, in contrast to Hamilton's view, Tucker's vision of concurrence amounted to a special invitation to the federal courts, not the state courts, to take jurisdiction over a select group of cases. The two theorists thus differed in their default assumptions as to which level of courts was the norm and which the exception, but they both presented some degree of judicial concurrency as necessary to the larger federal system.

But the fact that concurrence was a frequent topic of discussion

---

[79] St. George Tucker, however, took the view that concurrent powers of legislation were not a benison to state authority but rather a means of chipping away at the power of the states. Describing the "some few instances"—such as bankruptcy—in which "the grand boundary between the limits of federal and state jurisdiction . . . has not been strictly adhered to in the federal constitution," Tucker observed that such encroachments were "in derogation of the municipal jurisdiction of the several states" and therefore should be "strictly construed." St. George Tucker, *View of the Constitution of the United States with Selected Writings* 127 (Liberty Fund, 1999).

[80] Id at 128.

in the ratification period does not mean that contemporaries had uniformly warm regard for it. Some observers opposed any form of concurrence, believing that any overlap between the state and federal judiciaries would only lead to confusion and either centralization or disintegration, depending on the observer's particular array of anxieties about federalism. Virginia judge Joseph Jones wrote to Madison in July 1789 to note his discomfort with the draft judiciary bill, which he believed muddied rather than clarified the relationships among the various courts. "[T]he different powers and jurisdictions of the Courts would have been more clearly seen had they been taken up in several bills, each describing the province and boundary of the Court to which it particularly applied," he observed. But his objections extended beyond the form of the bill. To Jones, even the act's few references to the state courts (i.e., Section 9's language regarding concurrent jurisdiction to state courts for cases involving tort claims by aliens in violation of the law of nations or a treaty and Section 25's provision regarding appeals to the Supreme Court) obscured the true scope of the federal courts' reach. "[W]here there is danger of clashing jurisdictions, the limits should be defined as acurately [*sic*] as may be, and this danger will exist where there are concurrent jurisdictions," Jones contended.[81] Congressman John Brown, who represented the Kentucky district of Virginia, sounded a similar note of caution, describing his fear that "great difficulties will arise from the concurrent Jurisdiction of the Federal with the State Court, which will unavoidably occasion great embarrassment & clashing." Brown followed this statement with a guarded endorsement of the act, however, calling it "as good I believe as we at present could make it."[82]

Edmund Randolph's 1790 plan to amend the 1789 act, meanwhile, offered reforms while also attempting to correct some of the act's ambiguities concerning concurrence. As has been noted, the attorney general's proposals failed to gain sufficient support to be adopted. Nevertheless, they demonstrate the ways in which observers were working to reconceptualize and reconfigure jurisdiction in the years following the passage of the 1789 act. Randolph's scheme offered several significant changes to the structure

---

[81] Jones to Madison (July 3, 1789), 4 *DHSC* 441–42 (cited in note 32).

[82] Brown to Harry Innes (Sept 28, 1789), id at 519–20.

erected by the act. First, the plan whittled away the states' jurisdiction over nominally federal matters to such a degree that concurrent authority was rendered virtually nonexistent. As Maeva
Marcus notes, Randolph's "central premise" was that "federal and
state jurisdictions should be completely separate."[83] From this
premise followed a much more sweeping grant of authority to the
district and circuit courts as well as language that explicitly
stripped the state courts of the power to take cognizance of several
of the most common federal causes of action.

The plan's broad grant to the inferior federal courts included
original jurisdiction "of all cases in law and equity, arising . . .
[under] the Constitution of the United States . . . [t]he laws of
the United States . . . and [t]reaties made, or which shall be made
under their authority."[84] In other words, Randolph sought to vest
the lower federal courts with the full range of original jurisdiction
under Article III—that is, general federal question jurisdiction.[85]
State courts, meanwhile, were expressly prohibited from hearing
a number of types of cases, including admiralty and maritime cases,
cases in which the United States or a particular state was a defendant (except in cases of consent by the state), cases involving
land grants by different states, treason cases, federal criminal cases
(absent a specific congressional provision establishing state courts'
jurisdiction), and cases involving congressionally created rights
with federal remedies.[86] Moreover, an apparent narrowing of the
Supreme Court's power to review state-court decisions accompanied this expansion of the lower federal courts' jurisdiction,
although the precise contours of the restriction are not entirely
clear.[87]

---

[83] 4 *DHSC* at 122–23 (cited in note 32).

[84] Report of the Attorney-General to the House of Representatives, id at 140.

[85] See 4 *DHSC* at 123 (cited in note 32).

[86] Report of the Attorney-General to the House of Representatives, id at 140.

[87] Randolph's attitude toward the Supreme Court's appellate review of state-court decisions appears somewhat ambivalent. On one hand, in the preface to the report Randolph
refers to "convert[ing] the supreme court of the United States into an appellate tribunal
over the supreme courts of the several states," suggesting that such a relationship would
be novel; moreover, in discussing the phrase "appellate jurisdiction," Randolph contends
that "this phrase must be pressed close to the matter of the third article of the Constitution,
which is the *judicial power of the United States*, without blending state courts." Id at 132.
Both these observations are offered as the arguments of those who object to the granting
the Court appellate power over state-court decisions, but Randolph at times appears to
adopt these arguments as his own. The report itself did provide for the issuance of writs
of certiorari from the Supreme Court to the circuit and state courts. See id at 153. Marcus

Randolph's proposals appear to have confounded his contemporaries. Alfred Moore, a future Justice of the Supreme Court, remarked to North Carolina senator Samuel Johnston that "there appears an utter confusion in M͏ʳAttorney's Ideas," noting in particular the apparent conflict between Randolph's claim that "the State Courts ought to be <u>excluded</u> because <u>not under the Control</u> of the federal Courts" and his claim that the state courts' proceedings "are in some instances subject to the federal Judiciary, because that Judiciary must <u>ex natura rei</u> control determinations that counteract the operation of the Constitution."[88]

Despite these apparent ambiguities, Randolph's plan is important because it demonstrates the degree to which the scope and nature of federal jurisdiction remained a contested issue in the 1790s. Furthermore, the proposal clearly shows Randolph endorsing an expanded vision of "arising under" jurisdiction at the same time that he was struggling to articulate clearer boundaries between federal and state courts than those set forth in the 1789 act.[89] In this way, Randolph's plan eschewed the relatively welcoming attitude toward concurrent jurisdiction that Hamilton had adopted in his *Federalist* essays, moving instead toward a notion of the judicial power of the United States as something extraordinary and perhaps beyond the ken of state courts.

Of course, Randolph's plan did not mandate that cases arising under the laws of the United States fell *exclusively* within the jurisdiction of the federal courts; the report merely stated that the lower federal courts possessed original jurisdiction over such cases.

---

reads the report as prohibiting the Court from hearing appeals from the state courts, however, and as substituting a broadened power for parties to remove cases from state to federal court. See 4 *DHSC* at 124 & n 14 (cited in note 32).

[88] Moore to Johnston (Feb 23, 1791), id at 555–56 (translating the Latin phrase as "by the nature of the thing").

[89] Writing in 1794, James Kent articulated a similarly broad vision of federal jurisdiction, although his reasoning differed somewhat from Randolph's. Kent compared the judicial power with the legislative power and concluded that the scope of federal courts' authority necessarily had to at least match that of Congress. "This power in the Judicial, of determining the constitutionality of Laws, is necessary to preserve the equilibrium of the government, and prevent usurpations of one part upon another," Kent wrote, adding that "of all the parts of government, the Legislative body is by far the most impetuous and powerful." The judicial power, however, being "the weakest of all . . . ought not in sound theory to be left naked without any constitutional means of defence." Thus, he concluded, the judiciary and the legislature should be regarded as "co-ordinate powers." James Kent, *An Introductory Lecture to a Course of Law Lectures* in 2 *American Political Writing During the Founding Era, 1760–1805* at 943 (Liberty Press, 1983) (Charles S. Hyneman and Donald S. Lutz, eds).

This capacious view of the federal judicial power, however, heark-
ened to the subject-matter-driven analyses of the 1760s and 1770s,
insofar as it looked not to the nature of the parties or the jurisdiction in which their case arose but rather to the character of
the claim at issue. Randolph's conception thus also represented a
shift away from the 1789 act's focus on the parties' identity or
location, and toward the underlying subject of the cause of action
as decisive of jurisdiction.[90] In other words, the jurisdictional lines
drawn by the attorney general resembled the prewar notion of
sovereignty as attaching to specific subjects of regulation.

B. STATE COURTS AS FEDERAL COURTS; OR, DEPUTIZING THE
   STATES

In addition to contemplating concurrent arrangements, in which
the judicial powers of the federal and state governments overlapped, some theorists in the 1790s considered whether the state
courts could themselves be integrated into the emerging judicial
structure. In this scenario, the state courts would in effect function
as inferior federal courts. The idea had circulated since the Philadelphia and ratifying conventions; after all, the language of the
Supremacy Clause singled out "the Judges in every State" to be
bound by "the supreme Law of the Land."[91] Because the state
courts were thus already obliged to follow and enforce the laws
of the United States, the argument ran, inferior federal courts
were not necessary to the constitutional structure; on the contrary,
Congress could permissibly refrain from establishing such courts
altogether.[92]

Such an argument appealed especially to Antifederalists who
worried that the creation of inferior federal courts amounted to
the thin edge of the nationalizing wedge, intruding and encroach-
ing on the reserved powers of the states. Indeed, outspoken critics
of broad national power such as Luther Martin had initially sup-

---

[90] Consider on this point Casto, 26 BC L Rev at 1116 (cited in note 53) (noting, in the
context of general federal question jurisdiction, that under the 1789 act, "the circuit courts
were vested with jurisdiction keyed to the nature of the parties rather than the nature of
the dispute").

[91] US Const, Art VI, cl 2. For a recent discussion of the propriety of state courts' acting
as inferior tribunals, see James E. Pfander, *Federal Supremacy, State Court Inferiority, and
the Constitutionality of Jurisdiction-Stripping Legislation*, 101 Nw U L Rev 191 (2007).

[92] On the related question whether Article III requires Congress to establish some inferior federal courts, see the sources cited in note 14.

ported the Supremacy Clause precisely because they believed that its reliance on state courts threatened less intrusion on state prerogatives than did the federal negative.[93] "[W]hat is there left to the State Courts?" George Mason inquired of his colleagues in the Virginia ratifying convention as they debated Article I's grant to Congress of the power to establish inferior federal courts. "When we consider the nature of these Courts, we must conclude, that their effect and operation will be utterly to destroy the State Governments. . . . The discrimination between their Judicial power and that of the States, exists therefore but in name."[94] For Mason and others who advocated a general government with circumscribed powers, the prospect of swelling ranks of federal courts—with concomitant growth in claims of federal jurisdiction—threatened nothing less than "the annihilation of the state judiciaries."[95]

In the 1790s, following ratification, some commentators continued to make the case for relying on state courts to conduct the first level of federal judicial business. "[T]he whole judicial system is a giddy profusion, and quite unnecessary," lamented the pseudonymous "Rusticus" in Boston's *Independent Chronicle*.

> The business might have been done in the State Courts, with a balance or check, raised by giving a Court of the Union, power to examine and correct those cases where foreigners or persons of different States are concerned. And all this unweildy [sic] and useless machinery of Circuit, District and Supreme Courts might have been omitted.[96]

Such criticisms briefly gained momentum in March 1791, when New York congressman Egbert Benson introduced a set of amendments to Article III that echoed Rusticus's sentiments. The centerpiece of Benson's plan was a provision requiring Congress to

---

[93] See generally Charles F. Hobson, *The Negative on State Laws: James Madison, the Constitution, and the Crisis of Republican Government*, 36 Wm & Mary Q 215, 228 (3d ser, 1979). The final version of the Supremacy Clause failed to win Martin's support, however. In a related vein, "Federal Farmer" opposed the 1789 act's establishment of federal diversity jurisdiction, arguing that such jurisdiction was unnecessary, as such suits could also be brought in state court with appeal to the Supreme Court. *Letters from the Federal Farmer*, 1 *The Debate on the Constitution* 271 (cited in note 31).

[94] 2 id at 720.

[95] Centinel Revived, No 26, Independent Gazetteer (Philadelphia) (Aug 29, 1789).

[96] "Rusticus," Independent Chronicle (Boston) (Aug 26, 1790).

establish in each state a "General Judicial Court," either by de-
nominating the highest existing state court as such or by creating
a new court. The general judicial court, which was to be "regulated
as the Congress shall prescribe," would have original jurisdiction
"in all cases to which the judicial power of the United States doth
extend," as well as appellate jurisdiction over cases from other
courts within the state.[97] Moreover, although the judges of this
new court would receive their salaries from the federal government
and be subject to the good behavior standard, they could be impeached by either the House of Representatives or the state legislature. Judges from state courts that were declared general judicial courts by Congress would become judges of the new courts
"by force of their appointments" as state-court judges, and the
powers and duties of the state court would "devolve on the judges
of the general judicial court."[98] The plan concluded with an explicit
statement of the new courts' dual nature: state judicial officers
would be "held to execute their respective offices for carrying into
effect the laws of the United States" as well as "the duties assigned
to them by the laws of the state."[99] Benson's amendments thus
shunted aside fine distinctions relating to concurrence between
state and federal courts and instead essentially deputized the state
courts to serve Congress and the federal judicial power.

Although the Benson proposal received widespread attention in
the press, it too was dispatched to committee and never heard
from again.[100] Despite this ignominious fate, Benson's amendments highlight a tension in the arguments for increased reliance
on state courts. The arguments of anticonsolidationists such as
Martin and Mason could easily slide into plans such as Benson's;
putative goals of state autonomy might quickly give way to
schemes to subordinate the states into mere departments, administrative subdivisions of the general government. State courts
might be able to hear diversity cases, cases involving congressional
statutes, treaties, and other federal causes in the first instance, but
would not such an arrangement amount to the state courts' becoming co-opted by the general government rather than main-

---

[97] 4 *DHSC* at 170 (cited in note 32).

[98] Id at 170–71.

[99] Id at 172.

[100] Id at 168 n 4. Marcus states that the amendments were likely intended "less as a
topic for debate than as a political statement" by the Hamiltonian Benson. Id at 168.

taining their prized autonomy? Some commentators, such as one writing under the nom de plume "Curtius," expressed suspicion along these lines in considering the Benson amendments and similar plans:

> [O]n taking a candid and impartial survey of the amendments in question, it is obvious that the sole scope and intention of them is to absorbe [*sic*] and annihilate those very governments, to which the general one owes its existence; or at best, to convert them into extensive but feeble CORPORATIONS.[101]

Throughout the 1780s and 1790s, observers with a wide array of agendas and commitments argued that the state courts ought to have an institutional place in the new federal edifice. Some hoped that the state courts, as already extant and functioning adjudicatory bodies, could be folded directly into the federal apparatus. Others wanted robust state judiciaries to act as buffers against what they viewed as the creeping expansion of federal question jurisdiction (and, with it, the homogenizing, centralizing force of union). Opponents of a broader brief for the state courts, however, offered a wide array of arguments against further incorporating them into the federal structure. While some of these critics hoped that the state courts might for their own protection be cordoned off from the federal judiciary, others argued that the state courts must be kept out because they were untrustworthy and might corrupt the federal system.

Taking the former, protective view of state courts, Pennsylvania congressman William Maclay suggested that the states were already implicated in the federal structure, whether they liked it or (as in his case) not. Just as the Constitution had "meant to swallow up all the state Constitutions by degrees," he insisted, the 1789 act aimed to "Swallow by degrees all the State Judiciaries."[102] Despite his role as a member of the committee that had drafted the 1789 act, Maclay ultimately could not bring himself to vote for the act, which he called "a Vile law System, calculated for Expence, and with a design to draw by degrees all law business into the federal Courts."[103]

---

[101] "Curtius," Augusta (Ga) Chronicle (May 28, 1791), in 4 *DHSC* at 559 (cited in note 32).

[102] Id at 473.

[103] Id.

Federalist Fisher Ames of Massachusetts had different concerns, however. Ames contended that the state courts possessed the power to range freely over the full landscape of both federal and state matters. But how, if at all, Ames wondered, could the state courts ever be checked? Vesting state courts with any significant jurisdiction over federal questions risked profound problems of representation, insofar as it lodged decision-making power in officials whose allegiance was only to their local community, not the interests of the Union as a whole. "Will the state judges act quasi state judges or as federal[?]" Ames inquired. "If as state judges, how can you add duties not required by the states who commissioned them and how can you compel them to perform such duties, or punish for the violation or neglect."[104] Furthermore, Ames wondered, would one even be able to determine in what capacity a state judge was acting in any given moment? "The jurisdictions being concurrent, how will you distinguish when they act as state, and when as federal judges_sometimes a nice question this."[105]

The map created by the 1789 act expressed this prevailing uncertainty as to how the state courts ought to be treated. The act's structure not only accepted the states as preexisting polities but actually overlaid the new federal districts onto the existing map of the states—even borrowing the states' names. Thus, the districts described in the act comprised "one to consist of the State of Connecticut, and to be called Connecticut District; one to consist of the State of New York, and to be called New York District," and so forth through the other nine states and two subsets of states (Maine and Kentucky).[106] This overlap between the state and federal maps appears not to have raised significant objections during the debates on the act. Notably, an amendment to breach state boundaries by creating a multistate district covering portions of Maryland, Virginia, and Delaware failed in the House, suggesting that maintaining the states' territorial integrity—rather than drawing entirely new political boundaries solely for federal purposes— was important to members.[107]

Was this political and legal congruence evidence of the federal government's desire to press the states into its service, or was it

---

[104] Ames to John Lowell (July 28, 1789), id at 481.

[105] Id.

[106] Judiciary Act of 1789 § 2.

[107] 4 *DHSC* at 39 (cited in note 32).

an acknowledgment of the states' importance, perhaps even a sign of respect? Many contemporaries regarded the layout of the districts, and their number, as an attempt to ensure that the judicial power of the United States could be felt throughout the nation while also establishing it as superior to the judiciary of any one state.[108] During the 1790s, however, many observers complained that the seats of federal government within any given state were too remote. One commentator suggested that the upshot of this arrangement—which created, in the words of Julius Goebel, "a species of artificial federal entity"—was confusion leavened with a lack of popular identification with the federal government.[109] "The laws of the United States, coming into discussion only in one court in each state, are but little known, and, at a distance from that court they are considered as foreign laws," lamented "A Citizen" in the *Washington Federalist*. "The contrast between the state and the federal administration of justice appears strong, and the advantage manifest against the federal judiciary."[110] Thus, despite efforts by Randolph and others to keep separate the multiple levels of judicial power, the complexities of concurrence—both of subject matter and of territorial space—were very much on commentators' minds throughout the 1790s.

Here was another respect in which the debates of the post-ratification period echoed the arguments of the 1760s and 1770s: commentators in the early Republic employed a similar vocabulary of line drawing and *imperium in imperio* to that of their predecessors a few decades earlier. Even as they experimented with concurrence and considered deputizing state courts to act as inferior federal courts, early republican theorists continued to think about governmental structure in terms of the boundaries between different sovereigns and different sources of authority. The drive to delineate governmental spheres had preoccupied Thomas Hutchinson and the members of Boston's colonial opposition in

---

[108] See, for example, "A Citizen," Washington Federalist (Jan 26, 1801) (noting that "[t]he difficulty of organizing the Judiciary of the U. States, so as, agreeably to the Constitution to vest in the General Government a judicial authority over individual States; and, at the same time to establish a commodious administration of justice, was early foreseen"). See also Federalist 81 (Hamilton) in *The Federalist* 546–57 (arguing for the establishment of "four or five, or half a dozen districts" instead of relying on state courts to serve as inferior courts) (cited in note 13).

[109] Goebel, *Antecedents and Beginnings* at 471 (cited in note 41).

[110] "A Citizen," Washington Federalist (Jan 26, 1801).

1773, and it continued to needle Americans in the postratification period.

The urgency was even more profound in the later years, as "the judicial" (as Ames and others termed it) increasingly became the institutional site for hashing out the competing versions of federalism that had emerged since the 1760s.[111] In this anxious context, the old tropes of sovereignty gained new force and meaning. During the 1789 debates, William Paterson conjured up the *imperium in imperio* specter: "We are a Combination of Republics_a number of free States confederated together, & forming a social League." Within this league, Paterson went on, the Union and each of the several states possessed "a Head_each operating upon different Objects."[112] Given such an arrangement, could the state courts reach outside the state realm to take cognizance of federal causes of action? No, Paterson answered. Granting federal authority to judges "chosen by the respective States; in whose Election the Union has no Voice, and over whom they have little or no Control" was nothing less than "a Solecism in Politicks—a Novelty in Gov[t]."[113] By 1791, Massachusetts Federalist Theodore Sedgwick was bemoaning the problems that "arise from an administration of justice by two distinct & independent sovereignties over the same persons, in the same place and at the same time."[114] Sedgwick made his observations just a few weeks before Justice James Wilson wrote to Washington with a proposal for a digest of federal law, observing that "the difficult and delicate Line of Authority . . . must be run."[115] Born in the provincial legislatures of a mercantile, transatlantic empire, the vocabulary of federalism found new salience among the multiple judiciaries of the early Republic.

The ongoing constitutional debates of the 1790s demonstrated the fragile nature of the definitions of political and legal authority that many Americans believed they had worked out in the course of the conflict with Britain. Now, conscious of their inheritance as the second generation since the founding, early republican observers turned anxiously back to old themes of *imperium in imperio*, multiple sov-

---

[111] See, for example, Ames to Lowell (July 28, 1789), 4 *DHSC* at 481 (cited in note 32).

[112] Id at 414.

[113] Id at 415.

[114] Sedgwick to Peter Van Schaack (Nov 20, 1791), id at 566.

[115] Wilson to Washington (Dec 31, 1791), id at 572.

ereigns, and line drawing.[116] At the same time, however, they became fascinated with ideas of concurrence—of multiple and overlapping powers, especially judicial powers.[117] These warring impulses gained intensity throughout the 1790s until, fueled by partisan rancor that few in the first generation had anticipated, they exploded in the tumults of 1800 and 1801.

III. FROM FEDERAL TO FEDERAL JUDICIAL POWER: THE JUDICIARY ACT OF 1801

As the preceding discussion has suggested, beginning in 1789, judicial power emerged as the focus of both practical and theoretical disputes about the nature of multilayered authority. The judiciary became the key site of federalism during this period, with jurisdiction as the tool by which theorists and politicians carved up the levels of power among governments and people.

That was the scene in 1789 and for much of the subsequent decade. Around 1800, however, that picture changed. From the domain of federalism in the 1780s and 1790s, judicial power became the redoubt of Federalism in the 1800s. The story of the presidential election (or "revolution," as Jefferson termed it[118]) of 1800 is well known, as is the subsequent rise of the Jeffersonian-Republican party and the eclipse of the Federalists.[119] A familiar part of this tale is the flight of the Federalists to the judiciary in the wake of the schism that resulted in the first party system and the "loss" of the presidency and Congress to the Jeffersonians.[120]

---

[116] On the burdens that second- and later-generation Americans perceived themselves as bearing, see, for example, Joyce Appleby, *Inheriting the Revolution: The First Generation of Americans* (Harvard, 2000) (discussing Americans born between 1776 and 1830); Perry Miller, *Errand into the Wilderness* (Harvard, 1956) (describing the spiritual crisis of second-generation Puritans in New England); Henry Adams, *The Education of Henry Adams: An Autobiography* (Houghton Mifflin, 1935) (describing and illustrating later generations' sense of anxiety and fears of declension).

[117] On discussions of concurrence in the ratification debates, see Hulsebosch, *Constituting Empire* 223, 241–42, 382–83 nn (cited in note 10).

[118] Jefferson to John Dickinson (March 6, 1801), in 33 *The Papers of Thomas Jefferson* 196–97 (Princeton, 2007) (Barbara Oberg, ed).

[119] See generally Stanley Elkins and Eric McKitrick, *The Age of Federalism: The Early American Republic, 1788–1800* (Oxford, 1993); David Hackett Fischer, *The Revolution of American Conservatism: The Federalist Party in the Era of Jeffersonian Democracy* (Harper & Row, 1965).

[120] The outlines of this story appeared early. One day before Jefferson's inauguration, James Monroe—then Virginia's governor—wrote to the president-elect that the Federalist party "has retired into the judiciary in a strong body where it lives on the treasury, &

This story, however, often treats the Judiciary Act of 1801 as an artifact of the election of 1800, a manifestation of partisan rancor with little to tell us about constitutional thought. Hence the emphasis, as suggested in the quotation from Kathryn Turner Preyer above, on the Judiciary Act's passage in 1801 as a mere prelude to its repeal in 1802.[121] But there is more to the 1801 act than this narrative of Federalist overreaching and Republican chastisement suggests. Like the 1789 act, the 1801 act should be viewed not simply from the modern perspective of the forward march of the federal courts to the twenty-first century, but rather from the early republican angle of making divided government work. To be sure, party politics are central to this account; as Joanne Freeman points out, a "crisis mentality" had seized the American political scene by 1800, stemming in large part from the hardening of party lines in a time when "normalcy" was understood as "the *absence* of organized national parties, *not* a well-functioning national party system."[122] But more was at issue in the 1801 act than the partitioning of the federal empire between Federalist and Republican claimants to rule. *Ideas* were at stake in the debates surrounding the 1801 act, just as they had been in 1789.

The turn-of-the-century constitutional struggle was not merely a cover for partisan conflict; to interpret the period in that light does a disservice to the depth of the beliefs at issue. Such an interpretation also falls prey to the temptation to paint the 1790s as the fall from grace, the sullied and sordid aftermath of the edenic moment of 1787–89. Certainly, the rancor of the 1790s was real; the allegiances had hardened, and the threat that ongoing warfare in Europe would engulf the United States added a new level of global consequence to the continuing uncertainty about the Republic's future. And I do not mean to suggest that politics and ideas are separate categories, with "mere" politics bearing no relationship to the realm of ideas. My point is that the partisan din of the 1790s should not trick jaded modern observers into thinking that the

---

cannot therefore be starved out. [W]hile in possession of that ground it can check the popular current which runs against them, & seize the favorable occasion to promote reaction, which it does not despair of." Monroe to Jefferson (March 3, 1801), 4 *DHSC* at 720 (cited in note 32).

[121] See Turner [Preyer], 22 Wm & Mary Q at 3 (cited in note 5).

[122] Joanne B. Freeman, *The Election of 1800: A Study in the Logic of Political Change*, 108 Yale L J 1959, 1961, 1990 (1999).

source of the conflict was political gain or power alone.[123] Rather, the source of the conflict was political gain and power, as well as ongoing and fundamental disagreement about just what the "federal" in "federal republic" was to mean, and what role the judiciary would play in that federal republic.

The debates that culminated in the passage and repeal of the 1801 act demonstrate the degree to which early nineteenth-century theories of jurisdiction took on the full weight of the sovereignty discourse of the eighteenth century, transforming questions of political authority in the broadest sense into issues of judicial power and the degree to which the federal and state systems would or would not overlap. By 1801, jurisdiction had replaced sovereignty as the lodestar of American constitutional debate. The 1801 act thus continued the 1789 act's project of adjusting federal judicial structure as a means of adjusting the structure of federalism—the relationship between the states and the general government—itself.

Yet many of the premises underpinning the 1801 act differed markedly from those that informed the 1789 act. One crucial difference concerned the scope of the federal judicial power in the respective acts. As we have seen, the 1789 act took a cautious, even conciliatory, approach to the states' claims to jurisdiction. For example, the federal districts replicated the boundaries of the states rather than asserting new districts that swallowed or subdivided the states; in addition, supporters of the act pointed to its acknowledgment of concurrent state and federal jurisdiction as evidence that the lower federal courts were not intended to supplant the state courts. The drafters of the 1801 act, in contrast, spent little time reassuring the states and instead presented a significantly more robust federal judiciary—both in terms of the number of courts and in the nature of their jurisdiction—with the potential for far greater intrusion into the states. The 1801 act, in other words, combined the colonial impulse to draw lines between levels of authority with the ratification era's focus on the judiciary as the principal axis of that division.

A. DEBATING THE JUDICIARY ACT OF 1801

Throughout the 1790s, Congress engaged in relatively modest

---

[123] One influential recent study of the political battles of the 1790s and 1800s situates partisan struggle in a broader cultural and ideological context. See Joanne B. Freeman, *Affairs of Honor: National Politics in the New Republic* (Yale, 2001).

reforms of the federal judiciary, despite complaints from many quarters regarding the 1789 act. The chief criticism centered on the requirement that Supreme Court Justices ride circuit, which meant not only fatigue for the Justices but also occasional conflicts insofar as a given Justice might hear the same case twice, once at the circuit level and once in the Supreme Court.[124] Following John Adams's December 1799 address to Congress, the members of the Sixth Congress began to consider a comprehensive overhaul. In his address, the president insisted that "a revision and amendment of the judicial system" was "indispensably necessary" to "give due effect to the civil administration of Government, and to ensure a just execution of the laws."[125] Congress appeared to take Adams's recommendation seriously. In February 1800, a House committee met with Justices William Paterson and Bushrod Washington to receive their recommendations for reform. The committee comprised five members, all Federalists: Robert Goodloe Harper of South Carolina, Chauncey Goodrich of Connecticut, James A. Bayard of Delaware, Samuel Sewall of Massachusetts, and John Marshall of Virginia.[126] Shortly thereafter, on March 11, Harper introduced the committee's draft bill to the House.

The centerpiece of the Harper bill, as it was known, was a proposal to increase the number of federal judicial districts from thirteen to thirty, and the circuit courts from three to nine.[127] As these numbers suggest, the districts in the Harper bill did not conform to state boundaries; instead, most states were divided into multiple districts. The bill also proposed new names for the districts, given that they could no longer share nomenclature with the state with which they overlapped. The counties of Essex, Suffolk, Norfolk, Middlesex, Bristol, Plymouth, Barnstable, Duke, and Nantucket in Massachusetts were to constitute the district of Boston. The remaining Massachusetts counties (Berkshire, Hampshire, Worcester), meanwhile, would be combined into the district of Warranoch. Virginia's counties were to be divided among the Potowmac, Fluvanna, Kenhawa districts. Rhode Island would not be divided but would constitute the district of Narragansett; similarly, Vermont would constitute the single district of Champlain,

---

[124] See Turner [Preyer], 22 Wm & Mary Q at 5–6 (cited in note 5).

[125] Quoted in 4 *DHSC* at 284 (cited in note 32).

[126] Unfortunately, no official records of the committee's deliberations have survived.

[127] Harper Judiciary Bill of 1800, §§ 7 & 10, in id at 312–14.

although Connecticut's district would be called Connecticut.[128] As for the nine circuits, each was described according to the districts it comprised:

> The first circuit shall consist of the districts of Kennebeck, Merrimac, Boston, and Narragansett; the second, of the districts of Connecticut, Warranock [*sic*], and Champlain; the third, of the districts of Hudson, Saratoga, and Ontario; the fourth, of the districts of Rariton, Schuylkill, Delware, and Choptank; the fifth, of the districts of Chesapeake, Susquehanna, and Alleganey; the sixth, of the districts of Potomac [*sic*], Fluvannah [*sic*], and Kenhawa; the seventh, of the districts of Pamplico, Catawba, and Saluda; the eight, of the districts of Santee, Alatamaha, and Savannah; and the ninth, of the districts of Holston, Cumberland, Ohio, and Rockcastle.[129]

Besides this realignment of the districts and circuits, the bill proposed to expand the circuit courts' jurisdiction over several types of cases, including "all actions and suits, matters or things, cognizable by the judicial authority of the United States, under and by virtue of the constitution thereof," as long as the amount in question was at least one hundred dollars and exclusive jurisdiction was not already vested in the Supreme Court by the Constitution or in the admiralty courts pursuant to the new bill.[130]

Despite the committee's efforts (including John Marshall's "lengthy defence of the new system" on the floor of the House), the Harper bill immediately stirred enormous controversy both inside and outside Congress.[131] Much of the criticism focused on the provision to increase and rearrange the district courts. Georgia senator Abraham Baldwin, writing to his brother-in-law Joel Barlow (then the American ambassador to Algiers), characterized the Harper bill as intended "to new model the judiciary" and called it "a very broad stroke to draw all the powers to the general government and to do away as far as possible not only state powers, but even boundaries."[132] The Philadelphia *Aurora*, meanwhile, lambasted the reorganization of the districts, chortling, "instead

---

[128] Id.

[129] Id at 314.

[130] Id § 16 at 317.

[131] 10 *Annals* 646 (1800) (cited in note 39).

[132] Baldwin to Joel Barlow (March 26, 1800), 4 *DHSC* at 640–41 (cited in note 32).

of calling *Jersey* by that name the district is to be denominated
(*alamode de Paris*) the *department* or *district of Rariton*, and so on
throughout the United States!"[133] Given the frequency with which
Federalists accused the *Aurora* and other Republican newspapers
of "jacobin" sympathies, this critique of the Harper bill as carrying
out renaming projects akin to those of revolutionary France's
Committee of Public Safety is particularly noteworthy. In a letter
to his brother John Quincy Adams, U.S. minister to Prussia,
Thomas Boylston Adams despaired of such suspicions but expressed some of his own. "[T]here is an evident reluctance in many
gentlemen towards these great national acts, because they tend to
strengthen the bonds of union & give an influence to the general
Government, that interferes with their malignant designs," the
president's younger son wrote.[134]

Facing this opposition, on March 31 Harper introduced an
amended bill in which the number of districts was reduced to
nineteen and the circuits to six. In the amended bill, the names
and boundaries of the district courts followed the names and
boundaries of the states (with the exceptions of Massachusetts,
New York, Pennsylvania, Virginia, and Tennessee, each of which
was divided into two districts). This scaling back of the federal
courts' presence was accompanied, however, by an extension of
their jurisdiction.[135] Pursuant to the amended bill, the circuit
courts' jurisdiction would encompass "all cases in law or equity,
arising under the constitution and laws of the United States, and
treaties made, or which shall be made, under their authority."[136]
The scope of this grant stood in sharp contrast to the 1789 act's
grant of original jurisdiction to the circuit courts in, first, "all suits
of a civil nature at common law or in equity" in which the amount
in controversy is at least five hundred dollars, and the United
States is a plaintiff or petitioner, or an alien is a party; and, second,
diversity suits.[137] The amended bill's jurisdictional grant was not
as broad as that of the original Harper bill, however, which as we
have seen proposed expanding the scope of federal jurisdiction to
"all actions and suits, matters or things, cognizable by the judicial

---

[133] Philadelphia Aurora (March 18, 1800), id at 637.

[134] T. B. Adams to J. Q. Adams (Feb 25, 1800), id at 627.

[135] Id at 288.

[136] Judiciary Bill of 1800, § 13, in id at 340.

[137] Judiciary Act of 1789, § 11.

authority of the United States, under and by virtue of the constitution thereof"—that is, to the full extent of judicial power under Article III.[138]

The amended bill made little progress in the first session of the Sixth Congress. In the second session, however, a new committee—including some Republicans—took up the judiciary question again and presented a substantially similar bill to the full House.[139] At the beginning of the session, Adams had again pressed for judicial reform in a speech to Congress that Marshall—now secretary of state—had helped prepare.[140] Following some discussion of the propriety of permitting state courts to exercise jurisdiction over federal cases, the bill passed the House on January 20, 1801, and the Senate on February 7. Titled "An Act to provide for the more convenient organization of the Courts of the United States," the bill became law upon receiving Adams's signature on February 13. The final form of the provision regarding the circuit courts' original jurisdiction closely tracked the language of the amended Harper bill. Section 11 of the act provided "[t]hat the said circuit courts respectively shall have cognizance . . . of all cases in law or equity, arising under the constitution and laws of the United States, and treaties made, or which shall be made, under their authority."[141] In addition, the act provided for easier removal of cases from state to federal court.[142] Four days after the law's enactment, on February 17, the House finally settled the disputed presidential election by electing Jefferson on the thirty-sixth ballot.

As this chronology demonstrates, and as several scholars have noted, the movement that led to the Judiciary Act of 1801 predated the election of 1800 by several months. Thus, as Preyer notes, "the Act was clearly not occasioned by the Republican victory in 1800."[143] Indeed, commentators on both sides of the partisan di-

---

[138] Harper Judiciary Bill of 1800, § 16, in 4 *DHSC* at 317 (cited in note 32).

[139] Id at 289.

[140] See Marshall to John Adams (Nov 17, 1800), in 6 *The Papers of John Marshall* 11–12 (North Carolina, 1990) (Charles F. Hobson, ed).

[141] Judiciary Act of 1801, § 11.

[142] Id § 13.

[143] Turner [Preyer], 22 Wm & Mary Q at 3 (cited in note 5). See also Linda K. Kerber, *Federalists in Dissent: Imagery and Ideology in Jeffersonian America* 136 (Cornell, 1970) ("Contrary to its subsequent reputation, the Judiciary Act of 1801 had been the subject of a full and responsible debate during the preceding session of Congress, and its terms represented an attempt to correct the inadequacies of the first Judiciary Act of twelve years before.").

vide had anticipated an attempted expansion of the federal judicial power for some time before the 1801 act came to pass. In August 1799, Jefferson had confided his fears about the expansion of the federal government—in particular, the federal judiciary—in a letter to Edmund Randolph. Specifically, Jefferson worried that the growth of federal courts' jurisdiction would lead to a body of federal common law separate from state law that would become a tool of federal oppression. Jefferson's use of pronouns to refer to the government—and thus to the Federalists—is particularly illuminating:

> Of all the doctrines which have ever been broached by the federal government, the novel one, of the common law being in force & cognizable as an existing law in *their* courts, is to me the most formidable. All their other assumptions of un-given powers have been in the detail. The bank law, the treaty doctrine, the sedition act, alien act . . . &c., &c., have been solitary, unconsequential, timid things, in comparison with the audacious, bare-faced and sweeping pretension to a system of law for the U S, without the adoption of *their* legislature, and so infinitely beyond *their* power to adopt.[144]

For Jefferson, jurisdiction was a mere cover for the spread of substantive federal law, objectionable not only because it could potentially serve as an agent of nationalization but also—and perhaps more important—because such a body of law could not be checked by the people in the states.

Jefferson's democratic critique of the trend toward broader federal jurisdiction finds an echo in the writings of some leading Federalists, who harbored similar but differently directed concerns about the relationship between the people and the federal government. In contrast to Jefferson's claim that the general government was covertly absorbing the powers of the states, and therefore of the people, Federalists such as Hamilton and Sedgwick envisioned the spread of federal power as conducive both to the public good and, not incidentally, to the power of the current government. "An accurate view of the internal situation of the UStates presents many discouraging reflections to the enlightened friends of our Government and country," Hamilton lamented in October

---

[144] Jefferson to Randolph (Aug 18, 1799), in *Thomas Jefferson: Writings* 1066 (Library of America, 1984) (Merrill D. Peterson, ed) (emphasis added).

1799.[145] Despite the "instructive comments afforded by the disastrous & disgusting scenes of the french Revolution," he observed that "sentiments dangerous to social happiness have not been diminished."[146] Given this situation, "vigorous measures of counteraction" were required of the friends of the government, including the "Extension of the Judiciary system" by dividing each state into smaller districts and appointing federal justices of the peace in local areas.[147]

Sedgwick recommended a similar program of extending federal power further into the states. "If the real federal majority can act together much may and ought to be done to give efficiency to the government, and to repress the efforts of the Jacobins against it," he wrote to Rufus King. "We ought to spread out the judicial so as to render the justice of the nation acceptable to the people, to aid national economy, to overawe the licentious, and to punish the guilty."[148] And, like Hamilton, Sedgwick noted that these lofty goals also offered more immediate benefits: "[W]e ought, at the same time, that we promote the real happiness & welfare of the people, to court thereby their favor."[149]

These comments from Hamilton and Sedgwick emphasize the nature of the Federalists' program of expanded federal judicial power. In contrast to Hamilton's earlier acceptance of concurrent powers when writing as Publius in *Federalist* 32, by 1799 he was no longer attempting to thread the needle of concurrent power while still maintaining a forceful general government. Instead, Hamilton—and Sedgwick as well—embraced a vision of federal power that resembled the one that Randolph had struggled to articulate in his report of 1790. That vision in turn owed a debt to the opposition theories that colonists had deployed against parliamentary power in the 1760s and 1770s, according to which each level of the composite imperial government would possess the authority to regulate a defined set of subjects. Common to these early approaches and the views of Hamilton, Sedgwick, and others

---

[145] Hamilton to Jonathan Dayton (Oct–Nov 1799), in 25 *The Papers of Alexander Hamilton* 599 (Columbia, 1976)) (Harold C. Syrett, ed).

[146] Id.

[147] Id at 601.

[148] Sedgwick to King (Nov 15, 1799), in 3 *The Life and Correspondence of Rufus King* 145 (G. P. Putnam's Sons, 1896) (Charles R. King, ed).

[149] Id at 147. On Hamilton and ideas of the public good, see Cecelia Kenyon, *Alexander Hamilton: Rousseau of the Right*, 73 Polit Sci Q 161 (1958).

in the 1790s and 1800s was a belief that the federal and state governments would operate best as parallel powers, each with its own area of competence, with little concurrence or crossover. A decade earlier, however, as we have seen, many commentators had emphasized the opposite, insisting that concurrent powers of legislation as well as adjudication were inevitable and perhaps even desirable in the new federal republic.

The language of the two judiciary acts illustrates this difference in emphasis. While the 1789 act makes multiple references to concurrent state- and federal-court jurisdiction, the only mention of concurrence in the 1801 act concerns the concurrent jurisdiction of district and circuit courts with respect to bankruptcy proceedings.[150] Similarly, contrast the apparatus of inferior federal courts established by the 1789 act with that of the 1801 act. While the drafters of the 1789 act took pains to make the new districts track state boundaries as much as possible, thereby avoiding the suggestion that the general government was working to subsume the states within its own artificial boundaries and structures, the drafters of the 1801 act broke the states down into smaller, more administrable districts, showing little concern for the integrity of the states as they did so. Indeed, the Harper bill provides an even more striking example of this apparent lack of respect for state boundaries, selecting regional, geographic, or Indian names for the districts rather than adopt the titles of the states. Thus, the goal of separating the levels of government—with the dual effects of undoing past blurring and asserting national power—increasingly informed the Federalists' federalizing policy after 1789. And they viewed the expansion of the federal courts' general federal question jurisdiction, which had begun with the Randolph and Harper proposals and culminated in the "arising under" jurisdiction of the 1801 act, as the key to this separation.

B. REPEAL

Of course, the Federalists did not long enjoy the fruits of their plan. Upon the election of Jefferson by the House of Representatives in February 1801, many observers predicted the course of subsequent events. The events leading up to the repeal of the Judiciary Act of 1801 are well known and do not require extensive

---

[150] Compare Judiciary Act of 1789, §§ 9, 11, with Judiciary Act of 1801, § 12.

description here.[151] The 1801 act was repealed on March 8, 1802, by a repealing act[152] that "annulled the 1801 act's broad grant of federal question jurisdiction and discarded the newly created circuit courts, forcing the Supreme Court justices again to ride circuit and act as circuit judges."[153] In 1803, six days after handing down the decision in *Marbury*, the Supreme Court upheld the validity of the repealing act.[154]

In the waning days of the Adams administration, as the president filled the sixteen new circuit judgeships that the act had created,[155] murmurings of repeal had already begun to surface.[156] In his first annual message to Congress, Jefferson said, without really saying, the obvious. "The Judiciary system of the United States, and especially that portion of it recently erected, will, of course, present itself to the contemplation of Congress," the president said, noting that he had already requested an account of all the cases that had been decided since 1789 and of the number of cases that had been pending when the 1801 act took effect.[157] The act of 1801 had established six new circuit courts and seven new district courts.[158] Jefferson and his associates insisted that the Federalists had erected this apparatus as a means of entrenching their power in the face of popular opposition.[159] In their view, concurrence was not a bone to be thrown—or not—to the cowering states at the pleasure of a mighty federal government, but quite the opposite: a gesture of

---

[151] On the repeal of the act, see generally George Lee Haskins and Herbert A. Johnson, *Foundations of Power: John Marshall, 1801–15* (Macmillan, 1981) (especially chaps 4 and 5); Kathryn Turner [Preyer], *The Midnight Judges*, 109 U Pa L Rev 494 (1961).

[152] "An Act to repeal certain acts respecting the organization of the Courts of the United States; and for other purposes" (March 8, 1801), 2 Stat 132.

[153] 4 *DHSC* at 294–95 (cited in note 32).

[154] *Stuart v Laird*, 1 Cranch 299 (1803). Despite the repeal, however, at least one case brought pursuant to the 1801 act's grant of federal question jurisdiction managed to survive the repeal. See Wythe Holt, *The First Federal Question Case*, 3 Law & Hist Rev 169 (1985).

[155] These were the so-called "midnight judges." See Turner [Preyer], 109 U Pa L Rev at 495 (cited in note 151).

[156] See 4 *DHSC* at 295 (cited in note 32).

[157] Jefferson, First Annual Message to Congress (Dec 8, 1801), in 25 *The Papers of Alexander Hamilton* at 448 n 1 (cited in note 145).

[158] Id at 477 n 4.

[159] Some Federalists, such as Gouverneur Morris, agreed. But Morris took a more benign view of his colleagues' strategy, observing, "They are about to experience a heavy gale of adverse wind; can they be blamed for casting many anchors to hold their ship through the storm?" Morris to Robert R. Livingston (Feb 20, 1801), in 3 *The Life of Gouverneur Morris* 153–54 (Gray & Bowen, 1832) (Jared Sparks, ed).

goodwill on the part of the states as they shared a measure of their plenary power, their sovereignty, with the general government.

Hamilton, writing as "Lucius Crassus" in the *New-York Evening Post*, sneered at Jefferson's attempt to prove that the new courts were unnecessary. "No bad thermometer of the capacity of our Chief Magistrate for government is furnished by the rule which he offers for judging of the utility of the Federal Courts," Hamilton said of Jefferson's plan to tally the number of federal-court cases decided as a means of assessing the need for additional courts. "There is hardly any stronger symptom of a pigmy mind, than a propensity to allow greater weight to *secondary* than to *primary* considerations."[160] Hamilton and his allies contended that expanding the federal judicial power was the best solution to the problem of multiple authorities, the problem of *imperium in imperio*, that had dogged the republic since before its founding. In an address to the New York City bar shortly before the repeal of the 1801 act, Hamilton warned of the consequences that he feared would follow. According to a newspaper report,

> He declared in the most emphatic manner, that if the bill for the repeal passed, and the independence of the Judiciary was destroyed, the constitution was but a shadow, and we should, e'er long, be divided into separate confederacies, turning our arms against each.[161]

"*Separate confederacies, turning our arms against each*"—the famously eloquent Hamilton appears to have selected his words carefully to elicit a response from his audience. But Hamilton's choice of the language of confederation at this moment reveals more than simply rhetorical talents. For many observers in the early years of the nineteenth century, the murky abstraction of Article III's "judicial power of the United States" had taken shape only through the institutions of the courts themselves, and only through the device of federal jurisdiction. The years between 1789 and 1802 saw a constant drive to reshape and reconfigure the courts and their jurisdiction, in a period of institutional transformation that was unique to the judiciary. Interestingly, the early

---

[160] [Hamilton], *The Examination No. V*, New-York Evening Post (Dec 29, 1801), in 25 *The Papers of Alexander Hamilton* at 477 (cited in note 145).

[161] Hamilton, *Remarks on the Repeal of the Judiciary Act*, New-York Gazette & General Advertiser (Feb 13, 1802), in id at 523.

Republic witnessed few debates of similar scale regarding the meaning and form of the legislative or executive powers. The language of Article III, combined with the Madisonian compromise, had deliberately left a lacuna in the constitutional structure. By choosing not to fill that gap at Philadelphia, the drafters of the Constitution had ensured that any institution that eventually did fill it would always be seen as provisional, as an attempt but not necessarily a complete solution. The gap was visible from the beginning and would remain so, despite contemporaries' efforts to fill it—with the 1789 act, with the Harper bills, with the 1801 act, with the 1802 repealing act. In some sense, then, the judiciary of any particular era might always appear to its contemporaries as nothing more than "a new wheel . . . introduced into the federal machine to which the union was before a stranger, and which is not necessary to its genuine motives."[162]

IV. CONCLUSION

By 1789, the concept of jurisdiction had become one of the principal contested terrains of constitutional discourse. Instead of the emphasis on the legislature that had fascinated colonial and Revolutionary-era commentators, Americans of the ratification period and the early Republic devoted substantial thought to the structure of the judiciary. The lines of judicial authority thus replaced sovereignty as the great mystery to be unraveled by lawyers, politicians, and thinkers. Yet contemporaries' normative conception of jurisdiction was not stable throughout the period of the early Republic; rather, conflicting visions of jurisdiction—specifically, federal-court jurisdiction—collided and shifted throughout the period between the passage of the Judiciary Act of 1789 and the repeal of the Judiciary Act of 1801 in 1802.

The 1801 act must be understood not as an outlier but on its own terms, as—among other things—an attempt by Federalists to install a particular version of small-"f" federalism in the Constitution. That small-"f" federalism built on theories that colonial commentators had developed beginning in the 1760s, during the struggle with the British Empire. Colonial spokespeople had argued for a system of divided authority in which power was allocated along subject-matter lines, allowing for multiple levels of

---

[162] "A Citizen," Dunlap's American Daily Advertiser (Philadelphia) (Dec 20, 1791).

government to exist in the same system while each exercising a sovereignty defined by the subject of the regulation in question. In the 1801 act, unlike the 1789 act, Federalists sought to return to this idea of subject-matter jurisdiction by establishing broad federal jurisdiction over cases arising under the Constitution, the laws of the United States, and treaties made under their authority. This subject-matter focus was necessarily limited by the Supremacy Clause, which explicitly contemplated some interaction between state judges and federal law and therefore precluded all federal questions from being vested exclusively in federal courts. Yet the Federalists succeeded briefly, most notably by broadening "arising under" jurisdiction and easing the requirements for removal of cases from state to federal court. The election of 1800 and the ensuing repeal of the 1801 act, however, spelled the temporary demise of this idea of jurisdiction and the return of the type of concurrence and overlap that had characterized the system set up by the 1789 act. After 1801, Jeffersonian Americans pulled back from the federal idea that British North Americans had developed in the imperial crisis of several decades earlier. The fate of Federalism, therefore, fundamentally altered the landscape of federalism.

My goal has in some sense been to bring the 1801 act back into the mainstream of American constitutional history. Admittedly, this is something of a difficult task, owing to the act's truncated lifespan and to scholars' tendency to treat it as an anomaly, the result of a sudden burst of partisan fervor that disturbed the otherwise smooth unfolding of the federal judicial power. But that is precisely why this story matters. By demonstrating that one of the supposed modern endpoints of the teleological account of constitutional history—general federal question jurisdiction—was actually achieved for a brief moment in 1801, and that that achievement can be tied back to colonial ideas of the proper division of authority in a compound government, this account suggests that many ostensibly modern currents in constitutional thought are in fact recycled from earlier debates, and that older ideas can remain compelling in vastly changed circumstances from their original ones.